WITHDRAWN

THE EXTENDED CARE FACILITY:

A Guide to
Organization and Operation

The Extended Care Facility:

A Guide to Organization and Operation

Dulcy B. Miller

Assistant in Administrative Medicine
School of Public Health
and Administrative Medicine
Columbia University

Administrative Director
Nursing Home and Extended Care
Facility of White Plains, Inc.
(Miller Center for Nursing Care)
White Plains Center for Nursing Care
White Plains, New York

The Blakiston Division
McGRAW-HILL BOOK COMPANY
New York St. Louis San Francisco
London Sydney Toronto Mexico Panama

THE EXTENDED CARE FACILITY: A GUIDE TO ORGANIZATION AND OPERATION

Library of Congress Catalog Card Number: 69-14756

41985

234567890 MAMM 76543210

Dedicated To

M. B. M.

Foreword

Although new in name and unique in function, the extended care facility has had a long period of development. Many nursing homes providing skilled patient care have been developing programs aimed at the accelerated level of care now identified as the product of the extended care facility, and hospitals have been working toward the same basic concepts within programs frequently identified as "progressive patient care." Despite this degree of interest, despite the frequent steps into the administration of a post-acute extension of the intensive care aspect of institutional health care, there is little published material which can guide or even interest those working so stoutheartedly to fulfill the community's need for extended care facilities.

Management of an extended care facility involves the provision of numerous forms of therapy and treatment, mixed generously with inspiration, motivation, and appreciation. The proportion of each form varies with the needs of patients and varies in intensity from hour to hour. It therefore follows that there is no *one* method of organizing or administering an extended care facility or any of its components. However, a giant step forward has been taken with the publication of this book, which can serve, so effectively, those who would build the body of knowledge in this particular aspect of health care.

The author, an administrator, sees this publication as a manual. Her descriptions of methods of operation—forged in the crucible of reality—are made available in an orderly fashion to those who have similar responsibilities. Some readers will see the book as an educational tool, from which they can learn and from which they surely will want to teach. (Those readers who feel they have acquired superior knowledge and experience are hereby invited and urged to make this knowledge and experience available in print. All this shared information can only benefit the patient.)

Mrs. Dulcy Miller has filled the pages of this volume with details, specifications, program descriptions, and techniques. Wisely she has chosen to describe two types of nursing units, a concentrated care unit and a skilled nursing care unit. This approach permits, and in fact requires, the reader to understand the adjustments necessary to operate properly at, at least, two levels of care within what has been identified as an extended care facility.

This volume is a most welcome addition to the sparse supply of constructive literature available and should be of importance for many years to come. Dulcy Miller has given generously of herself in writing this volume but not more generously than she has given of herself in achieving success as an administrator, an educator, a lecturer, and a participant in numerous activities related to health and geriatrics. Her boundless energy and great capacity for work are coupled with a unique ability to observe and understand the needs of those with prolonged illness. She has earned the right to publish this fine book.

Harold Baumgarten, Jr.
Associate Professor
Administrative Medicine
Columbia University

Preface

The Extended Care Facility: A Guide to Organization and Operation documents the organization and actual day-to-day method of operation of a relative newcomer to the constellation of medical care organizations—the extended care facility.

Spurred by the rapid growth of the aged population in this country and by the associated problems of health, housing, and finances, Public Law 89-97 made available in January of 1967 Medicare extended care benefits to Americans over sixty-five.

Great professional and community interest has developed as a result of this federal legislation. General hospitals, homes for the aged, and public and private agencies have evinced interest in the construction of extended care units to complement their present facilities and in the development of new freestanding extended care institutions.

It is hoped that this volume will serve as a guide to those who are responsible for the planning, financing, development, supervision, and management of health care institutions—included governing boards, planning agencies, developers, medical and dental staff, administrators, department heads, unions, and representatives of government agencies, ranging from the Social Security Administration to the various health and welfare departments responsible for certifying extended care facilities to receive Title 18 and 19 patients. Section 1908 of Public Law 90-248, providing for compulsory licensing of nursing home administrators, serves to accentuate the need for text material for educational programs in the field.

It is further hoped that this book will prove useful to professionals in related disciplines—to the clergy in their work with the institutionalized aged; to hospital administrators contemplating transfer agreements with extended care facilities; and to social workers in family agencies working with the elderly. Third-party payers and fiscal intermediaries can plan appropriate reimbursement formulas only if they are familiar with the daily activities of the extended care facility.

The Extended Care Facility: A Guide to Organization and Operation has been developed as a direct result of clinical experience at the Miller Center for Nursing Care (Nursing Home and Extended Care Facility of White Plains, Inc.). The book presents a complete description of the functioning of an extended care institution as expounded in the Conditions of Participation of the Medicare legislation, including all the prescribed services and departments. In addition, the Administrative Residency Program, in effect with the Department of Health Care Administration of George Washington University, the field placement of social work students of the New York University School of Social Work, and the clinical work experience of the Mental Health Internes Program of the Department of Psychiatry of the Albert Einstein College of Medicine, and Miller Center have encouraged an intellectual climate resulting in a high level of performance and an analytical approach, helpful to this author.

I wish to thank all staff members of the Miller Center for their pioneering efforts in recording and analyzing data in their respective departments. Special acknowledgment is due Mina Klein for her contribution and supervision of the photography, Dian Elliott and Mary Murray for their careful typing, and Ada Jacobs for her help in proofreading galleys and pages and in preparing the index. The cooperative efforts of Dorothy Keller, R.N.; Barbara Greenberg, R.N., B.S.; Audrey Harris, A.C.S.W.; Alice Clay and Patricia Ellerbe, A.D.A.; Mary Saldicco, Activities Coordinator; Judith Krongold, O.T.R.; Carrol Wardlaw, R.P.T.; Sidney Goda, Ph.D., Speech Therapist; Sy Rook, Registered Pharmacist; Maurice Singer, C.P.A., and Shirley Woodruff, Business Procedures; William Woodruff, Building and Grounds; and Lawrence Cohen, Administrative Resident, are acknowledged with appreciation. Lastly and most importantly, my interest in working with the aged is a direct result of the involvement and longstanding concern of my husband, Dr. M. B. Miller, in rehabilitation of the chronically ill and aged.

With the projected figure of 24 million persons over sixty-five in the U.S. population by 1980, the need for all services to the aged must grow. I sincerely hope that this book will prove useful as a reference, a role definer, and a communications tool to professionals working with the ill aged in extended care settings.

Dulcy B. Miller

Contents

Section 1

Administration

Introduction

An extended care facility primarily should be concerned with providing medical care, nursing care, and rehabilitative services for inpatients no longer in an acute phase of illness. Its chief interest should be to help each patient to recover as fully as possible by assisting him to function to the best of his ability physically, socially, and emotionally. The extended care facility must also be concerned with the development of a close working relationship with families of patients, a vital element of a successful rehabilitation program as well as an important aid to families of patients in identifying and resolving problems accentuated by placement of a family member in an institutional setting.

Together with general hospitals and other social and welfare agencies, the extended care facility should function as part of the network of community health agencies. Whenever possible, local civic, social, and educational groups should be encouraged to use the facilities of the extended care facility. Professional seminars, meetings, and training programs should be conducted by the extended care facility, alone or in conjunction with other community agencies. Appropriate articles should be contributed to lay and professional publications to disseminate information on aspects of extended care with special reference to the efficient utilization of extended care units.

I. EXTERNAL AND INTERNAL ENVIRONMENT

A. The Site. The site of the extended care facility, if it is not attached to or located on the grounds of a general hospital, should be selected to afford:

1. Proximity to a general hospital and to professional offices, to expedite close medical supervision and ready access to special services
2. Accessibility to the cultural, social, and religious activities of the community
3. Availability of public transportation for staff and visitor convenience

4. Free movement of ambulatory patients in an outdoor area with proper safeguards for the more physically and intellectually handicapped residents
5. Sufficient area for parking for families, visitors, attending physicians, and staff
6. Protected parking approachable from the building, with no stairs, in order to encourage patients to go out into the community in cars, taxis, or buses
7. Appropriate areas for delivery and service vehicles

B. The Physical Structure. The physical structure should be a safe, fire-rated elevator building planned to provide areas for:

1. Patient activities of daily living including sleeping, bathing and toileting, dining, walking, socializing, and recreation
2. The isolation of patients with special problems and of the bodies of deceased patients until the arrival of the undertaker
3. Nursing, medical, dental, and pharmaceutical services
4. Restorative and social services
5. Clinical laboratory and diagnostic x-ray services

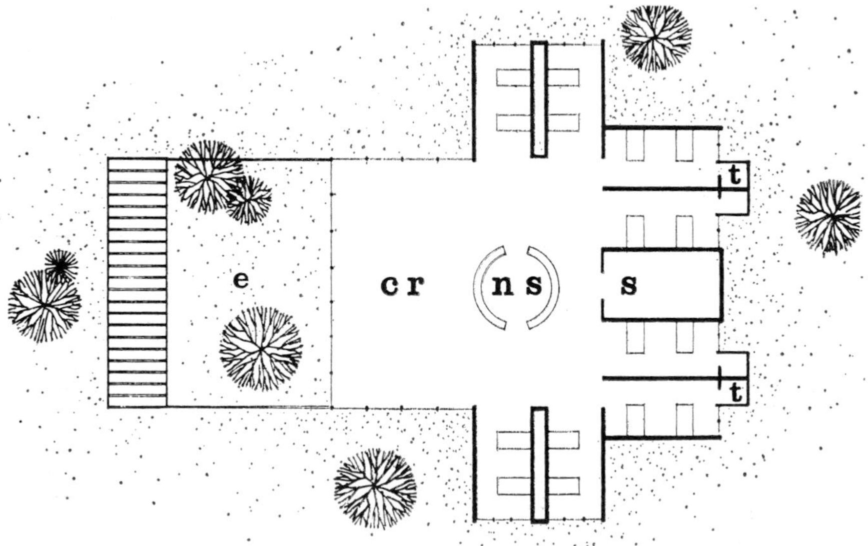

Fig. 1-1. The concentrated care unit for the severely physically handicapped patients is arranged to provide close nursing supervision. Symbols represent the following facilities: cr, community room; ns, nursing station; t, training toilet; s, services (i.e., utility rooms, treatment, bathing, pantry, nonpatient storage); e, outdoor environment. (*From Mod. Hosp., October,* 1966. *By permission of the publisher.*)

6. Personal grooming of patients
7. Dietary, housekeeping, laundry, maintenance, and business departments
8. Storage for supplies, equipment, and patients' possessions
9. Staff accommodations such as staff rooms, baths, lockers, and for dining and lounging

C. The Architecture. The building should be designed to serve as a tool in patient management with:

1. The nursing units planned for different levels of care commensurate with varying patient needs

a. A compact 30-bed concentrated care and easily supervised entity for the more physically handicapped (Fig. 1-1)

b. A less controlled, more expansive care unit for 35 less obviously disabled patients (Fig. 1-2)

c. And possibly a third closely controlled section for the mobile physically ill with associated mental impairment (Fig. 1-3)

2. Bedrooms sufficiently spacious to facilitate movement by handicapped persons dependent upon wheelchairs, crutches, walkers, and canes
3. The toilets arranged for easy accessibility of wheelchairs and at the proper height to encourage self-help on the part of the patients

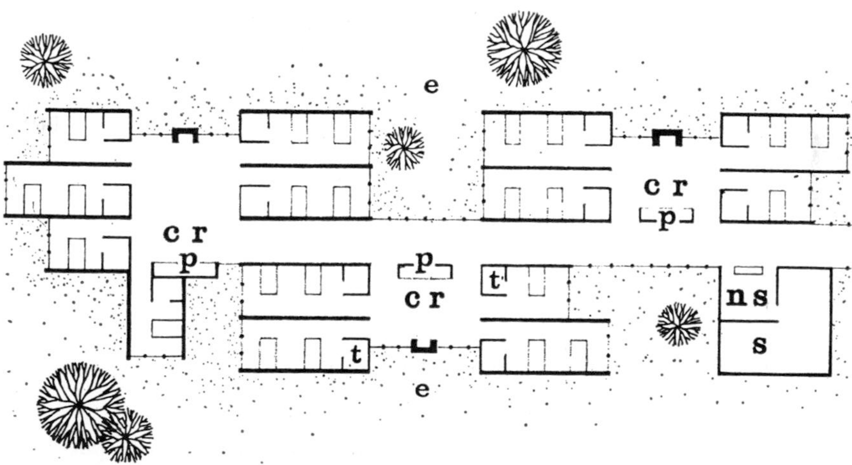

Fig. 1-2. The skilled nursing care unit is designed to encourage socialization of patients in therapeutic community groupings. Symbols represent the following facilities: cr, community room; ns, nursing station; t, training toilet; s, services (i.e., utility rooms, treatment, bathing, nonpatient storage); p, pantry; e, outdoor environment. (*From Mod. Hosp. October,* 1966. *By permission of the publisher.*)

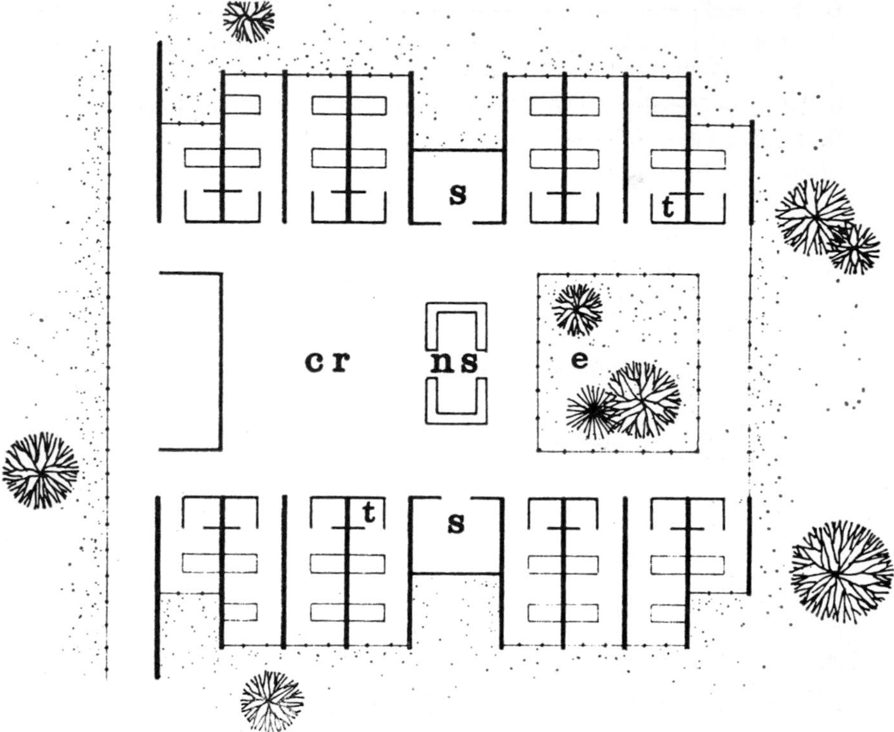

Fig. 1-3. A unit for ambulatory, intellectually impaired patients allows free movement of patients indoors and outdoors, with controls. Symbols represent the following facilities: cr, community room; ns, nursing station; t, training toilet; s, services (i.e., utility rooms, treatment, bathing, pantry, nonpatient storage); e, outdoor environment. (*From Mod. Hosp., October,* 1966. *By permission of the publisher.*)

4. Community and dining areas of various sizes located to encourage the social rehabilitation of the patients

5. Appropriate spaces to generate physical rehabilitation through the restorative services

D. Furniture and Equipment. The furniture and equipment in the extended care facility should be planned to meet:

1. The physical requirements of the patient population, with particular reference to patient safety, including:

a. Adequate weight for chairs and table to preclude tipping

b. The proper height for chairs

c. The use of arms on all chairs

d. Elimination of aprons and the use of pedestals in lieu of legs on tables used by wheelchair patients for dining or recreation (Fig. 1-4)

e. A minimum of freestanding, easily overturned items like lamps

f. The use of rounded edges on all furniture and equipment rather than sharp corners

g. Lighting appropriately located and sufficiently intense to compensate for visual deficits

h. The substitution of push plates or other types of facilitating hardware for doorknobs

2. The aesthetic needs of the patients, their families, the staff, and the community, with particular reference to:

a. The deft use of bright, gay colors

b. Furniture that is contemporary and airy in appearance

c. The use of artistic and decorative accessories to deinstitutionalize the interiors

d. The provision of plants and flowers to lend warmth to the ambience

e. Judicious utilization of carpeting in selected areas

Fig. 1-4. Dining tables without aprons and with pedestals instead of legs are more comfortable for patients in wheelchairs.

3. The administrative needs of the institution, with the emphasis on trouble-free maintenance and ease of housekeeping:

a. Dining chairs should not have crevices in which food particles can collect.

b. Fabrics in direct contact with patients should have a plastic finish.

c. Window hangings should be of a nonflammable material or should be professionally flameproofed and easily washable.

d. Surfaces should be selected in accordance with the amount and type of anticipated wear and tear.

e. Counters of plastic should have a suede rather than a smooth finish to prevent their being scratched.

f. Metal tips on chairs should be removed when the chairs are used on resilient flooring to prevent the floors from being damaged.

g. Indented areas should be used on furniture drawers and doors to eliminate the need for drawer pulls, doorknobs, and latches.

II. ORGANIZATIONAL STRUCTURE

A. Sponsorship and Organization

1. In conformity with *the suggested constitution and bylaws for a voluntary hospital,*[1] the extended care facility may be sponsored by:

a. A nonprofit corporation whereby:

(1) A constitution and bylaws should be promulgated.

(2) Members of the corporation may not receive any material or pecuniary benefit from the institutional corporation.

(3) Members of the corporation may not be held liable for any debts of the corporation.

(4) Exemption from federal and usually from state and local taxation should be the practice for legally constituted and managed corporations, or

b. A public agency whereby:

(1) Bylaws should be developed according to the statutes, rules, regulations, and policies governing the parent governmental agency.

(2) The same government bureau may direct the operation.

(3) An appointed representative of the parent agency may serve as the governing authority.

(4) A specially appointed or elected board of managers may serve as the governing authority.

(5) Members of the board may not receive any material or

[1] American Hospital Association, Chicago, Ill., 1968.

pecuniary benefit from the operation of the extended care facility.

(6) The members of the governing body may not be held personally responsible for any debts incurred by the institution.

(7) Exemption from federal, state, and local taxation may be anticipated, or

c. A proprietary agency whereby:

(1) Operating rules should be developed.

(2) The proprietors may derive material and pecuniary benefit from the operation of the extended care facility.

(3) The proprietors will be held liable for the debts of the agency.

(4) The institution as a commercial enterprise will be required to pay local, state, and federal taxes.

2. Irrespective of the sponsorship, the extended care facility may be organized as:

a. A separate and freestanding entity
b. A branch of a religious, charitable, or fraternal agency
c. An extension or addition to an existing organization
d. A satellite of an existing agency
e. A link in a chain of organizations

3. Whether the extended care facility be sponsored by a voluntary, public, or proprietary agency or by a board or corporation, the permission to operate such a facility can be expected to be dependent upon submission to the state licensing agency of the following information, as a minimum:

a. Full disclosure of ownership
b. A proposed program and staffing plan
c. Rules and regulations to ensure an orderly operation
d. A duly constituted constitution or a copy of the constitution of the parent body
e. Bylaws
f. A copy of the certificate of occupancy
g. A copy of the certificate of doing business (for a noncorporate organization)
h. A copy of the lease should the property be rented
i. Copies of any additional data required by local governmental units

4. After approval by the appropriate state body, the application for the charter to operate should become the constitution of the extended care facility, to be amended only with the acquiescence of the granting authority, and including the following information:

a. The title and location of the corporation

b. The objectives and purposes of the organization
c. The status (relating to nonprofit or proprietary)
d. When the corporation is a membership corporation:
(1) Qualifications of members
(2) The plan for membership dues
e. The size of the governing board:
(1) It is generally thought that an effective governing board should be composed of 8 to 15 members.
(2) The officers may be designated to function as the executive committee.
f. The method of election and term of office of officers and board members

5. The bylaws or rules and regulations of the extended care facility should discuss:
a. The details of membership in a membership corporation
(1) Qualifications for voting
(2) Qualifications for holding office
(3) Date of the annual meeting
(4) Number of members to constitute a quorum
(5) Techniques for calling special meetings
b. The details of a nonmembership corporation:
(1) Title and size of the governing board
(2) Method of electing or appointing board members, who may be representative of various segments of the population and talents of members of the community
(3) Number of consecutive terms of board service permissible and the time lapse required between terms of service
(4) Date of the annual meeting
c. A listing of the duties of the governing board, such as:
(1) Supervision of the property, affairs, and finances of the corporation
(2) Appointment of members of the governing board to fill unexpired terms of officers
(3) Selection of the administrative and medical directors
(4) Appointment of the medical staff
d. The specifics of the regular and special meetings:
(1) The regular monthly meeting should not be scheduled until the middle of the month or later to permit the preparation of reports for presentation to the board.
(2) Special meetings may be called by the president or at the written request of one-fourth or one-third of the board.
(3) A written notice must be sent in advance of the special meeting specifying the purpose of the meeting.

(4) Only the stated topic may be discussed at the special meeting.
(5) Half the members of the board should constitute a quorum.

e. The officers of the governing board should be composed of:
(1) The chairman or president to preside at meetings and to serve as ex officio member of all board committees
(2) The vice-chairman or vice-president to serve as chairman or president with the appropriate authority in the absence of the chairman
(3) The secretary to maintain records of all meetings, to notify board members of meetings, and to be responsible for all records and reports of the board
(4) The treasurer to be the custodian of all funds of the extended care facility, assuring proper methods of accounting and reporting of all financial affairs to the appropriate committee of the board and the presentation of bills to the designated person for approval of payment
(5) Other officers sanctioned by the governing board

f. The officers may be elected or appointed by the governing board from its own members:
(1) At the first regular meeting directly after governing board elections
(2) For a term of 1 year

g. The standing committees of the governing board should include:
(1) The executive committee, composed of the chairman, the secretary, the treasurer, and two other members of the board, whose duties should comprise the transaction of all institutional business between board meetings, examination of monthly financial reports, and the presentation of an annual operating budget
(2) The finance committee, consisting of the treasurer and two other board members, who should supervise the proper investment of trust and endowment funds and the proper handling of the income of these monies in accordance with the trust arrangements
(3) The medical staff committee, to be composed of three members of the governing board, to review and make final determinations on recommendations from the medical staff for medical staff appointments, to approve the specific professional area of concern of each medical staff member, to serve as the governing board representatives to the joint conference committee, and to act as the board's representative in all matters pertaining to the medical staff
(4) The nominating committee, to present nominations at the

annual meeting or at meetings during the year should vacancies occur

(5) A master plan committee and any other standing committees authorized by the governing board

(6) One-half of the committee members to constitute a quorum

h. Special committees should be appointed by the chairman as needed and should continue to function only until their specific charge has been completed.

i. The governing board should engage two administrative officers:

(1) A medical director to coordinate and supervise all professional activities of the extended care facility; to act as liaison in matters of patient care between the extended care facility, the medical profession, hospitals, and other health care agencies; to supervise clinical research; to administer the employee health program; to direct educational programs for the professional staff; to prepare scientific articles for publication; and to represent the governing board in medical administrative matters

(2) An administrative director to manage the physical plant and the business affairs of the facility; to implement all board policies; to prepare an organizational plan, personnel policies, and an operating budget; to be responsible for the selection, employment, and termination of personnel; to present financial reports on regular activities to the board; to cooperate with the medical director and medical staff, and to serve as administrative liaison between the governing board and the medical staff and between the extended care facility and the general hospitals

j. Bylaws for the governing board should provide for:

(1) Approval of medical staff and allied health professionals

(2) Granting of privileges

(3) Appointing the appropriate number of qualified persons to the medical staff for a period of 1 year

(4) Affording medical staff members who are not reappointed the opportunity of a hearing before the credentials committee of the medical staff whose determinations should be considered by the governing board before the final decision-making process

k. The governing board should delegate to the medical staff the responsibility for:

(1) Providing professional comprehensive patient care

(2) Continuously appraising the quality of care

(3) The routine functions of recommending appointments, reappointments, changes of status, and disciplinary action while reserving final approval rights as well as the right to handle special situations

l. Amendments for corporations with members may be approved by a two-thirds majority of members present at the annual or a properly announced special meeting.

m. Amendments for corporations without members may be approved:

(1) By a two-thirds majority of the governing board (*a*) provided that the proper procedure and written notice of 7 days be followed; (*b*) so long as the proposed amendment is included in the written notification of the meeting

B. Policies

1. Where sponsorship does not predetermine admission policies, it is recommended that patients be accepted and staff engaged without regard to sex, race, creed, national origin, or geography.

2. The admission of patients should be limited to persons over 18 years of age, not suffering from mental illness, tuberculosis, communicable or contagious diseases.

3. Patients should be admitted to the extended care facility by physicians who are members of the medical staff and who should present a completed transfer form upon admission and discharge.

4. The patient and/or his family should designate a responsible party with whom all financial transactions should be conducted.

5. Due notice should be given to patients and/or sponsors before rate changes are effected.

6. The extended care institution must abide by all rules and regulations set forth by the various governmental agencies concerned with the supervision of health care facilities.

7. Transfer agreements or affiliations should be developed between freestanding extended care facilities and general hospitals.

8. The extended care facility should cooperate with all appropriate health, governmental, and civic agencies.

9. The community should be requested to participate in the activities program and should be invited to engage in educational field trips to the extended care facility.

10. The staff should be encouraged to take part in intra- and extramural educational experiences and to become members of the appropriate professional societies.

11. Relatives and friends of patients should be encouraged to visit and to participate in programs whenever feasible.

12. The extended care facility should communicate with patients, their families, staff, volunteers, and friends by the regular utilization of various communications media.

13. Professional staff and volunteer workers should be subject to written policies developed for staff members and volunteer workers.

14. Accurate and complete medical, financial, and personnel records on all patients, staff members, and volunteers should be maintained in the strictest confidence.

15. The extended care facility should operate under policies developed by the medical staff, the pharmacy, personnel, safety, patient care policy, utilization review, and joint conference committees as approved by the governing body.

16. Operational policy should be determined by the governing body, which may be a board of directors, a board of managers, a partnership, or a proprietor, depending upon the ownership and control, with the authority delegated by the governing authority to a medical director for professional services and an administrative director for business management (Fig. 1-5).

C. Management

1. Executive Management. The staff of the extended care facility should properly function as a team, skills of members being intermeshed to provide a network of rehabilitation services and executive management carefully selected by the governing body to consist of:

a. A medical director, whose functions will be elaborated upon in the chapter on medical and allied health professionals

b. An administrative director to:

(1) Implement all policies of the governing body

(2) Program a staffing plan commensurate with the needs of an extended care facility

(3) Be responsible for the proper maintenance of the building, grounds, and equipment

(4) Supervise, select, and terminate employment of staff in the dietary, housekeeping and laundry, business, and maintenance departments, and the recreation, volunteer, publication, and reception services

(5) Require weekly verbal reports and monthly written reports from the heads of these departments and services, including statistical summaries, activities, special areas of concern, and apparent trends with deviations from routine experiences to be noted

(6) Be responsible for the development of written personnel policies and for all employee policy

(7) Prepare, supervise, or approve all reports to professional and governmental agencies

(8) Prepare the annual operating budget using departmental budgets, worked out in cooperation with department heads, and

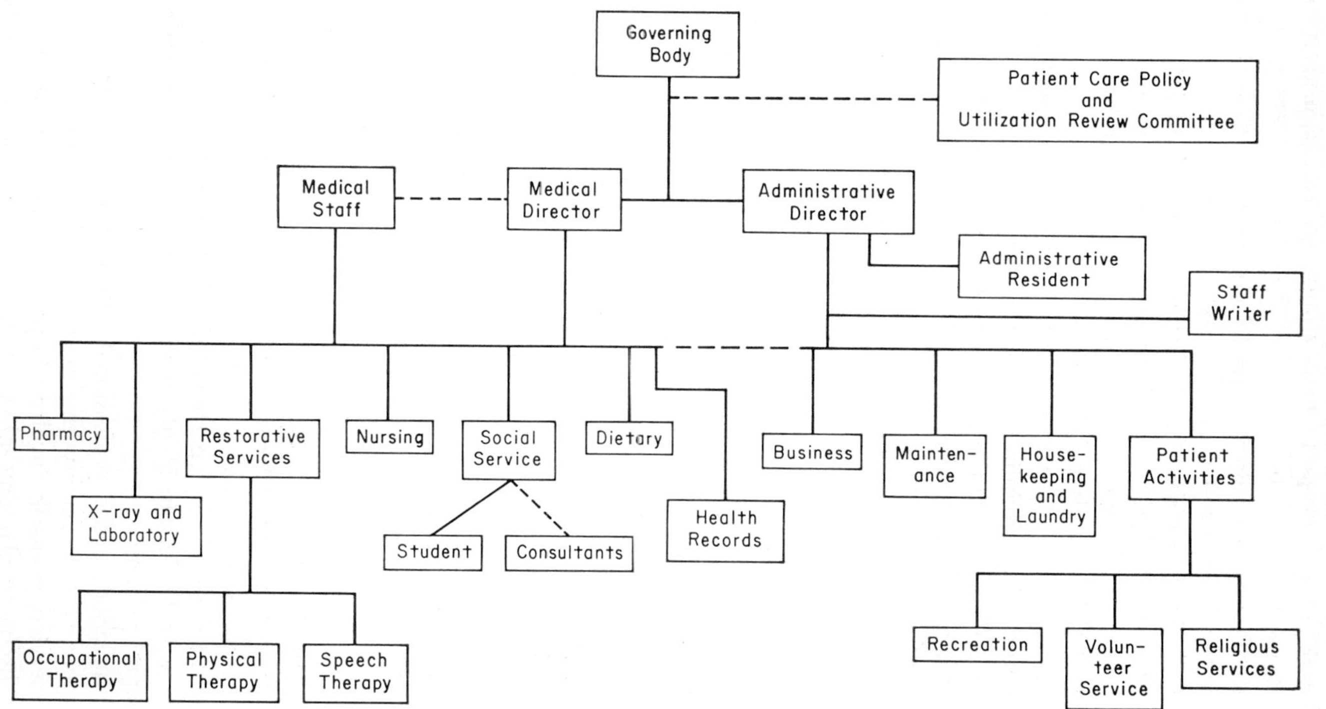

Fig. 1-5. The suggested organizational pattern of an extended care facility.

with adherence to budgets by the department heads to be stressed

(9) Present periodic and special progress reports to the governing body concerning activities and finances

(10) Be responsible for the general financial affairs of the extended care facility, including the purchase of major equipment and the development of a comprehensive insurance program

(11) Study trends and change services to meet unfilled needs

(12) Work jointly with the medical director and members of the paramedical disciplines to effect improved patient care

(13) Consult with the director of nursing on problems of personnel, schedules, and coordination; with the director of social service on problems concerning admissions, transfers, discharges, room assignments, and relationships to patients' families; and with the therapists on problems of scheduling and major equipment needs

(14) Be concerned with community relations by interpreting the extended care facility and its work to the professional and lay public, by representing the institution and participating in the work of related professional and community organizations (or by delegating appropriate staff members to do so), by contributing articles to professional publications, by attending out-of-town conferences and seminars, and by serving as administrative liaison between the hospitals and the extended care facility

(15) Approve all material for publication to ensure uniformity and to ascertain appropriateness of content

(16) Encourage and approve attendance of staff members at meetings, seminars, and educational institutes

(17) Serve on the safety, personnel, and pharmacy committees

(18) Be present at meetings of the governing board and serve ex officio on the joint conference committee and the medical board

(19) Prepare letters of appointment to members of the medical staff to be signed by the chairman or president of the board or comparable official

2. Departments. Each department should be directed by a competent person with leadership ability who may be classified as professional or nonprofessional:

a. Included in the professional category are nursing, in the extended care facility the matrix of all patient services; social service, primarily involved in patient admission, adaptation, and discharge planning; physical, occupational, and speech therapy, the restorative services; clinical laboratory, and diagnostic x-ray and medicine.

b. Dietary, housekeeping and laundry, maintenance, business, and recreation may be listed in the nonprofessional category. (Although dietary and recreation also may be included in the former classification, it is preferable to have these departments primarily responsible to the administrative director.)

3. Order of Responsibility. It is suggested that the governing body develop policies relating to the order of responsibility to be followed by management which could state that:

a. In the absence of the medical and administrative directors, the assistant director should make decisions and should conduct the affairs of the institution.

b. The director of nursing should follow the assistant director in the order of responsibility.

c. Next in the order of responsibility should be the charge nurse, registered nurses taking precedence over licensed practical nurses.

D. Personnel Policies

1. To provide the required care and services, a ratio of almost one staff member to each patient should be maintained by the extended care facility.

2. Information should be supplied to all personnel in the following two ways:

a. A personnel handbook (Fig. 1-6) should be presented to each member of the staff at the onset of his employment, describing the goals of the institution, the needs of the patients, the staff complement, and the specifics of employment including medical examinations, work schedules, salaries, benefits and holidays, uniforms, personnel committees and meetings, lines of communications, and safety.

Fig. 1-6

THE WELCOME MAT IS OUT

First, may we welcome you to the extended care facility as a new member of our staff. We are glad to have you with us, and we hope that you will find your work satisfying and rewarding.

To help you get off to a good start, here are a few basic facts about us that you should know. Please take a few minutes to study these pages so that you may understand our purposes as well as our simple rules and regulations.

Fig. 1-6 (Continued)

Our Aim

Our aim is to help our aged and chronically ill patients as much as possible. This means not only to try to improve their health, but also to encourage them to function to the best of their ability in *all* ways—physically, mentally, emotionally, and socially. To accomplish this difficult task, the understanding and cooperation of every member of the staff are necessary. For only through your pride in your work will our patients receive the superior sort of care they require. And only through the concerted efforts of all of us will we continue to be recognized as a leading facility for nursing care.

Everyone, in every capacity, is important to us. If you do your job with good spirit and a friendly smile, you are contributing your own kind of "treatment" to patients.

Our Patient Population

Our institution is a 65-bed nursing care facility, with women patients generally outnumbering the men 3 to 1. Average age of the patients is eighty.

Our Staff

A ratio of 1 staff member to 1.3 patients is maintained, and the staff includes a medical director, an administrative director, a nursing staff of approximately 30 persons, departments of Social Service, Diet, Housekeeping and Maintenance, Business, plus a physical therapist, a full-time recreation director, an occupational and a speech therapist, and also a staff writer.

Our Facility

Located in a residential section of the city, convenient to business and shopping areas, the facility is a two-story building. Patients requiring intensive care live on the first floor, with ten 2-patient, two 4-patient, and two 1-patient bedrooms. A large recreation room and an administrative office are also on this floor. The second floor has ten 2-patient, four 3-patient, and one 4-patient bedrooms, plus four community rooms, one at each corner, and a separate medical and social service suite. The ground floor includes kitchen and pantries, a staff dining room, business office, recreation and volunteer office, laundry and maintenance, storage and mechanical equipment rooms, lockers and lavatories, and two resident staff rooms. A parking lot for staff members' cars is located at the rear of the building.

GETTING TO KNOW YOU

Security Is a Two-way Street

To maintain a smoothly operating facility, we must have a loyal and experienced staff. But security is a two-way street. All employees should realize

Fig. 1-6 (Continued)

that just as permanence is part of our policy, we expect that loyalty and efficiency will be part of theirs.

Introductory Period

You become a permanent member of the staff upon satisfactory completion of a 3-month introductory period. At this time you become eligible for all employee benefits.

Medical Exam

A preemployment physical examination, including a chest x-ray and blood chemistries, is required of all new employees. This may be done by a physician of your own choice or by our own medical director, and must be repeated annually.

Work Schedule

An extended care facility, like a hospital, must be "on duty" around the clock . . . around the calendar. For this reason, weekends and holidays are part of a standard work week. Rotation of duty at times may be necessary. Schedules are carefully planned in advance for efficient and uninterrupted running of the nursing center. Employees work a 5-day week, a few persons being employed on a part-time basis.

Time Schedule

You are responsible for checking the employee time schedule for your hours and days of assignment. A time schedule for nursing department personnel is posted on the bulletin board at the first-floor nurses' station. There is also an attendance record book located at that station. The time schedule for dietary and housekeeping personnel is posted on the bulletin board in the staff dining room on the ground floor, and the attendance record book for these two departments is located on the same bulletin board. The laws of the State Department of Labor require that *you personally* sign in and out of these books each time you go on and off duty.

Immediately upon signing in, please report to your charge nurse or supervisor for assignment. Also, please remember to report to these department heads if you leave the building and when you go off duty. This is a safety measure. In case of emergency, we must know exactly where each staff member is as well as the whereabouts of each patient.

Be a Clock Watcher

Punctuality is a *must.* Our patients need you, and if you are not on duty exactly as scheduled, their welfare is bound to be affected. In addition, your fellow workers suffer if you are late, as our personnel do not leave their posts until they are relieved. For these reasons, frequent or habitual tardiness will result in the loss of your position.

Fig. 1-6 (Continued)

SALARIES AND SUCH

Your Salary

You will receive your salary check weekly, on Tuesdays. It will be distributed to you by your department head or, in the event that this is not possible, it will be kept safely for you at the first-floor nursing station.

Our work week runs from Sunday through Saturday, and hours are calculated according to employee attendance cards. For this reason, be sure to sign in and out accurately and regularly.

Deductions

As you know, deductions are required for federal income tax, state income tax, social security, and for disability insurance benefits, as well as for meals and lodging when appropriate. The extended care facility contributes its share toward social security and disability insurance.

Increments and Advance Pay

Increments are given on the basis of length and quality of service, plus attendance at staff training sessions, and are determined by conferences between the personnel committee and administration. For obvious reasons, requests for salary advances may not be granted.

Bonuses

After completion of the 3-month introductory period and a subsequent 6-month perfect attendance record, you will receive a bonus of 5 days' salary. Thereafter, you will receive 6 days' salary for each 6 months of perfect attendance. If you should be absent through illness during the next 6 months, you are entitled to a bonus of 6 days' salary for the second 6 months, plus a bonus for the first 6 months minus the days you were absent.

Gratuities and Gifts

It is a policy of the extended care facility that employees are not to accept cash or gifts from patients or families for services rendered.

INSURANCE VIA THE CENTER

Blue Cross and Blue Shield

After satisfactorily completing your 3-month introductory period, the nursing center purchases an individual Blue Cross–United Medical Service contract for each full-time employee as insurance toward hospital and associated medical and surgical bills. Your family may be included in the contract; the additional

Fig. 1-6 (Continued)

cost is borne by you and is deducted from the first two payrolls of each month.

Workmen's Compensation Insurance

The nursing center maintains a workmen's compensation insurance policy to insure employees for loss of salary due to personal injury, sickness, or death suffered in the course of their employment. Injuries must be reported at once to be eligible for compensation. In this state the amounts prescribed by law are two-thirds of the weekly salary earned by the employee, but not more than $— per week, payable from the eight day of disability. However, if the disability continues beyond 14 days, payments will be made from the first day of disability. All medical expenses will be reimbursed.

In the event that the Workmen's Compensation Board should determine that an injured employee is entitled to a specific award, such award will be made in addition to the above-mentioned benefits.

Disability Benefits

Through the extended care facility disability insurance is available to employees against loss of salary due to personal injury or sickness suffered by them *not* in the course of their work at the center. Disability benefits begin on the eighth day of disability and cover 50 percent of the average weekly wages, not exceeding $— per week, for a maximum period of 26 weeks.

AND AWAY WE GO!

Days Off

Whenever possible, employees will be assigned regular days and weekends off, with personal preferences and special requests taken into account if feasible.

Holidays

The nursing center gives its staff seven holidays with pay each year. These seven holidays are assigned to our staff according to the best interests of patients. If not on the actual holidays themselves (see list below), they are given during the month of the holiday.

1. New Year's Day
2. Easter
3. Decoration Day
4. Independence Day
5. Labor Day
6. Thanksgiving Day
7. Christmas Day

Two more words on this subject: First, the seven paid holidays are not cumulative. Second, pay in lieu thereof is permitted for personnel who prefer to work on their stipulated holidays.

Fig. 1-6 (Continued)

Vacations

Nonprofessional workers are given 2 weeks of annual vacation. Members of the professional and supervisory staff receive 3 weeks of vacation each year. However, the following apply to all personnel:

1. You must have a record of 12 months of steady service before you are eligible for an annual vacation.
2. Vacations due you in a single year must be taken during that year.
3. A minimum of 1 week must be taken at a time.
4. Preference for vacation time will be given to employees with most seniority. Please make requests to your department head as far in advance as possible.
5. Should you leave after one or more years of service—unless discharged for cause—you will be eligible for accrued vacation time upon termination of employment.

POLICIES ON ABSENCE

Sick Leave

You become eligible for paid sick leave after satisfactory completion of your 3-month introductory period. One day per month for personal illness is allowed. Presentation of a doctor's certificate upon your return to work after 3 days' absence is required, stating the nature of your illness and certifying that you are able to perform your job. Remember, your charge nurse or supervisor must be informed by phone 3 hours in advance of your tour of duty if you are to be absent due to illness.

Sick leave is not cumulative and can be taken before or after a stipulated holiday or scheduled day off *only* upon presentation of a doctor's certificate on the day or your return to the job.

Leave of Absence

Leaves of absence are granted for special reasons satisfactory to your department head and the administrative director. A month's advance notice must be given except in cases of personal emergencies. No salary is paid during a leave of absence, and the leave is granted with the understanding that the staff member will return as soon as his agreed-upon leave is over. Duration of leave of absence cannot be credited toward seniority.

Absentees

Since someone always must be assigned to your job, please be absent only when absolutely necessary. Whatever the reason for absence, be sure to notify your department head by phone 3 hours in advance of your tour of duty so that a replacement for your job may be obtained. Failure to

Fig. 1-6 (Continued)

do so will mean that you are not eligible for sick leave. Repeated absenteeism and/or negligence in informing your charge nurse or supervisor of your absence may result in loss of your position.

HOME, SWEET HOME

Meals

Nourishing, tasty meals are available to all staff members, both resident and nonresident. Should you desire to purchase your meals at the center, a charge of $0.— per meal will be deducted from your salary in accordance with the state labor regulations, effective January, 19—. If you prefer to bring in your own sandwich, coffee is available free of charge in our staff dining room, where a soft drink machine is also located.

When you finish your meals, please take your tray to the kitchen and leave the dining area tidy. Meal periods are half an hour; coffee breaks are 15 minutes.

Resident Staff

When you are a member of the resident staff, we want you to feel that the nursing center is your home. We hope that you will guide yourself accordingly and keep your living quarters neat and orderly. A charge of $0.— per day is deducted from your salary if you desire to live in, in accordance with the state labor regulations effective January, 19—.

HANDLE WITH CARE

Care of Equipment

Economical use of supplies, careful handling and use of equipment, and alertness to prevent loss or damage will enable the nursing center to utilize the savings for improvements which will benefit everyone. Faulty equipment should be reported at once to your department head.

PERSONAL MATTERS

Professional Behavior

Please refer families and interested friends to the charge nurse when they ask you about the patients' condition. Refrain from engaging in discussions with visitors about the patients—always refer visitors and comments to the charge nurse.

Fig. 1-6 (Continued)

Uniforms

Name pins are obtained free of charge from your charge nurse or supervisor and should be worn at all times while on duty.

The professional nursing uniform includes white stockings and shoes, school cap, and pin. The nonprofessional female uniform is white stockings and shoes, nonsheer white uniforms and, for dietary personnel, hair nets. Male nursing and dietary departments personnel wear white pants and shirt and black shoes. Male housekeeping personnel wear khaki slacks and shirts.

For your own morale, as well as the morale of patients and the facility, please have your uniform immaculate at all times.

Lockers

Lockers are issued by department heads. Male and female locker rooms with showers are located on the ground floor. Keys must be returned prior to receiving your final paycheck should your employment terminate.

Smoking

Please smoke only in the staff dining room. Be sure that your cigarette is out when you leave. Smoking by staff members is not permitted anywhere else on the premises, including patients' rooms, corridors, stairways, laundry, and storerooms. These regulations were deemed necessary by the fire department.

Personal Phone Calls

Please use the public phone provided for your personal telephone calls, and ask your friends and family not to call you at work except in an emergency. Nursing center lines must be kept clear for urgent and emergency calls.

Solicitors

The presence of unauthorized strangers or persons on the premises for the purpose of solicitation is not permitted and should be reported to your department head or the administrative director immediately.

FOR PERFECT HARMONY

Staff Meetings

All personnel are required to attend staff training sessions and meetings for our mutual benefit. As decided by the personnel committee, attendance at these training sessions will be one of the factors used in determining annual salary increments.

Fig. 1-6 (Continued)

PERSONNEL COMMITTEE

For the purpose of discussing matters of interest to the staff and the center, a personnel committee composed of representatives of each nursing shift and of each department and special services meets monthly, or as often as required, with the administrative director. Members of the committee will keep you informed of their activities and will ask your opinion and decisions on various subjects, to report back to the meetings.

COMMUNICATION LINES

Newsletter

"Center Talk" is a monthly newsletter issued for patients, families, and staff. Copies are placed at the following locations: the nursing stations, the staff dining room, and the counter of the recreation room opposite the elevator. Please feel free to pick up a copy at your convenience and keep it to read carefully for information on current happenings, programs, and news. All contributions of news items as well as original poetry, stories, and articles will be welcomed by the editor.

Bulletin Board

In addition to the center's newsletter, personnel are kept informed about activities and events by notices posted on bulletin boards located at the first floor elevator, as well as at nursing stations, in the administrative office, and in the staff dining room. Make a point of studying these bulletin boards frequently.

Suggestions, Please

If you have a personal problem or a complaint, grievance, suggestion, or comment, we are always ready to discuss it with you. This "open door" policy is important because we know that the spirit of service on which we pride ourselves can continue only as long as confidence and freedom of discussion prevail. Don't let problems grow and multiply. They will be listened to sympathetically and in confidence.

We welcome your suggestions for improvement of patient care, for reduction of expense, time savers, and ways to increase job satisfaction. Your suggestions can be of value to us.

TERMINATION OF EMPLOYMENT

Resignations

Two weeks' notice is required when you intend to leave the employ of the nursing center in order to receive your final paycheck on your last day of

Fig. 1-6 (Continued)

work. Otherwise, your final paycheck will be available to you at the next regular payroll period. Locker key and name pin must be returned before leaving.

Dismissal

Termination of employment is at the discretion of the employer and is automatic and immediate should you mistreat a patient in any way, walk off the job, or refuse a duty specified in your job description. After the 3-month introductory period, you will be given a 2-week notification of dismissal. Or a 2-week pay period in lieu of the 2-week notification may be given by the employer.

PLAY IT SAFE

Safety and Fire Protection

Safety meetings with instruction on proper use of equipment, followed by a written quiz, are held quarterly. Safe working conditions and safe practices in performing duties are of prime importance to all personnel. If you notice any condition that seems questionable or dangerous, you should report it immediately to your department head who will contact the maintenance director in an emergency, or leave a written report on his clipboard in the administrative office. Any suggestions you may have for improvement of safety rules or regulations will be welcomed.

Be sure to know the location of the nearest alarm box, fire extinguisher, and exit, and study the evacuation plan posted on the bulletin boards at both nursing stations. Fire drills are held regularly on each of the three shifts.

OUR REAL PURPOSE

Finally, we want to remind you once again that first, last, and always the objective of this extended care facility is to furnish the finest available treatment and care for our patients.

Your courtesy, tact, and sympathy are of prime importance in our achieving this goal. If throughout the day you approach patients, families, and your coworkers with cheerfulness and kindness, we will be doubly assured of success.

b. Job descriptions should be prepared by department heads after consultation with staff and should be approved by the administrative director and kept up to date by periodic review.

3. Personnel should be assigned to one department only and should not be shared by two or more departments such as Nursing and Housekeeping.

4. All department heads and supervisors should keep lists of names, addresses, and telephone numbers of key personnel at their homes for speedy communication in case of emergency.
5. Parties (departmental) should be cleared in advance with the administrative director and planned in accordance with the needs of the patients and the facility.
6. In addition to the traditional garb worn by nursing, medical, dietary, housekeeping, and maintenance personnel in a health care setting, other staff including social workers, health-record librarians, physical, occupational, and speech therapists should be encouraged to present a professional demeanor by wearing their own white coats or jackets. The recreation staff should don brightly colored smocks and the administrative staff identifying coats or jackets. Volunteers should wear pink, and candy stripers, pink and white striped pinafores. All personnel should be required to launder their own uniforms and to wear name pins at all times.

III. GENERAL PATIENT PROGRAM

A. Recreational Activities. The program of social rehabilitation for patients in an extended care facility should include an active recreation program to take place during both the morning and afternoon, and occasionally during the evening, under the supervision of the director of recreation and volunteers.

B. Religious Programs. The religious needs of the patient population should be served regularly by the neighborhood organizations of the three major denominations: Catholic, Jewish, and Protestant with weekly services conducted at the institution by:

1. The same clerical representative of each church on an ongoing basis to encourage the development of personal relationships between the particular minister and members of his faith (Fig. 1-7)
2. Clerical representatives of all the churches and synagogues in the community on a scheduled basis to provide for a broader representation of ministers without, however, the possibility of engendering a close involvement between minister and patient

C. Visitors. In order to allow sufficient time for nursing care, restorative services, and therapeutic recreation, definite visiting hours with a degree of flexibility should be established:

1. From 2:00 to 4:30 daily except Monday
2. Monday to be reserved for staff in-service training programs
3. Visiting at other hours to be permitted by special arrangement
4. Visiting of critically ill patients to be permitted at all times

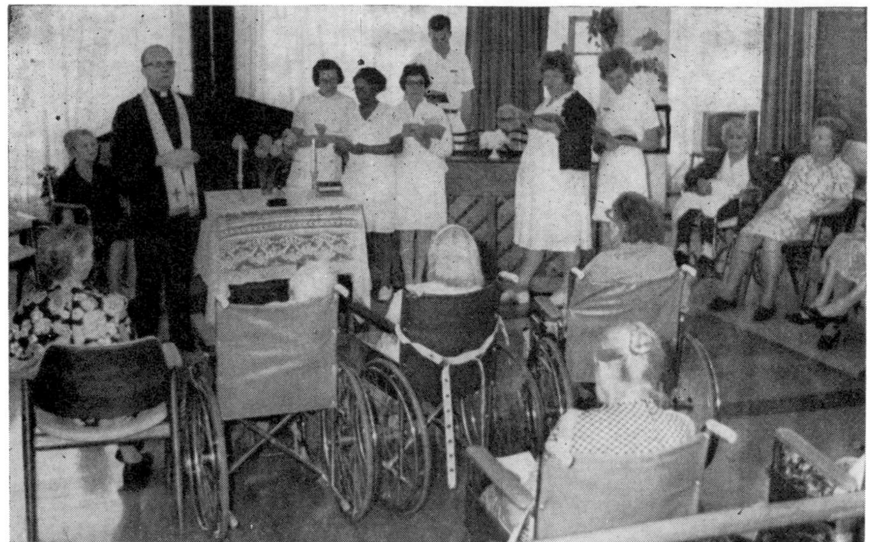

Fig. 1-7. A staff choir enhances the weekly religious services.

D. Outings. Written permission by the attending physicians should be obtained before patients are allowed to leave the premises alone or with responsible family members, authorized friends, or staff members, and the following procedures should be employed:

1. The time of departure and expected return as well as the signature of the person accompanying the patient and a notation of his relationship to the patient should be noted in a "Patient Outing Book" maintained at each nursing unit.

2. Should a patient join an outing directed by the Recreation Department, a release of responsibility form (Fig. 1-8) should be signed by the responsible family member or authorized friend.

E. Dining Arrangements. In a well-organized extended care facility, dining arrangements should vary according to the different needs of the patients:

1. Severely handicapped patients in the concentrated care units should be seated and served at tables in their rooms, not at overbed tables in their beds unless the patient is truly bedfast.

2. Patients in other units should be encouraged to dine in community or dining areas at tables accommodating four to encourage maximum sociability (Fig. 1-9).

IV. ADDITIONAL SERVICES (WITHIN THE FACILITY)

To implement the total program of the extended care facility, the following individuals should be included on the staff in addition to the depart-

Fig. 1-8

RELEASE OF RESPONSIBILITY FORM

I, the undersigned, do hereby authorize the ____________________ extended care facility, located at ____________________, to permit my mother/father, or ____________________, (name of patient)____________________ a patient at the extended care institution, to leave the facility under the supervision of a member of the nursing center staff. I relieve the extended care facility of any and all responsibility should accident or injury occur to my mother/father, or ____________________ while off the premises, as well as any and all responsibility from any adverse situation occurring as a result of this procedure.

____
Signature of Responsible Family Member

____
Date

ments described in the organizational structure section under management:

A. Receptionists. In order to cover the main entrance 7 days a week, two receptionists should be engaged, each to work a 5-day schedule, with the 3 overlapping days to be utilized for taking dictation by one receptionist while the responsibilities of the second receptionist assigned to the front entrance should include the following:

1. Greeting and offering necessary assistance and information to visitors of patients by referring to a file box containing names and assigned rooms of patients (Fig. 1-10)
2. Daily verification with Social Service and the health-records librarian to determine the names of discharged patients and the room assignments of newly admitted patients to maintain accurate information in the file box
3. Announcement over the intercom or by means of the public address system of all visitors to the staff

4. Helping to safeguard patients by preventing them from wandering through the front door
5. Informing the nearest staff member in the event of a patient accident or emergency
6. Unless a switchboard operator is maintained, the handling of incoming telephone calls for the staff to be announced by the telephone intercom or the public address system and, if the staff member cannot be located, a note, including the date, the time, the name of the caller, the message, the telephone number of the caller, and the initials of the receptionist to be placed on the appropriate clipboard or in the proper message box
7. Supervision of the showcase of gift items to sell to patients and visitors, located near the main entrance (This may be a project for a local philanthropic organization to develop.)
8. During large mailings, collating, addressing, folding, enclosing, sealing, and stamping the envelopes of materials like bulletins, newsletters, and announcements

Fig. 1-9. Community dining is part of the process of social rehabilitation.

Fig. 1-10. The receptionist assists visitors and safeguards confused patients.

B. Secretary. The secretary should work closely with the staff writer and the receptionist and should be responsible for:

1. Typing of letters, articles, manuals, and minutes

2. Duplicating of material to be reproduced on the premises

3. Distribution of mail to patients, staff, and administration

4. Relieving the receptionist at her post during her luncheon period and coffee breaks

5. Typing of medical records, dictated by the attending and consulting physicians (in a facility where this service is provided)

C. Staff Writer. The staff writer should concentrate on:

1. The development of a close working relationship with all local news media

2. Bringing information to inpatients, discharged patients, staff, families, and the general and professional community and establishing effective communication among these groups (Fig. 1-11)
3. The preparation of newsletters, bulletins, publicity releases, special announcements, and articles (Fig. 1-12)
4. The arrangement of photography for publicity purposes remembering that articles and photographs of patients to be published must be

Fig. 1-11. A program flyer is sent to discharged patients.

SENIOR CITIZEN ALUMNI OF THE EXTENDED CARE FACILITY

A Program of More Than Usual Interest
Is Coming to
the Nursing Center

MRS. JOHN JONES,
a member of the Peace Corps,
will show color slides
on West Africa

Be sure to come and learn about
this important and fascinating area
as well as to visit with your old
friends.

Thursday, April 6
from 2 to 4 P.M.

at

The Extended Care Institution

It's another Thursday social afternoon for discharged senior
citizen patients

Sponsored by the Extended Care Facility

Fig. 1-12. A press release should follow this general format.

FROM: The Extended Care Facility

Address

WRITTEN BY:

FOR IMMEDIATE RELEASE

SENIOR CITIZEN HONORED AT NURSING CENTER

SENIOR CITIZENS MONTH was launched by an open house on Sunday afternoon, May 1, at the extended care facility of ________.

The program included chamber music by members of the Community Symphony Orchestra, Inc., an address by City Councilman Joe Miller, and the second annual presentation of a citation to an outstanding senior citizen.

Honored was Mrs. Jennie Brown, active volunteer at the extended care facility and professional musician and singer. The open house was attended by 85 visitors.

Pictured are, left to right, Commissioner of Recreation John Smith, Miss Marian Jones, associate minister of the Community Church and last year's award winner, Mrs. Brown, and Mr. Miller.

accompanied by a signed release from the patient and/or family with a copy maintained in the patient's file (Fig. 1-13)

5. The supervision of all general mailings

6. Maintenance of minutes of the interdisciplinary conferences

7. The compilation and keeping current of a variety of manuals and handbooks

8. The writing and circulation to former patients, board members, financial contributors, medical staff, volunteers, personnel, and professional and lay members of the community of the annual report presenting the vital statistics of the year's operation

Fig. 1-13

RELEASE FORM FOR USING PHOTOGRAPHS OF PATIENTS

I, the undersigned, do hereby give permission to the Extended Care Facility of ______________________________ to include myself or my mother/father, ______________________________, a patient at the Extended Care Facility, in photographs taken at the nursing center. It is understood that these photographs may be used to illustrate articles in public and private media relating to nursing center activities.

____
Signature of Patient or Responsible Family Member

____
Date

RELEASE FORM FOR USING PATIENTS' NAMES IN NEWS RELEASES

I, the undersigned, do hereby give permission to the Extended Care Facility of ______________________________ to include my name or the name of my mother/father, ______________________________, a patient at the nursing center, in news releases concerning the facility and its patient activities.

____
Signature of Patient or Responsible Family Member

____
Date

V. SPECIAL SERVICES (BROUGHT INTO THE FACILITY)

A. Direct Services to Patients. In addition to the professional rehabilitation services provided for patients by staff and therapists, the following services should be made available on a regularly scheduled basis:

1. Podiatric Care. A podiatrist should visit the institution periodically to treat patients upon written orders by physicians and written approval by patients and/or sponsors.

2. Beautician or Barber. The use and frequency of the services of a beautician and a barber should be approved in writing by the family and/or sponsor of the patient.

B. Consultative Services to the Institution. To perform effectively a complex organization like an extended care facility in addition to full-time staff will require the services of professional consultants in a number of areas, either for long- or short-term periods of time.

1. On a continuing basis, the following professional persons should be appointed as consultants in their respective fields:

- *a.* A certified public accountant
- *b.* An attorney
- *c.* An interior designer
- *d.* A safety expert
- *e.* A pharmacist

2. For special situations where an objective point of view should prove useful, the following persons may be employed on a short-term basis:

- *a.* A systems expert
- *b.* A nurse
- *c.* A physician
- *d.* An architect
- *e.* A computer specialist

3. Consultants may be selected by:

- *a.* Reputation
- *b.* Written material
- *c.* Personal interview

4. Consultative services may be required to:

- *a.* Assist the governing body in the development of future plans
- *b.* Effect a higher level of performance in a particular department
- *c.* Determine unmet needs with respect to the purchase of costly equipment
- *d.* Offer an objective assessment concerning the abilities of particular staff members

5. In order for the consultants to function efficiently, advance planning should be done regarding:

a. The proper notification of the staff as to the constructive purposes of the consultative service to ensure:
(1) The cooperation of personnel
(2) The elimination of suspicion and hostility
(3) The availability of staff time for interviews

b. Appropriate physical facilities for the study, including:
(1) Private office space
(2) Equipment, such as a telephone, typewriter, and dictating machine

VI. COMMITTEES AND MEETINGS

A. Committees. The utilization review, the patient care policy committee, and various committees of the medical board will be described in the medical section. Other interdepartmental committees should include:

1. Pharmacy Committee. Quarterly meetings should be held by the committee to review policy and procedures related to medications used at the extended care facility, the committee to be chaired by the consultant pharmacist and members to include: the medical director, the administrative director, and the director of nursing. (A full description of the drugs and pharmaceutical policy of an extended care facility is given in Section 3.)

2. Personnel Committee. A representative of each department, each shift of the nursing staff, and of the special services should be elected to this committee, which should meet monthly with the administrative director to discuss general and interdepartmental problems with elections held periodically to enable all members of departments to have an opportunity to serve on this committee (Fig. 1-14).

3. Safety Committee. The members of this committee, chaired by the maintenance director, should be composed of all department heads and the medical and administrative directors, meeting monthly to develop and implement a coordinated safety program throughout the institution. (The safety program will be discussed in greater detail in section 9.)

4. Joint Conference Committee. Matters of mutual and general interest should be discussed by this intrainstitutional committee meeting prior to the monthly governing board meeting, comprising representatives of the medical staff and the governing board with the president of the board acting as chairman and the administrative director a member ex officio.

Fig. 1-14. The personnel committee meets regularly.

B. Meetings

1. General Staff. Just after the monthly personnel committee meeting, a meeting for the entire staff of the facility should be held.
2. Department Heads. Once a week a meeting of department heads, chaired by the administrative director, should be held to discuss general and interdepartmental problems.
3. Interdisciplinary Clinical Conference. The medical director should chair a weekly multidiscipline meeting attended by the social work consultants, the administrative director, the heads of all departments, and students, with other staff members present by invitation. (A full description of this conference is given in section 4.)
4. Annual Meeting. This meeting of the governing body (and where appropriate members of the corporation) may be opened to interested members of the lay and profesional community to stimulate involvement in the extended care facility.

VII. COMMUNICATIONS

Various types of communications are advisable for the extended care facility to reach staff, patients, visitors, families, and the professional and lay public.

Fig. 1-15. The public address system is used to announce a fire drill.

A. Intercoms. The intercom instrument should be used:

1. To announce incoming telephone calls to staff members in their offices

2. To hold individual and group conferences by staff

3. By visitors to announce themselves to the main nursing station after hours when the receptionist is no longer on duty

B. Public Address System. A public address system with microphones located at the administration and business offices, at the reception desk, and at the nurses' stations should be used to:

1. Announce telephone calls and visitors to staff members not in their offices

2. Contact visitors and visiting attending physicians

3. Give directions during fire drills and emergency situations (Fig. 1-15)

4. Attach to a record player or tape recorder for dissemination of special entertainment material during the holiday season to the entire population of the building

5. Announce recreational activities

C. Telephones

1. In the absence of a switchboard, separate telephone lines should be installed for the nursing units and for the other departments in the extended care institution in order that:

a. Physicians may speak directly to the charge nurses
b. Families may speak to their relatives by portable telephones transported by nursing staff to patient bedrooms or recreation areas

2. Incoming staff calls should be announced by using the intercom or the public address system and if the person should be unavailable, a message should be taken, including the name, date, time, and telephone number of the caller, and together with the content of the message and the initials of the person taking the message, this should be placed on the appropriate clipboard or message box.

3. A public telephone should be installed at wheelchair height for the patients' convenience in making outgoing calls (Fig. 1-16).

4. Outgoing personal calls by staff members should be made at public telephones convenient to their departments.

D. Nurses' Call System. Several types of communication between patients' bedrooms, lavatories, and bathing areas and the nursing stations may be considered for use in an extended care institution:

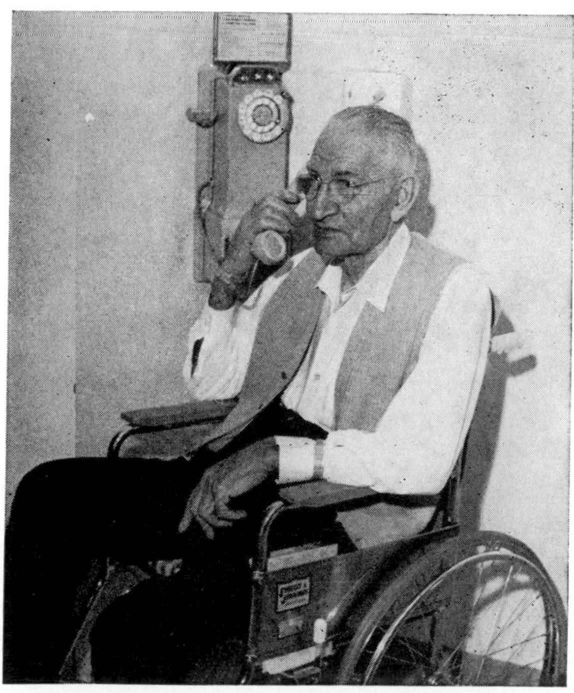

Fig. 1-16. A wheelchair-height public telephone allows disabled patients to make their own calls.

1. Closed-circuit television for rapid viewing of patients and their conditions
2. An audiovisual system where intellectually intact patients and nurses can converse with each other
3. An audiovisual call system for nurses without the above-described conversational factor, to enable intellectually impaired patients to be viewed personally by the nursing staff

E. Clipboards or Message Boxes. All messages for department heads and key administrative personnel should be placed on individually labeled clipboards or in individually labeled message boxes located at the receptionist's desk or in the business or administrative offices (Fig. 1-17).

F. Emergency Telephone Numbers

1. The home telephone numbers of the following key staff should be available to all department heads and supervising nurses:

a. Medical director
b. Administrative director

Fig. 1-17. Department heads communicate with each other via clipboards.

c. Director of nursing
d. Pharmacist
e. Social service director
f. Dietitian
g. Recreation and volunteer director
h. Physical therapist
i. Occupational therapist
j. Speech therapist
k. Staff writer
l. Secretary
m. Housekeeper
n. Maintenance director
o. Dietary director

2. In the absence of the maintenance director and his alternate, the telephone numbers of the following services should be available to department heads and supervising nurses in an emergency:

a. Plumber
b. Television
c. Furnace and boiler
d. Oil
e. Elevator
f. Gas and electric
g. Exterminator
h. Electrician
i. Freezer
j. Fire alarm
k. Incinerator
l. Linen supply
m. Typewriters
n. Laundry repair
o. Telephone
p. Auto repair
q. Fire extinguisher
r. Soda machine
s. Window cleaner

G. Bulletin Boards. A variety of bulletin boards should be placed in selected locations of the extended care facility including:

1. Each nursing station for the use of the nursing staff
2. The staff dining room or lounge for general staff information (Fig. 1-18)
3. The main entrance area to display selected news items and patients' activities programs to be noted by visitors, patients, and staff

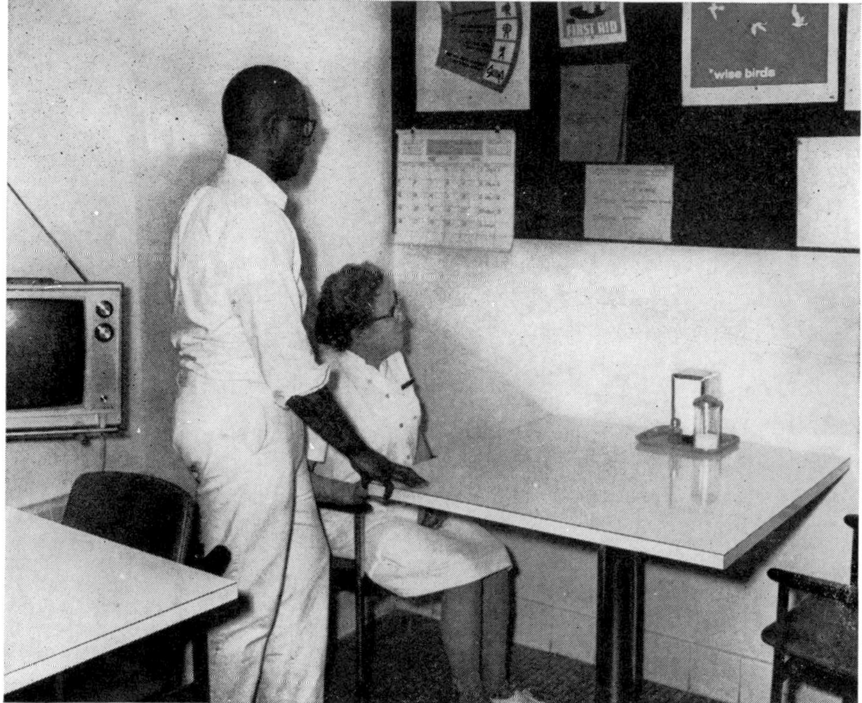

Fig. 1-18. The bulletin board in the staff cafeteria is seen by all personnel.

4. The medical director's office, the administrative director's office, and the offices of other staff members for items of specific professional interest

H. Publications. Two publications issued by the extended care institution can serve as an important form of communication for patients, families, staff, and members of the community.

1. A monthly newsletter for patients, families, staff, and members of the community

a. The staff writer should serve as editor (Fig. 1-19).

b. Contributing editors should consist of:

(1) A patient representative from each nursing unit

(2) A staff representative from each major department and each shift of the nursing staff

c. The contents of the illustrated bulletin should be designed to:

(1) Keep patients, families, and staff abreast of current and prospective program activities in the institution

(2) Exchange personal news items concerning patients, their

families, and staff members such as birthdays, anniversaries, engagements, and weddings

(3) Invite letters to the editor discussing certain topics in an attempt to develop policy decisions such as the use of first names of staff by patients and families

(4) Stimulate the use of the circulating library by including monthly book reviews

(5) Cement relationships with volunteer groups by an enthusiastic description of their activities in a special section of the bulletin each month

(6) Improve the understanding of the staff and the families of patients concerning the goals of the nursing center

d. The bulletin should be distributed to:

(1) Current patients and selected discharged patients

(2) Families of inpatients

(3) Staff members

(4) Persons mentioned in the bulletin

Fig. 1-19. The staff writer illustrates the monthly newsletter.

(5) Interested friends in the professional community

(6) Members of the communications media, particularly the editors of the local newspapers

e. The newsletter should be reproduced by the mimeograph process, illustrated and typed in capital letters with wide spacing to facilitate being read by patients with visual disabilities.

2. A bulletin for the professional community

a. The staff writer should act as the coordinator.

b. Contributing editors should consist of members of the program staff of the extended care facility including such professionals as physicians, social workers, nurses, physical, occupational, and speech therapists, ministers, recreation workers, and executive administrative personnel.

c. Contents of the professional bulletin should be designed to acquaint the professional community with:

(1) Newer trends in extended care

(2) Results of studies in the extended care facility

(3) Annual summaries of articles written by the staff and published in professional journals

d. The professional bulletin should be distributed to:

(1) Professionals in related disciplines in the community of the extended care facility

(2) Professional persons involved in health care problems on an organizational and national level

(3) Representatives of selected government agencies

(4) Legislators on a local, state, and national level

e. The professional bulletin should be reproduced by the mimeograph or printing process, depending on the size and cost of production.

I. Professional Articles

1. Articles and papers on aspects of patient care and rehabilitation, on social work, and on the administration of the extended care facility should be written regularly by staff members for publication in professional journals.

2. Reprints of these articles should be ordered at the time of the submission of the corrected galley proofs.

3. These articles should be summarized for inclusion in the annual issue of the professional publication of the extended care institution devoted to this purpose.

J. Releases to the Communications Media

1. Newsworthy information should be communicated to the news media by one authorized person:

a. The staff writer when employed

b. The administrative director or another staff member to whom the responsibility has been delegated

2. All releases should have the prior approval of the administrative director.

3. Material of interest to the communications media could include news:

a. Concerning patients
(1) Unusual backgrounds of patients
(2) Special events such as the wedding of elderly patients
(3) Newly discovered talents

b. About the program of the institution
(1) Special entertainers
(2) Prominent visitors
(3) Additional services to be provided
(4) Volunteer awards
(5) Annual or special meetings
(6) Purchase of unusual new equipment
(7) Building plans
(8) Fund-raising drive

c. Of the medical staff, governing body, and personnel
(1) Appointments to the medical staff and governing board
(2) Committee appointments of medical staff and board
(3) Announcement of new personnel in key posts
(4) Employee awards
(5) Special citations

d. Concerning research and education
(1) Reports of research projects and studies
(2) Grants received for purposes of research and education
(3) The selection of student trainees from universities and hospitals
(4) Field trips by student groups

K. Duplication. All material to be duplicated and distributed or mailed should be approved by the administrative director to ensure uniformity and appropriateness of content.

1. For large quantities duplication should be done by printing or mimeographing.

2. Photocopying should be used for small quantities.

L. Monthly Reports. Each department head should submit a monthly report to the medical and administrative directors, which should include a compilation of statistical data, activities, material relating to staff, plant, equipment, or expenditures, with specific emphasis on exceptions to normal operating procedures and suggestions for improvements.

M. Minutes of Meetings. Minutes of all meetings should be kept in a loose-leaf notebook in the administration office and should include the date, the time that the meeting began and ended, the attendance roster, the chairman, and signature of the designated recorder, and all pertinent discussion.

N. Repairs. All needed repairs should be reported in writing to the maintenance director via his clipboard except in cases of emergency, when they should be reported to him directly by the appropriate department head.

O. Mail. Incoming mail should be received and distributed by the secretary and outgoing mail processed in the business office, where a postage meter should be employed.

VIII. COMMUNITY RELATIONS

A. Community relationships can be developed on an individual, group, or agency basis.

1. An extended care facility's administrators and department heads should engage in seminars, conferences, and meetings with related professional and community groups.

2. In addition, transfer agreements with area hospitals, cooperative programs with the public library, the local recreation and parks department, and other community institutions and agencies should be maintained to provide services for patients, for the aged in the nearby community, for staff, and for student groups.

3. Key personnel should be encouraged to enlarge the public image of extended care facilities by giving talks to community organizations.

B. Communications with various communities might be encouraged by visits to the facility of:

1. The Lay Community. In addition to serving its patients and their families, the extended care facility has a vital interest in, and responsibility to, the community and should strive to increase public knowledge and understanding of the aged ill by regularly opening its doors to the lay community, with daily general visiting hours and special visits arranged for civic and cultural groups and local organizations encouraged to utilize the facility's community rooms for their meetings and conferences (Fig. 1-20).

2. The Professional Community

Fig. 1-20. Family and friends should be encouraged to visit the extended care facility.

a. Governmental representatives of city, state, county, and federal agencies should be asked for their credentials and should be referred to the administrative director unless prior arrangements have been made for them to visit specific departments. Upon completion of their survey, they should be asked to sign their names, titles, and dates of visits in a notebook labeled "Records of Inspections," kept in the administration office.

b. Social agencies and professional persons who visit should have either prearranged appointments with the administrative director or a particular department head, or should have permission to have a guided tour of the facility from the administrative director.

c. Educational programs for professional and special groups should be sponsored by the extended care facility several times a year and should be specifically designed to increase knowledge of the opportunities, problems, and new developments in the field of caring for the aged (Fig. 1-21).

d. Groups of students engaged in nursing, recreation, administration, and social work training should be encouraged to make field trips to the extended care facility, where the program should include (Fig. 1-22):

Fig. 1-21. A seminar in social work and chronic disease is held on the premises of the extended care institution.

Fig. 1-22. Students and their teacher on a field trip to the extended care institution.

(1) A guided tour of the facility

(2) Discussions with heads of various departments using guidelines for field trip programs for visiting students (Fig. 1-23)

(3) A record of visiting groups in a loose-leaf notebook labeled "Visiting Groups," kept in the administration office

3. Prospective Families and Friends

a. Families or interested friends inquiring about placement of patients should be directed to the Social Service Department where, if possible, prior appointments should be made with the social service director in order to receive professional guidance and direction.

b. In the absence of the social service director, the administrative director, or the director of nursing, unannounced visitors should be asked to leave identifying material to enable the social service director or other appropriate staff member to contact them.

c. Charge nurses should be directed not to give guided tours to visitors, as their responsibility should relate only to the care of patients.

d. Visitors should not be permitted to inspect the facilities unless accompanied by an appropriate staff representative.

Fig. 1-23

GUIDELINES FOR STUDENT FIELD TRIP PROGRAMS TO THE EXTENDED CARE FACILITY

I. Introduction to the Nursing Center
  A. External environment
    1. Advantages of urban site
      a. Proximity to hospitals
      b. Proximity to professional offices
      c. Proximity to community activities, e.g., shopping, churches, and movies
    2. Disadvantages of urban site
      a. External environment limited
      b. Difficulty in parking
  B. Internal environment
    1. Levels of care—groupings of patients
    2. Location of nurses' station—controls and supervision
    3. Therapeutic community groupings, including special dining arrangements
    4. Recreation rooms, religious services, physical therapy, occupational therapy, recreation
    5. Special features—toilets, bathing areas, hardware

Fig. 1-23 (Continued)

C. Facts regarding the institution
  1. Number of patients
  2. Source of patients:
    a. Geographical
    b. Type of facility—hospital, home, other facility
  3. Ratio of females to males
  4. Average residency
  5. Major goal is to help patients function at a maximal level commensurate with their ability to perform

II. Tour of Facility in Small Groups—On-the-Spot Explanation of Correlation Between Architectural Design and Patient Care

III. Return to Recreation Room for Discussion
  A. Description of social work program—director of social service
  B. Physical and occupational therapy with case presentation—physical therapist or occupational therapist
  C. Recreation program—Introduction of director of recreation and volunteers; description of activities program by two patients
  D. Speech therapy—speech therapist
  E. Nursing program: assistant director of nursing in charge of education
    1. Difference between nursing in general hospital and in an extended care facility
    2. Difference between nursing in a rehabilitation center and in an extended care facility
    3. Nature of patient population
    4. Distribution of outline and observations on nursing techniques and review of high points

IV. Distribution of the following material:
  A. Professional publication
  B. Recent copy of newsletter
  C. Reprints of articles by staff members in professional publications

IX. EDUCATION

A. Staff

1. In-service Training Program. The entire nursing staff should meet weekly for an in-service training program conducted by the medical director. (For more information, see Section 3.)

2. Courses, Seminars, and Meetings. Staff members should be encouraged to take courses and participate in educational activities related to their work so that they can improve their skills and keep abreast of new developments in their fields. These may be held in the community, in the area, and sometimes in other sections of the country, each department head being permitted at least one trip annually to attend an educational seminar or conference outside the home area, after appropriate clearance with the administrative director to ensure that no more than two key people will be absent simultaneously.

3. Libraries

a. Books and periodicals dealing with phases of operating an extended care institution should be maintained in a variety of convenient locations, and staff members should be encouraged to keep themselves informed on new developments and efficient practices and methods by making regular use of this material including the following periodicals: *Aging* (monthly publication of the Department of Health, Education and Welfare),

Journal of the Geriatrics Society, The Gerontologist, Hospitals, Modern Hospital, Nursing Homes, Modern Nursing Home, Professional Nursing Home, Parks and Recreation, Geriatric Nursing, Therapeutic Recreation, Institutions, Health Services Research.

b. Reading material should be readily available to patients, newspapers and periodicals being kept on a table or counter in the recreation rooms, and a bookmobile stocked with books regularly loaned to the facility by the public library, circulated several times a week. (A full description of such a bookmobile can be found in Section 6.)

B. Students

1. Administrative Resident. Residency training should be afforded by the extended care facility to a full-time graduate student in health care administration with satisfactory 12-months' residency to be completed by the student before he is admitted to master's degree candidacy in health care administration.

a. Purposes. The administrative residency should provide a student with a first-hand familiarity with the administrative operations of a representative health care institution and should be designed to give each student an opportunity to receive personal coaching and guidance from a well-qualified health care administrator, to apply and test administrative theory in practical work situations, and to develop ability to assume major administrative responsibility in a health care institution.

b. Procedures. The student could rotate and could be assigned projects among the various departments of the facility to familiarize him with the operations of each; he could attend administrative meetings, prepare monthly reports on his educational experiences and on the articles or books read and visits made to related community facilities, all to be done under the personal supervision of the preceptor.

c. Evaluation. A minimum of one site visit should be made during the residency year by a representative of the graduate programs in health care administration of the participating university; semester progress reports and a final evaluation and recommendations should be made by the preceptor, indicating whether the resident is ready for employment or whether additional training is required.

2. Social Work Students. The extended care facility should be utilized as a training center for students in the social and behavioral sciences, and the director of social service with the approval of the administration should be authorized to enter into agreements with colleges and universities for student field-work placement at the facility. (A full description of this student activity is included in Section 4.)

X. SECURITY PROGRAM

A. Emergencies

1. To review disaster plans and instruct new staff members, monthly fire drills and safety demonstrations should be conducted for the staff on different shifts by the director of maintenance, or other appointed staff member, together with the fire prevention and safety consultant, to ensure that every staff member will be educated to take action quickly and calmly to assure patient safety in an emergency. (The safety program will be described in detail in Section 9.)

2. Each staff member should be given an emergency plan handbook listing fire prevention rules, location of alarm boxes, types and locations of fire extinguishers and exits, procedures for patient evacuation, and responsibilities of the fire brigade and the on-duty personnel.

3. In case of fire, explosion or other disaster a written emergency plan should be followed by all staff members and should be developed for the extended care facility in cooperation with the local fire department and a safety and fire prevention consultant as follows:

4. At each nursing of staff bulletin board, a utility interruption and a floor plan showing the location of nearest exits, fire alarms, and extinguishers should be posted for easy reference and study by the staff.

B. Grounds and Building Security. To assure adequate protection of the persons and property of patients, the following security provisions should be made:

1. A receptionist should be on daily duty at the main entrance.

Fig. 1-24

DO YOUR PART

Naturally, no sane person enjoys a fire or explosion any place. But when a fire or other such emergency takes place in an extended care facility the seriousness of the situation is multiplied. Every staff member must keep in mind that the nursing center bears an enormous responsibility for the safety of over 60 aged, sick men and women. These helpless patients *depend* upon you and your coworkers for guidance and protection in case of fire or any other type of emergency.

Be sure that you know your P's (for prevention) and Q's (for quick action) so that you can do your part to prevent an emergency from becoming a disaster!

SAFETY FIRST IS THE RULE

A complete nursing center fire-safety program has four major parts:

1. An effective, continuing fire-prevention program
2. A speedy fire-alerting system
3. An efficient fire-control plan
4. A well-rehearsed method of evacuation

1. PREVENTION IS THE BEST POLICY

Primary aim of the entire staff must be to prevent fire from occurring. Here are 10 important prevention rules to follow:

No Smoking, Please

Where there's smoke, there's too often fire. The smoking regulations must be strictly observed, and staff members may not smoke in patient rooms, corridors, stairways, laundry rooms, or storerooms. Smoking is permitted *only* in the staff dining room.

Bug Those Litterbugs

Never drop, or permit to be dropped by patients or visitors, butts or matches in wastebaskets or on the floors. Ash trays or receptacles must always be used.

Tell-tale Smoke Signals

Personnel must report evidence of unauthorized smoking to the charge nurse. Such evidence might be matches or butts on the floor or burned wastebasket liners.

Fig. 1-24 (Continued)

Don't Be Slop-happy

Be a good housekeeper. Don't allow trash, papers, or dirt to accumulate anywhere in the facility to breed fire.

Keep the Shaft Clear

The elevator shaft is not a trash depository. Don't misuse it for throwing matches, butts, or trash.

Play It Safe

Such potential fire-starters as rags and matches must always be stored in covered metal containers.

Why Be a Handy Andy?

Well-meaning do-it-yourself repairs of cords, plugs, and appliances spell *danger.* So report all defective wiring or equipment to maintenance director promptly.

Also

Keep all stairwell doors closed at all times. Know your assignment in the event of fire.

Respond to the fire alarm quickly!

2. BE ON THE ALERT

Be a Star Reporter

This is one time when haste does *not* make waste! Should you discover a fire, no matter how small, immediately sound the alarm located on the floor of the fire. Any person discovering a fire is authorized to sound the alarm. Remember, visible smoke or flames may only be an external sign of a much larger hidden smoldering fire ready to burst into intense flames. So don't waste a minute—act quickly!

LOCATION OF FIRE ALARM BOXES

(All fire alarms are connected directly to the fire department)

Basement

At left side of elevator (facing elevator)

First Floor

a. Around the corner from the reception desk
b. End of hall at right of supply room door

Fig. 1-24 (Continued)

Second Floor

a. On hall wall between community room 1 and room 201
b. On wall to left of exit door in community room 2

"Musts" for All Employees

Learn the exact location of fire alarm boxes, fire exits, and fire extinguishers in your own working area.

Know how to operate fire alarm boxes and extinguishers.

Special to Supervisors

When fire is detected, the supervisor or person in charge of that particular area uses the public address system to summon male personnel to the scene, as follows:

"Attention all male personnel! Respond to (location of fire) with proper equipment. All other personnel clear corridors and close all doors and windows immediately."

Play it Cool

No personnel except supervisors are to use the public address system for any mention of fire. Such action might well result in panic on the part of patients and visitors. Instead, directly after sounding the alarm, inform the supervisor of the area of the exact location of the fire. Then telephone the administrative director by dialing 7 on the telephone intercom (in her absence, dial 5 for the director of nurses or the first-floor nurse, in that order). Now, in a clear, calm tone, describe the fire and its exact location.

Again, do not shout "*fire*" at any time. Be calm. Fear and panic can do more damage than the fire itself.

3. KEEP IT UNDER CONTROL

Fire drills are held once a month at the nursing center. They are planned in such a manner that there is a drill for each nursing shift at least four times a year. If every staff member is on the job and responds quickly, most fires can be extinguished before they are out of control.

Take First Steps First

Sound the alarm.

Quickly remove patients and combustible material from the area.

Turn off all ventilating fans, gas, and electrical appliances operating in the area immediately threatened by fire; also shut off oxygen tank valves.

Close all doors and windows in immediate vicinity.

Reassure patients who are aware of the fire that everything will be kept under control.

Fig. 1-24 (Continued)

Place wet blankets under closed doors if necessary to confine fire and smoke.

Keep fire doors in corridors and stairwells closed except when necessary to pass through for combating fire or evacuating patients. Be sure to close doors behind you if you must pass through.

Do not block stairways, exits, or corridors.

Do not turn off lights.

Stand by for assignment by the supervisor in the area.

Here Comes the Fire Brigade

The fire brigade consists of the following personnel:

7:00 A.M.–3:00 P.M.	Director of maintenance, who serves as chief fire marshal
	Porters
	Male kitchen personnel
	Orderlies
3:00 P.M.–11:00 P.M.	Orderly
	Porters
	All male personnel in building
11:00 P.M.–7:00 A.M.	Orderly
	All male personnel in building

It is of the utmost importance that all our personnel be *completely* familiar with the following information on fire extinguishers!

Fire Extinguishers

The fire extinguishers are all the easy-to-use trigger type. To work, simply pull the pin; then squeeze the trigger. They need not be turned upside down.

Four types of fire extinguishers are maintained on the premises:

1. Pressurized water fire extinguishers—used for fires created by paper, cloth, wood, and plastics
2. CO_2 fire extinguishers—for fires created by grease, electricity
3. Dry chemical extinguishers—used for fires created by oil, alcohol, grease, electricity, and volatile liquids
4. Foam extinguishers—used for fires created by oil

Location of Fire Extinguishers

1. Basement Hall

   One pressurized water extinguisher is on wall to left of elevator.

   One CO_2 extinguisher is on wall to left of elevator.

   One pressurized water extinguisher is in hall leading to the business office.

Fig. 1-24 (Continued)

2. Kitchen
   One dry chemical extinguisher is on right side of walk-in box.
3. Boiler Room
   One foam extinguisher is to the left of entrance.
   One dry chemical extinguisher is to right of entrance.
4. Laundry
   One dry chemical extinguisher is on wall facing basement hall door.
5. First Floor
   One pressurized water extinguisher is around the corner from the reception desk.
   One pressurized water extinguisher is on hall wall past medication room.
   One CO_2 extinguisher is at nurses' station.
6. Second Floor
   One pressurized water extinguisher is on wall opposite elevator to the right.
   One pressurized water extinguisher is at far end of hall between Community Rooms 2 and 3.
   One CO_2 extinguisher is at nurses' station.
   One CO_2 extinguisher is beneath the telephone in the x-ray room.

Facts for Fire Brigadiers

Call to Action: Though *all* personnel must cooperate in the event of fire, the fire brigade has definitely assigned duties to perform. When the alarm sounds, each member of the brigade must respond immediately by arming himself with the nearest fire extinguisher and proceeding to the scene by central stairway, guided by the area supervisor's instructions over the public address system. The assembled equipment should consist of at least two pressurized water extinguishers and one CO_2 extinguisher.

"Must-knows" for Fire Brigadiers

The proper procedure for locating the site of the fire
The location of all extinguishers in the facility
How to use each type of extinguisher
Which type of extinguisher to use on various types of fires

Respond to the scene quickly! Remember, your goal is to extinguish the fire before it becomes serious and uncontrollable.

Responsibilities of the Administration

Responsibility for overall supervision, coordination, and assignment of all personnel having no specific duties is assumed by the administrative director. In her absence, the responsibility rests with the director of nursing or, in turn, the supervising nurse. There are a number of definite steps that the administrative director or her substitute should take when fire is discovered.

Upon detection of fire, she makes sure that the fire department has been

Fig. 1-24 (Continued)

notified and that the necessary personnel have been summoned over the public address system.

She gives orders for removal of patients, if necessary.

If it is dark, she posts someone outside the building with a flashlight to direct firemen to the scene of the fire.

She assigns additional personnel as needed to assist in the removal of patients to a safety zone.

She posts guards and watchmen to keep all stairs and exits clear.

She keeps in touch with all areas, using office personnel as messengers if necessary. She issues reports to all areas as to progress of fire.

She notifies police or hospital if ambulance service is required.

If fire is minor, she reassures patients and personnel.

She cooperates with the fire chief.

4. FIRE EVACUATION PLAN

The great majority of patients require help; all are in various degrees of dependency. Thus the extended care facility differs from schools and factories, where the main objective when fire occurs is to clear the premises of all persons as quickly as possible. In the nursing center, leaving the building is the very *last* resort.

However, there is always the possibility that it may be necessary to evacuate patients and personnel, despite the fact that the building is well constructed and fire-protected. Though a situation of immediate peril will seldom occur, personnel must be familiar with procedure for direct evacuation of patients. These procedures, which are different from those recommended for other types of buildings, are described here in full detail for your benefit. Please study them carefully.

Location of Fire Exits

Basement	1. From central stairwell proceed left
	2. Main ramp is at rear service door
	3. Pass laundry room and proceed left
First Floor	1. Fire doors near rooms 107 and 108
	2. Main stairwell
	3. Front door
Second Floor	1. Community Room 2
	2. Main stairwell
	3. Stairwell by medical director's office

A plan of evacuation routes is posted at each nurses' station and on the bulletin board of the ground floor staff dining room.

Types of Evacuation

Evacuation does not necessarily mean the complete emptying of the building.

Fig. 1-24 (Continued)

There are several degrees of evacuation. The one to be used should be determined by the particular emergency.

Complete Evacuation

When the fire is of such volume that the whole building is endangered, a complete evacuation of patients from the building should be ordered, with directions given by the battalion chief or the ranking officer in charge of the fire fighting forces of the city. Complete cooperation and assistance should be given to members of the fire department. The charge nurses present should make themselves known to the ranking officer of the fire department who must know which patients need assistance in removal from the fire area or floor.

Horizontal Evacuation

1. Ambulatory patients are moved first as panic is less likely to be caused by nonambulatory people. Those who are ambulatory are instructed to line up outside their rooms, form a chain by holding hands, and follow a lead monitor into the safe area near a stairwell.
2. Next, nonambulatory patients are removed laterally by wheel stretchers, wheelchairs, blankets, or other conveyances, to the nearest and safest protected area near a stairwell. Patients in immediate danger are moved first, then others who might be subjected to danger if fire should enter their area.
3. Now, rooms and halls are searched for stragglers. All windows and doors are closed when the rooms are evacuated.
4. On arrival at a safe area, a resident count is made to make certain that no one has returned to the fire area. If refuge must be sought in a room, a window may be opened to get some fresh air, *provided the door is closed.*
5. All personnel must remain alert for further instructions during the fire emergency.

Vertical Evacuation

1. Vertical evacuation or downward movement of residents to a safe area below or out of the building may be necessary should the fire get out of control.
2. Ambulatory patients are instructed to line up, form a chain by holding hands, and follow a lead monitor into a safe area, stairway, or exit.
3. Nonambulatory patients are moved by wheel stretchers, wheelchairs, blankets or other conveyances to a safe area, stairway, or exit.

Handling of Patients

Ambulatory Patients: Ambulatory patients are gathered together and lined up first. They are wrapped in blankets and a monitor is appointed to accompany

Fig. 1-24 (Continued)

them. A fire department official directs the monitor where to take these patients if they must leave the floor. Ambulatory patients must not be left alone without guidance as they are subject to panic.

Wheelchair Patients: Wheelchairs are used to remove these patients to a safe place on the same floor. They must be wrapped in blankets before being placed in the wheelchairs. Upon reaching safety, they are removed from the wheelchairs so that this equipment may be quickly returned to remove additional patients.

Stretcher and Helpless Patients: Stretchers are used, if available, for these patients. If not, each patient is placed on a blanket on the floor. The top corners of the blanket are rolled in and the patient is pulled, head foremost, to a safe area on the same floor, near the stairwell, for evacuation to a lower floor. Actual tests have shown that quick removals by bed or mattress from a room or floor in a fire emergency are not practical, and are often impossible. Thus the blanket method is used.

Less Seriously Ill Patients: Patients not quite so ill or helpless are sometimes evacuated by various carrying methods, such as the back carry, the hip carry or the chair-seat carry. For the latter, two bearers cross hands to form a chair seat for supporting patients and carrying them to safety.

This is your own personal copy of the nursing center emergency plan.

2. Closed-circuit television and/or the use of buzzers on selected entrances and exits may also be employed.
3. After-hours visitors should announce themselves to the main nurses' station via intercom instruments, which should be placed at each entrance.
4. The parking lot should have gates that can be kept fastened to prevent patients from wandering, and lights should be clocked to turn on automatically at sundown.
5. A master key should be in the possession of the supervising nurse, and an elevator key should be kept at the main nursing station.
6. Solicitors should not be permitted on the premises.
7. A guard and/or night watchman should be employed to make regular rounds and security checks.

C. Staff and Visitor Accidents. Should a staff member or a visitor experience an accident on the premises, the director of nursing or, in her absence, the charge nurse should be notified and should offer immediate emergency treatment, or should expedite medical attention and write a report on the accident. (Further details on this procedure are given in Section 3 under Accident Procedure.)

XI. ADMINISTRATIVE RECORDS

The following administrative files and records should be kept in the administration office:

A. Loose-leaf Record Books or Files

1. Operations manual
2. Patient register
3. Patient daily census record
4. Staff schedules for past 6 months
5. Job descriptions
6. Interdisciplinary conferences
7. Health code and Conditions of Participation in Medicare
8. Utilization review and patient care policy committee minutes
9. Staff meetings
10. Staff publications
11. Community information
12. Visiting groups
13. Record of inspections
14. Fire drills
15. Monthly departmental reports

B. Bulletin Board

1. Bulletins and notices of pending meetings and conferences, etc., of health agencies
2. Licenses:
   - *a.* City license to operate extended care facility
   - *b.* State Department of Health narcotics registration number and narcotics license
   - *c.* United States Treasury Department of Internal Revenue special tax stamp for narcotics
   - *d.* State Department of Health license for maintaining depressant and stimulant drugs
   - *e.* State Health Department operating certificate
   - *f.* Department of Labor permit to pay wages by check
   - *g.* Medicare provider number

C. Patient Roster

1. Kept on the administration or admitting office wall, this roster should list, for convenient reference, patients' names, room numbers, and names of attending physicians.
2. New admissions should be indicated on the patient roster with a blue strip for male patients and a pink strip for female patients.

3. The name of the patient should be written on the appropriately colored strip, using a different color ink for a Catholic, Protestant, and Jewish patient.
4. The number corresponding to the number of the patient's physician, as listed on the roster, should be written on white magnetic squares and placed to the right of the patient's name on the roster.

XII. FINANCES

A. Budgets

1. Each department head should submit a written proposal for consideration by the administrative director before the preparation of the annual operating budget (see Section 10).
2. Department heads should stay within their budgets or should obtain prior approval for unbudgeted expenditures from the administrative director.

B. Purchasing. Purchasing should be a centralized procedure with:

1. All purchasing routed through the purchasing agent or other designated staff member via department heads
2. Each department head required to maintain and record an adequate inventory
3. The responsibility for informing the purchasing agent in sufficient time to place new orders for supplies assigned to the respective department heads
4. Purchases made in writing; when time does not permit written orders for supplies, orders to be made by telephone and immediately confirmed in writing
5. Equipment and supplies for all departments to be standardized
6. Joint purchasing among a group of health care institutions inaugurated

XIII. OPERATING INFORMATION

A. Rate Information. Complete rate information should be available in printed form in the following ways:

1. The daily rate for patient service limited to room and board, routine nursing service, and patient participation in religious services and in the regular activities of the Department of Social Service and Recreation and Volunteers, with medical care, drugs, diagnostic laboratory and x-ray services, and physical, occupational, and speech therapy not to be included in the daily charges
2. The daily charge for patient service an inclusive rate providing for total comprehensive patient care

3. A combination of the two above-mentioned methods

B. Gratuities. The extended care facility should not encourage the special treatment of patients through the practice of tipping.

1. Employees should not be permitted to accept individual presents of cash or gifts from patients or their families for services rendered.
2. A common staff fund may be instituted and the funds distributed by the personnel committee to the entire staff at Christmas time.

C. Fiscal Intermediary. For those extended care facilities participating in Title 18 of Public Law 89–97:

1. A fiscal intermediary approved by the Department of Health, Education, and Welfare may be selected by the institution to serve as the third party payor.
2. The extended care facility may elect to deal directly with the Social Security Administration with no fiscal intermediary.

D. Licensure. An extended care institution, depending on its geographical location, generally is licensed by:

1. The state department of health
2. The county or city department of health
3. The municipal department of public safety
4. Individual elements in the building such as the cafeteria, the elevators, incinerators, and the boilers require special permits for operation from any of the above-mentioned agencies.

E. Certification. A certified extended care facility is eligible to accept Medicare patients:

1. By dint of adhering to the published Conditions of Participation of the United States Department of Health, Education, and Welfare of Public Law 89–97
2. With certification usually effected by a team of professionals from the state department of health, unless the governor of the particular state should designate another agency to direct this survey program

F. Accreditation. In addition to certification for Medicare purposes, a professional medical care facility should strive to be accredited by the Joint Commission on Accreditation of Hospitals—a national member organization comprising the American College of Physicians, the American College of Surgeons, the American Hospital Association, and the American Medical Association, composed of commissioner representatives of the four above-mentioned organizations plus the American Nursing Home Association and the American Association of Homes for the Aging devoted to the standardization and elevation of patient care in hospitals and related facilities by delineating requisites in the following areas:[1]

1. Administration, including the governing body, the administrator, management practices, personnel management, and the physical plant and equipment
2. Organized medical and dental services with appropriate standards set for the regular care of the patient
3. Laboratory and radiology services with stipulated criteria for these diagnostic services
4. Relationships with hospitals with particular reference to the transfer of patients and appropriate information concerning the patients
5. Nursing services with criteria for staffing and patient care
6. Medical records and their quantity, quality, style, and confidentiality
7. Medical control with specific reference to narcotic control and storage
8. Dietary services including therapeutic diets and the proper management of the department
9. Housekeeping with special staff assigned only to this department
10. Restorative services including the equipment and professional staff to serve the physical, occupational, and speech therapy needs of the patient
11. Other patient services to provide for the social service, the recreational and spiritual drives of the patient population

G. Membership in Professional Organizations. To keep in the mainstream of development in the field:

1. The extended care facility should enjoy membership and all its ramifications in such related professional organizations as the:
   a. National Council on Aging
   b. American Hospital Association
   c. American Nursing Home Association
   d. American Association of Homes for the Aging
   e. National Safety Council
2. The professional staff of the institution should be encouraged to join and participate in the activities of organizations such as the:
   a. Geriatrics Society
   b. Gerontological Society
   c. National Association of Social Workers
   d. American Society for Hospital Social Work Directors

[1] "Standards for the Accreditation of Extended Care Facilities, Nursing Care Facilities, and Resident Care Facilities," January, 1968, Joint Commission on Accreditation of Hospitals.

e. American Nurses Association
f. American College of Nursing Home Administrators
g. American Dietetic Association
h. Association of Food Service Supervisors
i. National Recreation and Parks Association
j. American Occupational Therapy Association
k. American Physical Therapists Association
l. Association of Directors of Volunteers

Section 2

The Medical Staff and Allied Health Professionals

Introduction

Medical care is the key to all other clinical services provided by the extended care facility. Nursing, restorative services, and social work can perform only to the level of the leadership provided by medicine. To attain the goal of optimal patient function, the medical staff is obligated to serve as the coordinator of the professional persons in all disciplines. Physicians should also be expected to participate in the educational program of the institution.

Although the medical staff is the leading agent in assisting the extended care facility to achieve its objectives in patient care, it must function within the guidelines established by the governing body and in close working relationship with administration. In addition, the medical staff must review, develop, evaluate, and adhere to its own standards of practice in the extended care institution. It should engage in self-criticism, self-government, and clinical research, and should be available to offer guidance and support to the administration and to the governing board of the institution to implement improved patient care.

I. DEFINITION

The words "medical staff" should be interpreted to include all physicians and dentists who are privileged to attend patients at the extended care facility.

II. SCOPE OF RESPONSIBILITY

The medical staff should be responsible to the patient, the patient's family and/or sponsor, and the governing body for the quality of all medical care provided within the institution and for the ethical and professional practices of its members consonant with the stated principles of medical ethics of the American Medical Association.

III. PURPOSE

A. Patient Care

1. To provide regular and emergency care for all patients admitted to the extended care facility in accordance with the directives of the medical staff organization
2. To ensure that all patients admitted to the facility receive quality care, as defined by the standards for care established by the medical staff
3. To provide a vehicle for the consideration of problems of a medical-administrative nature by the medical staff

B. Medical Administrative

1. To review, develop, and evaluate the medical practices of the extended care facility
2. To provide advice and recommendations to the governing body on medical and administrative matters affecting the institution

C. Clinical Research. To administer the research in the extended care facility

D. Educational Responsibilities. To direct those educational endeavors related to patient services

IV. STAFFING PATTERN

A. Organization. This chart should serve to illustrate the organizational structure of the medical staff within the framework of the extended care facility (Fig. 2-1).

B. Qualifications of Physicians. The applicant for membership on the medical staff of the extended care institution should be:

1. A physician of good character, having graduated from an approved school of medicine and having a current unrestricted license to practice in the state where the facility is located
2. A member of the medical staff of the hospital or hospitals with which the facility enjoys a transfer agreement
3. An intern or resident in an approved training program within the extended care facility
4. A licensed resident working as house staff away from his own educational institution
5. A house staff physician who is a foreign medical school graduate properly licensed and certified to practice in the state

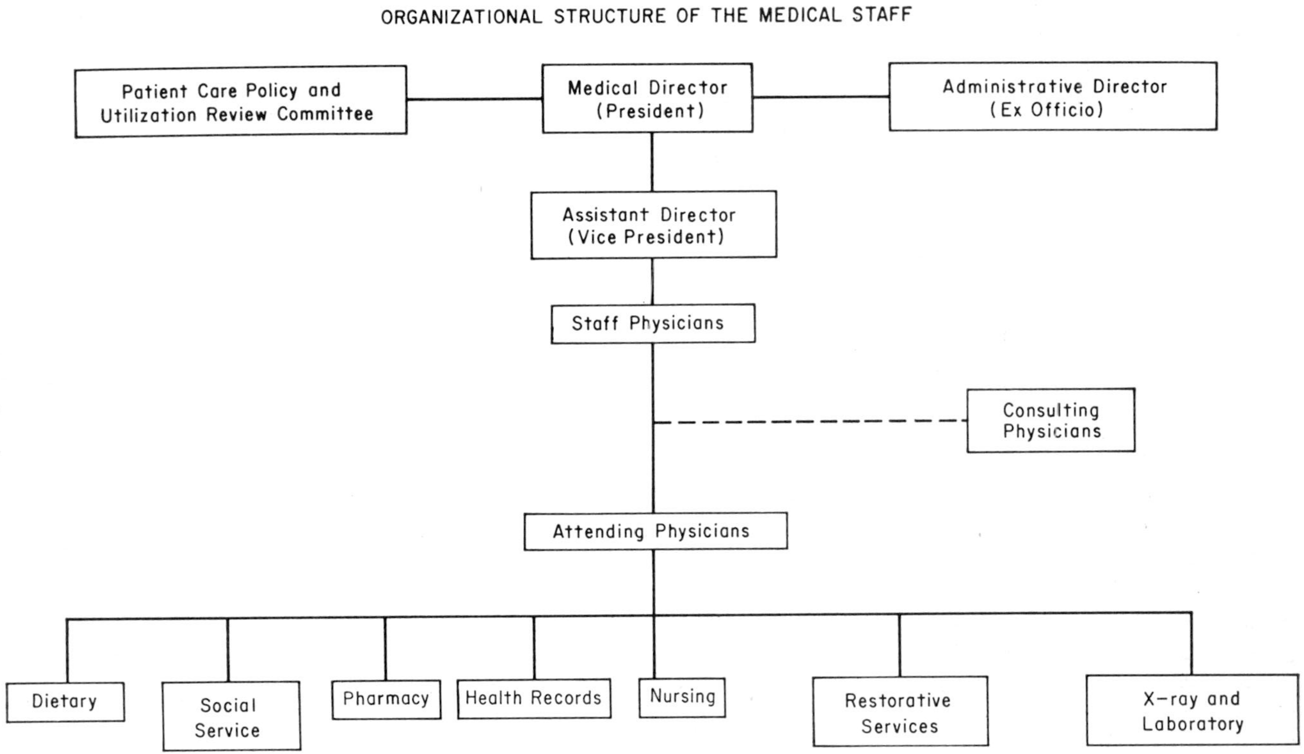

Fig. 2-1. The organizational structure of the medical staff in the extended care facility.

V. BYLAWS

A. Rules and Regulations

1. The medical staff should recommend such rules and regulations as may be necessary for the proper conduct of its work, using the "Model Medical Staff By-laws, Rules and Regulations of the Joint Commission on Accreditation of Hospitals"[1] as a guide.
2. Such rules and regulations should form part of the bylaws, except that they may be amended at any regular meeting without previous notice on motion of a two-thirds vote of the membership of the medical staff present.
3. Such amendments may be effective only after approval by the governing body.

B. Amendments

1. Bylaws may be amended after notice has been given at any regular meeting of the medical staff.
2. Such notice should be referred to the special committee which should report at the next regular meeting.
3. A two-thirds majority vote of the total membership should be required for adoption of amendments.
4. Amendments so made should be effective only after approval by the governing body.

C. Adoption

1. The bylaws, together with the appended rules and regulations, may be adopted at any regular meeting of the medical staff and should replace any previous bylaws, rules, and regulations.
2. They become operative when approved by the governing body of the institution.
3. When adopted and approved, bylaws should be equally binding on the governing body and the medical staff.

VI. ADMINISTRATION

A. Appointment of Members

1. The President
   - *a.* The president of the medical staff should be appointed by the governing body for a 3-year term of office with reappointment to be made every 3 years thereafter.
   - *b.* The 3-year term should afford an opportunity for purposeful development and organization of the medical staff.

[1] Chicago, Ill., January, 1964.

2. Other Members

a. Appointments of other members of the medical staff should be made annually by the governing body, subject to the approval of the medical staff.

b. Reappointments should be made annually thereafter at the discretion of the governing body.

3. Approval. In no case should the governing body be permitted to take action on any application or reappointment, or to alter the status of a member of the medical staff, without prior consultation with and subsequent approval by the medical staff.

4. Procedure

a. The president of the medical staff should nominate each applicant for membership on the medical staff.

b. The written application should be presented in the form of a statement of qualifications and references of the applicant and his affirmation to abide by the bylaws and rules and regulations of the medical staff (Fig. 2-2).

c. The application should then be directed to the administrative director of the extended care facility for transmission to the medical staff for study and consideration.

d. With the approval of the president of the medical staff, and with the recommendations of the medical staff members, the application should be offered to the governing body for appropriate action.

e. The administrative director should be authorized by the governing body to transmit the final decision to the applicant in the form of a letter.

B. Officers and Duties. A president and vice-president should suffice as officers of the medical staff of a 65-bed institution, although a larger organization should consider the positions of treasurer and/or secretary.

1. The President. The president should also function as the medical director and chief of the medical staff of the extended care facility with the following responsibilities:

a. To call and preside at all meetings of the medical staff

b. To be a member ex officio of all committees

c. To have general supervision over the work of all professional staff of the institution

d. To act as liaison between the extended care facility, the medical profession, the hospitals, and other health-related agencies in matters relating to patient care

e. To be responsible for emergency coverage for other physicians

f. To engage in preadmission evaluation and family counseling

Fig. 2-2

APPLICATION FOR MEDICAL STAFF

Name ______________________ Date ______________
Age _____ Sex _____ Marital Status _______ No. of children _______
Office address ______________________ Phone ______________
Home address ______________________ Phone ______________
Medical school ______________________ Year graduated _________
Internship ______________________ Year ______________
Residency ______________________ Year ______________
Licensed in ______________ License No. ______________
(state)

Date of license ______________________________________

Present hospital staff membership ______________________________

____

Professional societies or boards ______________________________

____

Substitute physicians to be called in an emergency ______________

List published material ______________________________

____

____

I agree to abide by the Bylaws, Rules and Regulations of the Medical Staff of the ______________________________.

______________________ M.D.

g. To serve on the safety and pharmacy committees

h. To work jointly with the administrative director in:

(1) Effectuating policy decisions

(2) Research and development relating patient needs to administration, architecture, etc.

(3) Medical administrative matters

(4) Developing joint educational programs with hospitals and universities

i. To conduct research in:
(1) Techniques of geriatric nursing
(2) Social gerontology
(3) Selected areas of study in geriatric medicine
(4) Methods of training professional and nonprofessional personnel

j. To participate in and/or conduct:
(1) Nurses' in-service training programs
(2) In-service training for physical and occupational therapists
(3) Training for nurses in local schools of nursing
(4) Training of social work students

k. To submit scientific articles for publication regularly

l. To keep accurate and complete minutes of all meetings and to attend to all correspondence

m. To serve on the joint conference, safety, and pharmacy committees

2. The Vice-President

a. The vice-president should act on behalf of the president in his absence.

b. He should act as treasurer of medical staff funds.

C. Committees

1. The Executive Committee

a. The executive committee should be composed of the president and the vice-president of the medical staff and additional members who may be appointed by the president.

b. The duties of the executive committee should comprise:
(1) Acting for the staff as a whole under such limitations as may be imposed by the staff
(2) Presenting at each meeting of the medical staff a report of all actions taken by the executive committee since the previous meeting
(3) Representing the medical staff on the joint conference committee with the administrative director and two representatives of the governing body of the extended care institution
(4) Functioning on the patient care policy and utilization review committee

2. Patient Care Policy and Utilization Review Committee

a. The president and the vice-president and additional medical staff members appointed by the president should serve on this committee with one or more registered professional nurses and other related professional health care personnel.

Fig. 2-3. In addition to the other physicians, it is advisable to include a psychiatrist, the directors of nursing and social service, and the health-records librarian on the patient care policy and utilization review committee.

b. The patient care policy and utilization review committee should conduct (Fig. 2-3):

(1) All functions of utilization review, in conformity with the standard requirements as defined by United States government Medicare requirements and the Joint Commission on Accreditation of Extended Care Facilities for 1968 (Fig. 2-4)

(2) A program to develop, improve, and implement standards of inpatient care

c. This committee should meet monthly and more often should additional meetings be required.

3. Credentials Committee

a. Members of this committee should be the president and the vice-president of the medical staff and additional members selected by the president.

b. The credentials committtee should be concerned with:

(1) The examination of the credentials of all applicants for medical staff privileges, advice to the medical staff on recommendations of appointment to, changes in privileges, or removal from the medical staff of the institution

(2) The study of the credentials of dentists, podiatrists, and all members of other allied health professions and medical sciences, advice to the medical staff on recommendations for appointment to, contracts with, changes in privileges or removal from the medical staff of the extended care facility

Fig. 2-4

UTILIZATION REVIEW FORM

(This section to be completed by person responsible for health records)

1. ______________________________
Patient's name and extended care facility number

2. ______________________________
Health insurance claim number

3. ______________________________
Admission date to extended care facility

4. Admitted to extended care facility from (please circle)

a) Hospital — Number of days' stay______
b) Home after hospital discharge — Number of days home______
c) Another ECF — Number of days' stay______

5. ______________ 6. ______________
Age — Sex

7. Admitting diagnosis:
(primary) ______________________________
(secondary) ______________________________
(additional) ______________________________

8. Present diagnosis:
(same as admitting) ______________________________
(changed to/additional) ______________________________
____

9. Days in extended care facility to current date______
Date of last review:______

____
Date — Signature

Fig. 2-4 (Continued)

(This section to be completed by nursing staff)

10. Mental status:________________________________

11. Behavior:___________________________________

12. A.D.L.:____________________________________

13. Incontinence:________________________________

14. Self-care:___________________________________

15. Medications:________________________________

16. Treatments:_________________________________

17. Diet and feeding:____________________________

18. Patient's condition has improved_______deteriorated________remained the same______since admission to extended care facility.

19. Patient's condition has improved_____deteriorated_____remained the same_____since last review_____
Date

____
Signature of Nurse

(Add additional information here if space is needed)

20. Supplemental information from paramedical staff:

Fig. 2-4 (Continued)

21. Name of attending physician:____________________

(To be completed by reviewing physician)

22. Was admission to extended care facility necessary for patient's welfare?

________ Yes ________ No

23. Is appropriate use of ancillary services being made?

________ Yes ________ No

24. Are there any additional services necessary and available to shorten patient's length of stay?____________________

____

25. Is further stay recommended?

________ Yes ________ No

If yes, complete the following:

a) Reason for continued stay:____________________

____

____

b) Date of next review____________________.

If no, complete the following:

c) Reason discontinuation is recommended:____________________

____

____

d) Recommendation of other type care (if any):____________________

____

26. Date of review____________ ____________________ Signature of Reviewing Physician

27. ____________________ Date of Next Review ____________________ Signature of UR Chairman

28. *To be Completed if Continued Stay Is Disapproved:*

a) Letter sent to attending physician ________________ Date

b) Letter sent to administrative director ________________ Date

c) Letter sent to responsible relative ________________ Date

4. Professional Activities Committee

a. This committee should be composed of the president and vice-president and other members of the medical staff appointed by the president.

b. Duties of this committee include:
(1) The regular review of the medical records and other evidence of professional activities in the institution
(2) A report of its findings to the medical staff and the governing body

5. Special Committee
a. The special committee should have as its membership the president and additional members of the medical staff nominated by the president under terms of reference established by him.
b. The special committee should be accountable for:
(1) The study and presentation of recommendations for amendments to the bylaws
(2) The engagement in any special activities

D. Staff Meetings

1. Annual Meeting
a. The medical staff should meet annually before the end of the fiscal year of the extended care facility.
b. The committees should report to the medical staff, and recommendations should be made for executive positions and reappointments to the medical staff.
c. Any new business should be discussed.

2. Special Meetings. Special meetings of the medical staff may be called at any time by the president or at the request of two members of the staff, with reasonable advance notice thereof to medical staff members.

3. Attendance and Voting
a. Members of the medical staff should be expected to attend all meetings.
b. Fifty percent of the total membership of the medical staff should constitute a quorum.

4. Agenda at Regular Meetings
a. Call to order
b. Reading of the minutes of the last regular and all special meetings
c. Unfinished business
d. Reports of committees
e. Communications
f. New business
g. Adjournment

5. Agenda at Special Meetings
a. Reading of the notice calling the meeting
b. Discussion of the business for which the meeting was called
c. Adjournment

VII. DUTIES AND PROCEDURES

A. Patient Care

1. Scope of Responsibility. The attending physician should be responsible for giving guidance, direction, and supervision to all medical, paramedical, nursing, and other staff involved in the care of the individual patient.

2. Regular Procedures

a. Admission

(1) Patients should be admitted to the extended care facility only on the recommendation of a physician licensed to practice in the state, who should provide the facility at admission with: (*a*) a complete diagnostic statement and admitting diagnosis; (*b*) a medical summary of all previous laboratory work and x-ray data; (*c*) a transcript of the patient hospital record, including a history, recent physical examination, and a discharge summary; (*d*) current medications, diet, and treatment; and (*e*) a description of patient's functional status.

(2) Patients admitted to the extended care facility should be attended by their own physician, provided that he/she has been accepted as a member of the medical staff.

(3) Patients and/or their designee unable to present the name of an attending physician so qualified should be asked to choose an attending physician from the medical staff.

b. Postadmission information. Within 48 hr following admission the following information should be provided and/or ordered by the attending physician:

(1) Family history
(2) Past history
(3) Physical examination
(4) Chest x-ray
(5) X-ray of patient with known bone pathology
(6) Electrocardiogram and interpretation
(7) Urinalysis
(8) Laboratory tests including, but not limited to, blood sugar, blood urea nitrogen, complete blood count, and sedimentation rate
(9) Psychiatric consultation on patients with brain disease, past psychiatric history, and/or current behavioral disorders
(10) Statement of functional capacity
(11) Rehabilitation potential and prognosis
(12) Drug and medication orders
(13) Therapy orders

(14) Orders for modified diet

(15) Nursing orders with respect to patient management and patient safety

c. Medical visits. All patients should be seen by their attending physicians at least once monthly, or as often as warranted by their condition.

d. Consultations. All attending physicians should seek consultative advice with respect to unclear diagnostic and/or treatment programs.

e. Monthly review. Each month the attending physician and the charge nurse should review orders and the total plan of patient care for every patient.

f. Orders:

(1) Written orders. Documentation of patients' records of medical supervision should be evidenced by signed written orders, progress notes, and discharge notes.

(2) Telephone orders. Telephone orders may be accepted by the nurse in charge who should report the orders, sign the physicians' orders, with their names followed by her own initials, and doctors must countersign such orders at their next visit.

(3) Permission for outings. Permission for a patient to leave the premises should be obtained by a form signed by the attending physician.

g. Semiannual reevaluation. Patients should be given semiannual comprehensive reevaluation of their health status, including all data under *b.* above documented and included in the patients' medical records.

h. Alternate physician

(1) Each attending physician should designate an alternate physician from the medical staff to provide emergency medical care in the event the attending physician is not available.

(2) The administrative director should be informed of his dates of absences and his substitute.

(3) Should the alternate be unavailable, the medical director should be contacted.

3. Emergency Procedures

a. Critical illness

(1) In the event that a patient should develop a critical illness, and the attending physician should elect to continue to treat the patient within the facility, the attending physician should be responsible for establishing a diagnostic basis for the critical illness; then providing the patient with every prudent, reasonable and medically sound therapeutic and nursing agent de-

signed to maintain life, including the use of intravenous fluids, nasogastric tube feedings, special-duty nursing, special appliances, restorative services, etc.

(2) It should be the responsibility of the attending physician to respond promptly to nursing staff emergency calls.

(3) It should be the attending physician's responsibility to inform the patient's family and/or designee of any change in the patient's medical or functional status.

b. Death. The attending physician or his physician designee should respond to a call from the nursing staff and should appear on the premises to make the diagnosis of death, sign the death certificate and other necessary papers, within a 2-hr period from the time of the nurse's call.

c. Autopsies

(1) Every member of the medical staff should be actively interested in obtaining autopsies whenever possible.

(2) Arrangements for autopsies should be made in conformance with state law, following the written consent of a legally responsible relative.

B. Employee Health Service

1. A member of the medical staff should be assigned to engage in:

a. Preemployment physical examinations of employees, including chest x-rays and blood chemistries

b. Annual employee physical examinations, including chest x-rays and blood chemistries

c. Emergency care

2. Written records should be maintained of all employee medical care.

C. Laboratory Work

1. Within the Facility

a. The following laboratory procedures should be performed on the premises of the extended care facility: complete blood count, routine urinalysis, and stool examination for occult blood.

b. These laboratory tests should be executed by written order of the attending physician and the results thereof entered on the patient's chart.

2. Outside the Facility. All other biochemical, hematologic, agglutination, serologic, bacteriologic, and pathologic studies should be effected by an approved and licensed laboratory, when ordered by the attending physician.

3. Reports. Reports of all laboratory studies and findings should be entered on the patient's medical records.

4. Laboratory Technician

a. For a 65-bed institution a laboratory technician should be available on the premises for the drawing and collecting of specimens, on a part-time basis.

b. For an extended care facility of 100 beds or more, serious consideration should be given to the employment of a full-time laboratory technician.

D. Diagnostic Radiology and Electrocardiography

1. The extended care facility should provide routine diagnostic radiology and electrocardiography on the premises (Fig. 2-5).

2. All x-ray studies should be ordered in writing by the attending physician and results thereof added to the patient's medical records.

3. All x-ray studies should be executed by a technician supervised by the medical director of the institution or by a consulting radiologist.

4. X-ray films should not be removed from the premises.

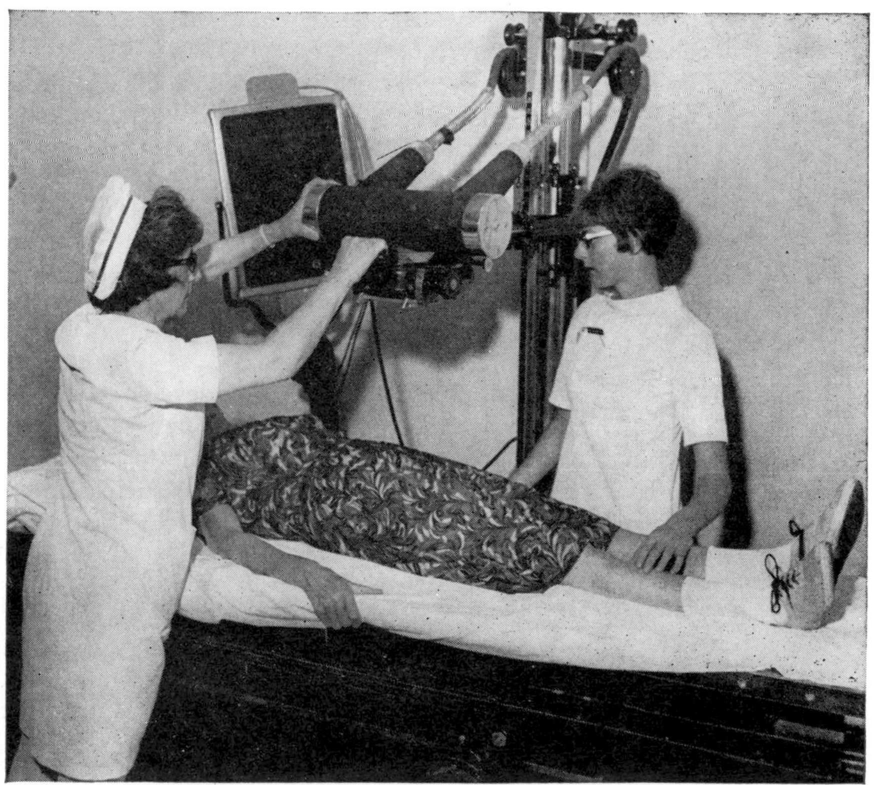

Fig. 2-5. Diagnostic x-ray is available to patients in the extended care facility.

5. X-ray films should be utilized in the facility by the medical staff for teaching purposes, consultation, staff meetings, and clinical demonstrations.

E. Other Diagnostic Procedures

1. Instruments for the following procedures should be available on the premises of the extended care facility at the request of the attending physician:

- *a.* Proctoscopy
- *b.* Anoscopy
- *c.* Sigmoidoscopy
- *d.* Ophthalmoscopy
- *e.* Indirect laryngoscopy

2. Consultations for the above procedures should be arranged by the attending physicians with the appropriate specialists.

F. In-service Education Programs

1. The in-service training programs conducted for all nursing and paramedical personnel and other designated staff should utilize the skills of members of the medical staff.

2. The medical staff should offer guidance and should conduct clinical sessions on restorative care programs, nursing procedures, dietary, oral hygiene, pharmaceutical, social, and diversionary programs related to patient care.

VIII. RELATIONS WITH ALLIED HEALTH PROFESSIONALS

A. Supervision. The medical staff should supervise the services performed by those in allied health professions and should be responsible for treatment involved.

B. Contracts. The extended care facility should develop contracts (Fig. 2-6), and should have on file completed curriculum vitae (Fig. 2-7), with allied health professional staff according to the same criteria as pertain to the regular medical staff, with particular reference to the state health code and the Conditions of Participation of Medicare.

C. Responsibilities. Allied health professional staff should be expected to:

1. Exercise independent judgment within their areas of competence, the ultimate responsibility for patient care to be shared by a member of the medical staff

2. Participate directly in the management of patients

3. Write orders and progress notes within the scope of their licensures

Fig. 2-6

CONTRACT FOR ALLIED HEALTH PROFESSIONALS

I agree to perform all services and to accept all responsibilities, within my professional discipline, as set forth in the Manual of the Extended Care Facility and the Code of the State Department of Health.

____________________ Date

____________________ Signature

____________________ Title

4. Be available for consultations on request by the medical staff
5. Offer direction and direct clinical training sessions related to patient care

D. Arrangements for Dentistry

1. Written Agreement. A written agreement maintained with one or more duly licensed doctors of dental surgery or doctors of dental medicine should signify consent to perform the following functions:

- *a.* To advise and participate in an active oral hygiene program
- *b.* To arrange to handle oral emergencies
- *c.* To provide prophylactic, therapeutic, and emergency care
- *d.* To visit the facility regularly to examine patients at the written request of their families, designees, or physicians
- *e.* To enter notes of treatment on the dental sheets of the patients' medical records
- *f.* To participate in the in-service training program

2. Annual Oral Survey

- *a.* Each patient should have an annual oral survey of his/her dental needs, followed by completion of any necessary work by a member of the dental staff (Fig. 2-8).
- *b.* Special arrangements may be made with the patient's personal dentist, providing his qualifications are approved by the credentials committee.

3. Emergency Oral Care. The advisory dentist or his designated alternative should be available to provide emergency oral care when a patient's personal dentist is not available.

Fig. 2-7

CURRICULUM VITAE FOR ALLIED HEALTH PROFESSIONALS

Name	Age	Sex	Marital Status	No. of Children

Office Address ____________________ Phone __________

Home Address ____________________ Phone __________

Educational Background:

____
High School and Year Graduated

College and Year Graduated	Degree	Graduate School	Degree

List of Professional Experience and Job Situations:

1. ____________________
2. ____________________
3. ____________________
4. ____________________

List Membership in Professional Societies and Organizations:

____
____
____
____

List Published Material:

____
____
____

Present Hospital Staff Membership ____________________

If Licensed, License Number: ____________________ State: __________

E. Podiatric Treatment

1. A written agreement, as delineated in the state health code, should be maintained with one or more duly licensed doctors of podiatry, to provide advice and service in prophylactic and therapeutic foot care with the approval of the attending physician.

2. The podiatrist should agree in writing to assume responsibility along with the attending physician in the podiatric care and treatment involved within the scope of his professional licensure, including the maintenance of proper clinical and administrative records (Fig. 2-9).

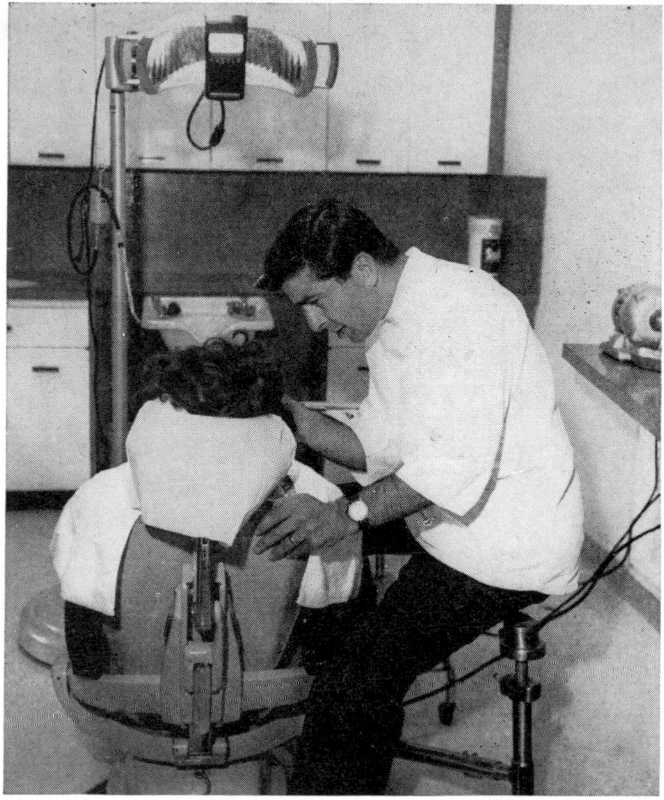

Fig. 2-8. Routine and emergency dental care is provided on the premises of the extended care institution.

IX. FINANCIAL ARRANGEMENTS

A. Charges for attending physicians, consulting physicians, dentists, podiatrists, x-ray, and laboratory work should be the direct responsibility of the patient or his designee.

B. Either the above providers should bill directly for services rendered or arrangements should be made for the extended care facility to handle this billing.

C. These bills should be submitted in such form as to be appropriate for Medicare reimbursement.

X. RELATIONS WITH FAMILIES OF PATIENTS

In addition to informing the director of nursing, the attending physicians, and where appropriate, the allied health professionals should be accountable to the families of patients for notification of:

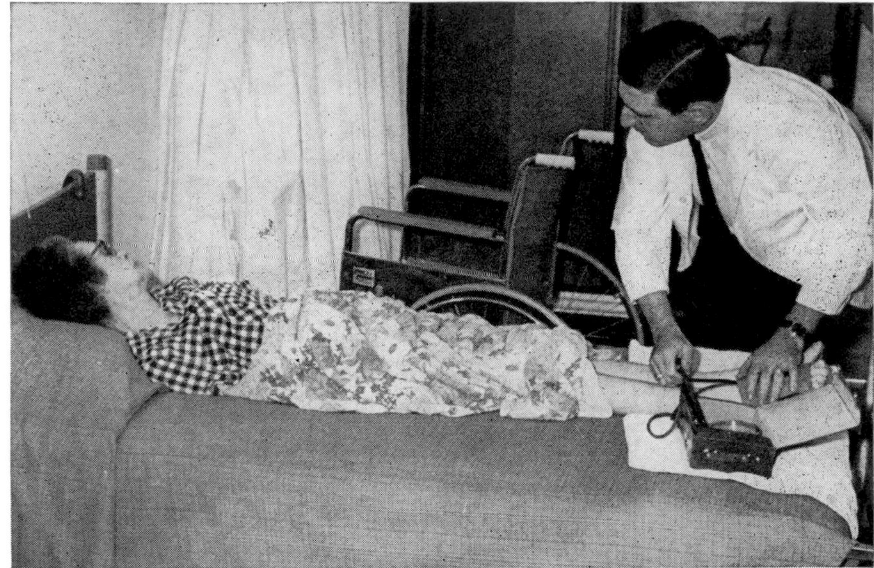

Fig. 2-9. A podiatrist attends patients on a regularly scheduled basis.

A. The changed condition of patients under their care

B. The need for transfer of patients from the nursing facility to hospitals

C. The need for special care services or equipment for patients

XI. INTERDEPARTMENTAL COMMITTEES

A. Safety Committee

1. Members of this committee, chaired by the maintenance director of the extended care facility, should include all department heads and the medical director.
2. The safety committee should be committed to analyzing accidents, teaching staff members methods of prevention of accidents, and setting forth and implementing safety rules and regulations.
3. The safety committee should meet monthly.

B. Pharmacy Committee

1. Members of this committee should be the president of the medical staff, the "consultant" pharmacist (chairman), the administrative director, and the director of nursing.
2. The pharmacy committee should be devoted to:

a. The formulation, evaluation, and review of policies concerning the prescribing, administering, and dispensing of medications at the extended care facility

b. The evaluation of pharmaceutical procedures

3. The pharmacy committee should meet quarterly to fulfill the responsibilities described.

C. Joint Conference Committee

1. This committee should be composed of two members of the executive committee of the governing body, two members of the executive committee of the medical staff, and the administrative director ex officio, the president of the governing body serving as chairman.

2. It should act as liaison between the medical staff, the governing body and the administrative director to consider medico administrative matters and to offer pertinent recommendations.

3. This committee should meet monthly before meetings of the governing body.

XII. INTERDEPARTMENTAL COOPERATION

To ensure that a high level of medical care is maintained, it is essential that the medical staff cooperate with all departments in the extended care facility.

A. Medical Director

1. A weekly interdisciplinary conference, including rounds of patients and/or patients with special problems, should be conducted for all professional services within the facility by the medical director (Fig. 2-10).

2. He should maintain an ongoing liaison with the attending medical staff and allied health professionals.

B. Administrative Director

1. Information. Should clarification be required regarding a physician's or allied health professional's duties and/or responsibilities to patients and to the extended care facility, the matter should be referred to the administrative director.

2. The administrative director should serve as ex officio member of the medical staff.

3. Annual letters of appointment and reappointment to the medical staff, as well as renewal of contracts with allied health professionals should be within the purview of the administrative director.

4. Major Equipment. Requests for major equipment should be submitted to the administrative director for consideration.

Fig. 2-10. Individual patients are assessed medically, socially, emotionally, and functionally at the interdisciplinary clinical conferences.

C. Nursing Department. To assure that the nursing staff maintains a high level in direct patient care, the medical staff should engage in the following:

1. Teaching

a. In-service education. A weekly in-service education program should be conducted by the medical director for the entire nursing staff with regular participation by members of the medical staff (Fig. 2-11).

b. Individual training. Each physician, as an essential part of his treatment of the patient, should describe his patient to the nurses in charge, including but not necessarily limited to the following information:

(1) Identification of patient's medical problems

(2) Medications to be used and their effects on the particular patient

(3) Development of a comprehensive nursing care plan to include all aspects of an overall nursing program

c. Patient care policies. The medical staff should aid the nursing staff in ensuring that the patient care policies are fulfilled.

D. Social Service Department. It should be the responsibility of the medical staff to aid the Social Service Department in the following areas:

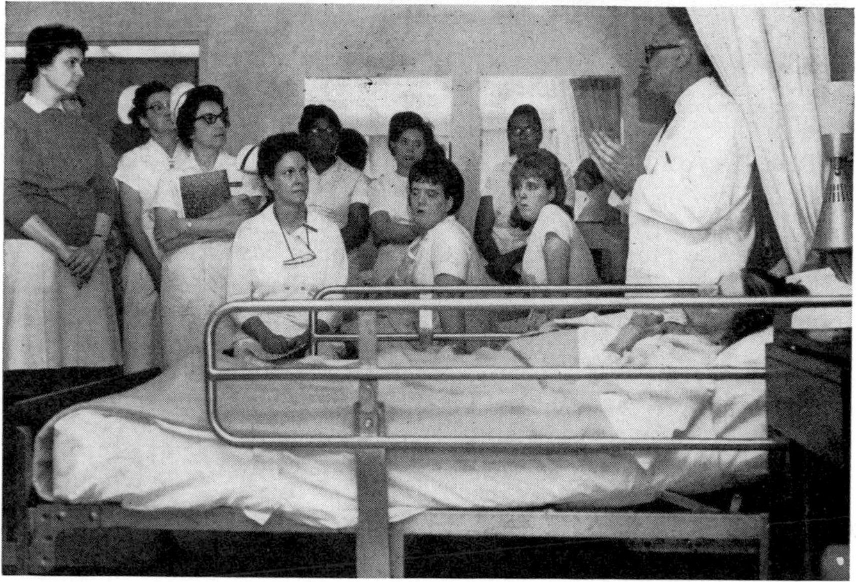

Fig. 2-11. The skills of the medical staff are utilized in the in-service educational programs.

1. Admission and/or discharge planning
2. Resolving problems of a "social nature" with patients and/or their families
3. Sharing information regarding Medicare as well as other financial aspects of patient care
4. Assisting in planning a therapeutically sound social program to fit the individual needs of patient and family

E. Restorative Services. For the physical, occupational, and speech therapists to do meaningful work in the overall rehabilitative program, the attending physicians should assist by:

1. Describing to each therapist involved with a particular patient the rehabilitative potential of that patient
2. Writing complete orders for each therapist involved with a particular patient and making changes as necessary, or at least monthly
3. Teaching the therapists any unusual techniques which may be useful when working with a particular patient

F. Recreation Department. As recreational therapy should form an integral part of the rehabilitative program, the medical staff members should confer with the director of recreation, especially when more involvement or curtailment in activities for a particular patient is desired by an attending physician.

G. Dietary Department. When special diet orders are written for patients, it is recommended that their attending physicians confer with either the consultant dietitian or the food-service manager of the institution.

H. Housekeeping Department. On a regular basis, designated members of the medical staff should confer with the executive housekeeper regarding the matter of "infection control" and continually review all infection control techniques in operation at the facility.

I. Maintenance Department. All requests for repairs of equipment or appliances should be made to the Maintenance Department via the administrative director or a charge nurse.

XIII. HEALTH RECORDS

A. All health records should be the property of the extended care facility and cannot be taken off the premises without permission of the administrative director.

B. Records should be made available to attending physicians in good standing for bona fide study and research consistent with preserving the confidentiality of personal information concerning patients and their families (see Section 11, Records).

XIV. TRANSFER AGREEMENTS WITH HOSPITALS

The extended care facility should have at least one transfer agreement with an area hospital to facilitate the continuity of patient care and the timely transfer of patients and records between the extended care facility and the hospital, the administrative director serving as liaison between the extended care facility and the hospital (Fig. 2-12).

Fig. 2-12

TRANSFER AGREEMENT BETWEEN THE COMMUNITY HOSPITAL AND THE EXTENDED CARE FACILITY

To facilitate continuity of care and the timely transfer of patients and records between the hospital and the extended care facility, the parties named above agree as follows:

1. When a patient's need for transfer from one of the above institutions to the

Fig. 2-12 (Continued)

other has been determined by the patient's physician, the institution to which transfer is to be made agrees to admit the patient as promptly as possible, provided customary admission requirements are met.

2. The transferring institution will send with each patient at the time of the transfer, or in the case of an emergency as promptly as possible, the completed transfer and referral forms mutually agreed upon to provide the medical and administrative information necessary to determine the appropriateness of the placement and to enable continuing care to the patient. The transfer and referral forms will include such information as current medical findings, diagnosis, rehabilitation potential, a brief summary of the course of treatment followed in the transferring institution, nursing and dietary information, ambulation status, and pertinent administrative and social information.
3. The transferring institution will be responsible for the transfer of other appropriate disposition of personal effects, particularly money and valuables, and information related to these items.
4. The transferring institution will be responsible for arranging the transfer of the patient, including arranging for appropriate and safe transportation and care of the patient during the transfer.
5. Neither the hospital nor the extended care facility shall assume any responsibility for the collection of any accounts receivable other than those incurred as a result of rendering services directly to the patients; and neither institution shall be liable for any debts, obligations, or claims of a financial or legal nature incurred by the other institution; and each institution assumes full responsibility for its own maintenance and operations.
6. Neither party shall use the name of the other party in any promotional or advertising material unless approval of the intended use shall first be obtained from the party whose name is to be used.
7. This agreement shall be in effect to and including the 31st day of December, provided it may be terminated by either facility upon 10 days' written notice, and shall be automatically terminated should either facility fail to maintain its license or certification.

Signed:

____

The Extended Care Facility Administrative Director

Date____________________

____

The Community Hospital Executive Director

Date____________________

XV. MEDICAL FACILITIES AND EQUIPMENT

The following listed equipment and facilities should be available to the medical and dental staff:

A. Examining Room

1. Examining table
2. Standing blood pressure unit
3. Electrocardiogram machine
4. Diathermy machine
5. Scale
6. Sink with foot pedals
7. Examining light
8. Cabinet with medical supplies

B. Dental Area

1. Hydraulic chair
2. Light
3. Drill
4. Buffing and grinding machine
5. Ultrasonic denture cleaner
6. Instrument tray on wheels
7. Automatic timer
8. Work shelf
9. Cabinets for supplies

C. X-ray Area

1. X-ray unit with fluoroscope
2. X-ray view box
3. Dark room
   a. X-ray cassettes
   b. Developing tank
   c. Film cabinet
   d. Developing light
   e. Developing timer
   f. Developing hangers
   g. Cabinets for supplies

D. Laboratory

1. Microscope and light
2. Refrigerator
3. Sterilizer
4. Blendor

Fig. 2-13. The medical library has many books concerned with geriatrics and rehabilitation.

5. Sink
6. Cabinets and supplies

E. Medical Conference Area

1. Conference table
2. Chairs
3. Sofa
4. Medical library with medical reference books and journals (Fig. 2-13)
5. Blackboard
6. Lamp and table

F. Patient Waiting Room

1. Chairs
2. Tables

G. Medical Secretary Office

1. Typewriter
2. Dictating machine
3. Copier machine

4. Files and desk
5. Bookshelves

H. Nurses' Stations

1. Blood pressure units
2. Stethoscopes
3. Suture sets
4. Syringes
5. Flashlights
6. Gloves
7. Equipment for sugar and acetone tests
8. Alcohol sponges

I. Appliances and Self-help Devices

1. Available on order via the physical therapist:
   a. Wheelchairs
   b. Walkers
   c. Crutches
   d. Canes
   e. Bedrails
   f. Trapeze frames
2. Devices for self-help in activities of daily living may be ordered via the occupational therapist.

Section 3

Nursing

Introduction

The Nursing Department in the extended care facility must be planned with an understanding of the nature of the patient population to be served. The average age of the patient can be expected to be seventy-five to eighty years with the ratio of female to male patients approximately three to one.

The predominant patient disability relates to cerebral arteriosclerosis with organic brain syndrome of varying degrees and other organ involvement and vascular disease as the basis, as in heart, kidney, and peripheral arterial disease. Typical of the geriatric patient is the concurrent involvement of multiple organ systems such as chronic pulmonary edema, arthropathies, urologic disease, and neoplasms of various organs.

To provide comprehensive nursing for these complicated patient care problems will require more than expeditious execution of medical directions. It will require more than a combination of high standards of nursing with compassion and understanding for the patients and their families. In order to encourage the rehabilitation of these patients and to assist them to function at their maximum level—physically, socially, and emotionally—nursing must be integrated with other professional services so that patients may benefit from a total care program involving nursing and physical and social rehabilitation in a coordinated ongoing program.

I. OBSERVATIONS ON NURSING TECHNIQUES

A. Administrative Relationships of the Nursing Staff

1. In contrast to the daily medical supervision available in the general voluntary hospital, less frequent medical visits have placed the supervising nurse at the hub of virtually all patient activities.

2. The chief nurse must relate patient and family activities to the operating management and vice versa.

3. Thus, the Nursing Service has the responsibility of translating operational policies to all nursing and paranursing professional services.

B. Psychosocial Nursing

1. In contrast to the usual patient stay of 10 to 14 days in a general voluntary hospital, the average patient placement in an extended care facility should be considerably longer.

2. Consequently, the nursing staff must be deeply committed to the psychologic and social rehabilitation of the patient population in several areas:

- *a.* The personal psychologic status of the patient
- *b.* Interpersonal patient relationships involving other patients, staff, visiting families
- *c.* Intrafamily and family relationships often requiring medical, psychiatric, and nursing management for effective and stable patient placement on exposure to chronic illness

C. Patient Physical Diagnosis at a Nursing Level

1. In the absence of immediate availability of a medical staff, physical diagnosis can be an important tool in the nursing armamentarium.

2. Because of the frequency and degree of organic brain disease in the patient population, valid symptomatic complaints may be lacking.

3. Therefore, objective evidences of patient disability in terms of change in patient behavior require those nursing skills of sound observation, smell, hearing, feeling (palpation), and judgment.

4. Diagnosis of clinical shock, acute and small stroke phenomena, congestive heart failure, dehydration, Cheyne-Stokes and Stokes-Adams syndrome, certain cardiac arrhythmias, diabetic acidosis and insulin shock, and bone fracture states can be within a nurse's capabilities.

D. Pharmacology

1. A knowledge of the clinical use and toxicology of commonly used drugs can be of particular importance in the extended care facility because of the less frequent presence of a medical staff.

2. The clinical behavior of the various insulins and hypoglycemic oral medications, clinical behavior of the various tranquilizers, depressants and opiates, and their frequent paradoxical behavior and other toxic manifestations, a working knowledge of digitalis and its various derivatives, with and without the presence of intensive diuretics, oral and parenteral, can be important tools of nursing skills.

3. Familiarity with the various antibiotics, their clinical, toxic, and related allergic phenomena should be understood.

4. Understanding the relative advantages and disadvantages of intravenous administration of water and electrolytes versus administration of clysis in the agitated, noncooperative patient, with or without chronic cardiac disease, should be understood.

E. Nursing Techniques and Nursing Rehabilitation

1. In the chronically ill aged, body movement should be the cornerstone of physical rehabilitation and physical reconditioning, and it can be preventive of debilitating disease and disabilities.
2. The relationship of body movement to psychosocial rehabilitation, physical therapy, occupational therapy, and recreational therapy, and utilization of the physical environment of the institution should be distinctly a nursing function, related at least to the prevention of decubiti, motor hypotonia, loss of range of motion in various joints, and at most, related to the rehabilitation of a chair- or bedridden patient to a functional, social, and reasonably intact social individual.
3. In the presence of organic brain disease, the feeding, bathing, and dressing of the elderly may require special skills.
4. Bowel and bladder training associated with the use of either intermittent catheterization or the use of an indwelling Foley catheter can be either a lifesaving procedure or a life-threatening experience, requiring a firm understanding of the anatomy, pathology, bacteriology, and the pharmacology of the urologic tract.
5. Bowel training with the prevention or treatment of fecal impactions should be a fundamental nursing technique of particular importance in a patient population in which fluid intake may be low, particularly with the frequent use of diuretics, and in which physical activity is often limited.
6. The importance of good nursing techniques in bowel and bladder function can only be appreciated when breaks in those techniques literally threaten the patient's existence.

F. Training and Research

1. In view of the present early phase of the development of geriatric nursing techniques, the nursing director must engage in education and training programs of registered nurses, licensed practical nurses, nursing aides, and orderlies and should develop techniques for more effective liaison with other paramedical professions involved in the total care of the chronically ill aged.
2. A program devoted to clinical research of new nursing techniques and improvement of conventional tools of nursing care should be developed in the extended care facility.

II. STAFFING PATTERN

For two nursing units in a progressive care 65-bed facility—a 30-bed concentrated care unit and a 35-bed skilled nursing care unit

A. Recruitment. The recruitment of nurses should be the responsibility of the director of nursing, following the staffing pattern established with the medical director and engaging all personnel in her department.

B. Staff Complement

1. The equivalent of 9½ nurses should include:

a. A director and an assistant director of nursing (in charge of education)

b. Six licensed nurses per day, with one registered nurse on the concentrated care unit and one licensed practical nurse on the skilled nursing care unit for day, evening, and night shifts

2. The equivalent of 20 nursing aides and orderlies should include:

a. A minimum of eight nursing aides on the concentrated care unit during a 24-hour period, with four on the day shift, two on the evening shift, and two on the night shift, as patients on this floor should require more intensive care than those in the skilled nursing care unit

b. A minimum of six nursing aides on the skilled nursing care unit during a 24-hour period, with three on the day shift, two on the evening shift, and one on the night shift

3. An administrative assistant to the nursing department may be engaged to process Medicare material and to handle all health records.

C. Work Schedule

1. A monthly time card for each member of the nursing department staff should be kept at the main nursing station showing a daily record of the time signed in and the time signed out.

2. Nurses and aides should work in three shifts: 7:00 A.M. to 3:00 P.M.; 3:00 P.M. to 11:00 P.M.; 11:00 P.M. to 7:00 A.M. with two 15-min coffee breaks during each shift and a meal period of half an hour.

3. A weekly time and floor schedule should be posted on the bulletin board at the main nursing station which, at the completion of the week, should be placed in the loose-leaf staff schedule book and kept for a period of 6 months.

D. Orientation

1. There should be a 20-hr orientation program, depending upon the needs of new employees, skill training in performance to be stressed for the nonprofessional staff and clinical, psychologic, social, and rehabilitative aspects to be stressed for the nurses. Both groups should receive specific instruction in the principles of geriatric care, including attention to the emotionally disturbed and confused patients; ways to assist families in understanding the patient's problems and needs; and proper conduct in emergency situations (Fig. 3-1).

Fig. 3-1. An orientation session for nursing attendants.

2. The new staff member should be introduced to the nurse in charge who will undertake the responsibility of indoctrinating him or her to patients, routine, equipment, facilities, etc.
3. An effort should be made to orient all new staff members on the 7:00 A.M. to 3:00 P.M. shift, to better acquaint them with important procedures before regular assignment.

III. NURSING AND HEALTH RECORDS

A. Patients' Charts

1. Information on patients' charts, kept at nursing stations, must be treated as confidential and should be read only by professional staff members and should not be removed without proper authorization.
2. The following records are listed in the order in which they should be kept:

- *a.* Check sheet.
- *b.* Intake and output record.
- *c.* Weekly summary. Notes for the weekly summary are to be kept on each patient by charge nurses on all shifts and should include information on the patient's condition for the past week including: eating habits; sleeping habits, the use of the bedrail and night frequency; elimination; association with other

Fig. 3-2

PHYSICIANS' ORDERS AND PROGRESS NOTES

Patient ______________________

Attending Physician ______________________

Health Insurance Claim No. ______________________

Extended Care Facility No. ______________________

Please use this space for medication and drug orders, treatment orders, and progress notes.

Date: ______________________

Signature ______________________

Laboratory orders: ______________________

X-ray orders: ______________________

Physical therapy orders: (initial for order and complete P.T. form)

Occupational therapy orders: (initial for order and complete O.T. form)

Speech therapy orders: (initial for order and complete S.T. form)

Special procedures:

Plans for continued care/discharge:

Social service:

Diet (routine or special): ______________________

patients; activities of daily living; personal and oral hygiene; visitation and outside activities, such as outings with families; self-care; mental status; eyesight and hearing; how patient handles aids such as dentures and eyeglasses; progress notes or nursing care plan (an outline of care projection for present week).

d. Initial physical examination.

e. Social service.

f. Laboratory reports. Such reports should include the following information on separate sheets, in chronologic order: electrocardiogram, urinalysis, and blood chemistries.

g. X-rays.

h. Dental treatment.

i. Podiatric treatment.

j. Incident or accident report.

k. Admission and discharge information.

l. Transfer form. This form should be sent with the patient at transfer or discharge.

B. Nursing Administrative (kept at nurses' station)

1. Physicians' Orders and Progress Notes. These orders and notes on individual patients should be kept in a loose-leaf notebook, and should form the basis of nurses' reports from shift to shift (Fig. 3-2).
2. Certification and Recertification Forms. Certification forms of patients on Medicare should be placed in the physicians' order book to be signed on designated dates by attending physicians who will be reminded by charge nurses of the proper dates for recertifications (Fig. 3-3).

Fig. 3-3

CERTIFICATION AND RECERTIFICATION

CERTIFICATION of patient admission. Required at time of admission.

____________________	____________________	____________________
(Patient)	(Health Insurance Claim No.)	(Admission Date)

I certify that post-hospital ECF services are required to be given on an inpatient basis because of the above-named patient's need for skilled nursing care on a continuing basis for the condition(s) for which he was receiving inpatient hospital services prior to his transfer to the ECF.

Fig. 3-3 (Continued)

_______________________________ _______________________________

(Physician) (Time and Date)

RECERTIFICATION of continued ECF inpatient care. On or before the 14th day. Date____________________

I certify that continued ECF inpatient care is necessary for the following reason(s):

____

____

I estimate the additional period of ECF inpatient care will be________days (or ________weeks). Plans for post-ECF care are:
Home health agency________; Office care________; Other (specify)____________
Continued ECF care is for same condition for which patient received inpatient hospital services: Yes________ No________

_______________________________ _______________________________

(Physician) (Date)

SECOND RECERTIFICATION: On or before the 44th day of ECF inpatient care. Date____________________

I certify that continued ECF inpatient care is necessary for the following reason(s):

____

____

I estimate the additional period of ECF inpatient care will be________days (or ________weeks). Plans for post-ECF care are: Home health agency________; Office care________; Other (specify)______________________________
Continued ECF care is for same condition for which patient received inpatient hospital services: Yes________ No________

_______________________________ _______________________________

(Physician) (Date)

THIRD RECERTIFICATION: On or before the 74th day of ECF inpatient care. Date____________________

I certify that continued ECF inpatient care is necessary for the following reason(s):

____

____

I estimate the additional period of ECF inpatient care will be________days (or ________weeks). Plans for post-ECF care are: Home health agency________; Office care________; Other (specify)______________________________
Continued ECF care is for same condition for which patient received inpatient hospital services: Yes________ No________

_______________________________ _______________________________

(Physician) (Date)

3. Medical Consultation Notes. Consultations should be recorded on fresh sheets or special forms in the loose-leaf notebook containing physicians' orders and progress notes.

4. Narcotic-Sedative-Stimulant Sheets
   a. These records should include the narcotic-sedative-stimulant sheets of individual patients and should be kept in a loose-leaf narcotic-sedative-stimulant book.
   b. Should the patient die, the charge nurse is to give the narcotic-sedative-stimulant sheet to the director of nursing, who should complete the official form in triplicate to be mailed with unused narcotics, sedatives, or stimulants wrapped in a package, sealed at both ends, and sent via Railway Express to the Narcotics Control Bureau of the state department of health.
   c. Narcotics, sedatives, and stimulants may be given to discharged patients unless otherwise directed by their physician, provided that a signed receipt is obtained.

5. Narcotic and Sedative Record Book. This book should record the date, the patient's name, the pharmacy, the drug, directions, amount ordered, registration number, and the name of nurse giving the order, and the signature of nurse receiving the order.

6. Depressant and Stimulant Book. This book should record the same data as the narcotic and sedative book mentioned above.

7. Medication File. This file should be maintained on all drugs ordered and received for patients from the pharmacy.

8. Record of Patient Care. These detailed check sheets should be kept in a loose-leaf notebook by nursing attendants on all shifts.

9. Patient Movement. Completed notification of patient movement slips should be sent to the administrative director on discharge and transfer of the patient within or outside the facility and are then routed to Dietary, Business, and Social Service.

10. Special Services Book. This loose-leaf notebook with the name of each patient on a separate sheet in alphabetical order should record information on services relating to hearing aids, braces, optometry, the barber, the beautician, and the podiatrist, including the date, the service administered, and the title and signature of the person administering such service.

11. Restorative Services Book. This book should provide a record of physical, occupational, and speech therapy.

12. Patient Outing Book. This book should provide a record of time the patient leaves the facility, expected return, signature of the person accompanying him, his relationship to the patient and signature of the charge nurse.

C. General Administrative

1. Census Book. The census book should be kept by the director of nursing or her designated alternative on a daily basis.

2. Patient Register. The patient register should be maintained by the director of nursing or the admitting officer to note admissions, transfers, readmissions, and discharges of patients.

3. Patient Roster. The patient roster should be located on the wall of the administrative office, and may be kept by the director of nursing or administrative staff.

4. Minutes of staff meetings and attendance book of staff training sessions. These records should be kept by the director of nursing and/or the administrative staff.

IV. PATIENT CARE PROCEDURES

A. Admission

1. Preparation

a. Information. The social worker should inform the appropriate charge nurse of the expected time of the patient admission.

b. Preparation. The charge nurse should check the patient's room or unit for cleanliness and order and should ascertain that the bed has been made and that all necessary supplies—soap, towels, glass, hangers, and nursing equipment—have been furnished.

c. Alerting of staff. The nursing staff member assigned to take care of the new patient should be alerted by the charge nurse as to the anticipated arrival of the patient.

2. Procedure with Patient

a. Arrival. When patient and family arrive, the charge nurse should welcome them and escort the family to the social service office and the patient to his assigned room.

b. Settling. The assigned staff member should help the patient to unpack and arrange his possessions and should label his clothing with a laundry pen and place an identification bracelet on the patient's wrist with the following material to be written: the patient's name and the address and telephone number of the extended care facility.

c. Observation. The patient's physical condition, including his use of eyeglasses and dentures, and his mental and social attitudes should be observed, and the results of the observations should be reported to the charge nurse, to be included in the nursing records.

d. Orientation. The staff member should then orient the patient as to the location of the bathing and toilet areas, the recreation room, and community rooms, and she should familiarize him with the routine of the extended care facility and should introduce him to other patients and staff members.

e. Personal medication. All personal medication in the possession of the patient should be given by the staff member to the director of nursing, to be returned to the family.

f. Valuables. A report in writing must be made by the staff member on all valuables or funds on the person or in the possession of the patient on his arrival and, where possible, the family should retain these articles, any funds left for the patient to be locked in the safe immediately and the family informed that the extended care facility is not responsible for jewelry, cash, or other valuables that are not kept in the safe.

g. Notification of physician. The charge nurse should notify the physician of the patient's arrival and admittance and should request an admission examination and written orders for all treatments and medications required.

h. Postadmission. Within 24 hr after admission, the patient should be bathed or showered, and temperature, blood pressure, and weight should be noted and body conditions should be reported to the charge nurse for notation on admission records.

3. Admission Records and Forms

a. Admission and discharge notes. These notes should be written by the charge nurse and should include the following information:

(1) Admitted from home, hospital, other facility
(2) Admitted via ambulance, wheel chair, automobile
(3) General appearance and state of patient
(4) Aids, such as dentures, hearing aids, canes, and eyeglasses
(5) Special diet requirements
(6) Eating and sleeping habits
(7) Associations with other patients
(8) Elimination habits
(9) During the patient admission procedures of bathing or showering, weighing, and taking of temperature and blood pressure, the patient's general body condition is to be noted, especially pressure areas, with precise description of location, size, and depth

b. Nursing care plan. A nursing care plan should be completed for each patient to:

(1) Provide a central source of information on the total needs of the patient
(2) Communicate information regarding individual care to new

and nonprofessional nursing personnel and to personnel in other departments

(3) Be used as a teaching aid

(4) Record observation of the patient

(5) Define goals for his care

(6) Develop a care plan with an approach to the physical and emotional needs of the patient

(7) Be modified to meet the changing needs and/or condition of the patient (Fig. 3-4)

c. Medical and nursing records. The name of the patient is written on the following records:

(1) Nursing care plan and progress notes

(2) Initial physical examination

Fig. 3-4

Special Medication	Start	Stop	Special Instructions
Treatments:			

Goals

Physical Needs	Emotional Needs	Social Needs
Approach:	Approach:	Approach:

Diagnosis (Medical and Functional)

Name: Age: Admission Date: Religion:

Physician:

(3) Physician's orders and progress notes (including certification and recertification for Medicare patients)
(4) Check sheet

d. Patient census record. The new admission is entered in the patient census record.

B. Checking Vital Signs of Condition. The following conditions are to be recorded in the nurses' notes:

1. Apical-Radial Pulse
a. Purpose: To take the rate of apical beat at its apex and the radial beat simultaneously, for comparison
b. Method: Two nurses are needed for this procedure with one locating the apex of the heart, just below the (L) nipple in the fifth intercoastal space and the second nurse locating the radial artery as both start counting a whole minute at the same time.

2. Radial Pulse
a. Purpose: To determine the rate of contractions of the heart
b. Method: The pulse can be taken at any superficial artery against a bone by:
(1) Placing the index and second finger over the artery
(2) Counting the pulse for ½ min and multiplying by 2
(3) If pulse is irregular, by counting for 1 full min

3. Respirations
a. Purpose: To determine the rate of respirations
b. Method: Respirations are counted for ½ min, then multiplied by 2 and, if irregular, they must be counted for 1 full min.

4. Blood Pressure
a. Purpose: To measure the arterial blood pressure
b. Equipment: Sphygmomanometer; stethoscope
c. Method:
(1) The cuff is to be applied smoothly and snugly around the patient's arm, about 2 in. above the patient's elbow.
(2) The bell of the stethoscope is placed over the brachial artery, the valve is closed, and the cuff is inflated just below the bend of the elbow until the mercurial column rises above the level at which the pulse can be felt or heard.
(3) The valve slowly is opened and the first sound heard should be the systolic pressure and the last sound heard should be the the diastolic pressure.

5. Temperature
a. Purpose: To take the temperature of the body accurately and safely

b. Equipment
(1) A rectal or oral thermometer
(2) Lubrication for the rectal thermometer
(3) Tissue for wiping the thermometer
(4) Dial-a-Therm holder will necessitate following special accompanying instructions

c. Method
(1) The thermometer should be checked to make certain that it registers 95°F or below.
(2) The oral thermometer is placed under the tongue and kept in place for 3 min.
(3) The rectal thermometer is lubricated and inserted in the rectum for 3 min.
(4) The rectal thermometer is not lubricated and is placed in the axilla for 10 min.
(5) The nursing attendant should remain with the patient while the thermometer is inserted.
(6) The thermometer is wiped with tissue and the temperature is read.

d. Aftercare of thermometer
(1) The thermometer should be washed in soap and cool water.
(2) It should be soaked in green soap for ½ hr.
(3) It should be stored in a boat of alcohol and rinsed with cool water before using.

C. Assisting Physician in Examination and Treatment

1. Positions

a. Objectives of nurse: To assist the patient to assume and maintain the correct position for the examination and treatment

b. Psychological preparation of patient
(1) The patient should be prepared psychologically before the examination to ensure proper relaxation.
(2) Considerable help will be required from the nurse by the seriously ill or weak patients in assuming and maintaining a stated position.

c. Basic equipment: A sheet and adequate light

d. Specific positions for examination should include:
(1) The dorsal recumbent position (with the knees flexed) for rectal and vaginal examination requires that a sheet be placed over the patient with one corner over the chest; the opposite corner between the feet with the patient's knees flexed and each of the other two corners of the sheet wrapped securely around patient's feet and the patient to lie flat on his back, with his legs

flexed, the soles of his feet flat on the bed and his knees flexed and separated, the perineal area being covered with the corner of the sheet until the arrival of the physician.

(2) The lithotomy position for vaginal and urethral examination indicates that the patient be placed on the examination table or bed with stirrups in place or feet flat on bed and with leggings used if needed; the sheet draped as for dorsal recumbent position and the legs placed in stirrups or kept flat on the bed.

(3) The prone position for examination of the back and to relieve pressure on the back necessitates removal of the pillow, the patient placed on his abdomen, his face to one side and his toes off the edge of the mattress with his extremities placed in good alignment.

(4) Fowler's position for the examination of the chest, eyes, ears, nose, and throat in which the patient sits directly upward may also be used for the treatment of cardiac disease, for asthmatic patients, for patients with upper respiratory infection, and when pelvic drainage is desired.

(5) The orthopneic position for patients with advanced cardiac disease in which the patient is to sit up and forward, with his arms and head supported by pillows placed over the bed table and his back covered, may also be used in the examination of the posterior chest.

(6) The knee-chest or genupectoral position for rectal examination and for the replacement of pelvic organs following prolapse obliges the patient to rest on his chest and knees with the knees slightly separated; the thighs perpendicular to the bed; the face turned to one side; the arms free on both sides and, if possible, no pillow.

(7) The Trendelenburg position, used to increase circulation to the heart when the blood pressure is low or if patient is in state of shock, provides that the entire foot of the bed be elevated on shock blocks or other elevation method, the head of bed remaining flat.

(8) The reverse Trendelenburg position, in which blocks are placed at the head of the bed to raise the entire bed, is used to promote drainage.

2. General Physical Examinations

a. Objectives of the nurse: To prevent discomfort and unnecessary exposure of the patient, to conserve his strength during the examination, and to facilitate the work of the physician.

b. Psychological preparation of the patient: To reassure the patient and to allay tension and anxiety, an explanation of the procedure should be given to the patient and the nurse should assist the physician closely in a female examination.

c. Equipment should include a sheet, tongue blades, a stethoscope, a sphygmomanometer, a flashlight, tissues, percussion hammer, a paper bag, an oto-ophthalmoscope and adequate light.

d. Procedure

(1) Preparation of equipment: All the equipment should be assembled, brought to the bedside, and arranged for convenient use if the patient cannot be transported to the examining room.

(2) Preparation of the patient: The patient should be screened, his bladder emptied and catheterized (if ordered); he should be covered with a sheet folded in half across his chest with the open edge toward his face and the top edge of the sheet picked up along with the bedding and brought down to the foot, and the top bedding fanfolded neatly to the foot.

e. Technique

(1) For a head, face, throat, and neck examination, the patient should be placed in Fowler's position, the nurse assisting with the equipment as indicated by the physician and the soiled tongue depressor to be broken, wrapped in a paper towel, and discarded.

(2) For a chest examination all unnecessary noise should be eliminated, and the right and left side of the patient's chest should be draped and undraped as the physician proceeds with the examination. If the patient is instructed to cough, the nurse should ascertain that tissue is used and that the head is turned to one side; the patient is then helped to sit up for an examination of the dorsal chest, and the gown is held out of the way as the physician proceeds with the examination.

(3) For an abdominal examination the patient is placed in a horizontal position, his chest is covered with a gown or towel, and the sheet is withdrawn to the pubic crest.

(4) For an examination of the lower extremities the sheet is gathered between the patient's legs, leaving both legs and feet exposed at the same time.

(5) For a back examination the patient is turned to the prone position, the pillow is removed, the bed is made flat, and a towel or gown is used to prevent undue exposure as the examination proceeds.

f. Aftercare of the patient: The sheets are removed, order is restored, and the patient is left comfortable.

g. Aftercare of the equipment: All equipment should be cleaned, returned to the proper places, and a paper bag containing the used tongue blades and tissues discarded and the soiled sheet placed in the dirty laundry.

3. Vaginal Examination

a. Objectives of nurse: To provide complete privacy, to facilitate the examination, and to prevent contamination.

b. Psychological preparation of the patient: The fears of patient should be allayed, the patient should be given as much privacy as possible, and the procedure should be explained.

c. Equipment should include: a sheet, a rubber sheet and cover, a lab slip if a smear is to be taken, sterile forceps, adequate light, and a tray containing sterile disposable gloves, sterile water-soluble lubricant, sterile vaginal speculum, sterile vaginal forceps, sterile cotton balls, sterile applicators if smear is to be taken or medication applied, two slides hinged together at one end with a small label attached, and an emesis basin.

d. Procedure

(1) Preparation of the equipment: The equipment should be assembled on a tray and brought to the bedside or to the examining table.

(2) Preparation of the patient: The patient should be prepared by complete screening, by having the patient void before the examination and catheterized (if ordered), by placing the patient in a dorsal recumbent position with the knees flexed or in the lithotomy position as indicated by the physician, and by placing the bed protector in position.

e. Technique of the vaginal examination

(1) When the physician is ready, the sterile glove case is opened and an emesis basin is placed near for waste powder.

(2) A small amount of sterile lubricant is dropped into the emesis basin.

(3) Sufficient lubricant is dropped into the physician's glove which should not be in contact with the tube.

(4) A point of the sheet is raised between the patient's thighs.

(5) Light is directed over the physician's shoulders to shine into vaginal vault.

(6) The speculum package is opened and the sterile towel is left open for the applicators.

(7) The speculum is lubricated with sterile jelly as the physician picks it up (care being exercised not to contaminate speculum with tube).

(8) If smear is to be taken, lubricant is not put into physician's glove and the speculum is not lubricated, but two sterile applicators are withdrawn from the sterile envelope with sterile pick-

up forceps and are dropped onto the speculum towel; the hinged slide is held ready to receive the smear, and a small wedge is placed between the slides at the open end and is secured with a rubber band with a laboratory request slip for smear wrapped around the slide.

(9) The speculum is removed by the physician, placed in an emesis basin, the bimanual examination is completed, and the physician's glove is placed in the emesis basin.

4. Rectal Examination

a. Objective of nurse: To provide complete privacy and to facilitate the examination.

b. Psychological preparation of patient: The procedure should be explained to the patient.

c. Equipment should include a sheet, a rubber sheet and cover, unsterile rubber gloves, and lubricant.

d. Procedure

(1) Preparation of the equipment: The rectal examination tray should be brought to the bedside or examining table.

(2) Preparation of the patient: The patient should be screened, he should void before the examination and be catheterized (if ordered), the top bedding should be removed and at the same time the patient should be covered with a sheet and placed in the dorsal or lateral position, as directed by the physician, and instructed to breathe deeply.

e. Technique for a rectal examination: A glove should be lubricated by the nurse and offered to the physician to use when inserting the fingers into the rectum of the patient.

f. Aftercare of the patient (vaginal and rectal): The sheet is removed, order is restored, and the patient is left comfortable.

g. Aftercare of equipment (vaginal and rectal examination):

(1) The equipment is removed to the sink, the instruments are washed with green soap, and the glove is discarded.

(2) The instruments are placed in double thicknesses of towel or wrapper and wrapped as a sterile package.

(3) A tag is attached stating the type of instrument, the size, the date and initial, and the package is given to the nurse in charge.

D. Bed Care of the Patient

In a modern extended care facility the patient should remain in bed only under the most unusual situations and the out-of-bed regime should follow shortly.

1. Morning Care (to be given in the lavatory, whenever possible)

a. Purpose: To prepare the patient for the day.

b. Equipment should include a face basin half full of warm water, mouth wash as necessary, toilet articles, soap, emesis basin and clean linen if necessary.

c. Procedure for the morning toilet

(1) The top of the upper bedding is protected with a towel and the patient's face and hands are washed.

(2) He is given mouth care (see Oral Hygiene section following).

(3) His hair is combed and brushed.

(4) The unit is straightened.

2. Oral Hygiene

a. Objectives of the nurse should be:

(1) To remove decomposing particles of food and bacteria

(2) To promote the patient's sense of well-being

(3) To teach proper oral hygiene

b. Points to be emphasized include:

(1) The patient's teeth and dentures must be brushed after meals.

(2) The patient's head should be turned to one side to prevent aspiration of fluid while being assisted with oral care.

(3) Special oral care must be given at least every 3 hr to all patients who are mouth breathers, who have had oral surgery, who have diseases of the mouth, who are dehydrated, who have high temperatures, and who are unconscious.

(4) Hands must always be washed before and after caring for patient's teeth.

c. Equipment for general use should include a face towel, an emesis basin, an oral cup with solution, tooth brush and dentifrice, cleansing tissues, and a glass of fresh water, with a straw if necessary.

d. Procedure

(1) Preparation of the equipment: The equipment is assembled and brought to the bedside (when necessary) and placed within convenient reach.

(2) Preparation of the patient: The patient is screened, his head is elevated unless contraindicated, and a towel is placed across the patient's chest.

e. Technique

(1) The brush is moistened, dentifrice is applied (powder or paste), the brush is placed across the top of the oral care cup.

(2) A hand is placed under the patient's pillow and his head is turned to one side.

(3) When feasible the patient is encouraged to brush his teeth and is assisted with rinsing, but if condition indicates, the patient's teeth are brushed for him.

(4) Oral care is followed with a drink of fresh water unless contraindicated.

f. Aftercare of equipment

(1) The basin, cup, and brush are cleaned in the nearest sink.

(2) The clean articles are returned to the patient's stand.

3. Special Oral Care

a. Care of dentures:

(1) Points to be emphasized: Dentures must be cleaned as frequently as natural teeth and under no circumstances should they stand unclean at the bedside; dentures not kept in the oral cavity must be placed in a denture cup filled with water and kept in a drawer of the patient's bedside table and should be checked daily; and dentures must be removed from all patients not completely conscious.

(2) Equipment: Same as for natural teeth

(3) Technique: The upper dentures are removed from the patient's mouth by grasping with gauze and pulling gently forward and upward; the lower dentures may be removed by lifting forward and upward; the dentures are placed in an oral care cup and cleaned at the sink or grasped firmly with gauze and cleaned over the emesis basin using extreme caution.

b. Care of the mouth:

(1) The following equipment is required: a package of applicators, six padded tongue depressors, an oral care cup and water, a paper bag, mineral oil with lemon, an emesis basin, and cleansing tissues.

(2) Technique: The patient is screened; a wash basin is brought to the bed; a tongue depressor is moistened with water; as much oral debris as possible is removed; a fresh padded tongue depressor is used after each contact with the patient's mouth and the soiled depressor discarded in a paper bag. An applicator with mineral oil and lemon is used to moisten all surfaces of the patient's mouth; a 4×4 gauze is moistened at one end with mineral oil, and the patient's tongue is grasped and cleansed, staff member taking care not to cut her fingers on the patient's teeth.

(3) Charting: The procedure is recorded and any lesions are noted.

4. Ultrasonic Cleansing of Dentures. Daily all patient dentures should be mechanically cleansed to remove all foreign matter by:

a. Immersion of each denture in a separate labeled container filled with detergent

b. The use of an ultrasonic cleansing device for 10 min per denture

5. Physical Comfort of the Bed Patient

a. Changing the position of the helpless bed patient:

(1) Purpose: To give comfort to the patient by changing his posture in bed and to help prevent complications such as decubitus ulcers or hypostatic pneumonia

(2) Equipment: The equipment is indicated by the patient's condition and may include extra pillows, rubber rings, etc., which should be assembled beforehand.

(3) The procedure of turning a patient: Care should be exercised to prevent the patient from falling out of bed; the patient should be supported and guarded well when he is near the edge of bed; bedrails must be placed in the up position when the patient is left, should his condition indicate the need for side rails.

(4) The procedure of turning the patient on his side: One pillow is removed and the other pillow is left under the patient's head (if two have been in use); the attendant should stand at the side of the bed to which the patient is to be turned, the patient being kept as well covered as possible and his arms placed close to the sides of his body before he is turned. The nurse should reach across the patient and place one hand well under the shoulders and the other hand well under the buttocks; the patient should be gently rolled towards the nurse until he is on his side; both hands of the nurse are held in hoop fashion under the buttocks and are lifted toward the middle of the bed, and shoulders are adjusted in similar fashion; the patient's knees are flexed, the uppermost knee considerably more than the lower knee, and a small pillow is placed between the knees making sure that the upper foot is neither unsupported nor resting on the lower foot by placing a small pillow or doughnut between the feet. The pillow is adjusted under the head, a large pillow is placed lengthwise at the patient's back, putting one edge well under back and rolling the rest of the pillow under to afford good support, and the end of the head pillow is pulled down and rolled under the shoulder for support; the upper bedding is readjusted.

(5) The procedure of turning the patient on abdomen: The above procedure is modified so as to turn the patient comfortably over onto his abdomen with his head turned to one side, the thighs and legs placed in line with the rest of the body, the arms

adjusted in the most comfortable position for the patient, and the upper bedding readjusted.

b. Back care

(1) Purpose: To provide protection, care, and comfort to patients who are confined to bed or who remain in the bed or the chair for long periods of time.

(2) Procedure: The skin areas should be washed and skin-care procedure followed when changing clothing or bed linen of the incontinent patient; the patient should be turned frequently to relieve pressure; lotion may be applied to his back with light friction rubbing. Specific orders are written by the physician if the skin should be broken, decubiti should be present, or if infection should set in.

c. Prevention of decubitus ulcers

(1) Symptoms: A reddened area, heat, and a dark blue color followed by an abrasion which may become infected.

(2) Predisposing causes include: poor general condition of the patient, prolonged illnesses, poor circulation, incontinency, and plaster casts and bandages which may cause continuous pressure or friction on a body part.

(3) Purpose of care: To use all prophylactic measures for prevention of a breakdown of tissues from pressure or malnutrition, to treat pressure areas when they develop so as to promote a rapid growth of new tissue, and to ensure the comfort of the patient.

(4) Prophylactic measures of prevention: The following preventive measures are the responsibility of both the doctor and the nurse: The patient supported with pillows should be turned at least every 2 hr except by special medical orders; all abrasions appearing on newly admitted patients should be reported and recorded; bony prominences such as heels, elbows, shoulder, and sacrum should be closely observed; pressure signs should be noted on any areas where pressures are made by casts, braces, or splints; circulation of patients in casts, splints, traction, or tight bandages should be observed; the patient should be kept dry and clean and his bed free from wrinkles and crumbs. The skin of the incontinent patient should be protected by bathing with soap and water, by rinsing and drying well, and by massaging with alcohol; protective devices should be used to relieve pressure (see following sections); patient should be carefully removed from the toilet or bedpan and cleansed thoroughly; the bedpan should be powdered to reduce friction between the pan and skin, and the patient should not be left for long periods on the toilet or bedpan, as this may cause bruising of the tissue.

(5) Therapeutic measures of prevention: The charge nurse should be notified as soon as any symptoms of a pressure area are noted, such as discoloration, tenderness, or swelling. Should the skin be broken and an abrasion be present, the area should be bathed with soap and water, rinsed well, and dried thoroughly by patting; the surrounding area should be rubbed with alcohol or given prescribed treatment. Special orders must be written by the doctor if the ulceration should be deep.
(6) Charting: Any symptoms of pressure and the location of the lesion should be charted; the time, frequency and type of ordered medication or treatment is charted; the daily condition of the decubitus, stating the topical size and the internal depth of the area and the reaction of the patient to the use and type of mechanical device, are charted.
(7) Mechanical devices for the relief of pressure, including the rubber ring, the infrequently used bed cradle, square gauze, and alternating pressure or water mattress should help to relieve pressure and to ensure the patient's comfort but may not be substituted for position change (Fig. 3-5).

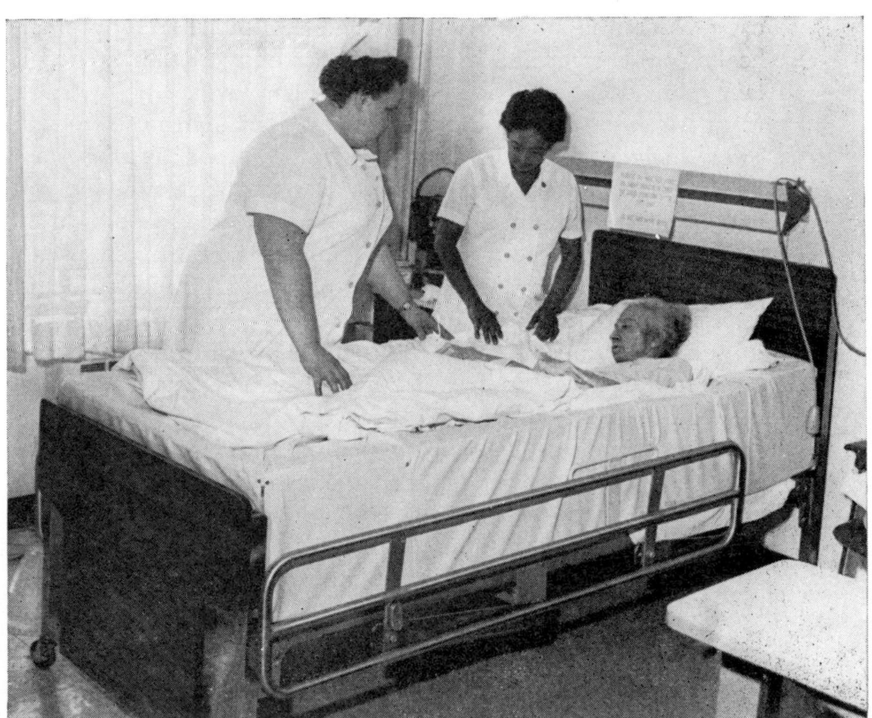

Fig. 3-5. Staff must be carefully instructed in the use of the water mattress.

(8) Procedure for the rubber ring: The ring is inflated about one-third full of air with an air pump and is protected with a cover, powdered to reduce heat and friction, assembled, and taken to the bedside of the screened patient. The procedure is explained, the ring is placed under the pressure area with the valve covered. When the ring is no longer needed, it should be washed, rinsed, dried, and inflated for storage.

(9) Procedure for bed cradle: The patient is screened; the procedure is explained and the cradle is placed on bed frame, across the foot and, when no longer needed, properly washed and stored.

(10) Procedure for the alternating pressure mattress: The patient is screened and the procedure is explained; the alternating pressure mattress is placed on the bed over the regular mattress; the patient is placed on the mattress, making sure that there are no pins or sharp objects on the patient; the instructions accompanying the mattress should be followed.

(11) Procedure for the water mattress: The instructions accompanying this device should be carefully followed during and between periods of use for proper flotation therapy.

(12) Devices for immobilization and support: These devices are used to rest the affected part of the body and thereby promote healing; to correct and maintain proper body alignment; to obtain more evenly distributed body weight by means of water, foam, or air mattress; and to relieve abdominal muscle strain. They include sandbags, fracture boards, foot boards, small knee roll and cover, or rolled bath blanket, trochanter hip roll, and air or water mattress.

(13) Care of devices for immobilization and support necessitates that sandbags be covered and bony prominences padded before application; that a continuous high knee roll be avoided due to permanent muscle contraction and danger of circulatory impairment; and that air or water mattresses not be punctured or filled more than indicated.

(14) Procedure for devices for immobilization and support: The covered equipment is brought to the screened patient; the procedure explained; the covered sandbag placed so that it supports but does not exert weight upon the patient. The knee roll is adjusted to the patient's comfort; the fracture board put under the mattress; the foot board anchored at the foot of the bed and the patient's feet placed at right angle against the board; the patient placed on the stretcher and the air or water mattress put on the covered spring. The patient is then set comfortably on the air or water mattress.

6. Bedpan Administration

a. Purpose: To help a patient confined to bed relieve himself as comfortably and efficiently as possible (should be used only when it is impossible for patient to reach the toilet)

b. Equipment: Bedpan and cover; basin filled with water, towel, wash cloth, and soap for cleansing patient after the use of the bedpan

c. Procedure

(1) The patient is screened.

(2) The cover is removed from the bedpan and placed at the foot of the bed.

(3) The patient is assisted on the bedpan by placing a hand under the buttocks as the patient lifts hips, or the patient is lifted onto the bedpan entirely if his condition should warrant it.

(4) The bedpan is adjusted under the patient; the head of the bed is raised if condition permits.

(5) Toilet paper is left within the patient's reach, and he is allowed to finish his own toilet if his condition permits.

(6) To remove the patient from the bedpan, a hand is placed under the buttocks and the pan is brought to the edge of the bed, removed, and placed on chair and covered.

(7) The patient is cared for as indicated, the area is washed and cleansed after defecation, the patient's hands are washed, and he is left comfortable and the unit, tidy.

(8) The screen is removed from patient and the equipment is cleaned, dried, and put away.

7. Evening Care

a. Purpose: To refresh the patient and to make him comfortable

b. Points to be emphasized:

(1) Soiled or damp linen should be changed.

(2) The patient should be kept warm, and any unnecessary exposure should be avoided.

(3) All chair or bed patients should be given a back massage, even though not in bed continuously.

c. Equipment

(1) Bath towel; face towel

(2) Basin of water; soap

(3) Wash cloth

(4) Necessary clean linen

E. Tube Feeding or Gastric Lavage

1. Purpose: To provide nourishment when the patient cannot be fed in the normal oral fashion, as evidenced by unconsciousness, severe agitation and depression, or refusal of all foods

2. Equipment: Nasal gastric tube, Asepto syringe, liquid formula prescribed by doctor and warmed to body temperature

3. Procedure

a. The clamp is removed from the tube and the Asepto syringe tip is put into the lumen of the tube.

b. The solution is allowed to flow in by gravity if possible, or water should be given to clear the tube before and after feeding.

c. The formula should not be given immediately to a severely malnourished patient but should be preceded by 200 cc of water for the first six feedings.

d. The tube is clamped, the Asepto syringe is removed when the feeding is completed, the cleaned equipment is wrapped in a clean towel and placed on the bedside stand.

F. Application of Heat

1. Purpose: To provide local applications of heat when needed on a doctor's order, including the temperature of water used (heating pads and electric blankets not to be used)

2. Procedure with Warm Water Bag

a. The temperature of water should not exceed 100°F and the bag should be filled about two-thirds full and wrapped in a bath towel.

b. After the bag is filled, it is held upside down to check for leaks.

c. The area to which heat is applied should be observed frequently, and the bag should be removed after the prescribed length of time or if the skin appears reddened.

G. Chair Care of the Patient

1. Purpose: To help the patient to move from the bed to the chair (and back to bed again) with a minimum of exertion and with as much safety to both patient and nurse as possible

2. Equipment: A comfortable chair or wheelchair, a blanket or large sheet if the patient is incontinent

3. Preparation of the Equipment

a. The chair is placed at the convenient side of the bed with the back of the chair even with the foot of the bed.

b. The blanket or sheet is placed with top edge level with back of chair.

c. If a wheelchair is used, it must be properly locked, with the footrest up.

4. Preparation of the Patient

a. The patient is offered the bedpan or is toileted.

b. The patient is assisted to dress in street clothes.

5. Procedure A (for patients who can help themselves to some extent)
   a. The patient's knees should be flexed.
   b. One of the nurse's arms is placed under the patient's shoulders and near to his head, and the other arm is put under his knees.
   c. The patient is lifted and turned into a sitting position; his feet are brought over the edge of the bed.
   d. The nurse should stand in front of the patient with a hand under each axilla to help the patient to stand up.
   e. The patient should be steadied so that his back is to the chair, and he should be seated in the chair gently, with his feet placed on footrests if available.
6. Procedure B (for patients who are helpless)
   a. Two people should be used for this job.
   b. The steps outlined above to get patient into a sitting position should be followed.
   c. Both helpers should stand on the same side of the bed, facing each other, with one person on either side of the patient.
   d. Each helper should place an arm under the patient's thigh simultaneously, grasping each other's wrists.
   e. With the other arm, each helper should support the patient's back and shoulders, and the patient is asked to put one arm around each helper's shoulder.
   f. The helpers should place their feet apart and bend their knees slightly.
   g. Together they should lift the patient and place him in the chair, which is held in place at the same time by each putting one foot in back of the front leg of the chair (if wheelchair is used, it should be locked).
   h. The patient should be transported to a community area or a call bell should be placed within patient's reach, if he is to remain alone in his room.

H. Use of Restraints

1. Purpose
   a. To control behavior when patients are out of contact with reality so that they will not endanger themselves, other patients, or personnel
   b. To prevent physically ill patients from tearing off dressings, contaminating wounds, or pulling out hypodermoclysis
2. Points to Be Emphasized. Three types of restraints are used:
   a. Manual restraints should be used to control the patient for brief periods only, with holds of various kinds.
      (1) A patient should never be harmed knowingly.

(2) A manual restraint is used only until another form of restraint can be administered.

b. Mechanical restraints are fashioned of cloth or of some other material.

(1) These may be used only under doctor's written orders.

(2) Sufficient personnel should be on hand to prevent harm to the patient before the application of restraints.

(3) Patients in restraints must be watched carefully every half hour to see that the restraints are not too tight.

(4) The restraints should be well padded to prevent rubbing of the skin.

(5) Patients in restraints should be offered fluids and should be released frequently to ambulate and to use the toilet.

c. Chemical restraints: Restraints in the form of drugs are used to control patient behavior.

(1) Nurses must be familiar with the toxic reactions of drugs administered.

(2) Nursing staff must watch for signs and symptoms of (a) excitement, (b) allergic reactions, (c) cardiac failure, (d) dehydration, and (e) delirium.

I. Bathing the Patient

1. Bed Bath

a. Purpose: To refresh the patient and to cleanse the skin (should be used only when it is impossible to bathe the patient in the tub or shower)

b. Equipment

(1) Bath blanket

(2) Clean linen as indicated

(3) Clean face towel, wash cloth, and bath towel

(4) Bath basin three-fourths full of water at temperature of 110 to 115°F

(5) Soap and toilet articles

c. Preparation of equipment

(1) The top of the bedside stand is arranged to receive the equipment.

(2) The linen is collected in the reverse order of use and is placed on the chair.

d. Preparation of patient

(1) The patient is screened for privacy and freedom from drafts.

(2) The procedure is explained.

(3) The bedpan is offered.

(4) The bed is left elevated until after the patient's hands and face have been washed.

e. Procedure

(1) Beginning on the side opposite the bedside table, the sheets are loosened, the blanket, spread, and top sheet removed, and the patient covered with a bath blanket.

(2) Mouth care should be done if needed.

(3) The patient's gown is removed.

(4) The patient's face, neck, and ears are washed and dried after his pillow has been covered with the face towel.

(5) The bath towel is placed under the patient's arm, and his forearm is supported and washed with soap and water, with particular attention paid to the axilla and bony prominences; the arm is dried and the same procedure is used for the other arm.

(6) The chest and abdomen are washed and dried, towels being used as covering, to prevent exposure.

(7) The patient is covered with a blanket and turned on his side; his back is washed and dried, with careful attention given to pressure areas. Then lotion may be applied.

(8) The patient is again turned on his back, and a clean gown may now be put on.

(9) The patient's legs and feet are washed, the bed is covered with a towel, and one leg is washed at a time with particular attention paid to areas between the toes and toenails and careful observation for pressure areas on the knees, heels, and ankles.

(10) The patient is washed and dried between the legs and buttocks; powder is not applied between the patient's legs.

(11) The bed is remade; the patient's fingernails are cleaned, and his hair is combed.

f. Aftercare of the patient: The screen is removed, the patient is made comfortable, the bedside table is placed within easy reach, and the unit is left in order.

g. Aftercare of the equipment: The equipment is removed from the unit, the water is emptied, the equipment is cleaned and returned to its proper place, and the towels and face cloth are replaced.

2. Tub Bath

a. Purpose: To refresh the patient and to cleanse the skin

b. Points to be emphasized

(1) A tub bath should be given only with the permission of the charge nurse.

(2) Patients with elevated temperatures and cardiac patients should not be given a tub bath.

(3) Bathroom temperature should be 75°F.

(4) Bath water should be 100 to 105°F and should be checked with a bath thermometer.
(5) Both hot and cold water should be run simultaneously.
(6) The patient should be assisted but not lifted when stepping into and out of the tub.
(7) No one should bathe unattended, and every patient is to be supervised at all times during the bathing procedure.
(8) Should the attendant need help, the nurses' call bell located adjacent to tub and shower should be used.
(9) The bath should be discontinued immediately if the patient shows any change in pulse quality or in color, or other untoward signs.
(10) If a patient should feel faint when in the tub, the water should be let out of the tub.
(11) Patients should remain in tub for no longer than 15 min.
(12) Tubs should have a nonslip interior surface.

c. Equipment
(1) Bathrobe
(2) Sheet
(3) Gown
(4) Slippers
(5) Two bath towels; washcloth
(6) Soap
(7) Chair or stool at side of tub
(8) Bath thermometer

d. Preparation of equipment
(1) The necessary articles are brought to bathroom.
(2) The tub is filled one-third full of water at 100 to 105°F.
(3) A chair or stool is placed near the tub, and a bath towel is placed on the floor for a bath mat.
(4) The bath thermometer must be in the water at all times, and the attendant must assume the responsibility for regulating the temperature of the water to keep it constant.

e. Preparation of the patient
(1) The patient is taken to the bathroom in a wheelchair if he is unable to walk.
(2) The patient is seated on a chair.

f. Procedure
(1) The hands of the nursing aide should be washed.
(2) The patient is helped to disrobe, the nurse standing directly behind the patient to assist him into the tub.
(3) Instructions are given to the patient who takes tub bath unassisted concerning (a) not turning on the hot water in tub,

(b) not touching any electric fixtures while in contact with water, (c) taking every precaution against slipping.

(4) The attendant should observe and report to the charge nurse any lesions or abnormalities on the patient at this time.

(5) The patient should be assisted in getting out of tub.

(6) A sheet should be wrapped around the patient when he is out of the tub, and he should be helped to sit on a chair or stool.

(7) The patient should be dried thoroughly with a bath towel.

g. Aftercare of patient. The patient is helped to dress and is brought back to his room to rest, if indicated.

h. Shower: The same procedure should apply as for the tub bath; patients who have difficulty standing in the shower should be

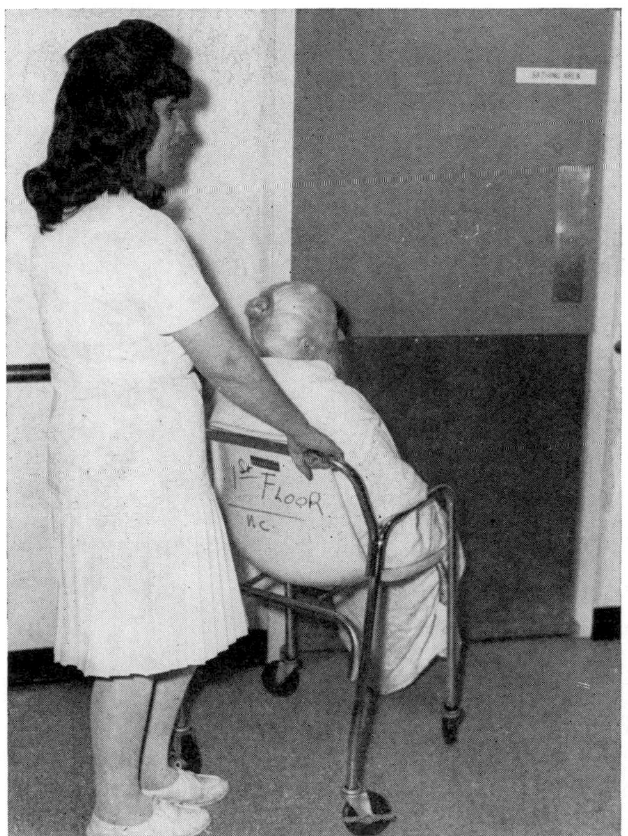

Fig. 3-6. Patients who experience difficulty in standing may remain seated in the shower chair after they have been transported to the bathing area.

seated in shower chairs, but no patient should be permitted to shower unattended (Fig. 3-6).

J. Therapeutic or Sitz Bath

1. Purpose

a. To induce voiding in urinary retention

b. To relieve pain, inflammation, and congestion

(1) For hemorrhoids or after hemorrhoidectomy

(2) After proctoscopic and cystoscopic examination

c. To promote healing

2. Points to be Emphasized

a. A nurse or attendant must always remain with the patient.

b. The tub must be absolutely clean before the treatment is started.

c. A covered rubber ring is indicated in rectal or vaginal conditions.

d. The temperature of water should not exceed 110°F.

e. The patient should not be chilled.

f. Hemorrhages, especially in rectal conditions, must be carefully watched for.

g. Perspiration and change in color or pulse should be noted.

h. Should a patient become weak or faint, the water is let out of the tub, the patient is covered with a sheet, assistance is obtained, and the patient is removed from the tub.

i. The patient should remain in the tub no longer than 20 min.

j. The patient may remain in bed for 1 hr following the treatment.

3. Equipment

a. Bath thermometer

b. Large sheet, safety pin

c. Two bath towels

d. Rubber ring and cover

e. Clean perineal or other dressing needed

f. Chair or stool

g. Wheelchair, if necessary

h. Newspaper if perineal pad or dressing is worn

4. Preparation of Equipment

a. The necessary articles are brought to bathroom.

b. The tub is cleaned, and a rubber ring is placed in the bottom of the tub and covered with a bath towel.

c. The tub is filled one-fourth full of water at 105°F and the bath thermometer kept in the water at all times.

d. A chair or stool is placed near the tub; a bath towel is placed on the floor for a bath mat.

5. Preparation of the Patient

a. The procedure is explained, especially if it is the first time the patient is receiving this treatment.
b. The patient is transported to bathroom as his condition indicates and is seated on a chair.

6. Procedure
a. The hands of the nurse should be washed.
b. The patient's clothing is removed; he is draped with a sheet, secured with a safety pin at the back of the neck, and the bottom edge of the sheet is rolled up.
c. The patient is assisted into the tub very carefully, and the sheet is draped over the edge of the tub, closed over the patient's back, and secured with a safety pin.
d. When the patient has become accustomed to the warmth of the water, the water is allowed to flow into the tub to the patient's waist, being guided by his comfort, and the temperature is increased to 110°F.
e. At end of 15 min, the patient is assisted out of tub, the sheet being used as a robe.
f. All parts of the body are dried thoroughly.
g. The dressing is replaced as indicated.
h. The gown and robe are replaced, and the patient is assisted back to his room.

7. Aftercare of the Equipment
a. The rubber ring should be washed with soap and water, rinsed, dried, inflated, and returned to its proper storage place.
b. The tub should be rinsed thoroughly with hot water, scoured with abrasive, washed with soap and water, and rinsed well.
c. Soiled linen should be placed in the hamper.
d. The thermometer should be washed in cold water followed by soapy water, rinsed, dried, and soaked in disinfectant for 10 min.
e. The bathroom should be left in order.

8. Charting
a. On the check sheet
b. On the nursing care plan and progress notes:
(1) Duration and temperature of the bath
(2) Pulse on return to bed and general reaction
(3) Nurse's signature

K. Eye, Ear, and Nose Care

1. Eye Drops—Procedure
a. The type and amount of solution is prescribed by the physician.
b. No more solution than is needed should be drawn into the eyedropper.

c. After the solution is drawn into the dropper, the dropper is held with the bulb uppermost.
d. The patient is given a piece of tissue so that he may have it ready when the drops are instilled.
e. The dropper is held close to the eye, but should not touch the eyelid or eyelashes in order to avoid injury if the patient is startled by the drops.
f. The lower conjunctival sac should be exposed and the prescribed number of drops allowed to fall into the center of the sac.
g. The patient is asked to close his eyelid and to move his eye, to distribute the solution over the conjunctival surfaces and anterior eyeball.

2. Ear Drops—Procedure
a. The solution should be warmed to body temperature.
b. The patient should be instructed to lie on his side and to remain this way after the treatment so that the drops will not escape from the canal.
c. An eyedropper should be used, the ear canal should be straightened, and the prescribed amount of drops should be allowed to fall on the side of the canal.

3. Nose Drops—Procedure
a. The patient is provided with a piece of tissue.
b. The patient is assisted to a sitting position with his head tilted back, or asked to lie in bed with his head tilted back.
c. The solution for both nares should be drawn into the medicine dropper which should be placed inside the nares ⅓ to ½ in., and the prescribed amount of drops should be instilled.
d. The patient should be instructed to keep his head back for a few minutes to prevent escape of the drops.
e. When nose drops are instilled into nares of confused patients, the end of the dropper should be protected with a rubber tip.

L. Respiratory Treatment

1. Care of Tracheotomy
a. Purpose: To keep the tube in the patient and in the proper position
b. Equipment
(1) Suction equipment at bedside
(2) Tracheal dilator or curved hemostat
(3) Scissors should be kept at the bedside to be used to maintain the opening until assistance arrives, should the outer tube come out.

(4) 0.25% peroxide to soften secretions

(5) Cold water, soap, pipestem cleaners, and brush, for cleaning

c. Procedure:

(1) The inner tube must be changed every 3 hr for the first 48 hr after the tracheotomy is done.

(2) The tube is cleaned by soaking in peroxide to soften the secretions; then using cold water, soap, and a brush; rinsing and boiling for a few minutes; and cooling.

(3) The patient should always be suctioned before reinserting the tube.

(4) The inner tube should be changed as often as necessary.

(5) The patient should be observed to note the need to change the outer tube to clear the airway, in which case a doctor must be called.

(6) The patient should be suctioned as often as needed; the tube should not go beyond the inner cannula, and the suction should be cut off as the tube is inserted.

(7) The patient should be observed for hemorrhage through the tube or around it during the first 48 hr.

(8) The dressing should be changed as needed.

(9) Fluids should be forced and proper mouth care maintained.

2. Suctioning

a. Purpose: To maintain a clear airway by removing excessive mucus in the nasal, oral, and pharyngeal passages

b. Equipment:

(1) Electric suctioning machine

(2) Catheter

c. Preparation of the patient: The patient should be placed in a lateral or semi-prone position with the bed flat or the head slightly elevated. If patient is conscious, the procedure should be explained.

d. Procedure:

(1) The catheter should be attached to the connecting tube.

(2) The cord is plugged into an electric outlet.

(3) The switch is turned to the *on* position.

(4) The catheter is lubricated with water and inserted into the nasal or oral passage to the epiglottis to initiate the cough reflex and to make the suctioning procedure more effective.

e. Aftercare of the equipment:

(1) With the machine turned to *on* position, clear water should be suctioned through the catheter to remove all mucus from the tubing.

(2) The drainage bottle should be detached, cleaned thoroughly

with green soap and water, then replaced in the proper position.

(3) The catheter is removed and, if disposable, discarded, and the charge slip is made out to the patient. If the catheter is rubber, it is to be soaked in green soap and water, then wrapped for sterilization in the autoclave.

(4) The suction machine is to be wiped off, the catheter replaced in the drawer in the stand, and the machine returned to its storage place.

(5) The maintenance director should be notified of any inoperable parts.

3. Oxygen Therapy

a. Purpose: To provide and maintain a normal supply of O_2 for blood and tissues, and to correct any deficiencies that may exist in the removal of carbon dioxide.

b. Equipment: Small emergency tank and mask, to be applied in emergency.

c. Preparation of the patient: The patient should be observed carefully and the process explained to him, if possible.

d. Procedure:

(1) The cylinder of oxygen is opened.

(2) The liter gauge is turned up to 6–8 liters; and flow of O_2 should be tested against the back of the hand.

(3) The facial mask is applied, and the facial straps are secured, care being taken to adjust the mask properly so that the patient is comfortable.

(4) If the mask is in the proper position, the breathing bag should deflate and inflate alternately, and the flow should be regulated so that the breathing bag is not completely collapsed during inspiration.

(5) This should be checked frequently.

e. Aftercare of equipment:

(1) The mask should be cleaned thoroughly with alcohol.

(2) The supplier should be notified at a convenient time of day so that the equipment may be serviced after use.

f. Maintenance: The tank and mask must be checked weekly by the service department of the supplier, and this should be supervised by 7:00 to 3:00 charge nurse in each nursing unit.

g. Precautions in the use and storage of oxygen equipment:

(1) A "no smoking" sign should be displayed.

(2) Oil and grease should not come in contact with the cylinder gauge or the regulator.

(3) A tank should be strapped to the bed or cart; when it is strapped to the bed, the wheels of the bed should be locked.

(4) Oil or alcohol rubs should not be given while the patient is in an oxygen tent.
(5) No electrical appliances should be used by a patient in an oxygen tent, and this includes such devices as radios, heating pads, electric razors, and call buttons.
(6) The nurse should discontinue the oxygen therapy whenever electrical equipment is used in the care of the patient.
(7) The nurse should check the cylinder gauge when reporting on duty, and at specific intervals thereafter, to assure the patient of an adequate supply of oxygen.
(8) When a cylinder gauge registers 500 lb, the nurse has an obligation to make certain another tank is on hand.
(9) If the oxygen supply should run out, the nurse should remove the mask from the patient's face; or, if he is in a tent, take him out of the tent immediately.
(10) Oxygen tanks must never be placed or stored next to radiators or heating equipment.
(11) When a tank is empty, it should be so marked.
(12) The cylinder protection cap should be in place. (This cap should be on whenever a tank is not in use.)
(13) Empty tanks should be stored separated from the full tanks.

M. Irrigation of Patient

1. Enema

a. Special purpose: To aid evacuation of the large intestine by stimulating peristalsis with particular reference to patients suffering from organic brain syndrome who may become impacted and require regular rectal examinations and observation for distention

b. Equipment:
(1) Enema can with solution to be used
(2) Rubber sheet
(3) Lubricated toilet tissue and dry toilet tissues
(4) Bedpan and cover
(5) Basin, washcloth, and towel
(6) Bath blanket

c. Preparation of equipment:
(1) The equipment is assembled in the utility room.
(2) The tube is lubricated about 4 in., and the enema can is filled with solution at a temperature of 105 to 107°F.
(3) This is taken to the bedside on a covered tray.

d. Preparation of the patient:

(1) The patient should be told what is to be done.
(2) The patient should be screened, the top covers should be removed, and the patient should be draped with a bath blanket.
(3) A rubber sheet and draw sheet should be placed under the patient's buttocks.
(4) The patient should be placed in a modified Sims' position.

e. Procedure:

(1) The pinch clamp should be released, some solution should be allowed to run through the tubing into the bedpan to expel air from the tubing, and the tubing should be clamped.
(2) A well-lubricated rectal tube should be inserted into the rectum of the patient, about 4 in.
(3) The irrigating can should be held so that the level of liquid above the anus does not exceed 18 in.
(4) The pinch clamp is released to allow solution to run in slowly.
(5) The patient is asked to retain the fluid until the enema is completed if possible, but should the patient complain of discomfort, the tubing should be clamped off until the patient is relieved.
(6) When the desired amount of solution has been given, the tube is pinched off and withdrawn from the rectum.
(7) The equipment is placed on a tray and covered.
(8) The patient is turned on his back and the bedpan placed in position.
(9) When the enema is expelled, a basin of warm water should be taken to the bedside, and if the patient is unable to expel the enema, a rectal tube is inserted and the solution is allowed to drain off into the bedpan.
(10) The bedpan is removed, covered, and placed on a chair.
(11) If the patient is unable to care for himself, he should be turned on his side if possible, and the areas around the anus should be cleansed with toilet tissue, washed with soap and water, rinsed, and dried.
(12) The rubber sheet, bath blanket, and upper bed covers are replaced, the patient being left comfortable.
(13) The equipment is removed, cleaned, and put away.

f. Enema procedure in the dorsal recumbent position: This position is used when patient cannot retain the fluid, and the enema is given to the patient while on the bedpan.

g. Enema procedure on toilet (the preferable style for the aged):

(1) The pinch clamp is released, and some solution is allowed to run through the tubing into the toilet to expel air from tubing, and the tubing is clamped.

(2) A well-lubricated rectal tube is inserted into the rectum of patient about 4 in.
(3) The irrigating can is held so that the level of liquid above the anus does not exceed 18 in.
(4) The pinch clamp is released, and the solution is allowed to run in slowly.
(5) The patient is asked to retain the fluid until the enema is completed, if possible, but should the patient complain of discomfort, the tubing should be clamped off until the patient is relieved.
(6) When the desired amount of solution has been given, the tube is pinched off and withdrawn from the rectum, and the equipment is placed on tray and covered.
(7) When the enema is expelled, thorough cleansing of anus area by toilet tissue is followed by cleansing with soap and water if necessary.
(8) The equipment is cleaned and put away.
(9) The patient never is left alone in the bathroom.

2. Retention Enema

a. Purpose: To give fluid or medication by rectum
(1) To relieve flatulence or distention
(2) To soften fecal impactions

b. Equipment
(1) 500 cc graduate with the solution prescribed
(2) Catheter No. 14-16 French with funnel attached
(3) Lubricant on a square of toilet tissue
(4) Treatment sheet (rubber or plastic) and draw sheet

c. Preparation of equipment
(1) The tip of the catheter should be lubricated, leaving paper around the tip of the tube.
(2) All other equipment should be assembled and the prescribed solution prepared in a graduate, heating the water to body temperature (testing on the wrist).
(3) The equipment should be taken to the bedside.

d. Preparation of patient
(1) The unit should be screened.
(2) The upper bedding is replaced with a bath blanket.
(3) The area under the hips and surrounding the buttocks is protected with treatment and draw sheets.
(4) The patient is placed in a modified Sims' position.
(5) The patient is instructed to retain fluid according to the therapeutic effect desired.

e. Procedure
(1) The tubing should be pinched off and the funnel filled with

solution, some solution being allowed to return to the graduate to expel air from the tubing.
(2) The tubing should be pinched off and the funnel refilled.
(3) The catheter should be inserted into the rectum about 4 in.
(4) The funnel should be held about 6 to 8 in. above the anus and the solution allowed to run in slowly, the fluid in the funnel to be replenished before it is completely empty.
(5) When the desired amount has been given, the tubing should be pinched off and removed from the rectum.
(6) The upper bedding should be replaced and the treatment sheet removed.
(7) The patient should be left comfortable and the unit neat.
(8) All equipment should be cleaned and stored.

3. Douche

a. Purpose: To cleanse the vaginal canal or for medication

b. Equipment
(1) Solution at 105°F as ordered by doctor
(2) Douche set
(3) Rubber sheet and draw sheet if given in bed; bedpan

c. Douche procedure in bed:
(1) The equipment should be brought to the patient's bedside.
(2) The patient is screened, and the bed is protected with a treatment and draw sheet.
(3) The patient should lie in the lithotomy position on the bedpan.
(4) Lubricant may be used if patient desires it.
(5) Some solution is allowed to flow through tubing to expel air.
(6) The douche tip is inserted into the vagina and the solution is allowed to run in slowly.
(7) The douche tip is rotated as the solution flows in.
(8) When procedure is completed, the douche and bedpan are removed, covered, and placed on a chair.
(9) If patient is unable to care for self, the area should be cleansed with soap and water, rinsed, and dried.
(10) Air should be permitted to circulate between the legs to avoid rashes.
(11) The treatment and draw sheets are removed and the patient is left comfortable.
(12) The equipment is removed and cleaned.

d. Douche procedure out of bed: A douche may be given in a bathtub or on a toilet.
(1) The equipment is brought to the patient's lavatory or shower rooms.

(2) Some solution is allowed to flow through the tubing to expel air, and, if desired, the douche tip is lubricated.
(3) The douche tip is inserted into the vagina and the solution is allowed to run in slowly.
(4) The douche tip is rotated as the solution flows in.
(5) When procedure is completed, the douche tip is removed.
(6) If the patient is unable to care for herself, the area should be cleansed with soap and water, rinsed, and dried.
(7) Air should be permitted to circulate between the legs to avoid rashes.
(8) The equipment should be removed and cleaned.
(9) The patient should never be left alone during the procedure.

4. Irrigation of Foley Catheter

a. Purpose: To cleanse the bladder of irritating products

b. Equipment (all must be sterile):
(1) Asepto syringe
(2) Small round basin
(3) Kidney basin

c. Preparation of patient: The patient should be prepared as for a catheterization.

d. Procedure:
(1) The patient should be catheterized.
(2) The bladder should be irrigated by means of the Asepto syringe, one syringeful at a time injected slowly and allowed to run out completely before another syringeful is injected.
(3) The above is repeated until the returns are clear.
(4) The procedure is finished as in a catheterization.

5. Irrigation of Colostomy

a. Purpose: To help regulate and control the drainage of a colostomy, thereby making the patient physically more comfortable

b. Equipment:
(1) Irrigating can (2-qt can or bag), tubing, glass connection, catheter, clamp, colostomy irrigator
(2) Solution (warm tap water, 105°F)
(3) Petroleum or lubricating jelly to lubricate the catheter
(4) Tissue
(5) A paper bag or newspaper
(6) Clean dressing or colostomy bag

c. Preparation of equipment:
(1) The tubing is attached to the can; the clamp is closed.
(2) The can is filled with warm water.
(3) The catheter is lubricated, wrapped in tissue, and brought to the bathroom with the other equipment.

d. Procedure:

(1) The patient is put on the toilet and the equipment is placed within reach so that the patient can assist as much as possible.

(2) The soiled dressing is removed, and the opening is cleaned with tissue.

(3) A small amount of fluid is allowed to run through the tubing to expel air, and the tubing is clamped.

(4) The catheter is inserted through the opening in the irrigator cup and is inserted gently into the colostomy opening 4 to 8 in.; the cup is held firmly against the abdomen and the outlet tubing allowed to hang between the legs into the toilet.

(5) The clamp is released; about one-fourth to one-half of the solution is allowed to enter the colon. The clamp is tightened and the solution allowed to return through the outlet into the toilet, with enough solution used so that drainage does not occur between irrigations (½ to 3 qt), and the can is refilled if needed while the return flow of the solution is being awaited.

(6) When the irrigation is completed, the bottom of the irrigator is closed off, and the patient wears it as a bag while showering or engaging in morning care to be assured that all drainage has ceased.

(7) The area around the colostomy bud is cleansed with soap and water, and when the skin is dry and clean, powder and a clean dressing are applied.

(8) The equipment is removed, cleaned, and put away, and the patient is left comfortable.

(9) This procedure is modified when the irrigation is to be performed in bed.

N. Catheterization of Patient

1. Female Patient

a. Purpose: To remove urine from the bladder under aseptic technique

(1) To relieve urinary retention

(2) To obtain an uncontaminated specimen for laboratory use

(3) To relieve incontinence temporarily

b. Equipment

(1) Sterile catheterization tray and sheet

(2) Sterile catheter

(3) Drainage bag and tubing if necessary

(4) Sterile gloves, sterile cotton balls

(5) Kidney basin

c. Preparation of patient

(1) The patient should be screened and draped, and her knees flexed and separated.

(2) Treatment should be discontinued if there is any difficulty in inserting the catheter or if the equipment becomes contaminated, when sterile equipment will again be needed.

d. Procedure

(1) The top dressing sheet should be removed from the catheterization tray and placed on the bed up to the edge of the patient's buttocks.

(2) Sterile gloves should be worn by the nurse.

(3) The catheter should be lubricated and placed on sterile cotton balls.

(4) The labia should be separated with left hand of the nurse.

(5) One cotton ball is extracted from the solution and is sponged downward on the far side of the labia.

(6) The above step should be repeated, this time sponging downward on near side of the labia.

(7) Sponging is repeated with a third cotton ball, this time sponging downward over the meatus.

(8) The kidney basin should be placed between the patient's legs on the dressing sheet.

(9) The catheter is grasped with the right hand, about 3 in. from the edge.

(10) The catheter should be inserted in the meatus about 2 in. or until the urine begins to flow.

(11) The urine should be allowed to flow into the kidney basin until the flow ceases, with the drainage bag kept below the level of the bladder.

(12) The catheter should be withdrawn slightly and additional flow watched for.

(13) If a Foley catheter is used, it should be attached to the drainage apparatus.

(14) The catheter should be withdrawn immediately if only a specimen is needed.

(15) The equipment should be removed, the bed straightened, and the patient covered and left comfortable.

(16) The equipment should be removed, cleaned, and stored.

(17) The cotton balls should be discarded.

2. Male Patient

a. Purpose: To remove urine from the bladder under aseptic technique for previously described reasons

b. Equipment

(1) Sterile catheterization tray, sterile dressing sheet

(2) Sterile catheter
(3) Drainage bag and tubing if necessary
(4) Sterile cotton balls, sterile rubber gloves
(5) Kidney basin

c. Preparation of patient. The patient should be screened, draped, and placed on his back.

d. Procedure (usually this is done by a doctor, assisted by nurse or by two nurses or a nurse and an orderly):

(1) The sterile top dressing sheet is removed from the catheterization tray and placed across the thighs of the patient.

(2) The glans is cleansed with cotton balls in the solution and is placed on the sterile sheet.

(3) The kidney basin is placed on the sterile sheet between the thighs.

(4) The sterile lubricated catheter should be placed on a sterile field.

(5) Sterile gloves are worn by doctor or nurse.

(6) The catheter is inserted until the sphincter muscle is reached.

(7) The procedure is halted for about 1 min, and the patient is asked to relax and breathe through his mouth.

(8) The catheter is inserted gently through the sphincter into the bladder.

(9) The urine is allowed to flow into the kidney basin until the flow ceases; the drainage bag must not be raised above the level of the bladder.

(10) The gloves should be removed and attached to the drainage apparatus if indicated, or the catheter is pinched and removed slowly.

(11) The equipment is removed from the bed, the bed is straightened, and the patient is covered and made comfortable.

(12) The equipment is removed, cleaned, and stored.

(13) The cotton balls are discarded.

O. Blood Transfusion–Hypodermoclysis

1. Purpose: To supply the body with fluids

2. Equipment

a. Sterile sets for blood administration or clysis
b. Solution prescribed by the physician
c. A treatment pole
d. Restraints as necessary
e. Drapes as necessary
f. Alcohol and sponges
g. Adhesive tape

3. Preparation of the Patient. The patient should be positioned, draped, and restrained as necessary.

4. Procedure for the Blood Transfusion

a. The doctor should give the transfusion, assisted by the nurses.

b. After the blood transfusion has been started, the patient should be observed carefully for any reaction such as headache, tingling sensation, rash, dyspnea, or lumbar pain.

c. The patient's temperature should be taken during the transfusion, as an elevation could indicate a blood reaction.

5. Procedure for Clysis

a. The area should be prepared with alcohol wipes:

(1) On a female, directly below the breasts or anterior thigh

(2) On a male, on the anterior thigh

b. Some fluids should be allowed to run through the tubing into kidney basin to expel air.

c. The needle should be inserted subcutaneously and the flow of the solution regulated.

d. The needle should be fastened with adhesive tape.

e. The patient should be checked often and the rate of solution and absorption observed and adjusted accordingly.

f. The patient should be left as comfortable as possible, with a minimum of exposure.

g. If the clysis is to continue for several hours, the position should be changed every ½ hr.

h. The needles should be removed quickly when discontinuing treatment and, if needed, a small sterile dressing should be applied.

P. Accident Procedure

1. Patients

a. Should a patient experience a mishap of any type, the charge nurse of the floor should be notified and she should immediately offer appropriate emergency treatment.

b. The charge nurse should complete an accident report in duplicate, the original to be added to the patient's chart and the duplicate to be filed in the administrative office.

c. The charge nurse should notify the director of nursing and, if appropriate, the patient's physician.

d. The incident must be described in the nurses' notes, and if it is at all significant it should be promptly reported to the insurance agent of the extended care facility.

2. Staff

a. Should a staff member experience an accident, the director of nursing should be notified and she should offer emergency treatment.

b. An accident report should be written in duplicate and the original taken with employee to the office of the medical director or, in the absence of medical director, the staff member should be sent with the accident report to the emergency room of the hospital by taxi, or, when necessary, by ambulance.

c. The duplicate of the accident report should be attached to the clipboard of the administrative director.

d. If the staff member required medical care, the incident must be reported to the insurance agent.

3. Visitors. The same procedure should be followed for visitors experiencing an accident as for staff members, as described in the preceding section.

Q. Evacuation Plan

1. Evacuation plans for each floor should be posted at floor bulletin boards with the direction to be taken from each patient's room and the exits clearly marked.

2. Nursing personnel should also study the emergency and utility interruption plans given to each new staff member. (See Section 1.)

R. Patient Transfer Procedure

1. A completed transfer form must accompany each patient to be transferred.

2. Should a patient be transferred to a hospital and be scheduled to return, the patient's name should be kept on the patient roster.

3. The name of patient should be marked as transferred in the patient register.

4. The transfer should be noted in the patient census book and on the patient record card.

5. The dietary director should be informed of the patient transfer.

S. Patient Discharge Procedure

1. Patients can be discharged only on the written order of their physician.

2. When patient and family insist upon discharge against medical advice, a signed release from the patient or family in the presence of witnesses should be obtained (Fig. 3-7).

3. If no one will sign the release, this should be noted and recorded in the presence of witnesses.

4. The nursing and medical records at nursing stations should be completed and stapled.

Fig. 3-7

RELEASE OF RESPONSIBILITY FOR DISCHARGE AGAINST ADVICE

Date____________________

Center for Nursing Care

This is to certify that I,______________________________ hereby assume full responsibility for being discharged against the advice of the attending physician and the extended care facility. I acknowledge that I have been informed of the risk involved and do hereby release the attending physician and the institution from all responsibility for any adverse effects which may result from this action.

____
Signature of Patient

____________________ ______________________________
Witness Signature of Responsible Family Member

Authorization must be signed by the patient. If the patient is physically or mentally impaired, the responsible family member is to sign.

5. The pages should be removed from the special services and restorative services book and attached to the nursing and medical records.
6. The patient record card should be completed and clipped to the records.
7. The records and attached card should be placed in a prearranged place.
8. The discharge should be entered in the patient register and in the patient census records.
9. The Dietary and Housekeeping Departments should be informed of the discharge of the patient.
10. The name of the patient is removed from the patient roster.
11. The chart should be assembled in the following order upon the discharge of a patient:
a. Admission, transfer, and discharge information

b. Medical abstract, if any
c. Initial physical examination
d. Social service notes
e. Physician's orders and progress notes
f. EKG, laboratory reports, and x-rays
g. Dental treatment
h. Podiatry treatment
i. Check sheets
j. Nursing care plan and progress notes
k. Record of patient care by nursing attendants
l. Narcotic-sedative record
m. Intake and output record
n. Accident report
o. Physical, speech, and occupational therapy
p. Special services

T. Terminal Care

1. The charge nurse should be notified immediately in the event of sudden illness, emergency, or death of a patient.
2. The charge nurse should check the patient for pulse, respiration, etc., and should notify the director of nursing and the patient's physician.
3. The charge nurse should remain with the patient in order to observe any change in his condition.
4. If patient is Catholic and has not received the last sacraments, the priest must be notified.
5. The physician must pronounce the patient dead and complete and sign the death certificate.
6. The deceased patient should be prepared by his body being straightened and his head placed on a pillow.
7. The body should be cleaned, and therapeutic devices, dentures, and jewelry should be removed, cleaned, and put in envelopes.
8. The body should be covered with a sheet.
9. A list should be made of all jewelry, to be put in the safe until called for by the patient's family.
10. The physician should notify the family when the patient dies.
11. The family of a deceased patient should notify the undertaker to remove the body, and the undertaker should sign the lower part of the admission and discharge form and indicate whether he has received jewelry and other possessions.
12. Belongings not accompanying the body should be kept by the director of social service in a safe place until they are removed by the family.

13. The Dietary Department should be notified when a patient has died.
14. The Housekeeping Department should be notified when a patient has died so that his room or unit may be properly cleaned.
15. The patient chart should be completed by the charge nurse and assembled and deposited in the discharge container in the administrative office.

U. Cleaning a Unit after the Discharge of a Patient

1. Purpose
- *a.* To thoroughly clean and inspect the unit for the protection of the entire facility
- *b.* To prepare a clean and orderly environment for the reception of another patient

2. Points to be Emphasized:
- *a.* All procedures should be carried out, remembering to keep the equipment away from the uniform and face.
- *b.* It is believed that a definite relationship exists between uncleanliness and certain types of diseases since microorganisms found in the air are carried in dust particles.
- *c.* Most organic substances are soluble in water and, therefore, should be removable with ordinary cleansing agents.
- *d.* It is important to know the material to be cleaned in order to select the proper cleaning agent, and the director of nursing should be consulted for specific directions on the treatment of mattress, pillows, and blankets.

3. Equipment:
- *a.* Cleaning basin with water
- *b.* Solution of ammonia and soap, 1 oz to a gal of water
- *c.* Whisk broom
- *d.* Two pieces of cleaning cloths—one wet and one dry
- *e.* Scouring powder and dish if necessary
- *f.* Two thicknesses of paper for mattress on floor

4. Preparation of Equipment:
- *a.* A utility cart should be obtained.
- *b.* The cleaning materials should be assembled on the top shelf.
- *c.* Clean linen should be placed on the middle shelf.

5. Preparation of Unit:
- *a.* The unit should be screened.
- *b.* The waste should be collected and deposited in a paper bag or newspaper.
- *c.* The utensils should be removed from the bedside table and placed on the table with paper bag.

d. The pillow cases should be removed and should be placed on the bed at the head end with the pillow placed on the seat of the chair.

e. The bedding should be loosened on all sides, starting at the far side first; the spread should be removed and placed at the head end; the blanket should be removed and placed on the pillow, and the rubber sheet should be removed and placed at the head end.

f. The bedding should be rolled compactly inward and placed in a hamper.

g. The utensils and paper bag should be deposited on the bottom shelf of the cart.

6. Procedure

a. The upper surface of the mattress is whisked with hot ammonia and water solution; the mattress should not be allowed to get too wet, and the tufts and seams should be inspected for vermin.

b. The mattress is slid from the bed to the newspaper on the floor, the mattress being kept on its side in an upright position.

c. The bed frame and springs are washed and dried.

d. The second side of the mattress and three sides should be cleaned.

e. With the aid of another person, the mattress is slid onto a spring overhanging the fourth side to be cleaned.

f. The fourth side is cleaned and the mattress turned from top to bottom.

g. The bedside stand is washed and dried inside and out.

h. The chair and table are washed and dried.

i. Clean linen is placed on the seat of the chair.

7. Aftercare of Equipment

a. The utility cart is removed to the utility room.

b. The water is poured down the hopper.

c. The equipment is cleaned and returned to its proper place.

d. The bath basin, emesis basin, and mouth cup are thoroughly cleaned and sterilized or discarded, if disposable.

e. The bedpan and urinal are cleaned, rinsed, and sterilized for 10 min, or, if disposable, discarded.

V. X-ray and Laboratory Procedure. Laboratory and/or x-ray work should be available when ordered by the attending physician and the following procedure should be used:

1. Each request should be made out in duplicate.

a. One color pad—for all x-rays

b. Another color—for all urinalyses

c. A third color pad—for all blood chemistries

2. The original should be sent to the medical director's office.
3. The duplicate should be kept at the nurses' station on the patient's floor until the report is returned.
4. The secretary should arrange appointments with the charge nurse on the appropriate nursing unit.
5. Results of x-ray and laboratory procedures should be entered in the patient's medical record.

W. Patient Outings Procedure

1. Patients should be permitted to leave the facility for short periods only upon the written order of their physicians.
2. The patient and his accompanying relative or friend should complete the information required in the patient's outing book kept at each nursing station which should note the signature of the person accompanying the patient, the time of departure, the expected return, the actual return of patient, the relationship of the person accompanying the patient to the patient, and the nurse's signature.
3. The charge nurse should inform the Dietary Department if the patient is to miss a meal.
4. Patients who are remaining away overnight or for several days may have families take their medication along, unless this is specifically prohibited by the physicians.

X. Special Services

1. Several types of special services should be available to patients in extended care units with arrangements approved by their families.

- *a.* Podiatry care
  - (1) A podiatrist should visit regularly and should be available on an emergency basis, a written order by the patient's physician to be obtained prior to rendering podiatry treatments.
  - (2) The podiatrist should note pertinent data regarding the treatment given on the podiatry treatment record sheet and the medical record.
- *b.* Beautician. A beautician should visit weekly to attend the women patients.
- *c.* Barber. A barber should be in attendance for male patients every week.
- *d.* A brace maker, hearing-aid maker, and optometrist should be available to serve patients on request to the director of nursing.

2. When any of the services described above is performed, it should be recorded in one of the special services books located at each nursing station.

a. Each patient should be listed in alphabetical order.
b. The person performing the service should indicate the date, the type of service performed, and should sign his name.

V. SCHEDULE OF ACTIVITIES OF THE NURSING STAFF FOR A 65-BED EXTENDED CARE FACILITY WITH TWO NURSING UNITS

A. The Director of Nursing

1. Typical Daily Schedule

7:00–7:15 A.M. The director of nursing may report on duty to receive reports with the two daytime charge nurses from the 11:00 P.M. to 7:00 A.M. charge nurses and to communicate with other night staff, (or she may alternately report at 9:00 A.M. and remain until 5:00 P.M.).

7:15–8:00 A.M. She should make rounds on both units.

8:00–9:00 A.M. She should do office work, such as daily census book, checking clipboard notes, ordering or canceling newspapers for patients, etc.

9:00–9:30 A.M. The director of nursing should meet with the charge nurses to discuss plans regarding patients, their families, and the staff.

9:30–11:30 A.M. She should complete her administrative work, including phone calls, personnel work, scheduling, interviewing, etc.

11:30–12:00 noon. The director should meet with the social service director to plan for new patient admissions and to discuss in-house patients and their families.

1:00–3:00 P.M. She should confer with physicians and families, and have a dialogue with nurses and aides regarding any unusual occurrences and should go off duty shortly thereafter, unless it is a 9:00 A.M. to 5:00 P.M. day.

2. Weekly Activities

a. Monday: The nursing director should participate in the in-training session, during which she should maintain a written record and a schedule of attendance of the nursing staff.
b. She should consult with the consulting dentist regarding patients to receive dental appointments and with the podiatrist concerning patients to receive podiatry services.
c. Tuesday from 6:00–7:30 P.M.: She should attend and participate in the interdisciplinary conference.

3. Monthly Duties

a. She should supervise the return of unused narcotics, sedatives, and stimulants to Narcotic Control Bureau of state Department of Health.

b. She should plan a meeting with all supervisory nursing personnel.

c. She should take inventory of medicines and supplies with the designated charge nurses.

d. She should be responsible for supervising contacting physicians for monthly examinations of all patients and for certification and recertification visits for Medicare patients.

e. On a stipulated day once a month, she should attend the personnel meeting.

f. Once a month on a designated day she should attend the utilization review and patient care policy committee meetings.

4. Quarterly Duties

a. She should check current physical examinations for the entire staff.

b. She should attend a meeting of the pharmacy and safety committees.

5. Semiannual Duty

a. She should schedule chest x-rays for the staff.

b. She should supervise updating of the nursing procedure manual.

6. Annual Duty

a. She should maintain a written record of employee performance on the reverse side of the employment application of all nursing department personnel.

b. She should prepare a master staffing plan with provision for holidays, vacations, illness, and anticipated variations in patient census.

B. Charge Nurse

1. All Shifts, Both Units

a. At each change of shift, the charge nurse of each unit should turn over the keys on the key ring to her relief nurse after the narcotic count.

b. At the same time, each charge nurse completing her tour of duty should report to the incoming charge nurse on the condition of each patient in her unit.

2. Charge Nurse for Both Units, 7:00 A.M.–3:00 P.M. Shift

The special duties and activities for both charge nurses on daytime shift should include the following:

a. Weekly

Monday

(1) The nurses should attend the in-training session conducted by the medical director.

(2) The aides' and orderlies' daily assignments for the week should be posted by the charge nurses.

Wednesday

The patients' weekly bathing schedule should be posted.

Friday

The charge nurses should check all medications carefully to see whether the supply is sufficient to cover needs through Monday P.M. and should order additional supplies if needed.

Monday, Tuesday, and Saturday

The charge nurses should verify the participation of specified patients in the speech therapy program.

Sunday, Wednesday, and Friday

The charge nurses should check on the participation of patients in religious services, scheduled as follows:

Sunday—Protestant services
Wednesday—Catholic services
Friday—Jewish services

Weekly Check-up

(1) The nursing care plan of each patient should be reviewed and corrected by the charge nurses according to the changing condition of the patient.

(2) The charge nurses should be responsible for the weekly inspection of the oxygen tanks and masks on both units by the service department of the supplier.

(3) She should verify the names of patients who require medical certification or recertification and should so notify the attending physicians.

(4) Every week the charge nurse on each unit should verify with the director of nursing the names of the patients who are to receive dental, podiatric, beautician's and barber's services.

b. Monthly

(1) The attending physicians should be reminded of the monthly examinations of their patients.

(2) The current conditions of the patients should be written in the summary note and the projected nursing care plan.

(3) The charge nurses should attend the meeting of all supervisory nursing personnel.

3. Concentrated Care (30 Beds) Charge Nurse, 7:00 A.M.–3:00 P.M. Shift *a.* Typical daily schedule:

6:45–7:00 A.M.

(1) She should report on duty.
(2) She should receive reports from 11:00 P.M.–7:00 A.M. nurse and should count the narcotics.

7:00–7:30 A.M.

(1) She should pour and distribute 7:00 A.M. medications.
(2) She should make patient rounds.
(3) She should supervise the bathing schedule.

7:30–8:30 A.M.

(1) She should prepare and pour the 9:00 A.M. medications.
(2) She should supervise the patients' breakfast routine.

8:30–9:30 A.M.

(1) She should distribute the 9:00 A.M. medications.
(2) The treatments should be administered by the charge nurse.

9:30–10:30 A.M.

(1) The charge nurse should check the physicians' orders and progress notes, the medication cards, and the nursing supplies.
(2) She should order any drugs needed for patients' daily use.
(3) She should direct the aides' carrying out of their assignments.

10:30–11:30 A.M. She should prepare and pour the 11:00 A.M. medications.

11:30–12:00 noon. Lunch should be eaten.

12:00–12:30 P.M. The patients' dinners should be supervised by the charge nurse.

12:30–1:00 P.M. The 1:00 P.M. medications should be prepared and administered.

1:00–2:45 P.M.

(1) The medications should be charted and the nursing care plans and progress notes written.
(2) The aides should be queried on patients' bowel movements.
(3) The record of patient care by the nursing attendants for each patient is examined.
(4) The patients are checked.
(5) She should determine whether aides have completed their special assignments.
(6) She should prepare the report for 3:00–11:00 P.M. nurse.

(7) She should oversee the transportation of patients to recreational activities and out of doors when weather permits.

2:45–3:00 P.M.
(1) She should give the report and count narcotics with the 3:00 to 11:00 charge nurse.
(2) She should go off duty.

b. Special daily activities: The charge nurse should validate the contents of treatment tray and should replenish it.

c. Special weekly activities:
(1) *Monday and Tuesday:* The weighing of the patients should be supervised.
(2) *Tuesday morning:* She should authenticate the consignment inventory with the representative of the pharmaceutical supply company.
(3) *Friday:* The charge nurse should check the emergency tray kept in medicine room, and any medication given to a patient from the emergency tray must be charged to the patient and reordered for replacement on the tray.

d. Special monthly activities
(1) She should assist the director of nursing with the monthly inventory of nursing department supplies.
(2) She should inspect and sterilize the supplies in the supply room and the contents of the small instrument boat kept in the medication room.

4. Skilled Nursing Care Unit (35 beds) Charge Nurse, 7:00 A.M.–3:00 P.M. Shift

a. Typical Daily Schedule

6:45–7:00 A.M.
(1) She should report on duty.
(2) She should receive the report from 11:00 to 7:00 nurse and should count the narcotics.

7:00–8:00 A.M.
(1) She should pour and distribute the 7:00 A.M. medications.
(2) Patient rounds should be made.
(3) The bathing schedule should be supervised.
(4) She should help aides if needed, checking to see that the tables are properly set and that patients are ready for breakfast.
(5) She should call the kitchen if any additional supplies for breakfast are needed.

8:00–9:00 A.M.
(1) She should pour the 9 A.M. medications.

(2) She should supervise breakfast in the community rooms.

9:00–10:00 A.M.
(1) She should distribute the 9:00 A.M. medications.
(2) Treatments should be administered.

10:00–11:00 A.M.
(1) Physician's orders and progress notes, medication cards, and supplies should be checked.
(2) Any drugs needed for patients' daily use should be ordered.
(3) She should supervise the aides in carrying out their assignments.

11:00 A.M.*-12:00 noon*
(1) She should pour and give out the 11:00 A.M. medications.
(2) She should see that the tables are properly set and that the patients are ready for dinner.
(3) She should have her lunch.

12:00–1:00 P.M.
(1) The 1:00 P.M. medications should be poured.
(2) Dinner in the community rooms should be supervised, the patient supper menus should be completed and sent to the dietary director.

1:00–2:45 P.M.
(1) The 1:00 P.M. medications should be passed.
(2) The charge nurse should chart the medications, the nursing care plan, and progress notes.
(3) She should check with the aides on the patients' bowel movements and should study the record of patient care by the nursing attendants.
(4) The patients should be visited and observed.
(5) She should note whether the aides have completed their special assignments.
(6) She should prepare the report for the 3:00 to 11:00 P.M. nurse.
(7) The transportation of the patients to recreational activities and out of doors when weather permits should be directed.

2:45–3:00 P.M.
(1) She should give the report and count the narcotics with 3:00 to 11:00 P.M. charge nurse.
(2) She should leave duty.

b. Special daily activities. The treatment tray should be examined and replenished, if needed.

c. Special weekly activities. On Wednesday she should supervise the weighing of the patients.

5. Charge Nurses for Both Nursing Units, 3:00–11:00 P.M. Shift. Special duties and activities:

a. Daily

(1) They should supervise the daily wheelchair washing schedule by aides, to take place at about 9:00 P.M.

(2) The delivery of drugs should be checked against the order, and the signature of the charge nurses and the extended care facility registration number listed on the label in the narcotic sedation and stimulant book should testify as to the accuracy of the amount of the order.

b. Weekly

(1) The nursing care plan of each patient should be reviewed and appropriate corrections made according to changes in the patient's condition.

(2) *Monday:* The charge nurses should post the aides' and orderlies' daily assignments for the forthcoming week.

(3) *Tuesday* 7:00 P.M.: They should supervise the attendance and transportation of the patients to the group therapy meeting.

(4) *Thursday:* They should verify the participation of specified patients in the speech therapy program.

c. Monthly

(1) The charge nurses should detail patient condition summaries in the nursing care plan and progress notes, following the same sequence of patients begun by the 7:00 to 3:00 P.M. shift charge nurses.

(2) The nurses should attend the monthly meetings of supervisory nursing personnel.

6. Concentrated Care Unit Charge Nurse, 3:00–11:00 P.M. Shift

2:50–3:00 P.M.

a. She should report for duty after having checked the evening patient recreational activities on the appropriate bulletin boards.

b. She should receive the report from the 7:00 A.M. to 3:00 P.M. nurse and should count the narcotics.

3:00–4:00 P.M.

a. The order book should be checked.

b. The aides should be supervised to ensure that their assignments are being carried out.

c. The charge nurse should visit patients, taking note of any special complaints or unusual symptoms.

4:00–5:00 P.M.

a. She should ascertain that all patients have been returned from the recreational activities and are in their own rooms to be prepared for supper.

b. All nursing phone calls should be taken, calls transferred, and messages given to patients.

c. Medications for 5:00 P.M. should be poured.

5:00–6:00 P.M.

a. Medications should be distributed.

b. The charge nurse should check special diets and see that meals are properly served to patients and that those patients who need help are properly fed.

c. She should check appetites and administer tube feedings.

d. She should verify and put away newly delivered refills and drugs.

6:00–7:00 P.M.

a. Catheters should be irrigated, and necessary enemas or suppositories should be given.

b. The charge nurse should proffer special skin care.

c. Temperatures and blood pressures should be taken and recorded.

d. She should continue to take phone calls, messages, and to report to families on the condition of their relatives.

7:00–7:30 P.M.

The charge nurse should have supper.

7:30–8:00 P.M.

a. She should assist in putting patients to bed.

b. Any special or new orders from doctors should be recorded in the physicians' orders and progress notes.

c. She should check with aides on the patients' bowel movements.

d. She should examine the nursing attendants' record of patient care.

8:00–9:00 P.M.

a. The charge nurse should dispense the 9:00 P.M. medications, bedtime sedations, and laxatives, noting any special complaints or unusual symptoms.

b. The sedations should be indicated in the narcotic-stimulant-sedation book when poured.

9:00–10:00 P.M.

a. Medications and nursing care plan and progress notes should be charted.

b. Any new orders from doctors should be verified.

c. She should supervise the cleaning of the wheelchairs, according to the posted schedule.

10:00–10:45 P.M.

a. She should make rounds to observe patients, noting if they are sleeping.

b. She should check with the aides on the patients' bowel movements and incontinence.

10:45–11:00 P.M.

a. She should give the report and count the narcotics with 11:00 P.M. to 7:00 A.M. charge nurse.

b. She should relay any special messages.

c. She should go off duty.

7. Skilled Nursing Care Unit Charge Nurse, 3:00–11:00 P.M. Shift

a. Typical daily schedule

2:50–3:00 P.M.

(1) The nurse should report on duty after having noted the evening recreational activities posted on the bulletin board listing patients' activities.

(2) She should receive the report from the 7:00 A.M. to 3:00 P.M. nurse and should count the narcotics.

3:00–4:00 P.M.

(1) The order book should be checked.

(2) Assignments for aides and orderlies should be verified.

(3) She should ascertain that all patients have been returned to their unit after the afternoon activities.

4:00–5:00 P.M.

(1) She should visit patients, taking note of any special complaints or unusual symptoms.

(2) She should pour and dispense medications.

5:00–6:00 P.M.

(1) The medications should be distributed.

(2) She should check to see that all patients are in the community rooms for supper.

(3) She should check any special diets and note the appetites of the patients.

6:00–7:00 P.M.

(1) The charge nurse should check with the aides on the patients' bowel movements and should note the laxatives to be given.

(2) She should visit with the patients, noting any complaints or irregularities.

(3) Temperatures and blood pressures should be taken and charted.

7:00–7:30 P.M.
She should have her supper.

7:30–8:00 P.M.
(1) She should assist in putting patients to bed.
(2) She should check assignments for baths and should supervise the bathing of the male patients by the orderly according to the bathing schedule.
(3) The charge nurse should supervise special treatments, soaks, and enemas.
(4) Some patients should be prepared for special evening programs when scheduled.
(5) The charge nurse should verify and put away any newly delivered refills or drugs.

8:00–9:00 P.M.
(1) The patients should be returned to their rooms after the special programs.
(2) New orders or messages from the attending physicians should be noted.
(3) She should walk with patients who require this special attention.
(4) The 9:00 P.M. medications and bedtime sedations should be poured.
(5) The sedatives should be marked in the narcotic-sedation book when poured.

9:00–10:00 P.M.
(1) The 9:00 P.M. medications and bedtime sedations should be dispensed.
(2) The cleaning of the wheelchairs should be supervised according to the schedule.

10:00–10:45 P.M.
(1) Medications and nursing care plan and progress notes should be charted.
(2) Any new orders from doctors should be checked.

10:45–11:00 P.M.
(1) She should give the report to and count the narcotics with the 11:00 P.M. to 7:00 A.M. charge nurse and should relay any special messages.

(2) She should go off duty.

b. Special weekly activities

(1) Monday: The charge nurse should post the aides' and orderlies' daily schedule for the week.

(2) Tuesday: She should supervise the patients' attendance at group therapy.

(3) Thursday: The patients' attendance at speech therapy should be supervised.

c. Special monthly activities

(1) Patient condition summaries should be written in the nursing care plan and progress notes.

(2) The monthly meeting of the supervisory nursing staff should be attended.

8. Charge Nurses on 11:00 P.M.–7:00 A.M. Shift on Both Units

a. Typical daily schedule

10:50–11:00 P.M.

(1) The nurses should report on duty.

(2) They should receive the report from 3:00 to 11:00 P.M. nurses and should count the narcotics.

11:00–11:30 P.M.

(1) Patient rounds should be made.

(2) Assignments for aides and orderlies should be checked.

11:30–12:00 midnight

(1) The charge nurses should check all door exits.

(2) The coffee pot in the staff dining room should be disconnected.

(3) The laundry room should be checked.

12:00–2:00 A.M.

(1) The physicians' orders and progress notes should be checked.

(2) Patient rounds should be made.

2:00–2:30 A.M.

Supper should be eaten.

2:30–3:00 A.M.

Patient rounds should be made.

3:00–4:00 A.M.

(1) Aides and orderlies should be checked on their special assignments.

(2) The charge nurses should supervise the daily sterilizing of bedside equipment schedule for aides.

4:00–5:00 A.M.
Patient rounds should be made.

5:00–6:00 A.M.
(1) Medications and nursing care plan and progress notes should be charted.
(2) The census for dietary director should be completed and placed on the kitchen door.

6:00–6:45 A.M.
The charge nurses should observe the patients for comfort, etc.

6:45–7:00 A.M.
(1) The report should be given and the narcotics counted with the 7:00 A.M. to 3:00 P.M. nurses.
(2) The night charge nurses should be relieved from duty.

b. Special weekly activities
Monday
(1) The aides' and orderlies' daily assignments for the week should be posted.
(2) The nursing care plan of each patient should be reviewed, and appropriate corrections according to the patient's condition should be made.

c. Special monthly activities
(1) The patient's summary notes and projected nursing care plan should be written.
(2) The monthly meeting of the supervisory nursing staff should be attended.

C. Nursing Aides and Orderlies. *A close working relationship between licensed and auixliary nursing personnel is mandatory. Nursing aides and orderlies should be reminded repeatedly that during their tour of duty the record of patient care should be completed and any unusual patient condition should be reported to the charge nurse immediately, for quality nursing care is dependent upon close clinical contact.*

1. Nursing Aides and Orderlies On 7:00 A.M.–3:00 P.M. Shift

a. Typical daily schedule

7:00–7:45 A.M.
(1) Aides and orderlies should report to the nurse in charge promptly at 7:00 A.M. to receive assignments.
(2) The patients should be prepared for breakfast, and tables should be set in the community rooms.
(3) The nursing attendants should start to shower or bathe patients according to the posted schedule.

7:45–8:30 A.M.
Concentrated Care Unit:
(1) The breakfast trays should be arranged with coffee, and the toast should be prepared.
(2) The trays should be distributed.
(3) The patients who require feeding should be assisted.
(4) The trays should be collected, the contents noted, and the tables should be cleaned.
(5) Any changes in the eating patterns of the patients should be reported to the charge nurse.
Skilled Nursing Care Unit:
(1) Breakfast should be served, and the toast should be prepared.
(2) Patients who require assistance should be fed.
(3) Any changes in eating patterns of the patients should be promptly reported to the charge nurse.

8:30–11:00 A.M.
(1) Patients should be bathed, dressed, and accompanied to the activity program.
(2) Patients' beds should be made, and bedside cabinets should be cleaned.
(3) All rooms, including drawers and closets, should be inspected for neatness and cleanliness.

10:00 A.M. Nourishment should be offered to all patients who so desire.

11:00–12:00 noon
The nursing attendants should have their lunch in two shifts of half an hour each, so that patients are not left unattended.

11:30 A.M.
The patients should be prepared for dinner.

11:45 A.M.–*1:00* P.M.
Concentrated Care Unit:
(1) The dinner trays should be set up with coffee, tea, bread, and butter.
(2) The trays should be distributed.
(3) The patients who require feeding should be assisted.
(4) The trays should be picked up and the contents examined, and tables should be cleaned.
(5) The charge nurse should be informed of any changes in the eating patterns of the patients.

1:00–2:00 P.M.

(1) The patients who wish should rest at this time.

(2) The patients should be toileted, cleaned, neatly dressed, and transported to the recreation room.

2:00–3:00 P.M.

(1) Extra assignments should be completed.

(2) The patients in the recreation room should be checked.

(3) One nursing attendant from each nursing unit should remain in the recreation area to assist the patients from 1:00–3:00 P.M.

(4) The record of patient care should be completed.

(5) The aides and orderlies should sign out.

b. Special weekly activities

Monday, Tuesday, and *Saturday:* The nursing attendants should transport specified patients to various locations for the speech therapy program.

Sunday, Wednesday, and *Friday:* Patients should be transported to various locations for religious services, scheduled as follows:

Sunday	Protestant services
Wednesday	Catholic services
Friday	Jewish services

Monday and Tuesday

Concentrated Care Unit

Patients should be weighed (Fig. 3-8).

Wednesday

Skilled Nursing Care Unit

The patients should be weighed.

Alternating Fridays and Saturdays

The aides and orderlies should cooperate in making patients available for the beautician and barber at the proper time.

c. Weekly, biweekly, or monthly activities

(1) Aides and orderlies should assist in making available patients who are to receive podiatry services.

(2) Aides and orderlies should transport patients who are to receive dental services to the dental treatment room.

2. Nursing Aides and Orderlies on 3:00–11:00 P.M. Shift. The nursing attendants should be reminded frequently that at any time during their tour of duty any unusual patient condition should be reported to the charge nurse immediately.

a. Typical daily schedule

3:00–5:00 P.M.

(1) The aides and orderlies should report to the charge nurse promptly at 3:00 P.M. to receive their assignments.

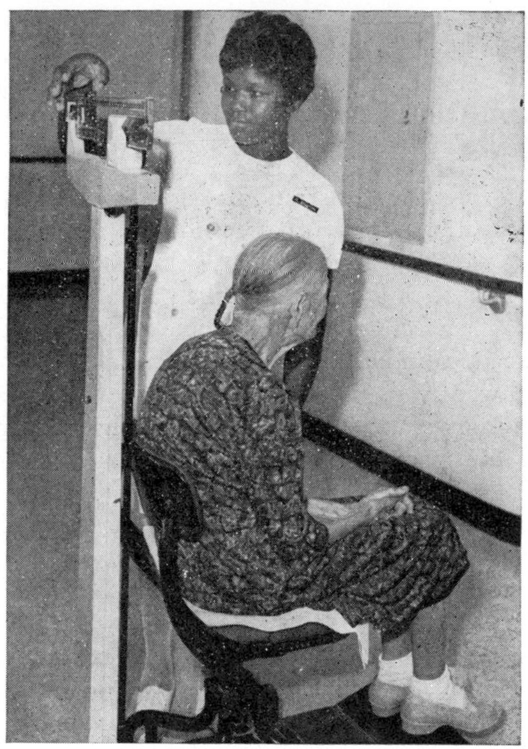

Fig. 3-8. Patients in the concentrated care unit who cannot stand should be weighed in a chair scale.

(2) The bulletin boards should be checked for the recreational activities scheduled for patients.
(3) One aide from each unit should be stationed in the recreation room until 4:00 P.M. (Fig. 3-9).
(4) Water should be put on for tea, using a low flame.
(5) All rooms should be checked to see that all patients are comfortable.
(6) All training patients should be helped on the toilets.
(7) Fluids should be distributed at 3:30 P.M.
(8) All rooms should be checked for neatness.
(9) The tables in the community rooms (in the skilled nursing care unit) should be set.
(10) All patients should be prepared for supper.
(11) All beds should be turned down.

5:00–6:30 P.M.
Concentrated Care Unit

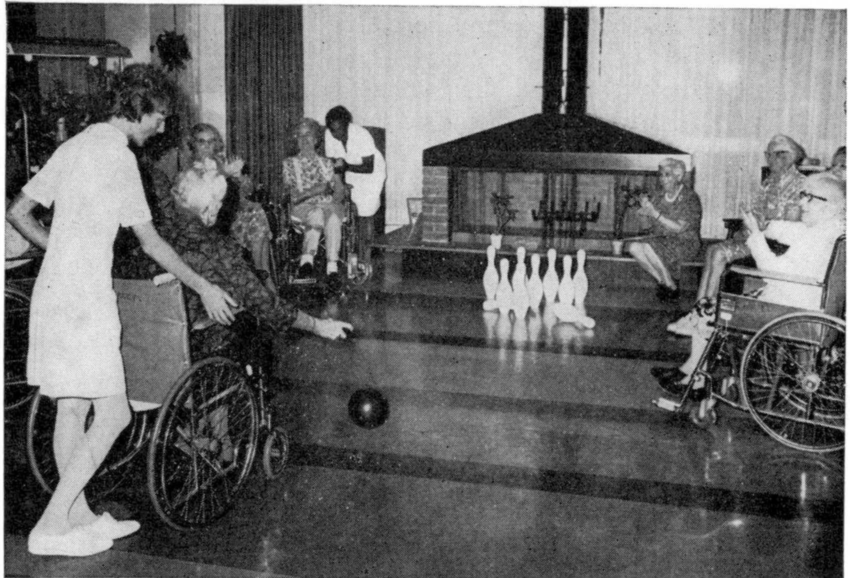

Fig. 3-9. Nursing attendants should be assigned to assist patients in their activities of daily living during recreational programs.

(1) All supper trays should be arranged with sugar, bread and butter, and water for tea and coffee.
(2) Supper trays should be distributed.
(3) Patients who require feeding should be assisted.
(4) All trays are collected and the contents observed.
(5) Any changes in the eating patterns of patients should be reported to the charge nurse.
(6) The tables should be cleaned.

Skilled Nursing Care Unit

(1) The supper should be served.
(2) Patients who require feeding should be assisted.
(3) Any changes in the eating pattern of the patients should be reported to the charge nurse.
(4) The tables and dining areas should be cleaned.

6:30–7:30 P.M.

(1) The patients should be undressed and prepared for bed if no evening activities are scheduled.
(2) All soiled clothing should be placed in the hamper.
(3) Clean dresses, trousers, etc., should be neatly hung up.
(4) The remaining clothes should be folded on a chair, never on the bed.

(5) The dentures should be cleaned and placed in proper containers.
(6) Back care should be administered to all wheelchair patients.
(7) All wheelchairs should be removed from the rooms.

7:30–8:30 P.M. The aides and orderlies should have their supper in two contingents of ½ hr each.

8:00–8:30 P.M. Extra duties, such as cleaning of the pantry, including the refrigerators, cupboards, and sink, should be performed.
Skilled Nursing Care Unit. The community room tables should be set for breakfast.

8:30–9:00 P.M. Patients should be toileted or offered bedpans.

9:00–10:00 P.M.
(1) Sheets to be left for 11:00 P.M. to 7:00 A.M. shift should be counted.
(2) Wheelchairs should be cleaned according to the posted schedules.

10:00–10:45 P.M. Patients should be toileted or offered the bedpan, and all patients should be left clean and dry.

10:45–11:00 P.M. The record of patient care should be completed.

11:00 P.M. The aides and orderlies should sign off duty.

b. Special weekly activities:
Tuesday: The specified patients should be transported to group therapy at 7:00 P.M.
Thursday: The specified patients should be transported to speech therapy at 6:30 P.M.

3. Nursing Aides and Orderlies on 11:00 P.M.–7:00 A.M. Shift. Nursing attendants should be frequently reminded that any time during tour of duty any unusual patient condition should be reported to the charge nurse immediately.

11:00 P.M. The nursing aides and orderlies should report to the charge nurse promptly at 11:00 P.M. to receive their assignments.

11:30 P.M–*12:00 midnight.* All patients should be checked.

12:00–1:00 A.M. Patients should be toileted or offered the use of the bedpan.

1:00–2:00 A.M. The bedside equipment should be sterilized according to the posted schedules and directions.

2:00–3:00 A.M. The patients' dentures should be cleansed in the ultrasonic device.

3:00–4:00 A.M. The aides and orderlies should be divided in two contingents, each to take a half-hour snack and rest period.

4:00–5:00 A.M. The patients should be checked and toileted if necessary.

5:00–5:30 A.M. The soiled linens should be collected and transported to the laundry.

5:30–6:45 A.M.
(1) The patients should be toileted and morning care offered to some.
(2) Certain assigned patients should be prepared for breakfast.

6:45–7:00 A.M. The record of patient care should be completed.

7:00 A.M. The night-duty nursing attendants should sign out.

VI. MEDICATIONS AND SUPPLIES

An extended care facility of 150 to 200 beds should justify the development of a free-standing pharmacy by a full-time pharmacist in the employ of the institution, although smaller facilities should work with a consultant pharmacist. In both instances, the principles enumerated below should be followed.

A. Pharmacy Committee

1. Purpose
- *a.* To evaluate the pharmaceutical policies and procedures of the extended care facility
- *b.* To make pertinent changes as required

2. Composition of the Pharmacy Committee
- *a.* Consultant pharmacist—chairman
- *b.* Medical director
- *c.* Administrative director
- *d.* Director of nursing

3. Meetings. The pharmacy committee should meet quarterly to fulfill the above mentioned purposes.

B. Medication Policies. The following policies concerning the prescribing, administering, and dispensing of medications should be approved by the pharmacy committee of the extended care institution.

1. Only medications listed in the *U.S. Pharmacopeia,* the *National Formulary, Accepted Dental Remedies, New Drugs,* and *U.S. Homeo-*

pathic Pharmacopeia, or those approved by the pharmacy committee should be used at the extended care facility.

2. Medications brought to the institution by patients or their families should not be used.

3. Medications should not be stocked unless the facility is sufficiently large to warrant the employment of a full-time pharmacist.

4. No medications, including aspirin, laxatives, etc., should be administered to a patient without a physician's written order.

5. No medication should be administered to a visitor for any reason (unless ordered by a staff physician).

6. The extended care facility should dispense no medications for sale, but, in an emergency, medication should be dispensed from an emergency tray by physician's orders.

7. Medications should not be stored in patients' rooms.

8. Medications should be given to the family of patients leaving the facility for a period of a day or several days, and a receipt for these medications should be obtained from the family member.

9. All medications, including narcotics, sedatives, stimulants, and depressants, should be returned to the patient and/or family at discharge unless specifically prohibited by the patient's physician, and a receipt for these medications should be obtained.

10. Individually prescribed and labeled medications only should be used for each patient.

11. A "stop order" policy should be in effect for all medications unless otherwise directed by a patient's physician.

C. The Consultant Pharmacist

1. Regular Duties

a. The consultant pharmacist should note the physician's orders and progress notes daily for new medication orders, and the pharmacist should remove the carbon copy of the orders for his own records.

b. He should arrange for all medication orders to be filled and delivered promptly.

c. The emergency medication trays should be checked.

d. A drug profile should be maintained on each patient, including:

(1) The medications used by each patient

(2) The known allergies of the patient

(3) The refill dates for the medications

2. Weekly Duties

Twice weekly the pharmacist should examine the individual medication containers to note the quantities of medications remaining for

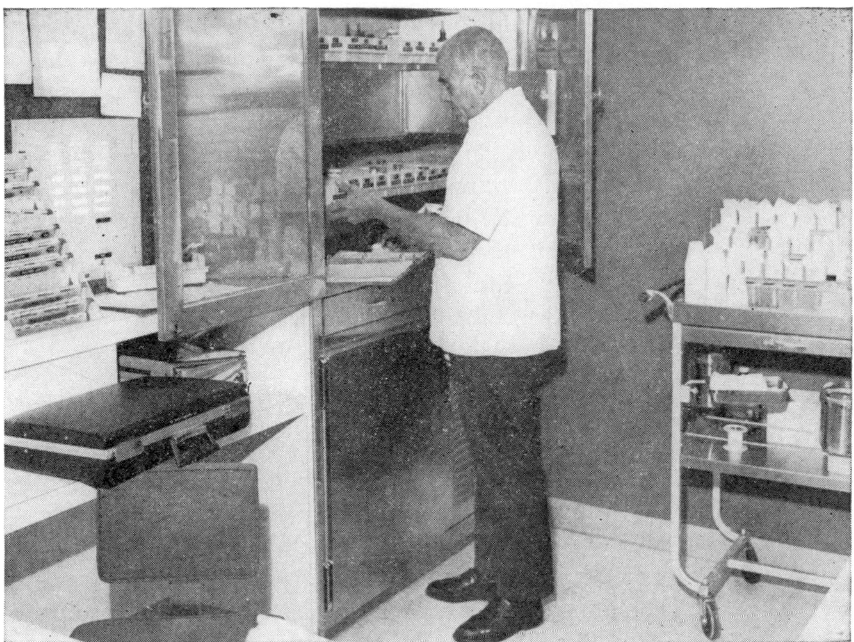

Fig. 3-10. Individual medication containers of each patient are checked by the pharmacist.

each patient and, when appropriate, these should be refilled (Fig. 3-10).

3. Other Responsibilities

a. The consulting pharmacist should alert the nurses to possible side effects of any new medications.

b. He should conduct regular in-service training sessions for the nursing staff on the administration and dispensing of medications and the clinical application of the newer pharmacologic agents.

4. Interrelations with Staff

a. Administrative Director

(1) The consultant pharmacist should confer with the administrative director on matters relating to new equipment, supplies, and storage.

(2) The consultant pharmacist should submit a copy of the bills sent to the patients' families or the responsible person at the end of each month, to be filed in the medication room and used as a checklist.

b. Business Department

(1) The consultant pharmacist should communicate with the office manager via the pharmacy notification cards, which should be located in the Kardex in the business office for the purpose of establishing the billing status of all patients should they be: (a) private patients, (b) potential Medicare patients, (c) Medicare eligible patients, or (d) patients no longer certified for Medicare.

(2) The consultant pharmacist should submit all bills to the business manager for Medicare-eligible patients. (Families should not receive statements from the pharmacist while the patient is eligible for Medicare benefits.)

D. Ordering and Administrative Procedures

1. Ordering Procedures

a. Physician's written order: Upon receiving the physician's written order and prescriptions for necessary medications, the charge nurse on each unit generally should be responsible for the ordering of these medications.

b. Telephone order: Should a physician telephone a medication order for a patient, the charge nurse is to:

(1) Write the order in the physician's orders and progress notes.

(2) Repeat the order back to the physician to establish its accuracy.

(3) Sign the order in the following manner.

Example: T.O. Dr. Smith/Doris Smith

The physician must sign the order within 48 hr after the telephone conversation.

2. Checking. When medications are delivered to the institution, the charge nurse should check them against the written orders for accuracy, and, if correct, she should sign and return the attached slip to the pharmacist.

3. Labeling and Storage

a. All medication containers should be labeled with the patient's full name, physician's name, prescription number, name and strength of drug, date of issue, expiration date of all time-dated drugs, and the name, address, and phone number of the pharmacy issuing the medication.

b. Any medication container with a blurred or missing label must be discarded unless the name, strength, etc., of the medication can be accurately verified by the consultant pharmacist.

c. All medications are to be stored in the medication room, which is to be kept locked except when authorized personnel are working there, and medication cabinets are to be locked except when medications are being dispensed.

d. A plastic container should be provided for each patient's medications, properly labeled with the patient's name and room number.

e. Medications for external use should be kept in an entirely different place, possibly on the swinging tray attached to the medicine carts.

f. Should medication containers be too large to be placed properly in the plastic containers, the name of the patient, the name of the medication, and a code to describe location of the medications should be noted on a small card so that to store the medication in cabinet C, a "C" plus the number of the shelf should be written after the name of the medication.

Example: Pint bottle of Kaon Elixir—C-2

g. If the medication should require refrigeration, an "R" should be noted next to the name of the medication as shown above.

h. The completed card should be placed in the patient's individual plastic medication container.

4. Stop Orders. The charge nurse on each unit should regularly check the physician's orders and progress notes to note how long

TABLE 1. STOP ORDER POLICY

Drug Type	Stop Order
Analgesic (internal)	2 weeks
Antianemia drugs	1 month
Antibiotics	3 days
Anti-emetics	3 days
Antihistamines	1 week
Antineoplastics	1 week
Barbiturates	1 month
Cardiovascular drugs	1 month
Cathartics	1 month
Cold preparations	3 days
Cough preparations	5 days
Dermatologicals	1 week
Diuretics	1 month
Hormones	2 weeks
Hypnotics	1 month
Narcotics	3 days
Psychotherapeutic agents	1 month
Sedatives	1 month
Spasmolytics	2 weeks
Sulfonamides	5 days
Vitamins	3 months

medication is to be continued, and in the absence of a specified time the charge nurse should effect the following stop order policy shown in Table 1 until new orders are received.

5. Recording. At admission time, and when appropriate during the patient stay at the extended care facility, the charge nurses, using the physician's orders and progress notes, should:

a. List on the check sheet the following information:

(1) Name of medication

(2) Dosage of medication

(3) Frequency of administration

(4) Other pertinent information such as weight, pulse, baths, etc.

(5) Their initials and full signatures at the bottom of the check sheet if they dispense medications

b. Complete a medication ticket for each medication ordered and should place this ticket(s) in the appropriate time slot in the medicine rack in the medication room, and as the medication ticket is completed, the nurse should check off the medication on the physician's orders and progress notes, with date ordered and her signature.

E. Dispensing Medications

1. On the Concentrated Care Unit. The charge nurse should dispense medications to patients in their rooms from the medication cart, and she should remain with the patients to make certain that the medications are swallowed.

2. On the Skilled Nursing Care Unit

a. The charge nurse should dispense medications from the medication cart, and patients who are able to wheel themselves or walk to the nurses' station for their medication should do so (Fig. 3-11).

b. Medications should be brought to patients who are unable to come to nurses' station, and in either case, the charge nurse should remain with the patient until the medication is swallowed.

3. At the time medications are to be dispensed, the charge nurses using the physician's orders and progress notes should:

a. Remove the proper medication tickets from the medicine ticket rack in the medication room and place them in the appropriate slots on the medicine carts

b. Place the correct dosage of the medication in the medicine cups and align the cup with the proper medication ticket on the cart

c. Dispense the medications, remembering that any medication directly affecting the heart requires that the pulse be deter-

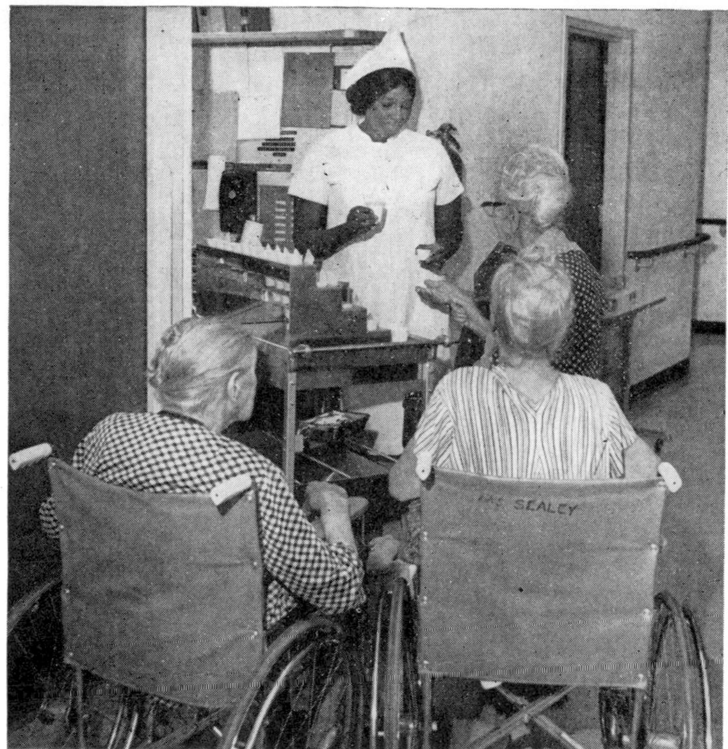

Fig. 3-11. Patients in the skilled nursing care unit are encouraged to present themselves to the nursing station for their medications.

mined and noted before the medication is administered to the patient, and that any medication that has a tendency to lower the blood pressure, e.g., Thorazine, requires the blood pressure to be taken twice a week

d. Replace medication tickets on the medicine rack after the medications have been dispensed

F. Narcotics, Sedatives, Depressants, and Stimulants

1. Ordering and Recording Procedures:

a. Upon receiving the doctor's written order and prescription, the charge nurse should order the narcotic, sedative, depressant, or stimulant from the pharmacy.

b. These drugs should be obtained for individual patients only with doctor's written orders and prescription which must be dated as of, and signed on, the day when issued, and must bear the full name and address of the patient, as well as the name and address of the physician.

c. Prescriptions which indicate registration numbers only of prior prescriptions for these drugs are not valid and should not be filled.

d. The narcotic-sedative record book, or the depressant and stimulant book at each nurses' station should be filled in according to headings, e.g., date, patient's name, pharmacy, drug, amount ordered, directions, registration number, and person placing order (nurse's name).

e. As soon as the narcotic, sedative, depressant, or stimulant is received, the prescription should be given to the delivery man from the pharmacy.

f. The nurse should count narcotic, sedative, depressant, or stimulant, fill in the registration number, and sign her name in the narcotic-sedative or depressant and stimulant book on same line as original order (see *d*).

g. She should then complete in proper form the narcotic-sedative-depressant-stimulant loose-leaf book at the nurses' station where each patient given one of these drugs should have a form in this book with all headings properly filled in so that whenever a narcotic, sedative, depressant or stimulant is given, the correct check of same is made on the patient's form, with the date and hour, name and quantity of the drug administered and prescribed, the patient's name, the signature of the nurse administering, and the balance of such drug remaining.

2. Prescription Refills: A prescription for narcotic, sedative, depressant, or stimulant drug may not be refilled.

3. Telephoned Orders: The furnishing of narcotic, sedative, depressant, or stimulant drugs by telephoned order is prohibited except in an emergency, when the pharmacist may deliver a drug in these categories pursuant to a telephone order, provided a properly prepared and signed prescription is supplied to him before the drugs are handed to the nurse.

4. Registration and Certification of Narcotics, Sedatives, Stimulants, and Depressants: The following certificates should be posted on the bulletin board in the Administrative office:

a. A certificate of approval for possession and use of narcotics issued by the state department of health, bureau of narcotic control

b. Registration after the receipt of certificate of approval required biennially by some states

c. The annual registration required before July 1 with the District Director, United States Internal Revenue Service, for a special narcotic tax stamp

d. A certificate from the state department of health, where required, for the custody and use of depressant and stimulant drugs

5. Disposal of Narcotics, Sedatives, Depressants, and Stimulants:

a. A receipt should be obtained for any narcotics, sedatives, depressants, stimulants, and all other medications given to families of discharged patients.

b. If narcotic, sedative, depressant, or stimulant drugs prescribed for patient are no longer required by the patient, they should be surrendered to the bureau of narcotic control, state department of health.

c. Surrendered narcotic, sedative, depressant, and stimulant drugs should be inventoried in triplicate, and the completed form with the unused drug should be wrapped in a package sealed at both ends and sent via Railway Express to the bureau of narcotic control, state department of health.

6. Safekeeping:

a. All narcotic drugs should be kept in a locked narcotic box permanently affixed to a locked cabinet in a medications room.

b. All depressant, sedative, and stimulant drugs should be stored in the medicine room under double-locked protection in stationary cabinets.

7. Records. All records relating to narcotics, sedatives, stimulants, and depressants should be kept for a period of 2 years from the date of transaction.

G. Nursing Department Supplies

1. Purchasing Supplies. Triplicate forms should be used by the Nursing Department, with the white sheet for the suppliers, the pink sheet for the business office, and the yellow sheet to be kept at the nursing office until the arrival of the supplies.

2. A small sterile instrument boat should be kept at each nursing unit containing the following:

a. 2 scissors—one large and one small

b. 2 large hemostats

c. 3 small hemostats

d. 2 thumb forceps

e. 2 probes

f. 1 scalpel and blade

g. four 4×4's

3. A treatment tray should be maintained at each nursing unit containing the following:

a. 1 small bottle of hydrogen peroxide

b. 1 small bottle of tincture Merthiolate

c. 1 small bottle of liquid green soap
d. 1 large jar of sterile gauze (Iodoform 5%) 1 in., and 5 yd of packing
e. 1 razor and blade
f. 6 alcohol sponges
g. 1 small plastic case containing safety pins
h. 1 roll of adhesive tape
i. 2 padded mouth depressors
j. 3 sterile packs of cotton balls
k. 1 sterile pack with 4 applicators
l. Several unsterile tongue depressors
m. 1 box of Band-Aids (including butterfly closure strips)
n. 1 sterile pack containing four 4 × 4's
o. 1 small bottle tincture benzoin
p. 1 tube lubricating jelly
q. 1 bottle alcohol

4. Emergency medication trays:

a. The emergency medication tray should be located in the medication room and must be sealed at all times.
b. Should the seal be broken on the tray due to the removal of a medication(s), the entire tray must be returned to the consultant pharmacist for replenishing the medication(s) and for resealing.
c. The name of the patient for whom the medication was needed should be noted in order to assist the pharmacist in billing.
d. Contents of the emergency medication trays should be as follows:

1—Dramamine 50 mg/cc 5-cc ampule
4—Adrenalin in oil 1:500 1-cc ampule
4—Adrenalin solution 1:1,000 1-cc ampule
4—Aminophylline 0.5 Gm intramuscular 2-cc ampule
3—Aminophylline 0.5 Gm intravenous 20-cc ampule
1—Amamine 1% 10-cc vials
2—Dilantin 250 mg/cc diluter #S-V 105
1—Calcium gluconate 10% 10-cc ampule
6—Digoxin 0.5 mg/2-cc ampule
1—Procaine HCL 1% injection 30-cc vial
1—Procaine HCL 2% injection 30-cc vial
1—Dextrose 50% 50-cc ampule
2—Synkavite 10 mg 1-cc ampule
2—Synkavite 75 mg 2-cc ampule
4—Coramine 25% 1.5-cc ampule

1—Atropine 0.4 mg/cc 30-cc vial
1—Isuprel 1:5000 5 cc-ampule
1—Pronestyl injection 10-cc vial
1—Glucagon 1 mg injection comb. pack #666
1—Thorazine 50 mg/2-cc ampule (6's)
1—Hydrocortisone intramuscular 50 mg/cc 5-cc vial
1—Hydrocortisone intravenous 100 mg/2-cc ampule
1—Aromatic ammonia vaporoles 1 box (12's)
1—Water for injection 30-cc vial
1—Normal saline for injection 20-cc vial
1—Benadryl 10 mg/cc 10-cc vial
3—Digitoxin 0.2 mg/cc 2-cc ampule
2—Plastic airways
1—Box Curity suture material
1—Rubber tourniquet
1—Percussion hammer
1—Sterile 50 cc syringe
1—Sterile 10 cc syringe
3 Sterile 2 cc syringe
2—Mercuhydrin 2-cc ampule

5. The supply room should contain:
  a. 1 sterile large instrument tray
  b. 1 sterile vaginal tray
  c. 1 stomach tray

6. Nursing Department Supplies (see Table 2)

VII. NURSING DEPARTMENT COMMUNICATIONS

A. Nurses Call System

1. An audiovisual system should be located:
  a. In each bedroom, easily accessible to the patient
  b. In each lavatory area
  c. At each shower and tub to permit staff to summon assistance, if required

2. The system should light:
  a. Over the door with a color code to indicate lavatory or bedroom
  b. At the nurses' station

3. The nurses call should sound a continuous buzz at the nurses' station until staff has responded to the patient.

4. The nurses' call system from the skilled nursing care unit should be able to be switched over to sound at the concentrated care unit, should all staff members in an emergency be required to leave the unit.

5. Unless the patients are completely intact intellectually, intercom

TABLE 2. NURSING DEPARTMENT SUPPLIES

Item	Reorder Point	Reorder Quantity
Water cups 3½ oz	25 boxes	50 boxes
Portion cups 1 oz No. 45	10 boxes	20 boxes
Portion cups 1¼ oz No. 47	10 boxes	20 boxes
Air deodorizer	6 cans	12 cans
Surgical soap	1 gal	4 gallons
Detergent	1 gal	4 gallons
Antiseptic soap	1 gal	4 gallons
Plastic trays	1 tray	6 trays
Plastic pitchers	1 pitcher	6 pitchers
Tongue depressors	1 box	2 boxes
Polypropylene syringes 22 Gm, 2½ cc, 1 in.	1 box	6 boxes
Plastic syringes 25 Gm, 2½ cc, ⅝ in.	1 box	6 boxes
Plastic syringes 20 Gm, 2½ cc, 1 in.	1 box	6 boxes
Disposable syringes 20 Gm, 12 cc, 1½ in.	1 box	6 boxes
Glass syringes 20 Gm, 2½ cc, 1 in.	1 box	6 boxes
Insulin syringes 26 Gm, 1 cc, ½ in.	1 box	6 boxes
Plastic straws	1 box	1 case
Sterile gloves (No. 150, size 7½, 2 doz. pair/box)	1 box	2 boxes
Unsterile gloves (right hand, No. V-5, 6 doz./ box Pylox Quixoms)	1 box	2 boxes
Adhesive tape (2 in. roll)	2 rolls	1 tube (5 rolls)
Band-Aids 100/box ¾ in. Water repellent	1 box	2 boxes
Alcohol preps (pads) 100/box	2 boxes	10 boxes
Autoclave paper		
20 × 20 in. 500 sheets/pkg	25 sheets	1 pkg
13 × 13 in. 1000 sheets/pkg	25 sheets	1 pkg
Thermometers—rectal	½ doz	1 doz
Bulb syringes (1 or 2 oz)	6 syringes	3 syringes

conversations between nurses and patients using the nurses' call system are not recommended.

6. Closed-circuit television may be useful in certain special situations when patients require close observation and are not mobile.

B. Telephone System for Patients and Nurses

1. The Nursing Department should have its own line for speed in incoming and outgoing calls.

2. Patients should have their own lines with jacks located in bed-

rooms and community areas for patients to receive incoming calls.
3. Some patients, with their families' and physicians' approval, should be encouraged to have their own telephone.
4. Other patients should use the wheelchair-height public telephones to make outgoing telephone calls.

C. Bulletin Board at the Nurses' Stations

1. On the bulletin board at the main nursing station should be posted:
a. Nursing Department attendance Kardex
b. Weekly schedule for duty
c. Assignment to unit or floor schedule
d. Floor evacuation and utility interruption plans
e. Daily assignment schedule
f. Bathing schedule, rectal examination schedule, patients to be ambulated
g. Wheelchair-cleaning schedule
h. Sterilizing-of-equipment schedule
i. Beauty service orders
j. Listing of attending physicians and on-call schedule
k. Special notices and memoranda
2. The bulletin board at the skilled nursing care unit should include all the above material except the attendance Kardex.

VIII. NURSING DEPARTMENT EQUIPMENT

Should include:

A. Autoclaves in the clean utility rooms

B. Bedpan sterilizers in the dirty utility rooms

C. Emergency oxygen tanks on both patient units

D. Side rails—located on all beds in the concentrated care unit and on half in the skilled nursing care unit

E. Scales—chair scale for the concentrated care unit and a regular scale for the skilled nursing care unit

F. Shower chairs—two in each bathing area

G. Patient lifter—for the concentrated care unit

H. Medication dispensing carts—one on each nursing unit

I. Wheelchairs of varying types on all patient units

J. An admission receiving chair for each patient unit

K. A stretcher for each unit

L. An electric suction machine on each nursing section

M. An ultrasonic denture-cleansing device for each nursing unit

N. A water mattress for flotation therapy at the concentrated care unit

Medical equipment that should be maintained at the extended care facility is described in Section 2.

IX. NURSING DEPARTMENT FACILITIES

A. The supply room on each unit should contain the following items:

1. Supplies
2. Trays
3. Extra syringes

B. The pantries on both units should contain the following items:

1. Refrigerators
2. Stoves
3. Toasters, etc.
4. Sinks and cupboards

C. Nursing Department storage room should contain an inventoried stock of all supplies used by the Nursing Department.

D. The medicine room should contain the following items:

1. Medications
2. Small sterile instrument boat
3. Treatment tray
4. Emergency tray

E. Utility rooms should be provided with instrument and bedpan sterilizers.

F. A ventilated closet on each unit should contain emergency oxygen tanks and extra tanks.

G. A linen closet should be located at each unit.

H. The nursing office file cabinet should have the following items:

1. An address and telephone book
2. Prospective employees' completed applications
3. Application forms for employees
4. Weekly time schedules for employees
5. Monthly time schedules for employees
6. Hospitalization applications
7. Monthly schedules
8. Personnel physical forms
9. Reference forms

10. Master staffing plan forms
11. Narcotic inventory forms and regulations
12. Depressant and stimulant inventory forms and regulations
13. Various forms for patient charts
14. Forms for special and restorative services
15. Dietary cards
16. Flashlights
17. Pharmacy cards

I. The nursing station reference shelf should be provided with:

1. Medical directory of the state
2. A medical dictionary
3. *Physicians' Desk Reference*
4. Hospital formulary
5. Administrative policies
6. Nursing service policies
7. Patient care policies
8. Procedure manual of the extended care facility
9. Conditions of participation for Medicare
10. State Health and Narcotics codes
11. Minutes of meetings involving the Nursing Department
12. *How to Be a Nurse's Aide in a Nursing Home*
13. Diets for use in the extended care facility
14. *Diet and Menu Guide,* American Hospital Association
15. *Safety Manual for Nursing Homes and Homes for the Aged*
16. Geriatric and rehabilitation nursing texts

X. STAFF RELATIONS WITH FAMILIES AND VISITORS

A. Should families and/or visitors question staff about the adjustment or the condition of the patient, these questions should be referred directly to the charge nurse, who should either handle the questions herself or should refer them to the director of social service or director of nursing.

B. Employees should be discouraged from witnessing affidavits, wills, etc., of patients.

C. Requests for presence of patient's attorney should be cleared with administrative director and/or the director of social service.

XI. INTERDEPARTMENTAL COOPERATION

The Nursing Department should function as the hub of all activities that take place at the extended care facility and should maintain good working relationships with the following:

A. The Medical Director

1. In-service Training Program: This weekly program should be conducted for the nursing staff by the medical director, with the assistance of the director of nursing, and topics should include those listed in Fig. 3-12.

2. Specific Patient Problems: Informal meetings should be frequently held by the director of nursing and the charge nurses with the medical director to discuss specific patients, their medical and social problems, and suggested solutions.

3. Coordination: The medical director should coordinate nursing with other professional services.

4. Staff Nursing Duties: The medical director should assist in the development of nursing procedures for the nursing staff.

Fig. 3-12

SCHEDULE OF IN-SERVICE TRAINING PROGRAM

Sessions are all scheduled for Monday afternoons at 1:00 P.M. Unless marked "General" (for entire staff) sessions are for Nursing Department.

Session 1: Discussion of the nature of the radial pulse and coordination with pulsations of the chest and neck

Session 2: Observations on respiration, dyspnea, and orthopnea

Session 3: Case presentation. Chronic pyelonephritis with relapse and particular reference to measurement and reporting of fluid intake and urine output in uremia and congestive heart failure

Session 4: Techniques on administration of enemas with particular reference to fecal impaction and its sequelae

Session 5: A program for management of decubiti

Session 6: Case presentation. Initial symptom of vomiting. The nurses' responsibility in differential diagnosis to exclude intestinal obstruction:

a Nature of vomitus and vomiting mechanism
b Description of abdominal conformation
c Auscultation of abdomen for presence of bowel sounds
d Presence or absence of flatus
e Rectal examination for presence of stool, color, and consistency
f Presence of fever
g Rule out presence of hernia

Session 7: Oral hygiene in the aged ill. Guest speaker: consulting dentist

Session 8: (*General*) Safety and fire. Written quiz. Speaker: maintenance director

Session 9: Nurses' responsibility in reporting phenomena associated with acute congestive heart failure

Session 10: Nurses' responsibility in reporting phenomena associated with nursing management of diabetes mellitus

Fig. 3-12 (Continued)

a Clinical features of hypoglycemia and insulin shock
b Clinical features of diabetic acidosis

Session 11: Nurses' responsibility in reporting potential differential diagnosis of acute congestive heart failure versus pneumonitis

Session 12: (*General*) Discussion of food handling. Speaker from County Department of Health

Session 13: Differential diagnosis in nursing diagnosis of acute congestive heart failure versus acute coronary thrombosis

Session 14: Syncope, coma, and seizures

Session 15: The stroke syndrome. Film: "Cerebral Vascular Disease—The Challenge of Management" (38½ min, ANA)

Session 16: Feeding and nutritional problems of the aged: consulting dietitian
a Low-salt diet
b Liquid, soft, and regular diet
c Gastric-tube feeding and aspiration pneumonia

Session 17: Nursing rehabilitation and the physical therapist. Film: "Teaching Crutch Walking" (13 min, ANA).

Session 18: Patient attitudes on fear, death, and family guilt. Speaker—director of social service

Session 19: The terminal patient and his care

Session 20: Relationship of nursing functions to other paramedical and paranursing activities, such as occupational therapy, recreational therapy, and utilization of the internal environment of the extended care facility

Session 21: Nursing psychiatry with reference to supportive therapy for patients and family. Film: "Psychiatric Nursing: Nurse-Patient Relationships" (35 min, ANA)

Session 22: The formation of a therapeutic community and the proper selection and placement of patients vis-à-vis physical structure and patient population

Session 23: Geriatric pharmacology. Consulting pharmacist. Film: "Techniques of Parenteral Medications" (23 min, ANA)

Session 24: Relationship of nurses, nursing aides, and visiting physicians

Session 25: Relationship of nursing staff to administration and other departmental functions of the extended care facility

Session 26: Accident prevention. Film: "Diagnosis Danger" (29 min, ANA)

Session 27: Relationship of nursing staff to religious services. Clerical representative

Session 28: Bladder and bowel care and management of intermittent catheterization and Foley catheter. Film: "Urethral Catheters" (30 min, ANA)

Session 29: Diagnosis and management of organic brain syndrome

Session 30: Infection Control. Film: "Role of Nursing in Infection Control" (25½ min, ANA)

Session 31: Relation of staff to community. Film: "Telephone Manners" (telephone company)

Session 32: Development of nursing plans. Film: "Mrs. Reynolds Needs a Nurse" (38 min, ANA)

B. Administrative Director

1. Staffing Pattern: The number of personnel employed on the nursing staff, their salaries, etc., should be worked out by the administrative director in cooperation with the director of nursing.
2. Coordination with Nonprofessional Services: The administrative director should assist in the development of effective working relationships between the nursing and dietary, housekeeping, maintenance, recreation, and business departments.
3. Major Equipment: Major equipment needed by the nursing staff should be ordered with the approval of the administrative director.

C. Director of Social Service

1. Admission of Patients: The admission of patients, their histories, and placement should be the responsibility of the director of social service, who should supply the director of nursing with a social history of each patient and should supervise their placement in the extended care facility.
2. Contacting of Physicians: The director of social service should contact each patient's physician before the admission of that patient and should give current information to the director of nursing.
3. Liaison with Families: Liaison between families of patients and the nursing staff should be maintained by the director of social service.

D. Dietary

1. Diet Requirements: The director of nursing should discuss with the dietary director the diet requirements of new patients.
2. Changes of Diet: The director of nursing should notify the dietary director in writing of any changes in diet directed by the doctors.
3. Notice of Discharge: Should a patient be discharged, absent during mealtime, transferred, or die, the Nursing Department should notify the dietary director immediately.
4. Delivery of Meals: The dietary staff should have the responsibility of delivering the setups and food trucks to patient floors, and the meals should then be served to the patients by nursing aides.
5. Refrigerators: Unit refrigerators and pantries should be kept stocked by the Dietary Department with items used for patients upon receipt of completed floor supply lists.

E. Housekeeping

1. Laundry: The housekeeping staff should cooperate with the nursing aides by supplying clean linens, caring for patients' personal laundry, etc.
2. Cleaning: The executive housekeeper should cooperate with the

director of nursing in working out the cleaning schedules of her staff, the director of nursing advising the executive housekeeper on admissions and discharges so that rooms may be thoroughly cleaned and prepared before the arrival of new patients.

F. Maintenance: All necessary repairs to nursing equipment should be reported in writing to the Maintenance Department by the director of nursing or charge nurses and should be placed on the appropriate clipboard in the administrative office.

G. Physical Therapy: The nursing department should relate doctors' orders to the physical therapist and should maintain continuity with patients during the course of treatment.

H. Speech Therapy: Nursing aides or orderlies should transport specified patients to assigned locations for speech therapy.

I. Occupational Therapy: Nursing aides or orderlies should transport patients to the recreation room or community rooms for occupational therapy.

J. Health Records: Unit charge nurses should offer information on patients to be used to complete the Medicare records for the utilization review committee by the health records librarian.

K. Recreational Therapy: Nursing aides or orderlies should encourage the attendance of patients in recreational activities and should transport them to proper locations for such activities (Fig. 3-13).

L. Business Office: The director of nursing should check the business records of the nursing staff with respect to salaries, insurance policies, vacations, stipulated holidays, sick leave, etc.

XII. EDUCATION AND TRAINING

A. In-service Training Program: This program should be held weekly and conducted by the medical director to include bedside demonstrations plus occasional talks by experts in the field of caring for the aged (see p. 86).

B. Group Therapy: Nursing staff members should be encouraged to attend the weekly patient and family group therapy sessions.

C. Seminars: Educational seminars on various aspects in the field of caring for the aged should be planned in the extended care facility with participation by members of the nursing staff.

Fig. 3-13. Nursing should encourage patients to participate in the recreation program.

D. Safety Education: For details, see Section 9 (p. 386).

E. Orientation sessions for all new nursing staff should be conducted at regular intervals by the assistant director in charge of education.

XIII. TELEPHONE LISTINGS

The telephone numbers of the following professional persons and services should be listed and appropriately displayed at each nursing station.

A. Attending physicians and dentists

B. Hospitals

C. Ambulance service

D. Laboratory

E. Special services to include:

1. Podiatrist
2. Optician
3. Hearing-aid consultant
4. Brace maker

5. Beautician
6. Barber

F. Clerical representatives

G. Fire department

H. Police department

Section 4

Social Service

Introduction

The primary goal of the Social Service Department should be the successful placement and psychosocial adaptation of the patient and his family to the extended care institution. Other important objectives should include the growth of appropriate social work skills to bring effective service to patients, their families, and the staff; the development of a therapeutic patient community in which the patient, his patient peers, the treating staff members, the administrative staff, the family and the community-at-large can function within a protective environment; the evolution of a long-term post-extended care plan for the patient; the expansion of continuing relationships with the health and welfare community. Finally, the objective is the acceptance of teaching responsibilities and the sharing of specific social work skills and techniques by the conduct of research and the study of the dynamics of family life under the stress of chronic illness and disability as related to the role of the aged ill in the family and in the community.

I. STAFFING PATTERN

The director of social service in a 65-bed extended care facility should be assisted by: one or two consultants in social work whose special area of interest should relate to patient and family group therapy; two social work students and one part-time typist (or the assignment of typing from the dictating machine to a typing pool or personnel in the administrative office).

II. SOCIAL SERVICE RECORDS

A. Patient Care Records

1. These records should be filed alphabetically and kept in the social service office, each manila folder to be marked with the patient's name and to include:

a. All material pertaining to initial inquiries for placement of the patient
b. A copy of the initial social service summary
c. Copies of all subsequent social service summaries
d. A copy of the patient's admission card with names, addresses, and telephone numbers of the patient's relatives, the attending physician, and other helpful locating information, including the patient's Medicare number
e. Notes of pertinent interviews, with dates
f. Any other information specifically related to the individual patient's management and progress

2. When a patient is discharged, the entire social service record may be placed with the patient chart and thus become a part of the permanent discharge file kept in the record room for 6 years or the proscribed duration of the statute of limitations in the state.

B. Records of Placement Inquiries

1. Records of all inquiries for patient placement, filed alphabetically under patients' names, should be kept in the social service office.
2. At the end of each calendar year, these inquiries should be removed from the files and placed in a large dated manila envelope.
3. This envelope should be placed in a file in the social service office to be used for long-range planning.

C. Numerical Records of Social Service Contacts

1. A running numerical record of all social service contacts performed by each member of the Social Service Department should include:
a. A monthly social service summary (Fig. 4-1)
b. A monthly patient group meeting attendance record
c. Monthly attendance record of family orientation sessions

2. The director of social service should tally all of these contacts and write a full report of the month's social service activities.
3. The original report should be presented to the administrative director, and a carbon copy should be kept in the social service office.

D. Special Projects File

1. On occasion the director of social service should engage in the investigation and inauguration of special projects.
2. The material gathered on these projects should be placed in manila folders, according to content, and filed alphabetically in the social service office.

Fig. 4-1

MONTHLY SOCIAL SERVICE SUMMARY

Worker ________________

Month ________________

Name	Patient Interview	Family Interview	Hospital or Home Visit	Staff Conference	Patient Integration Conference	Patient Group Meeting	Family Orientation Meeting

III. SOCIAL WORK PROGRAM WITH PATIENTS AND FAMILIES

A. Preadmission Process

1. Initial Inquiry. The initial inquiry is made by the prospective patient's family, his physician, a responsible friend, or a health and welfare agency by letter, phone, or visit to the director of social service or, in her absence, to an assigned staff member.

2. Visit to the Extended Care Facility. The prospective patient's family or other concerned person or persons should plan a visit to the facility, including an interview with the director of social service, or, in her absence, with the administrative director (Fig. 4-2).

3. Other Conversations and Meetings. After the initial conference, and before any definite decision on placement is made, multiple conversations and meetings between the patient's family, physician, or other concerned persons and members of the staff, usually represented by the director of social service, are held.

4. Contact with Physician. Should the family at this point indicate genuine interest in admission of the patient, the director of social

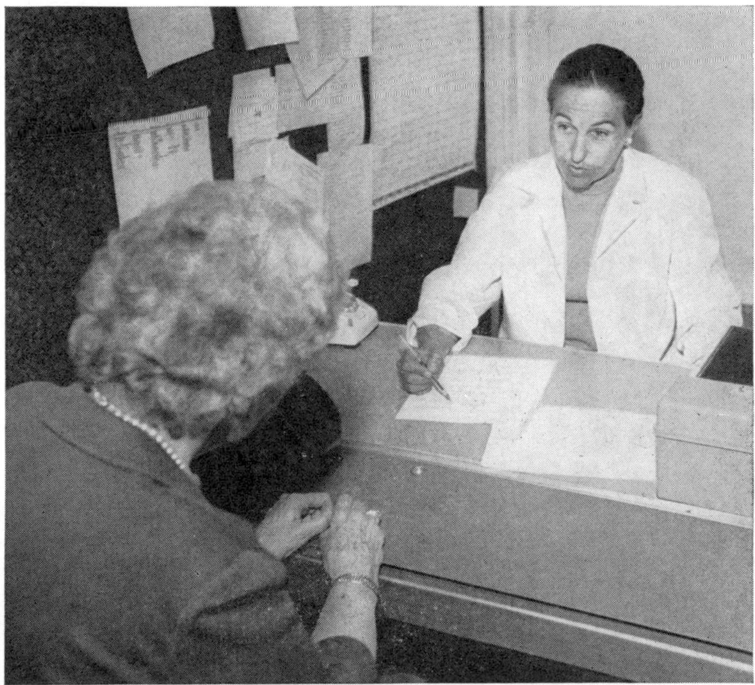

Fig. 4-2. An interview between the director of social service and a relative of a patient candidate is held to discuss the procedure of hospital discharge and admission to the extended care facility.

service should contact his attending physician for further medical information and, when feasible, obtain permission to visit his patient.

5. Visit to Candidate Patient. When time permits, a visit should be made to the candidate patient in the hospital or home by the director of social service alone, in conjunction with the medical director, or accompanied by other appropriate members of the staff.

6. Evaluation of Candidate Patient. The director of social service next should develop fuller medical and psychosocial evaluation of the candidate for placement to be presented for final decision by the medical and administrative director and the director of nursing.

7. Final Preadmission Planning

a. A definite admission time and date should be scheduled and a room appropriate for the individual patient selected.

b. The hospital and/or physician should be notified and a letter written to the family finalizing the admission plans and accompanied by:

(1) An "Information for Families Form" describing the details of extended care and pertinent financial arrangements to be read and retained by the sponsor, the final page to be signed and brought to the extended care facility at admission (Fig. 4-3).

Fig. 4-3

INFORMATION FOR FAMILIES

Please read the Information for Families form carefully. At admission, you will be asked to retain pages 0 to 0 for your own records, sign duplicate page 0, and present signed duplicate page 0 to us. We have attempted to clarify the policies and procedures or our institution as clearly as possible in these pages. If you have any additional questions regarding "Information for Families," please speak to us prior to the date of admission.

Admission

Admitting days are Monday through Friday from 9:00 A.M. to 12 noon. If you plan to have the patient admitted directly from the hospital, in order to avoid delay, arrange the discharge procedure in advance. Please consult with the patient's physician regarding the most appropriate means of transportation. If the patient is not ambulatory, it is advisable to use the ramp entrance at the side of the building.

A. The Medicare Patient

1. Transfer Form:

The patient desirous of receiving Medicare benefits at the extended care facility must present a completed hospital transfer form as a basis for Medicare eligibility. The patient's physician and the hospital Social Service Department will assist you in fulfilling this requirement.

Fig. 4-3 (Continued)

2. Medical Report:
   Please ask the patient's physician to furnish this institution with a complete report of recent patient studies, including a chest x-ray, an electrocardiogram, blood chemistries, and other appropriate data.
3. Certification for Medicare Benefits:
   Medicare patients must be certified for admission by the patient's physician and recertified when indicated. It is the responsibility of the family to demonstrate the patient's eligibility for Medicare benefits, and it is expected the family will facilitate the necessary certification by the physician.

B. The Non-Medicare Patient
1. Medical Report:
   The family must furnish the extended care facility with a recent written medical report.

C. Medical Supervision

On admission, it is expected that the patient's family will nominate a physician to supervise the patient while in residence. The physician is responsible for the performance of a comprehensive physical examination of the patient within 24 hours following admission, to include chest x-ray, electrocardiogram, blood chemistries, urinanalysis, and x-ray studies on patients with known disease. All patients must be examined at least once monthly by their personal physician. It is customary for physicians to bill families for services rendered.

Need for Additional Medical Examinations and Emergencies

In the event of change in the patient's medical status or emergency, the patient's attending physician will be promptly notified. The attending physician has the responsibility of determining the need for visiting the patient. Physicians are also responsible for drug management and prescriptions for preventive, restorative, and rehabilitative procedures and for ordering diagnostic procedures and hospitalization. The physician is responsible for notifying the family in the event of change in the patient's medical status or in the event of death. When the attending physician is not available, his prior designated substitute physician will be acceptable. When neither is available, the extended care facility has qualified physicians on call for medical emergencies.

Medications and Drugs

Drugs and medications in prior use cannot be accepted for patient use at the extended care institution. The patient's attending physician will be responsible for prescribing all medications and drugs. All drugs and medications ordered by the patient's attending physician will be purchased from the Community Pharmacy.

A. For Certified Medicare Patients

Bills for Medicare-covered pharmaceuticals for certified Medicare patients will be forwarded to the fiscal intermediary. Families will not receive such

Fig. 4-3 (Continued)

drug and medication bills during the patient's certified Medicare benefit days.

B. For Non-Medicare Patients

Families will be billed directly by the pharmacy for all drugs and medications prescribed by the patient's attending physician.

Laboratory and X-ray Fees

The following procedures will be considered routine at the time of admission of your patient:

A. Urinanalysis

B. Complete blood count, blood sugar, and blood urea nitrogen

C. X-ray of the chest

D. Electrocardiogram

E. X-ray studies of patients with known osteous disease

These diagnostic procedures will be ordered by the patient's attending physician at admission and repeated periodically when ordered. The attending physician may elect not to order these procedures by presentation of the results of the same studies performed no later than 1 week prior to admission to the extended care facility. All charges for laboratory and x-ray services will be billed directly.

Restorative Services

Physical therapy, speech therapy, and occupational therapy are available modalities of restorative and rehabilitative care when prescribed by the attending physician. Fees for such services are (1) physical therapy, ——— per treatment; (2) speech therapy, ——— per treatment; (3) occupational therapy, ——— per treatment.

A. For Certified Medicare Patients

Bills for physical therapy, speech therapy, and occupational therapy will be forwarded to the fiscal intermediary during patient's certified Medicare benefit days. Families will not receive bills for these therapeutic modalities during the patient's certified Medicare benefit days.

B. For Non-Medicare Patients

Families will be billed for all services performed and ordered by the patient's attending physician.

Special Appliances

When needed continuously and exclusively for the patient, special equipment and appliances such as wheelchairs, crutches, walkers, braces, traction apparatus, trapezes, etc., may be rented or purchased as prescribed by the physician. The patient's family may arrange for such rentals or purchase with the director of social service. These costs are the financial responsibility of the family.

Dental Service

A qualified dentist is in attendance at the extended care institution. If requested in writing by the patient's family or attending physician, the patient

Fig. 4-3 (Continued)

will be examined by the dentist. If a treatment plan is indicated, the dentist will communicate directly with the family in writing. Arrangements for completion of appropriate dental treatment, thus, will be made with the family. Dental charges are the financial responsibility of the family.

Podiatrist

A qualified podiatrist is also in attendance. Podiatry service is available on the physician's prescription and at the request of the patient's family. The current prevailing fee is ———. Arrangements may be made with the nurse in charge. Charges for podiatry service are the financial responsibility of the family. Families will be billed directly for services by the podiatrist.

Beautician and Barber Service

A trained beautician is in regular attendance. Arrangements may be made with the nurse in charge. The price list for beautician services is posted. Beautician bills are the financial responsibility of the family.

A trained barber is in regular attendance. Arrangements may be made with the nurse in charge. The fee for barber service will appear on the monthly statement and is the financial responsibility of the family.

Clothing and Toilet Articles

Patients wear street clothes during the day. All clothing for patient use should be marked with his or her full name, either by name tape or indelible laundry pen. Washable clothing is often easiest to handle. A minimum patient wardrobe should include:

A. Male

- 3 to 4 pairs of pajamas
- 1 robe
- 1 pair of slippers
- 6 shirts
- 4 pairs of trousers
- 6 sets of underwear
- 6 pairs of socks
- 1 sweater and/or jacket
- 1 to 2 pairs of shoes
- Electric razor only
- Regular toilet articles
- Appropriate outerwear

B. Female

- 3 to 4 nightgowns
- 1 robe
- 1 pair of slippers
- 3 to 4 dresses
- Appropriate underclothing
- 1 sweater

Fig. 4-3 (Continued)

Regular toilet articles
Appropriate outerwear

It is expected that the patients' family will plan the replacement of clothing and other personal articles with the nursing staff.

All clothing must be removed by the family at discharge. All unclaimed clothing and personal articles remaining at the institution after 30 days will be given to a local charitable organization.

Laundry and Dry Cleaning

The extended care facility will launder underclothing, nightgowns, pajamas, and other machine-washable articles without charge but will assume no responsibility for the intactness or loss of these articles. It is preferable that families be responsible for clothing requiring hand laundering, ironing, and dry cleaning. When requested, we will send clothing to professional dry cleaners and hand laundries. Families will be billed directly by the dry cleaner and the hand laundry for service.

Eyeglasses, Dentures, Hearing Aids, etc.

We shall take every reasonable precaution to safeguard eyeglasses, dentures, and hearing aids but cannot be responsible for their breakage or loss. If you wish, you may leave extra eyeglasses, batteries, etc., with the nurse in charge. When visiting, please check periodically to ascertain if replacement articles are needed.

Money and Valuable Jewelry

We suggest patients not bring jewelry or other valuable keepsakes. Prudence dictates that patients carry only nominal amounts of cash. The facility cannot be responsible for these items.

Visiting

A. Visiting the Patient at the Extended Care Facility

Families and friends are encouraged to visit their patient between 2:00 and 4:30 P.M. daily, except Mondays. Staff is not permitted to revise the visiting hours schedule except during unusual conditions or a medical emergency. Visitors are requested to enter and exit the building via the main entrance and to use elevators only to go above the first floor. No more than two persons may visit patients at one time. Children under fourteen years of age are not permitted. Young people over fourteen are welcome to visit in recreation areas only.

Food and candy in reasonable quantities, not requiring refrigeration, may be brought in to patients. It is expected that special diets will be respected.

Family and friends are requested to join their patient in the activities of the Department of Recreation during visiting hours. Programs sponsored by the Department of Recreation are planned therapeutically for patients, and family participation in these programs is encouraged.

Fig. 4-3 (Continued)

B. Off-premises Visiting

Physician's written approval is required to remove a patient from the premises for excursions, shopping trips, lunch, etc. Written permission from the responsible family member is required before the patient may leave the premises with other than family members. The approximate time of patient departure and return should be entered in writing in the Patient Off-premises Visiting Notebook at each nursing station.

It must be understood that premature or poorly planned off-premises visiting often impedes the patient's adaptation to the new environment. Please discuss your visiting plan with the director of social service as well as with the patient's physician.

Telephone Calls

A wheelchair-height public telephone is available for patient use in outgoing service. Telephone jacks for incoming calls are available in patient rooms.

If you wish to discuss the patient's progress with the nursing staff, you may call the charge nurse on your patient's floor at 2 P.M. daily. The telephone number for patients and nurses is 200-21-2110.

Newspapers, Magazines, Mail, Packages

Delivery of mail is a daily routine service. Packages, magazines, and periodicals are delivered as received. When requested, a subscription for daily newspaper delivery can be arranged with the director of nursing. The newspaper distributor will bill the family directly.

Smoking

Patients and their guests are permitted to smoke only in designated recreation areas.

Tipping

It is neither customary nor expected that patients and their families engage in tipping personnel. Some families have elected to contribute to the Staff Christmas Fund. At the appropriate time, funds received for this purpose are distributed by the personnel committee to all employees, following the Christmas holidays. All personnel are informed of the source of the contributed funds, but the amount is not disclosed. It is our impression that this practice has been successful to date.

Family Vacations and Changes of Address

It is expected that all changes in family addresses and telephone numbers will be registered with the administrative director or nurse in charge. Please observe this practice when the responsible family members will be out of town or traveling.

Please Do Not

Please do not make special requests of the staff to purchase personal items for patients.

Fig. 4-3 (Continued)

Please do not ask staff to present medical information. Medical information must come directly from the attending physician to families.

Financial Arrangements

The daily rate for patient care is limited to basic room and board, routine nursing service, laundry (as stated previously), and patient participation in the activities of the Department of Recreation, Department of Volunteers, Department of Social Service, and Religious Services Programs. Rates for patient care at the Community Extended Care Facility range from $——— to $——— per day and are established prior to the date of admission by the director of social service and the responsible family member. All financial arrangements are made between the extended care facility and the responsible family member. A trustee or other duly authorized person may be nominated by the patient to serve in this capacity. Financial arrangements with patients are generally not acceptable.

A. The Medicare-eligible Patient

It is understood by all parties participating in Medicare benefits that the extended care facility has, in effect, as prescribed by law, a utilization review plan. The recommendations of the utilization review committee must be supported by the agency. If, at admission, a patient requests Medicare coverage and meets the eligibility requirements for such coverage, the family is responsible for the $5.50 per day co-insurance factor as defined in the Medicare provisions. When Medicare benefits are terminated by decision of the patient's attending physician and/or authorized utilization review commitee, the responsible family member will be so notified and immediately assumes responsibility for all financial costs incurred by the patient. At all times during Medicare benefit days, the responsible family member is responsible for uncovered supplementary costs and co-insurance after 20 days.

B. For Non-Medicare Patients

Payment of extended care charges must be made 30 days in advance. Bills are payable monthly at the beginning of each month. The responsible family member is responsible for all charges incurred by the patient.

Discharge and Transfer

The extended care facility reserves the right to request the responsible family member to provide for the patient's immediate discharge and transfer from this institution should this institution find the patient's behavior harmful to himself or to others.

A. Hospitalization

If the patient is removed to the hospital, the extended care facility will not reserve the patient's bed unless notified otherwise by the family. Hospital charges are the financial responsibility of the family.

B. Discharge

Patients may be discharged by written physician's orders. Discharge days are Monday through Friday from 9:00 to 11:00 A.M. Patients remaining beyond the 11:00 A.M. time will be charged for an additional day. Notification of

Fig. 4-3 (Continued)

discharge is required 1 week in advance when permanent transfer of the patient is planned, except for emergency hospitalization. Prior to discharge of the patient, the responsible family member must present an approval slip from our business office to the nurse in charge. The nurse in charge will present the responsible family member with a list of current medication and drug orders, as well as with the patient's remaining supply of medications, as ordered by the physician. Patient discharge *must* follow the above-noted routines.

ADMISSION AGREEMENT

I am requesting admission of the patient noted below to the extended care facility.

I have read and agree to the Information for Families material regarding patient procedures and policies.

On behalf of the patient noted below, I certify that the information given in applying for payment under Title XVIII of the Social Security Act is correct. I authorize release of any information needed to act on this request. I request that payment of authorized benefits be made on this patient's behalf.

I authorize this extended care facility to engage in implementation of patient care as ordered by the patient's physician and shall refrain from holding the institution, its administration, or its staff responsible for any injuries or accidents which may develop as a result of carrying out of medical orders.

____
Patient's Name

____
Daily Rate

____
Responsible Family Member

____
Address

Special Services

Special Nursing Care__________	Dental Service__________
Physical Therapy__________	Podiatry__________
Occupational Therapy__________	Barber, Beautician__________
Speech Therapy__________	Newspaper__________

____________________	____________________
Date	Signature of Responsible Family Member

(2) A preadmission questionnaire describing the personal likes, habits, and abilities of the patient completed by the family and brought to the institution at admission

(3) A transfer form to be completed for presentation at the time of the patient's admission

c. The director of social service should assist the family, if requested, in making arrangements for the patient's transportation to the extended care facility.

d. The family should also be advised by the director of social service on the patient's clothing, furnishings, toilet articles, and other details mentioned in the Information for Families form for emphasis.

e. The director of social service should familiarize the appropriate department heads with the forthcoming admission.

8. Admission Set. The director of social service should complete an admission set as fully as possible with identifying information about the patient at this time.

9. Initial Summary of Patient. The initial social service summary (Fig. 4-4) should be prepared by the director of social service before the patient is admitted or shortly thereafter to form part of the patient chart and to:

a. Present a written record of the department's initial psychosocial interpretation of the patient's past medical, social, emotional, and functional history

b. Assess the current medical, social, emotional, and functional status of the patient

c. Furnish a description of the history of the patient's family and the current patient-family interaction

d. Help develop the plan for treatment of the patient

B. Financial Arrangements

1. Prior to Admission

a. The family of the candidate patient should be advised by the director of social service on the following:

(1) Medicare benefits

(2) The rate structure of patient fees and specific daily rate for the candidate patient

(3) The exact information on just what the rate covers and what items or services are available at extra charge

(4) Any admission financial requirements

(5) An explanation of the regular billing procedure

b. With the assistance of the director of social service, the family should nominate one of its members as the responsible relative who will be required to sign the Information for Families form, and where appropriate, the Extended Care Admission and Billing form, and to handle all financial matters.

2. During Residence

a. Financial status of the patient

(1) The director of social service should be regularly informed by the business manager on the status of all patient accounts.

(2) If a patient account should become overdue, the director of social service should bring this fact to the attention of the administrative director and together a plan should be made for discussion of the delinquent account with the responsible relative.

(3) The director of social service should be available to families for ongoing discussion of patient financial status.

b. Alteration of fee

(1) A change in the patient's condition may warrant a change in care, in room, etc., with a resultant adjustment in the daily rate.

(2) The director of social service should discuss the matter with the administration and inform the responsible relative in writing if adjustments are necessary, giving the family ample notice.

c. Changes in financial status

(1) The director of social service should serve as the liaison in interpreting any changing financial status of patient and family to the administration, insofar as these changes relate to patient care.

(2) If patient requires financial assistance to remain in the facility, this should be discussed by the director of social service and the administration who together determine whether it is feasible for the patient to remain under different financial arrangements.

(3) When a decision is reached, it should be relayed to the family by the director of social service who then should assist the family in making the necessary arrangements.

3. Following Transfer or Discharge

a. Holding fee. Should the patient require hospitalization and the family requests the extended care facility to hold the patient's bed, the director of social service should discuss a holding fee with the responsibile relative, and the sum agreed upon by Social Service and the family should be charged to the patient's account during the hospitalization.

b. Billing. The director of social service should inform the business

Fig. 4-4

SAMPLE INITIAL SOCIAL SERVICE SUMMARY

Mrs. Mary Jones
August 10, 1968
Social Service Summary

Mrs. Jones is an eighty-eight-year-old white, Protestant female who will be admitted to the extended care facility on Thursday, August 11, 1968 at 10:00 A.M., by ambulance from the Community Hospital, Morgan City, New York.

Medical History:

This eighty-eight-year-old female was reported as well, without any significant medical history, until the age of eighty-five at which time she is reported to have become forgetful and intermittently confused, and in the opinion of her family physician, unable to continue to live alone in her own apartment in New York City. She subsequently moved into the home of her daughter, Mrs. Eva Smith of 37 Deep End Lane, Morgan City, in 1963. The patient reportedly "did well" until 6 weeks ago, at which time it is reported she fell while getting out of bed and sustained a fracture of the left hip. She was subsequently hospitalized on July 1, 1968 at the Community Hospital and sustained surgery for hip-pinning. Following the surgery the patient became markedly forgetful, confused, and disoriented and required special duty nurses around the clock for management in the hospital. Her physician, Dr. John Barnes, has suggested that the patient may have sustained a cerebral vascular accident following surgery. No paralysis is reported. Hearing and vision are reported intact. No other significant medical information is reported.

Functional:

The patient was seen in an interview at the Community Hospital on Tuesday, August 9, 1968 at 10:00 A.M. Present at the interview were: the patient, her special duty nurse, Miss O'Gosh, her physician, Dr. John Barnes, her daughter, Mrs. Eva Smith of the Morgan City address, and this interviewer.

The patient presented as an attractive white-haired lady who looked somewhat younger than her stated age. She was seated in a chair and was dressed in a hospital gown and bathrobe. Although her social affect remained intact, the patient was unable to state accurately where she was or why she had gotten there. There was complete denial or forgetfulness of the recent surgical experience. The patient was confused about time and place and was able to identify her daughter after many errors. She seemed pleasant, good-natured cooperative. She appeared to have a memory content of somewhat less than 5 sec. Nurse reported patient is able to feed herself; is intermittently incontinent of urine and not incontinent of feces; is quiet and cooperative with nurses

Fig. 4-4 (Continued)

in nursing management. Patient must be watched or she will attempt to ambulate independently, which is not recommended at this time.

Dr. Barnes presented the patient as 6 weeks postsurgical repair of a fractured left hip; possible cerebral vascular accident. Dr. Barnes recommended placement in an extended care facility for patient management. He wishes a program in physical rehabilitation with independent ambulation as a goal, if the confusion and disorientation permit.

Social History:

The patient is a college graduate, was married at age twenty-two, and lived in New York City with her husband. The couple had one child, Mrs. Eva Smith. The patient's husband was employed by a toothbrush company as a vice-president and died in 1962 following a brief illness. Following his death, the patient remained in the New York apartment alone until 1963, at which time she moved in with her daughter.

The daughter appears to be genuinely interested in providing a great deal of care and nursing attention for her mother. The daughter also seems extremely anxious about her mother's medical status and especially worried about the possibility of the recent cardiovascular accident. Although the daughter is aware her mother has been forgetful and confused for at least 3 years, she is very much upset by the recent events and will probably need a great deal of reassurance from her physician (whom she trusts) that "I am doing the right thing." The daughter is having difficulty in permitting herself to understand that the patient is, and has been, ill for some time and is no longer the strong and vigorous maternal figure of previous years.

Plan:

Mrs. Smith has acquired power of attorney for her mother's affairs. Patient will be transferred from the Community Hospital on August 11, 1968, to the nursing center. Mrs. Smith has been invited to participate in the next series of family group therapy programs beginning in one week.

Mrs. Mary P. Jones, ACSW
Director of Social Service

---

manager of patient discharge and effective dates, for purposes of either:

(1) Termination of patient billing
(2) Revision to holding fee status

C. Admission Process

A folder holding data on "pending admissions" should be kept on the desk of the social service director at all times for convenient reference.

1. Arrival of Patient
   a. The director of social service or her designated alternate should be on the premises at the time of the patient's arrival.
   b. Independent arrival. If the patient should enter the extended care facility accompanied by his family, but requiring no further assistance, he should be greeted by the director of social service, and the charge nurse from the unit of the room assigned to the patient should be called to escort the patient to his room. Meanwhile the director of social service or her representative will take the family to the social service office.
   c. Assisted arrival
   (1) By ambulance. The patient should be brought into the building at the ramp entrance and the ambulance personnel, directed by the charge nurse of the assigned unit, together should conduct the patient to his room, and the family should be directed to the social service office by the director of social service or her representative.
   (2) By car. The patient should be helped from the car by his family or a staff member and taken to his assigned room by the charge nurse while the family is conducted to the social service office by the director of social service or her representative.
   d. Luggage should be brought into the structure by the family or the driver and taken to the room by a staff member.
2. Procedure for Family
   a. Admission set completion. In the social service office, the director of social service or, in her absence, an assigned staff member should complete the admission set with the help of the family, and these forms, the majority of which are the basis of the patient chart, should include: diet check list, check sheet for medications and treatments, admission and discharge information form, nursing care and progress notes, initial physical, social service summary, physician's orders and progress notes, preadmission questionnaire, transfer form and Medicare Extended Care Admission and Billing form questions 1-15, the pharmacy notification card, and the certification and recertification sheet when appropriate.
   b. Other patient data
   (1) The preadmission questionnaire, having been completed by the family, should be given to the director of social service or other admitting staff member.
   (2) The family should be requested to present a hospital transfer form and written medical report from the attending physician

for his patient and any special directions for the patient, such as special dietary orders or preferences or a description of previous nursing routine followed, which should be added to the chart.

(3) The patient record card, diet check list, health department form, release of responsibility for valuables form, and the last page of the Information for Families form should be completed with the family's aid, and the patient should be assigned an extended care facility admission number.

(4) The family should give the extended care facility representative a check covering 30 days' care for non-Medicare patient or should sign the Medicare Extended Care Admission and Billing form for a Medicare patient.

(5) Should the family wish to leave funds for the patient, the director of social service or other admission staff member should place the money in an envelope marked with the name of the patient and the date in the safety box, and a receipt should be made out and given to the family or patient before the family's departure.

(6) Instructions on special services, such as newspaper delivery, hairdresser, etc., should be rechecked with the family. (*a*) If any such services are requested, the director of social service or her representative should list them on a sheet of paper which is attached to the material for the patient chart. (*b*) In addition, those department heads who will be concerned with ordering these special services should be notified both verbally and in writing. (*c*) The charge nurse of the patient's unit (7:00 A.M. to 3:00 P.M. shift) should be given the complete list, the director of social service later following up to see that the services are being supplied as requested.

(7) The patient record card, pharmacy notification card, the health department form, the release of responsibility for valuables, the signed last page of the Information for Families form, the check, and where appropriate, the completed Extended Care Admission and Billing form should then be placed in the administrative office for proper handling and for listing in the patient registry and roster.

c. Family evaluation. During the admission procedure the director of social service should evaluate family function and add her observations to the family diagnosis.

d. Completion of admission

(1) The following material should be given to the charge nurse assigned to the patient: (*a*) diet check list, (*b*) preadmission

questionnaire, (*c*) admission and discharge information form, (*d*) initial physical examination form, (*e*) physician's orders and progress notes form, (*f*) nursing care plan and progress notes form, (*g*) check sheet for medications and treatments, (*h*) initial social service summary, (*i*) written medical report (if any), (*j*) special instructions (if any), (*k*) transfer form (if any), and (*l*) certification and recertification (if appropriate).

(2) Family should be escorted to the patient's room by the director of social service or her representative, who should remain generally available until the departure of the family.

D. Treatment of In-residence Patients and Their Families

The director of social service should work as a coordinator and catalyst in the development of the patient and family treatment plan under the direction of the patient's attending physician.

1. Preparatory Steps for Development of Treatment Plan

a. Initial interview. Shortly after admission, the director of social service could conduct a patient interview to establish the degree of functional abilities and in-residence social service goals (Fig. 4-5).

b. Staff consultations. She should consult with all staff members concerned with the patient to learn more about his functions

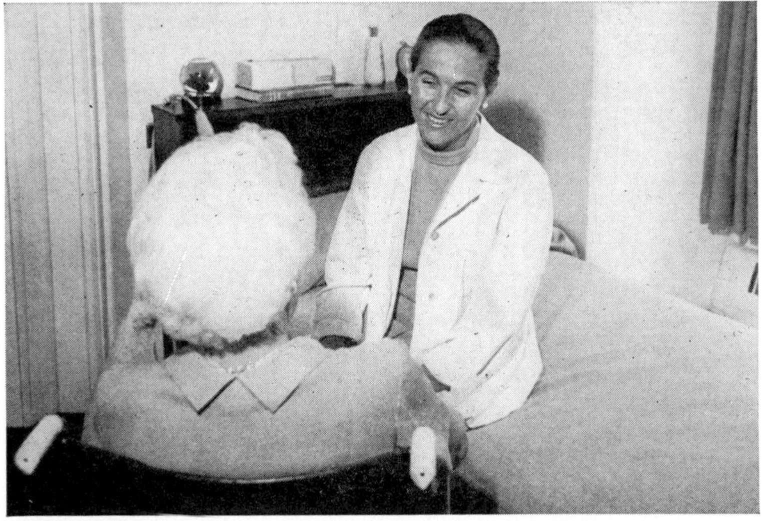

Fig. 4-5. The social service director meets with a newly admitted patient to determine her social needs.

and to obtain their assessments of his needs, abilities, and disabilities to assist her in designing the initial program for the patient.

c. Evaluations

(1) Observation by the director of social service should include patient interaction with patient peers to evaluate room and bed placement, as well as to determine treatment plan and patient-family interaction via visits and telephone conversations.

(2) Observations should be made and given to the social service director by the administrative director, the nursing staff, and other concerned staff members.

2. Social Work Treatment Plan for Patient and Family

a. Purpose of the treatment

(1) To help the patient and his family with their adaptation to the placement situation

(2) To determine the appropriateness of the patient's placement within the therapeutic environment

(3) To provide treatment oriented toward helping the patient and family work through their premorbid conflicts which preclude adaptation to the placement situation

(4) To help the family and the extended care facility develop similar goals for patient management

b. Location of treatment. All social service treatments should be conducted either spontaneously or by planned appointment in any appropriate location within the facility, with exceptions:

(1) Casework interviews for patients and/or families should be conducted in the social service office.

(2) Family therapy group meetings should be conducted in a conference or meeting room.

(3) Patient therapy group meetings should be conducted in a community room.

c. Times of treatment

(1) Individual, conjoint, and/or family sessions should be held regularly and as needed.

(2) Family group therapy should be held regularly one evening a week.

(3) Patient group therapy is held regularly one evening a week.

d. Modalities of treatment

(1) Individual therapy: (*a*) Director of social service and (*b*) a patient or a family member

(2) Conjoint therapy: (*a*) Two or more staff members who may be two social workers and/or other staff members; a physician and social worker, and/or other staff members; a nurse and a

social worker, and/or other staff members; the medical director and the social worker, and/or other staff members; the social worker and other staff members; and (*b*) one or two patients, the social worker, and/or other staff members

(3) Family therapy: (*a*) an individual family and one or more therapists and other staff members, with or without patient and (*b*) family groups with one or more therapists and other staff members and members of several families—with or without patients

(4) Patient group therapy: One or more therapists and other staff members, and approximately 12 patients, the number of patients varying but the treatment designed to utilize the dynamics of group process as a therapeutic mechanism (Fig. 4-6)

3. Weekly Interdisciplinary Clinical Conferences. Individual patients should be assessed medically, socially, emotionally, and functionally.

a. Goal of conference

(1) To provide a vehicle for the rehabilitation team

(2) To explore, plan, and coordinate effective treatment programs

b. Participants

(1) The conference should be coordinated by the director of social service and chaired by the medical director.

Fig. 4-6. A therapist leads a group discussion designed to help patients to adapt to congregate living.

(2) Others in attendance should include the (*a*) administrative director, (*b*) director of nursing, (*c*) social work consultants, (*d*) attending physicians (when available), (*e*) director of recreation and volunteers, (*f*) physical therapist, (*g*) occupational therapist, (*h*) administrative resident, (*i*) speech therapist, (*j*) social work students, (*k*) staff writer, and (*l*) dietitian.

(3) Other staff members should be invited to attend when appropriate.

c. Subjects and purposes

(1) Education and coordination. The conference should serve as an educational and informational experience for all concerned staff members and thus should assist in coordinating the program of the patient.

(2) Newly admitted patients. The conference should afford an opportunity for the staff to be familiarized with the medical and psychosocial history of each patient and to discuss his current functions and the goals of his treatment.

(3) Change in patient performance. The reasons for this change and possible methods of solving problems should be discussed.

(4) Patient with constant problems. The handling of this type of problem and goals should be discussed.

(5) Communcation between staff members. The meetings themselves should furnish an opportunity for department heads and others to communicate on the progress of each department's phase of treatment with the patient.

(6) Patient discharge. Possible discharge for appropriate patients should be planned at this multidisciplinary meeting.

4. Patient Care Changes

a. If a dramatic change in a patient's condition should occur, the attending physician should be notified by the charge nurse.

b. If requested by the physician, the director of social service should contact the family with the information on the patient's changed condition.

c. If the change in the condition of the patient should warrant a change of room, of roommate or -mates, or of program, the details should be worked out with the administrative director and the director of nursing, and the director of social service should take the following steps:

(1) She should inform and interpret the changes to the family.

(2) She should help the family and the patient work through the changes.

(3) She should implement the changes in the institution by cooperating with the director of nursing and the charge nurse.

d. The director of social service should make herself available throughout changes in a patient's accommodations or routine and should follow up the condition of the patient after the move or changes, keeping his family and the attending physician informed.

5. Extra Services for Patients and Families

a. The director of social service should interpret policies and procedures to families of patients, and certain services not included in the regular routine, such as eye examinations or hearing-aid repairs, are sometimes requested and implemented by the social service director.

b. The director of social service should exercise her judgment on requested extra services and should consult with the patients' attending physician and/or the administrative director before making the necessary arrangements.

E. Termination of Patient Care

1. Emergency Discharge

a. If a patient's condition should warrant immediate transfer to a hospital for medical or surgical reasons, his physician so informs the nursing staff.

b. At the request of the physician, the director of social service should assist in making the necessary transportation arrangements.

c. A transfer form prepared by the charge nurse must accompany the patient to the hospital, and the director of social service may be asked to include certain social data in this form.

d. The director of social service should inform the administrative director of the emergency discharge and date.

e. The business manager should also be informed so that financial records and accounts may be completed.

2. Planned Discharge

a. If the patient or his family should inform the extended care facility of its intention to have the patient transferred, the director of social service should initiate a conference with the family:

(1) To determine the basis for the planned discharge

(2) To provide counseling on procedure

b. Should the attending physician inform the extended care facility of a proposed patient discharge, the social worker should provide counseling to the patient and family on the procedure.

c. The director of social service should inform the charge nurse and the administrative director of the planned discharge and the date of transfer.

d. The business manager should also be informed of the date of transfer by the director of social service so that financial records and accounts may be completed.

3. Procedure on Death of Patient

a. The attending physician has the responsibility of informing the family when a patient dies.

b. If the director of social service is on the premises, it is her duty to consult with the nursing staff to make certain that the attending physician has reached the family with news of the death.

c. The director of social service should inform the administrative director of the death.

d. The director of social service should consult with the nursing staff to learn if the family has informed them regarding arrangements for the deceased patient to be removed from the premises by a funeral director.

e. She should make herself available by telephone to consult with the family regarding the details of the removal of the deceased patient's effects from the premises, such as clothing, drugs, and personal belongings.

f. The director of social service should inform the business manager of any special arrangements concerning the financial records and accounts of the deceased.

g. If appropriate, the director of social service may contact the family at a proper interval after death to offer therapeutic counseling and/or supportive service related to the patient's death.

4. Procedure with Patient Peers

a. The extended care facility and the director of social service should recognize the phenomena of the entire therapeutic community:

(1) Should a patient become severely ill and require hospitalization

(2) Should a patient become severely ill and require transfer to another section within the facility

(3) Should a patient die

b. The director of social service should help resident patients to deal with their fears and anxieties related to these occurrences, and she should remain responsive to the impact of any change in the function of one patient upon the functions and attitudes of all patients.

c. She should attempt to accomplish this by individual conferences with selected patients and by conferences with groups of patients.

5. Procedure with Staff. When appropriate, the director of social service shou'd counsel with concerned staff members.

6. Procedure with Families of Other Patients. The director of social service, when appropriate, should be responsible for the discussion of the recent death or change in a patient's functions with families of other resident patients.

F. Transfer of Patients

1. Within the Institution

a. Room transfers. Patients should be transferred to different rooms and units when their medical, social, and emotional conditions warrant.

(1) The transfer should be made at the request of the patient, the family, the nursing staff, the attending physician, or the social service staff.

(2) The planned patient transfer should be discussed with the attending physician for his approval, with the patient's responsible relative, and with the patient himself.

(3) All relevant nursing staff members should be informed and the patient move implemented.

(4) If appropriate, the patient move shou'd be discussed in the patient group therapy and/or with patient peers by a member of the Social Service Department.

b. Following death

(1) The director of social service may participate with the administration and the nursing staff in deciding where the body will remain until called for by the funeral director.

(2) If a delay in the arrival of the funeral director is anticipated a decision may be made to remove the body to a nonpatient area so that patients and visitors may be spared the experience of observing the arrival of the funeral director.

(3) Additionally, the director of social service should participate with the nursing staff in assuring performance of all required procedures related to a patient death, including notification by the attending physician that he has informed the family of the death, receiving information from the family for funeral arrangements as related to removal of the body, and discussion with the family with regard to disposition of the clothing and effects of the deceased patient.

2. Oustide the Extended Care Facility

If, upon physician's orders, the patient should be transferred to a hospital, the director of social service has several responsibilities:

a. Transfer procedure

(1) She should assist, if requested, in making transportation arrangements for the transfer.
(2) Within 24 or 48 hr following the transfer, she should contact the family and the physician to inquire of the patient's progress.
(3) She should discuss holding the bed (see Part B) with the family, arrive at a decision, and notify the business manager and the administration of the plan.
(4) She should discuss the transfer with patient peers and interested nursing staff members, if appropriate.

b. Arrangements for patient return
(1) The director of social service should maintain contact with the attending physician and the family to remain informed on the program of the patient and to determine the date the patient is expected to return to the extended care facility.
(2) When a definite date is agreed upon, the director of social service should so notify the administration and the nursing staff.
(3) The director of social service should check to see that the return of the patient is noted by Administration and Nursing in the patient register, the census book, and the alphabetical index card.
(4) The director of social service should notify the business manager of the patient return to inpatient financial status.

c. Death of patient. Should the patient die while in the hospital, the director of social service is notified by the family, and all charges, including the holding fee, should be discounted as of the date of the death.

IV. RELATIONSHIPS WITH COMMUNITY AGENCIES

The Social Service Department should assist in maintaining and developing integration of the extended care facility within the health and welfare community by:

A. Personal and telephone contacts with other social workers and with health and welfare agencies both within and outside the community

B. Attendance and participation at meetings, conferences, and seminars in the field of social work

C. Teaching and assistance in programming at universities and at health and welfare agencies

D. Maintaining a file of resources for patient referrals

E. Dispensing of information and referral services upon the request of agencies or of members of the community

V. DUTIES AND PROCEDURES

A. Director of Social Service

1. Hours

a. Monday, Wednesday, Thursday, and Friday: 9:00 A.M. to 5:00 P.M.

b. Tuesday: 1:30 P.M. to 9:30 P.M.

c. The director of social service should also be available by telephone evenings and weekends if in the area.

2. Daily Routine

a. She should check the clipboard in the administrative office for overnight messages.

b. She should consult with the director of nursing and with the charge nurses on the condition of patients, admissions, discharges, etc., and if any action is needed, she should take the necessary steps.

c. She should check with the administrative director and the medical director to report on patients and to work out problems and schedules.

d. She should perform regular administrative duties within the institution such as:

(1) Correspondence

(2) Telephone conversations, particularly in relation to patient intake

(3) Records and files

(4) Patients and family interviews

(5) Admission and discharge planning

(6) Staff consultations

(7) Attendance at conferences

(8) Tours of the facility

(9) Assignment of cases to the consultants

(10) Arrangements for consultants to see patients and families

(11) Arrangements for medical director to see patients and families

(12) Assignment and supervision of cases to social work students

e. She should perform regular duties outside the facility consisting of participation in preadmission home or hospital visits, alone or accompanied by the medical director or other staff members.

3. Weekly and Semiweekly Routine

a. At least once a week, the director of social service should visit all patients and should familiarize herself with the progress and status of each.

b. Two afternoons each week she should make herself available to families of patients for discussion of progress and assessment of placement.

c. The face sheet of the admission folder in the social service office should be reviewed once weekly and revised if necessary, with new admissions and discharges, as well as validated anticipated admissions, and their scheduled dates noted.

d. Plans for weekly interdisciplinary clinical conference should be made with particular reference to the selection of the patients to be presented by the medical director.

e. With the administration she should review the admission discharge pattern and the inpatient status.

f. She should supervise the work of each social work student for 1½ hr each week.

4. Monthly Routine

a. She should distribute the social work activities record forms to the consultants and the students.

b. She should complete the monthly statistics based on the monthly social service summary and the monthly patient and family group meetings.

c. Each month the director of social service should review the status of patient accounts with the business manager and, if necessary, with the administrative director.

d. She should participate in the meetings of the utilization review and patient care policy committee, where she may act as the committee secretary.

5. Periodic Duties

a. As needed, additional social service notes on patient and family situations should be written with the originals added to the patient charts and the carbon copies filed in the social service office.

b. The social service director should initiate interviews with patient, family, or physician, as needed.

c. She should periodically review the status of patient placement.

d. She should participate with the administration in research, review, and planning of new projects and current patient services.

e. She should collate and develop data into professional material for publication.

f. She should prepare written evaluations of the social work students and should consult with their respective university advisors.

g. She should participate in inservice training and in seminars held on the premises for the health and welfare community.

h. She should explain the role of the Department of Social Service in the total rehabilitation program to visiting groups.

6. Yearly Duties

a. The director of social service should prepare a yearly statistical compilation of the activities of the department, based on the monthly summaries.

b. A yearly survey of inquiries for placement that have not resulted in placement in the extended care facility should be made to help the administration to evaluate the course or direction of the institution, the public image, policies, etc.

c. The director of social service should cooperate with the administrative director in furnishing certain statistical information required by various governmental and health agencies.

d. The director of social service should review the total social work program with the administration, including budget, staffing, training patterns, and unmet needs.

B. Consultants

1. Hours. The social work consultants should have a schedule of approximately 40 sessions per year, each to be of 4-hr duration.

2. Weekly Duties

a. The consultants should attend and participate in interdisciplinary clinical conferences.

b. Consultant A

(1) Consultant A should serve as therapist for the weekly patient therapy group meetings.

(2) Consultant A in addition may serve as the cotherapist for the family therapy weekly meetings.

(3) He should also accept individual patient therapy by assignment, time permitting.

c. Consultant B

(1) Consultant B should function as the therapist for the family therapy group meetings held weekly for 1½ hr, preferably in the evening.

(2) He should be available also to serve as cotherapist with the medical director or the director of the social service for other family therapy service contacts by assignment only.

(3) He should accept individual patient therapy by assignment, time permitting.

3. Monthly Duties

a. The consultants should be responsible for preparing and submitting a record of their activities to the director of social service.

b. The consultants should submit monthly bills for services rendered to the business manager.

4. Yearly Duties

a. The consultants should review the total social work program with administration and the social service director.

b. The consultants should discuss their fee schedule for the forthcoming academic year.

5. Periodic Duties

a. The consultants should participate in the social work training seminars for the health and welfare community.

b. The consultants should contribute articles for the professional bulletin of the extended care institution.

C. Social Work Students

1. Training Center for Students

a. The extended care facility should be utilized as a training center for students in the social and behavioral sciences.

b. With approval from the administration, the director of social service should enter into agreements with colleges and universities for student field-work placement.

c. Students selected by their respective academic institutions should be interviewed by the administration and the director of social service prior to their acceptance for the training program.

2. Students in Social Work

a. Hours for field work and training

(1) Social work. Students are required to spend 400 hr per academic year at the extended care institution.

(2) They must receive 1½ hr of weekly supervision of their learning and practice experiences by a social work staff member certified by the Association of Certified Social Workers.

b. Program

(1) The director of social service should design a curriculum in conformity with the standards set by the Council on Social Work Education, the school of social work, and the extended care facility.

(2) The director of social service should select and assign appropriate student cases and should assign students to attend and participate in the interdisciplinary clinical conferences and training sessions, patient and family therapy programs, and other activities within the Department of Social Service of the extended care institution.

c. The director of social service should maintain an ongoing relationship with the students' academic institutions and should submit periodic written and oral evaluations of student activity.

3. Mental Health Interns

a. Hours required for field work

(1) Mental health interns are required to spend 500 hr per academic year at the extended care facility.

(2) They must receive 1½ hr of weekly supervision of their learning and practice experience by a social work staff member certified by the Association of Certified Social Workers.

b. Program

(1) The director of social service should design a curriculum in conformity with guidelines suggested by the Mental Health Rehabilitation Counselor Program of the particular university and the extended care facility.

(2) The director of social service should assign the mental health interns to appropriate student cases and activities and should assign attendance and participation in the interdisciplinary clinical conferences and training sessions, patient and family therapy programs, and other activities of the Departments of Social Service and Recreation.

c. The director of social service should maintain an ongoing relationship with the mental health interns' academic institutions, and should submit periodic written and oral evaluations of student activity.

VI. INTERDEPARTMENTAL COOPERATION

The Social Service Department should maintain working relationships with the majority of other departments in the facility.

A. General Responsibilities

1. The Social Service Department should implement administrative policy concerning the development and function of the therapeutic community.

2. To add the special skills of social work to the work of other departments and staff of the institution in the development, implementation, and innovation of programs within all departments, the Social Service Department should:

a. Be familiar with the functions of all departments with particular reference to their relationships to patient care and family contacts

b. Be prepared to help other department heads when needed to make decisions related to patient management and provision of service

c. Have an appreciation of the work responsibilities of the other staff members and their roles in providing their special areas of service

3. The director of social service should inform responsible staff members of anticipated social work activities in the event of her absence from the extended care facility.

B. Relations with Two or More Departments

1. New Patients. The director of social service should have the responsibility of planning with other department heads for patient admissions and for presenting appropriate detailed information.

2. Observations. Consultations initiated by the director of social service or various members of the staff should be held regularly with all staff members directly concerned with a patient, requesting their observations on his functioning, needs, abilities, and disabilities, and interaction with staff members and patient peers.

3. Interdisciplinary Clinical Conference. A weekly conference on patients should be attended by department heads, other invited staff members, the administration, and consultants.

4. Unplanned Patient Discharges. Implementation of unplanned discharges should be a shared responsibility between the medical and administrative directors, the director of nursing, and the director of social service, any of these people to be available for discussion with the interested community of the discharged patient.

5. Patient Meals. The director of social service and the director of nursing should work cooperatively with the Dietary Department and the administrative director to plan and coordinate aspects of patient meals, and to establish communication between patient, physician, family, nursing service, and dietary staff with respect to special food requirements and preferences.

C. The Administration

1. General Areas of Interaction

a. The Department of Social Service should be directly responsible to the administration, employment arrangements for this department's consultants being the responsibility of the medical director.

b. Periodically, when appropriate, conferences should be held between the director of social service and the administration for the purpose of consultation, evaluation, and survey into the functions of the extended care facility.

(1) Procedures and programs related to patient activities and services should be discussed, planned, organized, coordinated, and developed.

(2) Ongoing procedures related to patient and family management in an extended care facility should be reviewed.

2. Patient Inquiries and Admissions

a. The director of social service should provide the administration with a verbal report of recent and current inquiries for admission.

b. She should present a verbal admission plan related to a new patient admission and placement to consist of the following:

(1) Name and sex of the candidate for admission
(2) Comprehensive medical and psychosocial statement
(3) Suggested bed assignment and special services required
(4) Suggested rearrangements of other inpatients, if necessary
(5) Suggested patient financial arrangements

c. The above material should be jointly evaluated by the administration and the directors of nursing and social service, and a decision made on the patient admission.

3. During Period of Patient Residence

a. The director of social service and the administration should endeavor to meet regularly and as needed for discussion and planning related to the following:

(1) Clinical aspects of the patient's course
(2) Patient needs
(3) Significant changes in patient/family function and status
(4) Pattern of patient-family institution interaction
(5) Provision or elimination of additional services
(6) Possible discharge or transfer plans for the patient
(7) Patient financial status

b. The director of social service should counsel with individual patients and their families, and progress reports of these sessions should be made regularly to the administration.

D. The Medical Director

1. In September of each year, the medical director and the members of the Social Service Department should meet to:

a. Reevaluate the complete program of the Social Service Department

b. Study patient and family needs which could be implemented by the department

c. Plan continuation, discontinuation, or development of additional social service programs and methods

2. The medical director should advise the Department of Social Service in all its work.

3. When available, the medical director should accompany the director of social service on hospital visits to candidates for admission.

4. The medical director should participate as cotherapist with one or more of the social service staff during casework interviews with patients and/or families and, when appropriate, as cotherapist with one or more of the social service staff in the weekly patient group and family group meetings.

5. Periodically the medical director should meet with the director of social service:

a. To initiate planning

b. To evaluate patient and family progress as related to the social service treatment program

c. To discuss long-term programs of study, research, and activity within and outside the nursing center in relation to:

(1) Community and government progress

(2) Activities of the health and welfare community

E. The Administrative Director

1. Statistical Information

a. The social service director should prepare for the administrative director a yearly summary of inquiries for placement that were not followed through with admission.

b. She should cooperate with the administrative director in compiling information on patient care, census, etc., for governmental and health agencies.

2. Planned Discharges of Patients. The social service director should give the administrative director information on planned discharges of patients, and together they should develop plans for implementation of the discharge process.

3. Students. Utilization of the extended care facility for students assigned to the Social Service Department and subsequent arrangements with the university affiliation are finalized by the director of social service in consultation with the administrative director.

F. The Nursing Department

1. General

a. Social Service should work closely with Nursing in that roles often overlap, as:

(1) Nursing personnel become involved in family counseling and interpretation of patient behavior.

(2) The social worker becomes involved with the family in interpreting requirements for the patient's nursing care.

(3) The Social Service Department serves as liaison between the families of patients and the nursing staff, particularly with new admissions.

b. The nursing staff and social workers should frequently counsel together as to the most effective and/or useful manner of providing patient service and should discuss patients' daily activities of living and response to treatment, both medical and and nursing.

c. Members of the departments of Nursing and Social Service mutually should share the responsibility of keeping the directors of these two departments informed of new developments or changes in patient-family status and relationships.

2. Admission

a. The director of social service verbally should present germane information to the nursing staff before the patient admission.

b. The Nursing Department should cooperate with the director of social service when new patients arrive, the director of nursing greeting the new patients, and the charge nurse of the floor to which the patient is assigned escorting the new arrival to his room, while the director of social service completes the admission procedure with the family.

c. Upon completion, admission records are given to the charge nurse of the new patient's unit by the social service director, together with a list of special services required.

3. Consultations

a. With nursing staff

(1) The Department of Social Service should be available regularly and when needed to consult with members of the nursing staff on: (a) individual patient care and family management, (b) patient-peer relationships, (c) patient-family-staff relationships, and (d) other areas of concern to the Nursing Department in providing more effective nursing service with the aid of social service counseling.

(2) These consultations should occur prior to and following admission of patients and also during the period of patient residence, and may be initiated by members of either the Nursing or Social Service Departments.

b. Joint interviews

(1) Representatives of the Social Service and Nursing Departments (usually the director) should serve as cotherapists when needed with: (a) individual patients, (b) groups of patients, (c) individual patients and their respective families, and (d) physicians and others.

(2) Purposes of these interviews should be: (a) to receive orders and instructions related to patient care and management from physicians and families, (b) to discuss areas of mutual concern, and (c) to interpret, present, and discuss the administration's point of view and recommendations.

(3) Requests for these joint interviews may be initiated by: (a) members of the Social Service Department, the Nursing Department, or other departments; and (b) physicians, patients, or families.

4. Planning

a. The departments of Social Service and Nursing should function cooperatively in initiating planning for programs and procedures related to:

(1) Patient needs

(2) Patient activities of daily living

(3) Patient-family management

b. These areas of concern should include the following:

(1) Provision and maintenance of clothing and other personal articles

(2) Hairdresser and barber services

(3) Dentistry and podiatry services

(4) Special care to be included in regular routine nursing service

(5) Special care required or requested by patient, physician, or family

(6) Special diets and other problems related to patient meals

(7) On-premises visiting of patient by physician, family or others, and off-premises activities, including transportation arrangements, etc., that require written permission

c. The decisions resulting from these planning sessions should be effected by members of either of the two departments.

5. Dining Arrangements for Patients

a. Upon admission of new patients and at the other times as required, the departments of Social Service and Nursing should plan and structure patient group dining-table assignments.

(1) The director of social service and the charge nurses cooperatively should evaluate patient dining functions.

(2) Together they should plan and assign patients to selected dining areas and selected table positions.

b. The nursing staff should be responsible for keeping the director of social service informed as to the effectiveness of the assigned seating arrangements, and periodically these arrangements should be reevaluated and improved.

6. Rounds of Patients. The directors of social service and nursing should make regular patient rounds together (Fig. 4-7):

a. To observe patient function and performance

b. To consult with other department staff members with respect to patient status

7. Discharges of Patients

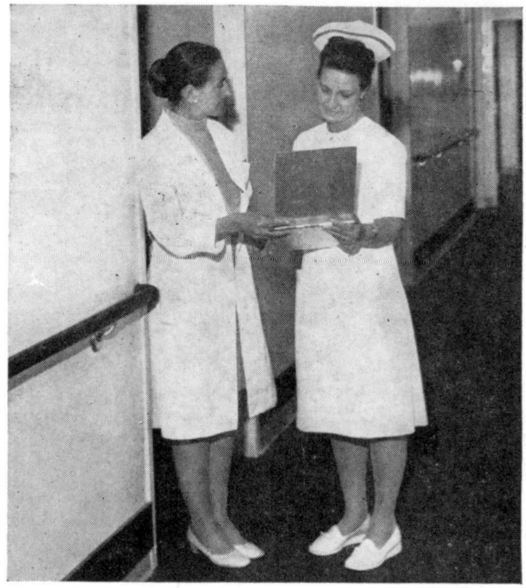

Fig. 4-7. The directors of social service and nursing make rounds to evaluate patients.

a. The director of social service should share the responsibility with the charge nurses for completing a transfer form to accompany any patient being transferred to a hospital.

b. In the case of a planned discharge, the director of social service should inform the charge nurse of the discharge and date.

8. Deaths of Patients

a. The director of social service should cooperate with the nursing staff to see that the treating physician reaches the family with news of the death.

b. She should also check with the nursing staff to determine whether the family has notified the extended care facility regarding removal plans for the deceased patient by a funeral director.

9. In-service Training

a. Time permitting, the director of social service and/or other members of the department should attend the weekly nursing training sessions.

b. When appropriate, the director of social service and/or members of the department should conduct discussions and prepare selected teaching material to present to the in-service training sessions to help members of the nursing staff understand:

(1) Psychosocial, cultural, and behavioral aspects of patient care

(2) Psychosocial and behavioral aspects of patient-family interaction and patient-family-institution relationships

c. The director of social service and/or other members of the department should attend bedside teaching rounds conducted for the nursing staff by the medical director.

G. The Business Department

1. Admission of New Patients. The director of social service should inform the business manager of the admission of new patients and should advise her of any special arrangements or services to be charged to the patients' accounts.

2. During Patient Residence

a. Once a month the director of social service and the business manager should confer on the status of patient financial accounts, and the director of social service should take appropriate action on those accounts judged delinquent.

b. Should financially responsible relatives of patients request explanations of billing procedures or account status, the director of social service and the business manager together should provide explanatory services to these persons.

c. Requests for completion of third-party payment forms are frequently directed to the director of social service by financially responsible relatives, and these forms should be completed cooperatively by the director of social service and the business manager.

d. The director of social service should keep the business manager informed of any fee alterations or other changes or adjustments that will affect patient billings.

e. The director of social service should notify the business office of patient discharges, and the financial account of each discharged patient should be checked, completed, and submitted to the fiscal intermediary, financially responsible relative, or other sponsor.

H. The Dietary Department

1. Admission of New Patients. The director of social service should be responsible for completion of the diet cards for newly admitted patients, which are then transmitted to the Dietary Department by the appropriate charge nurse.

2. During Patient Residence. The director of social service should meet as needed with the dietitian and the dietary director and members of other departments, to discuss:

a. Patient food intake
b. Suggested changes in patient diet
c. Other areas related to patient feeding

I. The Physical Therapy Department

1. The director of social service should inform the physical therapist of the medical, psychosocial, and functional aspects of newly admitted patients.

2. She should share with him any verbal or written requests for initiation of programs in physical therapy.

a. Written requests from physicians for physical therapy may sometimes be received for the physical therapist by the director of social service in conjunction with the director of nursing.
b. The director of social service should transmit recommendations from the medical director and the families of patients to the physical therapist.

3. The director of social service should work cooperatively with the physical therapist as a part of the rehabilitation team.

J. The Recreation and Volunteer Department

1. Admission of New Patients. The director of social service and the recreation director should meet together regularly upon the admission of a new patient:

a. To discuss the medical, psychosocial, and functional status of the patient
b. To develop tentative plans for patient involvement in the activities of the Recreation Department

2. During Patient Residence

a. The directors of social service and recreation should meet regularly to discuss and evaluate patient participation within the program of recreation.
b. When utilization of a student or a volunteer is a part of the total patient-treatment plan, the program should be discussed by the directors of social service and recreation, together with the student or volunteer involved.

K. The Occupational Therapy Department

1. Admission of New Patients. The director of social service and the occupational therapist should meet regularly upon the admission of a new patient:

a. To discuss the medical, psychosocial, and functional status of the patient
b. To develop tentative plans for patient participation in occupational therapy

2. During Patient Residence. The director of social service and the occupational therapist should meet as needed:

a. To discuss patient activities within the occupational therapy program
b. To evaluate individual and group patient needs
c. To discuss and evaluate the role of families in relation to patient activities in occupational therapy

L. Speech Therapy

1. Requests for speech therapy for individual patients should be made by the director of nursing, the attending physician, the medical director, or a member of the patient's family.

2. Arrangements

a. A written order for speech therapy should be obtained from the attending physician and permission obtained from the responsible family member by the director of social service.
b. Arrangements for financing should also be clarified by the director of social service with the responsible family member should the patient be non-Medicare.
c. The social service director should contact the speech therapist, who then will proceed to design and implement a speech program for the patient.
d. The director of social service should assist in supervising arrangements for such details as:
(1) Hours
(2) Treatment location
(3) Record keeping
(4) Billing

3. Conferences

a. The director of social service should meet regularly as needed with speech therapist to discuss patient progress within the speech program and to transmit recommendations for changes in aspects of the program received from other members of the staff.
b. The speech therapist should meet regularly with members of the Social Service Department, the medical director, and other department heads for study and evaluation of the speech program and evaluation of individual patients.

M. Religious Services Program

1. The director of social service should meet with the extended care facility's three attending clerical representatives, as needed, to discuss:

- *a.* Patient attendance at services
- *b.* Changes in patient status pertinent to the religious program
- *c.* Programs for development
- *d.* Other events related to the spiritual aspects of the therapeutic community

2. Counseling Services

- *a.* The three attending clergymen are frequently requested by the administration or the director of social service to function as pastoral counselors to patients.
- *b.* The director of social service occasionally should arrange counseling sessions with patients and families wherein she and a member of the clergy function as cotherapists.

3. Hospital Visits. Sometimes the director of social service should request a clergyman to accompany her on a preadmission visit to a candidate for admission to the institution.

N. The Receptionists

1. Patient Information

- *a.* The director of social service should inform the on-duty receptionist of new patient admissions and their assigned rooms.
- *b.* Any changes in patient room assignments and patient discharges should also be given to the receptionist by the director of social service.

2. Visitors

- *a.* The director of social service should advise the on-duty receptionist of special visiting plans relating to her department.
- *b.* She should inform the receptionist of special visiting restrictions.
- *c.* The on-duty receptionist should greet persons scheduled for appointments with the Social Service Department and should advise of their arrival.
- *d.* The receptionist should inform the director of social service of the arrival of visitors requesting information about the nursing center (Fig. 4-8).

3. Typing. Dictation by members of the Social Service Department may be typed by the receptionists in the absence of the department typist.

O. The Housekeeping Department

1. The director of social service should meet as needed with the

Fig. 4-8. The receptionist directs a visitor requesting information about the extended care institution to the Social Service Department.

housekeeping staff to discuss procedures related to the laundering and cleaning of patients' clothing, and any orders from families with respect to special handling of patient's clothing should be transmitted to housekeeping, sometimes via the Nursing Department.

2. The Housekeeping Department should assist in the transportation of the bulky or heavy items belonging to patients at the request of the director of social service.

3. The Housekeeping Department should cooperate with the Social Service and Nursing Departments in physically assisting patients and their luggage into and out of the building.

P. The Maintenance Department

1. Repairs. The director of social service occasionally should request the director of maintenance to see that certain repairs to patient's appliances be made.

2. Alterations. Changes in patient furniture arrangement or storage of articles are sometimes effected by the Maintenance Department at the request of the social service director after a written memorandum of approval from the administrative director has been obtained.

Q. The Health-Records Librarian

1. The social service director should inform the health-records librarian of planned patient admissions, transfers, and discharges to enable the records to be prepared.
2. The social service director should confer with the health-records librarian concerning information for Medicare records.

R. Special Services

1. Dentistry and Podiatry
   a. The social service director, as well as members of the nursing staff, may receive requests and written permissions for dental and podiatric services from attending physicians, patients, and families.
   b. The director of nursing should effect the necessary arrangements regarding the planning of patient appointments for dental and podiatry services.
   c. The director of social service should advise families or patients requesting these services of the necessary financial arrangements.

2. Hairdresser and Barber
   a. The director of social service should inform the director of nursing of requests for these services.
   b. She should advise families of the necessary financial arrangements and should receive their written permission for patients to receive these services.
   c. The director of social service should be available for consultation with the hairdresser and barber for discussion of patient performance during receipt of these services.

VII. TRAINING AND EDUCATION

A. Inside the Extended Care Facility. The director of social service should be asked to present material about the social components of care to the in-service training program for nursing and should participate in the interdisciplinary conferences.
B. Outside the Extended Care Facility. The director of social service should attend appropriate seminars and conferences on behavioral and social sciences sponsored by local, state, and national health and and welfare agencies and academic institutions.

VIII. EQUIPMENT AND FACILITIES

The Social Service Department should occupy a private office for consultations, and its equipment should include:

1 desk and chair
1 large formica-top worktable

1 typewriter
A dictating machine
Bookshelves
3 or 4 comfortable chairs
Files

IX. TELEPHONE NUMBERS

The telephone numbers of social work consultants, hospitals, ambulances, undertakers, attending physicians, social work students and their faculty advisers should be conveniently posted in the social service office.

Section 5

Restorative Services

Patient rehabilitation is an important goal of an extended care program. The staff should be trained to conduct its daily activities with particular emphasis on helping patients to maintain and improve their functioning on all levels—physical, psychologic, and social. This is especially true of personnel having direct contact with patients, such as members of the Nursing, Social Service, and Recreation Departments.

In addition, specific restorative services, including physical therapy, occupational therapy, and speech therapy, should be available to patients upon the written prescription of their attending physicians and with the approval of their families or of other responsible persons. The following section deals entirely with such services that may be rendered to patients by qualified therapists, thus developing a total plan of comprehensive patient care.

PHYSICAL THERAPY

Introduction

The physical therapy program in the extended care facility should be both preventive and treatment-oriented. Wherever possible, patient function should be maintained, developed, and restored with major emphasis on the avoidance or correction of deformity and the alleviation of pain at joints, muscles, or nerve centers. Implicit in the administration of a successful physical therapy program is an understanding of the psychosocial needs of the physically handicapped patient. A positive motivation on the part of the patient is a necessary concomitant to an optimistic attitude on the part of the treatment staff to effect a successful program of the physical rehabilitation of the chronically ill and aged.

I. DEFINITION

Physical therapy is essentially the skilled treatment of disabilities, disorders, and injuries, and the prevention or arresting of deterioration through the selective use of physical agents, procedures, and techniques prescribed by a physician, including:

A. The application of physical agents such as heat, light, water, and electricity by means of specialized equipment

B. Therapeutic exercise and massage

C. Training in ambulation and activities of daily living, specifically related to transfer activities and wheelchair usage, with appropriate aids or assistive devices

II. STAFFING PATTERN

One (1) licensed physical therapist may be employed and possibly assisted by a trained physical therapy aide.

III. RECORDS

A. Physicians' prescriptions for physical therapy should be kept in the physicians' order book (Fig. 5-1).

B. A daily record of treatment for each patient receiving physical therapy should be kept by the physical therapist in the book labeled "Restorative Services" at each nurses' station for easy reference by the medical and nursing staff.

C. A monthly progress report on these patients should be made by the physical therapist to form part of the patient's chart and also should be kept in the restorative services book.

IV. MODALITIES OF TREATMENT

Each of the following modalities of physical therapy must be prescribed in writing for patients by their attending physicians, to be carried out only under medical direction with the physical therapist evaluating the patient's motor skills, abilities, and rehabilitation potential, and subsequently preparing a treatment plan in conformity with the medical prescription. Treatment generally is offered on an individual basis, but group ambulation and exercises may be used in appropriate cases.

A. Whirlpool Bath

1. Description: A whirlpool bath is created by agitation of the water in a tub by the use of a special apparatus.

2. Purpose: To stimulate circulation and relieve pain, to relax spastic muscles, to cleanse and desensitize skin, and to promote a feeling of well-being, especially in the lower extremities, through mechanical massage given by heat and active water

Fig. 5-1

Patient's Name ________ Room No. ________ Case No. ________ Physician ________ Date ________

PHYSICAL THERAPY PRESCRIPTION

	Check Rx. Requested
1. Manual Muscle Testing	________
2. Therapeutic Exercises:	
a. Passive	________
b. Active-assistive	________
c. Active	________
d. Resistive	________
e. Shoulder wheel	________
f. Trapeze	________
g. Pulleys	________
3. Range of Motion	________
4. Ambulation:	
a. With prosthesis	________
b. Without prosthesis	________
c. Parallel bars (horizontal and wall type)	________
d. Walker	________
e. Stairs	________
f. Fractures:	
(1) Non–weight-bearing	________
(2) Partial weight-bearing	________
(3) Full weight-bearing	________
5. Tilt table	________
6. Whirlpool	________
7. Diathermy	________
8. Infrared lamp	________
9. Cryotherapy	________
10. Hydrocollator	________
11. Program for decubiti	________

Other (specify) ________________________

Precautions: ________________________

____

Physician's Signature

3. Preparation

a. Bath

(1) The physical therapist should consult with the attending physician concerning the circulatory status of the patient and with the charge nurse of the patient's unit to determine the condition of the patient, as patients with elevated temperatures or other special temporary ailments should not receive any type of tub bath.

(2) The temperature of the treatment room should be 75°F.

(3) In filling the tub, the physical therapist should allow for water displacement caused by the patient and should use a bath thermometer to maintain the water at 90 to 100°F.

b. Patient

(1) A nursing aide of the same sex as the patient should be assigned to assist the physical therapist, to remain on hand throughout the treatment, to transport the patient to and from the bathroom, to help the patient undress and dress and to enter and leave the tub.

(2) During the treatment, women patients should wear bathing suits; men patients should wear trunks.

(3) Details of preparatory procedures for bathing may be noted in Section 3.

4. Procedure

a. Once in the tub, the patient should never be left unattended and should be instructed to hold securely to the grab rails.

b. Directed and aided by the physical therapist, the patient should perform both active and passive exercises of the legs and the lower part of the body.

5. Period of Treatment: The whirlpool bath may be given daily or three times a week for an average of 15 min (or according to the toleration of the patient).

6. Location of Treatment: The whirlpool treatment may be administered in a special apparatus in a physical therapy room or in the bathing area of the extended care facility by the use of a portable whirlpool in a bathtub.

B. Infrared Lamp

1. Description: Infrared is a heat lamp.

2. Purpose: To provide heat that penetrates deeply into the body tissues, to relieve pain, and to promote reflex increases in circulation

3. Procedure: The treatment should be given to the patient in a bed or seated, using covering, portions of the patient's body to be exposed to the lamp. The physical therapist should be in continuous attendance for the duration of the session.

4. Period of Treatment: Infrared-lamp treatment generally is offered three times a week for length of time as prescribed by the physician.
5. Location of Treatment: The treatment may be given in the patient's bedroom or in a special treatment room.

C. Diathermy Machine

1. Description: A diathermy machine gives deep heat to the body tissues.
2. Purpose: To relieve pain in joints, muscles, etc.
3. Procedure: The patient should be assisted onto a table, pads to be placed on the exposed parts of the body to be treated, and the rest of the body covered.
4. Period of Treatment: Diathermy may be offered three times a week for periods ranging from 15 to 30 min under careful supervision by prescription.
5. Location of Treatment: Diathermy should be administered in a treatment room.

D. Hot Packs

1. Description: Individual packs of a special material, silica gel, should be placed in a Hydrocollator machine and removed and wrapped in 4 to 6 thicknesses of towels when the boiling point is reached, with the heat generally retained for 20 to 30 min.
2. Purpose: To furnish temporary relief from pain caused by fracture, arthritis, etc.
3. Procedure: The towel-wrapped packs should be applied to the sight of the pain, the knee joint, the shoulder, the hip joint, the back, etc. while the patient is in bed, in a position directed by the physical therapist, assisted by an aide or ordely.
4. Period of Treatment: The hot packs should be kept on the point of pain from 20 to 30 min, and may be applied daily while the pain exists.
5. Location of Treatment: The treatment may be given in the patient's bed or in a treatment room.
6. Supervision of Treatment: The application and duration of Hydrocollator should be closely supervised by the physical therapist as there is always a danger of burns due to the high temperature of the packs.

E. Cryotherapy may be similarly used, except that cold appliances should be substituted for heat.

F. Standing or Tilt Table

1. Description: A tilt table is a specially constructed table that may be gradually tilted from a horizontal to an upright position.

2. Purpose: To relieve pressure on specific parts of the body, to promote urinary drainage, to prepare and increase gradually the toleration of the previously bedridden patient to bear weight and changes in position, and to prevent osteoporosis of weight-bearing bones

3. Procedure: The table should be placed in a horizontal position with the patient strapped into place on the table, which is gradually tilted to an upright position (Fig. 5-2).

4. Period of Treatment: This table treatment may be conducted daily for a period up to 1 hr, depending on the toleration of the patient with particular reference to reassuring geriatric patients concerning the process of being moved while immobilized.

5. Location of Treatment: This treatment may be effected in the physical therapy room, in the patient's bedroom, or in a recreation area to afford the patient the opportunity of observing activities during the process.

G. Stall Bars

1. Description: Stall bars are a series of horizontal bars, 4 in. apart, affixed to the wall.

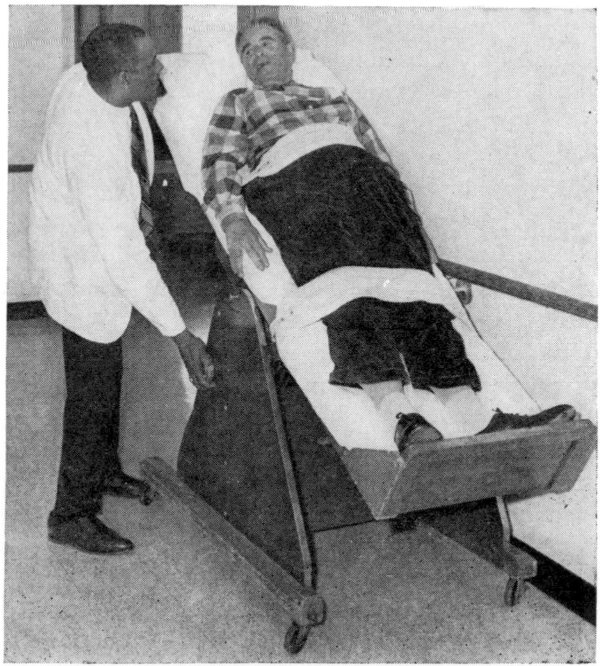

Fig. 5-2. The patient on the tilt table is inclined gradually to an upright position.

2. Purpose: Stall bars are particularly useful for stretching exercises for the upper extremities, the back, and the neck, and to help the patient to stretch his body into straight alignment.
3. Procedure: The patient should reach up to grasp the bars, thus pulling his body up and stretching at first under the direction of the physical therapist and, as he becomes more proficient, independently.
4. Period of Exercise: Patients may exercise on the stall bars daily and as frequently as possible.
5. Location of Treatment: The bars may be placed in a general activity area where they will be used more frequently than if they are in a separate location.

H. Shoulder Wheel

1. Description: A large wheel affixed to the wall, with a projecting handle for the patient to grasp to rotate the wheel
2. Purpose: To improve the range of motion in the shoulder joint
3. Procedure: The patient should be instructed in the operation of the wheel in a sitting or standing position.
4. Period of Activity: The wheel may be used daily, or several times a day, for lengths of time depending upon the patient's toleration.
5. Location of Treatment: The shoulder wheel may be located in a treatment room or community area where it will be used more frequently.

I. Parallel Bars

1. Description: This apparatus is a 15-ft wooden "walk" with adjustable hand bars along either side.
2. Purpose: To help disabled patients to learn to walk again and to straighten shoulders and arms in preparation for using walkers and crutches
3. Procedure:

- *a.* The wheelchair patient should be helped from his wheelchair by the therapist, who then should show him how to support himself by gripping the hand bars and bearing his weight on them with one foot slowly placed before the other, and the patient propelling himself down the length of the walk (Fig. 5-3).
- *b.* Gradually both the distance walked and the speed of the steps taken should be increased until the patient has regained enough strength and confidence to graduate to a walker or crutches.

4. Period of Activity: The parallel bar exercises may be done several times a day, according to the toleration of the patient.
5. Location of Treatment: The parallel bars may be located in the

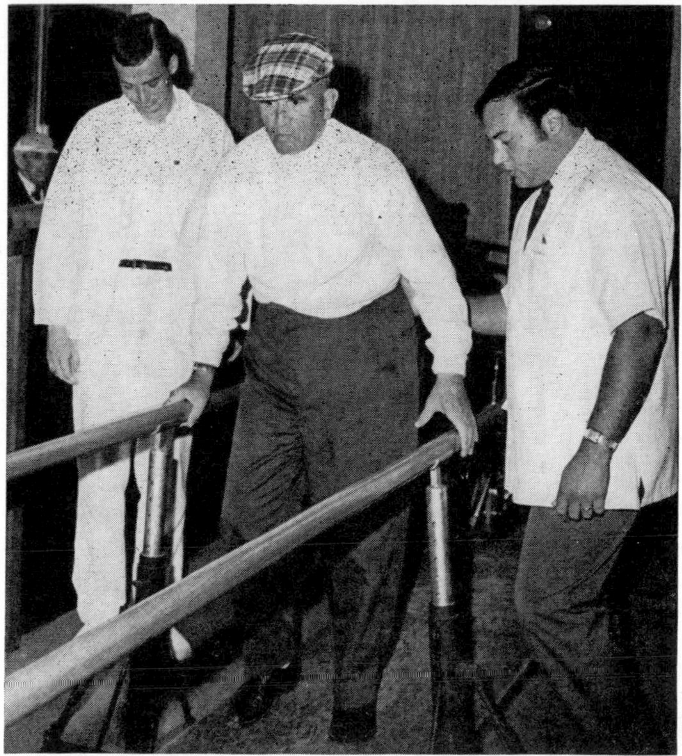

Fig. 5-3. The physical therapist trains a disabled patient to walk between parallel bars prior to using crutches or a walker.

Physical Therapy Department or in a recreation area, where they may be used more and where patients will be encouraged to perform without self-consciousness before other patients and visitors independently or with assistance.

J. Door Pulleys

1. Description: Hand rings on rope pulleys that are attached between the uprights of a door
2. Purpose: To increase the range of motion in shoulders
3. Procedure: The physical therapist should demonstrate the use of the pulleys, and the patient should exercise with them from either a standing or wheelchair position.
4. Period of Exercise: Pulleys may be used for periods ranging from 5 to 15 min, depending upon the toleration of patient.
5. Location of Treatment: Door pulleys may be affixed to doors in

various locations, depending upon the judgment of the physical therapist.

K. Sandbags

1. Description: Bags are filled with sand weighing from 5 to 10 lb.
2. Purpose: To hold the extremity or foot in the correct position
3. Procedure: The sandbag should be brought to the patient in bed and placed in the correct position.
4. Period of Use: Sandbags may be used continuously during the day while the patient remains in bed, and may also be used during the night.

L. Trapeze Bars

1. Description: A triangular bar that is attached to a permanent overhead bar above the bed
2. Purpose: To enable a patient to change position or to pull himself to a sitting position, to help him get in and out of bed, and for strengthening exercises of the upper extremities (Fig. 5-4)
3. Period of Exercise: When used for exercising, the periods should

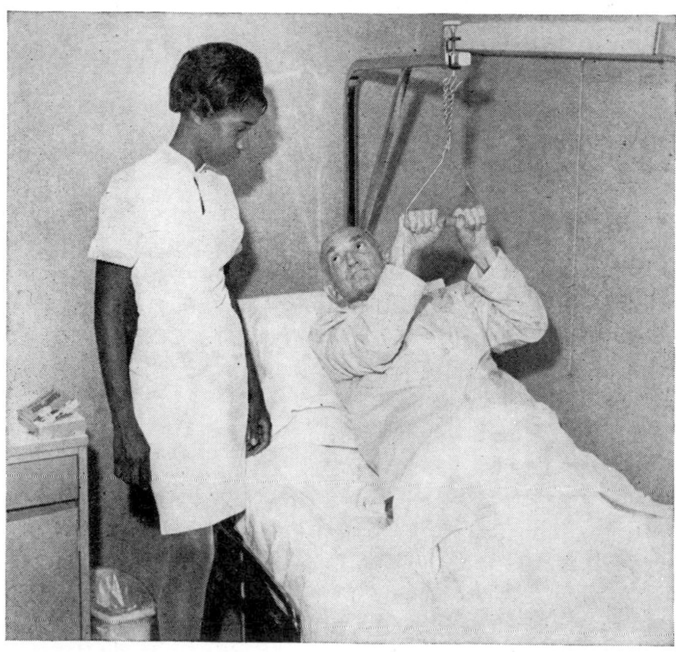

Fig. 5-4. A trapeze frame encourages a patient to help himself into a sitting position.

vary according to patient toleration, the trapeze bar being used frequently during the day or night to assist the patient in self-help activities.

M. Traction Apparatus

1. Description: Ankle cuffs on weighted rope pulleys that are suspended over buck extension
2. Purpose: To help straighten contracted legs (may be currently contraindicated since stretching may be painful, may facilitate tightness, may weaken muscles and cause the skin of the aged patient to break down under prolonged traction)
3. Procedure: The traction apparatus should be brought to the patient's bed and the cuffs placed around his ankles.
4. Period of Use: From 1 hr to the entire day and used daily during the duration of the prescription

N. Exercises

1. Purpose: To stimulate circulation, strengthen weak muscles, and keep the body in condition
2. Types
- *a.* Active: These should be performed by the patient himself, directed by the physical therapist, and mainly consist of abduction and adduction of arms and legs on an alternating basis.
- *b.* Passive: The therapist should exercise the patient's arms and legs with no assistance from the patient.
- *c.* Active-assisted: These are very limited exercises with the physical therapist assisting the patient in working within his range of motion.
- *d.* Ambulation: The physical therapist should help the patient to learn to walk with the use of a walker, crutches, or a cane on a one-to-one relationship, teaching him how to bear weight correctly while walking.

3. Period of Activity: In some instances, exercises are done several times a day, according to the toleration of the patient.
4. Location of Activity: Exercises may be done in the patient's room, in the Physical Therapy Department, or in a general activity area, in groups or individually.

O. Massage

1. Purpose: To stimulate circulation, to relax tight and spastic musculature, to ease pain and discomfort, and to engender a feeling of well-being
2. Procedure

a. Massage should be performed by the physical therapist assisted by a nursing aide or orderly.
b. The patient should lie on a bed, draped by towels, sheets, or clothing, with only the part of body to be treated exposed.

3. Period of Treatment: Massage should be given patients daily or three times a week, as prescribed by their attending physician.

4. Location of Treatment: Massage may be performed in a treatment room or in the patient's room.

V. WORKING SCHEDULE

A. The physical therapist should work a 5-day week, from 9:00 A.M. to 5:00 P.M.

B. He should be on duty on Saturday, off duty on a weekday so that the treatment of patients need not be interrupted for more than a single day and to afford visiting families on Saturdays an opportunity to consult the physical therapist.

VI. PAYMENT FOR SERVICES

The physical therapist may function as an employee of the extended care facility or as an individual practitioner.

A. When the physical therapist is employed by the extended care institution, charges for physical therapy service should be added to the general statement of charges for patients.

B. Should the physical therapist function as an individual practitioner as is the requirement for physical therapists in proprietary facilities in some states, he should check with the social service director as to the Medicare status of new patients for purposes of billing.

1. Private Patients. The physical therapy charges may be added to the monthly statement for each patient sent by the Business Department to the family or responsible relative, or the physical therapist may send his own bills on his letterhead.

2. Medicare Patients. Charges for physical therapy should be added to the statement of services rendered by the Business Department and transmitted to the fiscal intermediary for payment.

VII. PURCHASING

When prescribed by the patients' attending physicians for continuous use, the physical therapist should order appropriate braces or other equipment for patients, such as walkers, wheelchairs, crutches, and canes, from a local surgical supply firm. Should the physician or family request that the articles be ordered from some other specified vendor, their instructions should be followed as should their instructions concerning the rental or purchase of assistive devices.

A. Billing

1. The patient's attending physician should prescribe the equipment or appliance, and his family or the responsible person should give approval before the order is placed.
2. The patient's family or responsible person should be billed directly by the vendor for any equipment or appliances rented or purchased.
3. Medicare coverage for equipment rentals should be investigated.

VIII. EQUIPMENT AND FACILITIES

A. Equipment. The following equipment should be maintained for physical therapy use in an extended care institution:

Whirlpool bath
Infrared lamp
Diathermy machine
Hot packs and Hydrocollator
Standing or tilt table
Stall bars
Shoulder wheel
Parallel bars
Sand bags
Door pulley
Wheelchairs
Walkerettes, canes, crutches
Traction apparatus
Trapeze frames

B. Facilities

1. In an extended care facility of 100 beds or more where it can be anticipated that physical therapy will be ordered for 25 to 35 percent of the patient population, a separate physical area should be utilized for the Physical Therapy Department.
2. For an institution of 75 beds or less with a program of physical therapy appropriate for 25 or fewer patients, physical therapy modalities should be offered in:

a. A shared private area such as a treatment or examining room
b. Recreation and community rooms
c. Patient bedrooms
d. Bathing areas

3. Notwithstanding the size of the facility, 15-ft parallel bars (and possibly shoulder wheels and stall bars) should be located in a general recreation and community area to encourage more frequent practice by patients between physical therapy treatments assisted by the nursing staff, to lessen patient self-consciousness at performing before patient peers and visitors.

IX. INTRA- AND EXTRAMURAL COOPERATION

A. Outside the Nursing Center

1. Attending Physician

a. A program for an individual patient should include one or more of the modalities previously described as prescribed in writing monthly by the attending physician.

b. It is advisable before treatment begins and at intervals thereafter that patient ability tests be jointly conducted by the physician and the physical therapist.

c. The physician should review the progress of his patient on a monthly basis, both from the physical therapy progress report and in consultation with the physical therapist, and revisions should be effected in the treatment programming if the patient's condition should so warrant.

2. Family or Responsible Person

a. Family approval or approval of the responsible person should be obtained in writing before the onset of physical therapy.

b. Discussions with family

(1) The physical therapist should discuss the treatment of the patient, the program, and the established goals: (*a*) at the beginning of treatment and (*b*) at intervals thereafter.

(2) The social service director may make appointments for these interviews, which are conducted either by the physicial therapist alone or in cooperation with the attending physician or medical director.

c. Demonstrations for family: The physical therapist, upon request, should conduct patient demonstrations for families to show progress or lack of progress.

B. Within the Extended Care Facility. The physical therapist should transmit information on the patients' progress in the physical therapy program to the staff to encourage staff cooperation by integrating the physical therapy program into the comprehensive patient-care plan.

1. Medical Director. Frequent consultations should be held between the medical director and the physical therapist on such subjects as:

a. Overall treatment of patients

b. Specific treatment of individual patients

c. Patient load

2. Administrative Director. Various problems should be discussed from time to time by the administrative director and the physical therapist such as:

a. Needed physical changes in the facility

b. Storage problems

c. Specific patient or family problems

d. Arrangements for physical therapy demonstrations before visiting students *e*. Supply and equipment purchases or replacements

3. Nursing Department

a. Director of nursing

(1) The physical therapist and the director of nursing should meet to discuss the medical, psychosocial, and functional status of new patients receiving physical therapy treatment.

(2) The nursing director should alert the physical therapist to the physician's written prescription for treatment.

(3) A conflict in scheduling should be worked out between the director of nursing and the physical therapist.

b. Charge nurse on each unit. The charge nurse should verify daily the patients receiving physical therapy for the following purposes:

(1) To make sure the patients are prepared for the treatment

(2) To note patient progress, problems, and reactions

c. Nursing aides and orderlies

(1) Aides or orderlies should assist in transporting patients to treatment room or other locations, if needed.

(2) Aides of same sex should help patients to undress before the treatment and to dress at the conclusion of the treatment.

(3) In the absence of a physical therapy assistant, an aide or orderly should remain on hand throughout the treatment period, lending assistance if needed.

4. Business Department. A monthly quantitative record of patients receiving physical therapy should be transmitted by the physical therapist to the Business Department for billing purposes.

5. Social Service Department

a. The social service director should discuss patients with the physical therapist on admittance to acquaint him with their medical, psychosocial, and functional status.

b. In conjunction with the director of nursing, the social service director may receive written requests from physicians for physical therapy for their patients, and she should alert the physical therapist to these medical orders.

c. She should serve as liaison between the physical therapist and the patient's family in the following ways:

(1) She should keep the family informed of the patient's program and progress in physical therapy.

(2) She should consult the family or the responsible individual for approval when it is necessary to have the physical therapist order equipment.

(3) She should make appointments with the family for interviews and patient demonstrations in physical therapy activities.

(4) She should interpret the recommendations and opinions of the patient's family to the physical therapist.

6. Occupational Therapist. The physical therapist should work with the occupational therapist in planning programs for patients.

7. Recreation and Volunteer Department. The physical therapist frequently should consult the recreation and volunteer director on individual patient problems like:

a. The patient's ability to stand, walk, and transport himself

b. The patient's tolerance for physical activity

8. Maintenance Department. Upon the physical therapist's request, the maintenance director should install apparatus or repair such equipment as walkerettes, wheelchairs, etc.

9. Housekeeping Department. Fresh linens for use in physical therapy of patients should be supplied by the Housekeeping Department.

10. Health-Records Librarian. The physical therapist should transmit information on the progress of Medicare patients to the health-records librarian to assist in the completion of records for the meetings of the utilization review committee.

11. Weekly Interdisciplinary Clinical Conference. Every week the physical therapist should attend an interdisciplinary clinical conference with other professional staff members.

X. TRAINING AND EDUCATION

A. The physical therapist should attend the meetings of the local Physical Therapy Association, of which he should be a member.

B. He should attend conferences and symposia on physical therapy at hospitals and health centers in the general area.

C. He should read books and journals on physical rehabilitation, kept in the staff room and in the libraries of the medical office and the Nursing Department.

D. The physical therapist should attend the in-service training sessions of the Nursing Department when patients under his treatment are being observed for participation and demonstration at these sessions, should assist in staff education and in integrating physical therapy and nursing (Fig. 5-5).

OCCUPATIONAL THERAPY

Introduction

The goals of the occupational therapy program in the extended care facility should be closely related to the physical therapy and total reha-

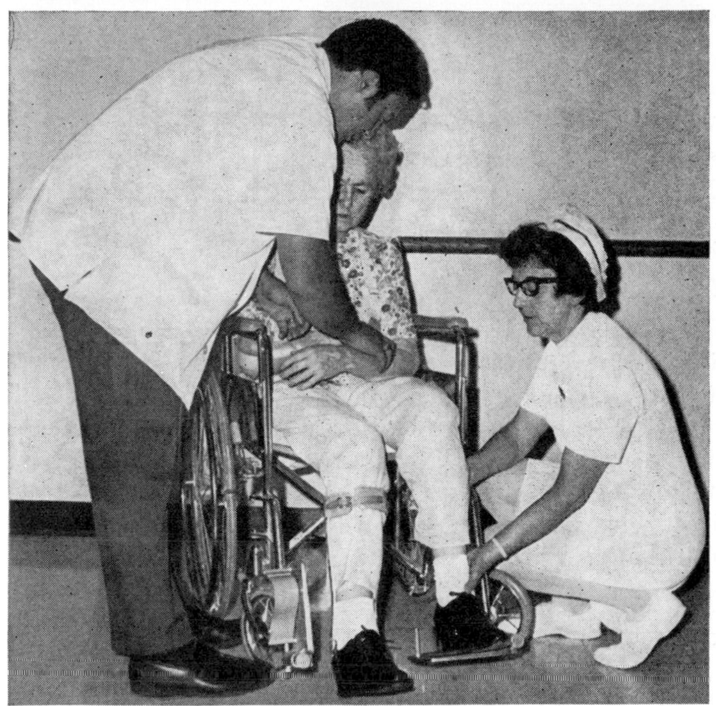

Fig. 5-5. The physical therapist trains a nurse in rehabilitation techniques to ensure a comprehensive treatment plan for the patient.

bilitation program, with the emphasis on encouraging the patients to help themselves—to perform the functions of daily living as independently as possible with specific reference to feeding, dressing, and bathing. Occupational therapy should be preventive and remedial and should promote and sustain the patients' social and psychologic well-being by discouraging social withdrawal and assisting the patient in becoming adjusted to the environment, including the staff and patient peers.

I. DEFINITION

Occupational therapy is the medically prescribed treatment of patients through the use of selected activities in order to achieve maximum physical and mental function in the activities of daily living.

II. STAFFING PATTERN

One occupational therapist registered by the American Occupational Therapy Association

III. RECORDS

A. The physicians' prescription for occupational therapy should be kept in the physicians' order book at the nursing stations (Fig. 5-6).
B. A record of treatment and progress report for each patient under treatment should be maintained by the occupational therapist in the book labeled "Restorative Services," at the nursing stations.

IV. PROCEDURES

A. Treatment Plan

1. The occupational therapist should evaluate all patients who are to receive treatment after she has been given a thorough briefing on their medical, social, and psychologic histories by the directors of nursing and social service, in order that a treatment plan may be prepared in accordance with the attending physician's prescription and the overall rehabilitative care objective established for each patient.
2. Treatments should be designed for individual as well as for group occupational therapy.

B. Recreational or Diversional Therapy

1. Purpose: To assist in the rehabilitation of patients with physical, social, and/or emotional disabilities, by encouraging their participation in a program of simple prescribed activities which may also promote general physical exercise (Fig. 5-7)
2. Types of Activities
- *a.* Individual projects should include working with copper, leather, tiles, ceramics, paints, weaving materials, jewelry, wood, needlework, and knitting.
- *b.* Group projects should include weaving rugs and garden therapy and may include games, dancing, and other types of projects that encourage socialization.

3. Periods of Activity. Most programs described should be held two to three times a week for 2 hr in cooperation with the director of recreation and volunteers.
4. Materials. Materials for patient activities should be provided by the extended care facility, and patients who are able to do so should be encouraged to help put materials away and clean up following this activity program.

C. Functional Therapy

1. Activities of Daily Living Program
- *a.* Purpose: To help patients achieve a maximum degree of independence in their daily functions such as dressing, feeding, bathing, grooming, and transfer activities

Fig. 5-6

Patient's Name	Room No.	Case No.	Physician	Date

OCCUPATIONAL THERAPY PRESCRIPTION

Check Rx. Requested

1. Kinetic:
   - *a.* Upper extremity ________
     - (1) Range of motion ________
     - (2) Muscle strength ________
   - *b.* Lower extremity ________
2. Activities of Daily Living:
   - *a.* Evaluation ________
   - *b.* Training ________
3. Self-help or Splinting Devices (List devices prescribed):

   ____

   ____

   ____

   ____

4. Diversional:
   - *a.* Individual ________
   - *b.* Group ________
     - (1) Arts and Crafts
       - *(a)* Gardening ________
       - *(b)* Weaving, sewing, knitting, crocheting ________
       - *(c)* Ceramics ________
       - *(d)* Painting ________
       - *(e)* Sculpture ________
     - (2) Community Exercises ________

Other (specify):

____

____

____

Precautions: ____

____

____

Physician's Signature

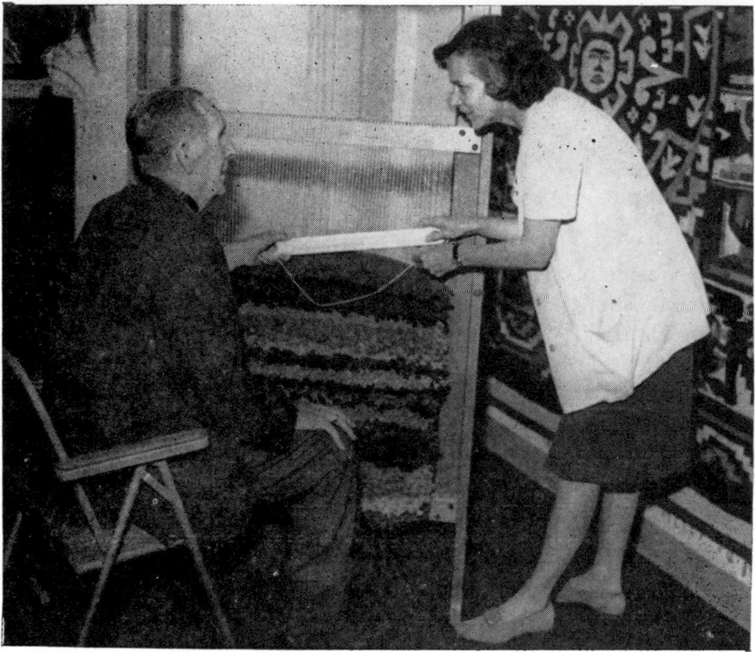

Fig. 5-7. Weaving is a diversional activity that also promotes physical exercise.

b. Procedure: The occupational therapist should evaluate the patient's performance in the activities of daily living and, when necessary, a self-help retraining program should be planned and carried out by the nursing staff under the therapist's supervision (Fig. 5-8).

c. Special Equipment

(1) Self-help devices for dressing, eating, and bathing activities should be available for testing and training purposes.

(2) Should a patient need these devices on an exclusive, long-term basis, they should be purchased by the patient's family or by the occupational therapist with the written consent of the family.

d. Periods of Activity: The occupational therapist should work with each patient three to five times a week for periods of up to half an hour, depending on the patient's tolerance with daily practice in self-help activity carried on under the direction of the nursing staff.

2. Kinetic Therapy

a. Purpose: To restore maximum joint and muscle function to the upper extremities, to prevent deformity from disuse, and to increase work tolerance

b. Procedure: The craft media which can be adapted to produce a desired result should be employed, the occupational therapist designing a treatment plan to be carried out by the Recreation Department with regular supervision by the occupational therapist.

c. Periods of Activity: The treatment program for each patient should be conducted according to the physician's orders and the patient's tolerance.

D. Splinting. Splintings should be provided when needed to prevent or correct the deformity of an upper extremity part; a physician's prescription is necessary.

V. WORKING SCHEDULE

The occupational therapist may be employed on a part-time basis in a 65-bed extended care facility, treatments to be carried out under her direction by the nursing or recreation staffs, and the occupational therapist seeing patients and staff for follow-up two to three times a week.

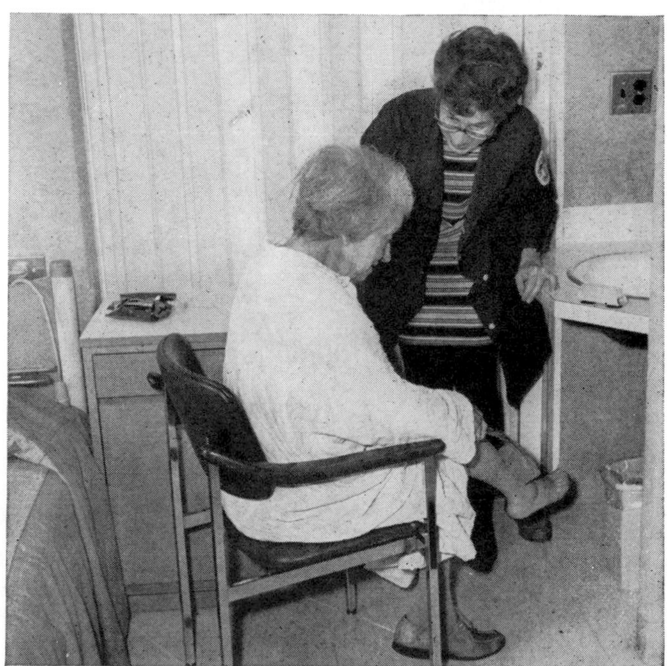

Fig. 5-8. The occupational therapist trains the patient to dress herself.

VI. CHARGES FOR SERVICES

A. Private Patients. The charges for occupational therapy ordered by physicians should be added to the monthly statement for each patient, sent by the Business Department to the family or responsible person.

B. Medicare Patients. The charges for occupational therapy ordered by the patient's physician should be added to the statement of services rendered by the Business Department and transmitted to the fiscal intermediary.

VII. EQUIPMENT AND FACILITIES

A. Equipment

1. Arts and Crafts Materials. The maintenance, storage, and purchasing of arts and crafts supplies and equipment should be the responsibility of the occupational therapist in consultation with the director of recreation, and the basic equipment should include a kiln and various types of looms. (Detailed information on equipment, supplies, and purchasing procedures may be found in Section 6.)
2. Special Equipment. Self-help devices that should be available in the extended care facility for the "activities for daily living" program include the following:

a. For dressing
(1) Elastic shoelaces
(2) Long-handled shoehorn
(3) Buttonhooks

b. For eating
(1) Flatware for the handicapped, including swivel spoons, built-up handle utensils, long-handled spoons and forks
(2) Compartmented dishes
(3) Utensil holders
(4) Plate guards
(5) Glass holders

c. For bathing
(1) Flexible shower arm attachment
(2) Hand brush with rubber suction cups
(3) Soap mitt

d. Other
(1) Book butler
(2) Scissor-type pickup sticks
(3) Wheelchair trays
(4) Wheelchair brake extensions
(5) Card holders

B. Facilities

1. In an extended care facility of 100 beds or more where vocational rehabilitation is part of the rehabilitation program and where special mechanical equipment is required for job retraining, the Occupational Therapy Department should be located in a distinct physical area.

2. For the retraining of handicapped housewives, an equipped kitchen should be included in the physical facilities.

3. For an institution of 100 beds or less where vocational rehabilitation is not a realistic goal for the 20 or fewer patient candidates for functional occupational therapy, occupational therapy should be offered in:

a. Recreation, community, and dining areas (Fig. 5-9)

b. Patient bedrooms and lavatories

4. Notwithstanding the size of the facility, diversional and recreational occupational therapy should take place in general recreational and community areas to encourage the socialization of patients and their adaptation to the social milieu.

VIII. INTRA- AND EXTRAMURAL COOPERATION

A. Outside the Institution

1. Attending Physician

a. The occupational therapy program for individual patients must

Fig. 5-9. The pantry and dining area may be used by the occupational therapist to retrain handicapped housewives.

be prescribed in writing by the attending physician (see Fig. 5-6).

b. Prescriptions for all occupational therapy should be written by the physician monthly, and the occupational therapist should be alerted to these orders by either the director of nursing or the social service director.

c. The physician should review the progress of his patient on a monthly basis, from the progress report and in consultation with the occupational therapist, advising revisions in the therapy program if the patient's condition so warrants.

2. Family or Responsible Person

a. Written family or responsible person approval should be obtained before any private patient is scheduled to receive occupational therapy.

b. Discussions with family

(1) The occupational therapist should discuss the progress of the patient, the program, and the established goals at the beginning of the program and at intervals thereafter.

(2) The social service director should arrange for these interviews, to be conducted either by the occupational therapist alone or in cooperation with the social service director.

c. Demonstrations for family. Upon request, patient demonstrations for families to show progress or lack of progress in occupational therapy should be conducted.

B. Within the Extended Care Facility. The occupational therapist should work closely with other departments to keep in contact with members of these departments for mutual exchange of information, recommendations, and guidance to use in the treatment program, spontaneous meetings between the occupational therapist and other staff members to be held frequently.

1. Administrative Director. The occupational therapist should discuss problems of various types with the administrative director:

a. Scheduling of the occupational therapy program

b. Special needs for occupational therapy equipment or supplies

c. Specific patient or family problems

2. Medical Director. The medical director should be consulted in the planning of occupational therapy programs for advice on such subjects as:

a. Overall treatment of patients

b. Specific treatment of individual patients

3. Nursing Department. The occupational therapist should keep the nursing staff informed of the progress of patients involved in the activities of daily living program, working with those nurses directly involved with patients under the activities of daily living retraining so that they may follow through daily with this program after having been introduced to any special equipment or techniques to be used by the patient.

a. Director of nursing

(1) The director of nursing and the occupational therapist should meet to discuss the medical, psychosocial, and functional status of new patients.

(2) The director of nursing and the occupational therapist should meet as needed to discuss patient activities in the occupational therapy program and to evaluate individual patient needs and performance.

(3) The director of nursing should alert the occupational therapist to the physician's written prescriptions for occupational therapy.

b. Charge nurse on each unit. The charge nurse should check regularly on patients receiving occupational therapy:

(1) To make sure that they are attending therapy sessions

(2) To note their progress, problems, and reactions

c. Nursing aides and orderlies

(1) Transportation to occupational therapy is effected by aides and orderlies.

(2) The nursing aides should be familiarized with special self-help devices for eating, dressing, and bathing by the occupational therapist.

4. Social Service Department

a. The director of social service and the occupational therapist should meet to discuss the medical, psychosocial, and functional status of new patients to familiarize the occupational therapist with the patient's family history and to develop plans for patient participation in the occupational therapy program.

b. Thereafter they should consult to discuss patient activities within the occupational therapy program and to evaluate individual patient needs and performance.

c. In conjunction with the director of nursing, the director of social service may alert the occupational therapist to written prescriptions from physicians for occupational therapy for patients.

d. The social service director should serve as the liaison between the patients' families and the occupational therapist by:

(1) Informing the family of the patient's program and progress in occupational therapy

(2) Arranging appointments with the family for interviews with the occupational therapist and for patient demonstrations in occupational therapy activities

(3) Interpreting the recommendations and opinions of the patient's family to the occupational therapist

5. Physical Therapy Department. The physical therapist and the occupational therapist should cooperate in planning programs for specific patient needs:

a. Recommending that a patient is ready to receive occupational therapy in conjunction with his physical therapy

b. Suggesting that a patient be encouraged to stand occasionally during occupational therapy activities

6. Recreation and Volunteer Department. The occupational therapist and the director of recreation and volunteers should work closely together by:

a. Cooperating in the planning and conducting of programs for arts and crafts activities

Fig. 5-10. The occupational therapist consults with a member of the dietary staff to plan for separate handling of self-help feeding utensils.

b. Cooperating in the planning and conducting of certain recreational programs

c. Joint conference with the health-records librarian to inform her of patient progress to assist in the preparation of Medicare forms for the utilization review committee meetings

d. Special projects for patient participation in handiwork for exhibitions and fairs

e. Joint consultation on the purchase of arts and crafts supplies and equipment

7. Business Department. A monthly quantitative record of patients receiving occupational therapy treatments should be forwarded by the occupational therapist to the Business Department for the purposes of billing.

8. Maintenance Department. The maintenance director may be requested by the occupational therapist to design and/or manufacture and repair special self-help equipment for patient use.

9. Dietary Department. The staff of this department should be alerted to self-help mealtime equipment for the purpose of separate handling (Fig. 5-10).

10. Weekly Interdisciplinary Clinical Conference. Each week the occupational therapist should attend an interdisciplinary clinical conference with other staff members.

IX. COMMUNITY RELATIONS

A. The occupational therapist should be called upon to exhibit and describe her work to various student groups and professional visitors as well as to family visitors.

B. Displays of patients' art work and crafts should be exhibited by the occupational therapist, in cooperation with the director of recreation and volunteers, in local art shows, at the state fair, and at various senior citizen exhibits.

X. TRAINING AND EDUCATION

A. Outside the Facility. The occupational therapist should attend conferences, meetings, conventions, and classes of the occupational therapy professional societies and other organizations pertinent to her work.

B. Within the Facility. The occupational therapist should be present at in-service training sessions of the Nursing Department when patients under occupational therapy are under scrutiny, to contribute to staff education by participation and demonstration of progress or to give talks on rehabilitation techniques for the nursing personnel.

SPEECH THERAPY

Introduction

The goals of speech therapy should be closely related to the total program of patient rehabilitation, emphasis to be placed on improving speech intelligibility and language functioning in order that the patient may communicate effectively. Since communication relates to all activities of living, formal speech therapy must be integrated into the comprehensive care plan to assist the patient to function as a social being to the best of his ability.

I. GENERAL DEFINITION

Speech therapy is essentially the provision of rehabilitative services for speech and language disorders for the purpose of restoring language functioning to the maximum level.

II. SPECIFIC PROBLEMS AND GOALS

In a setting of chronically ill aged patients, two types of language disorders resulting from organic brain damage present major challenges:

A. Dysarthria

1. Definition: A disturbance in sending messages so that patients cannot form words with any reasonable degree of clarity
2. Goal of Therapy: To improve intelligibility so that words can be understood

B. Dysphasia

1. Definition: A disturbance in linguistic functioning so that the patient cannot find words to express his thoughts
2. Goal of Therapy: To improve language functioning so that the patient is able to express himself

III. STAFFING PATTERN

One part-time speech therapist with a clinical certificate in speech and hearing from the American Speech and Hearing Association should prove sufficient for the usual case load of patients requiring speech therapy in the extended care institution, and he may function as a part-time paid employee of the institution or as an independent practitioner.

IV. RECORDS

A. Physicians' prescriptions for speech therapy should be kept in the physicians' order book at the nursing station on each unit.

B. A record of each individual speech therapy session with a patient and a monthly progress report should be maintained in the book labeled "Restorative Services" at the nursing stations, forming part of the patient's medical record (Fig. 5-11).

V. PROCEDURE

Requests for speech therapy for individual patients should be made by the medical director, the attending physician, the director of nursing, or the patient's family.

A. A written prescription must be obtained from the attending physician and written approval from the patient's family (only in the instance of private patients).

B. There should be access to an audiometric examination for patient candidates for speech therapy.

C. The procedure in speech therapy should differ with each patient, according to his age, disabilities, etc.

D. Each patient receiving speech therapy should be treated by the therapist three to five times a week, for half-hour sessions.

E. When useful, group speech therapy should be offered to two or more patients.

VI. WORKING SCHEDULE

The working schedule of the speech therapist should vary according to the case load of patients whose physicians have prescribed this therapy.

VII. PAYMENT FOR SERVICES

The speech therapist should verify the Medicare status of new patients with the social service director for the purpose of billing.

A. Private Patients

1. If the speech therapist functions as a paid member of the staff, the fee for speech therapy should be added to the monthly statement.
2. Should the speech therapist function as an individual practicing practitioner, the family or sponsor of the patient should be billed for speech therapy by the therapist for services rendered.

B. Medicare Patients

1. The speech therapist should submit a monthly statement to the nursing center.

Fig. 5-11

SPEECH THERAPY RECORD

Date No. Patient Age Sex

Responsible Family Member Address Phone

Attending Physician Diagnosis

Date	Speech Therapy Treatment Plan	Signature

Record of Treatments

Month	1	2	3	4	5	6	7	8	9	10	11	12	13	14	15	16	17	18	19	20	21	22	23	24	25	26	27	28	29	30	31	Total

Fig. 5-11 (Continued)

Date	Progress Notes	Signature

2. The business office should add this amount to the billing form, transmitted to the fiscal intermediary for payment.

3. The extended care facility should reimburse the speech therapist for services rendered.

VIII. EQUIPMENT AND FACILITIES

A. Equipment. The equipment used by the speech therapist may include: a tape recorder, a record player, a slide projector for audiovisual material, and printed cardboard visual aids (Fig. 5-12).

B. Facilities. Speech therapy should be conducted in a private, soundproofed room with a sufficient number of chairs for group as well as for individual therapy.

IX. INTRA- AND EXTRAMURAL COOPERATION

A. Outside the Extended Care Facility

1. Attending Physician

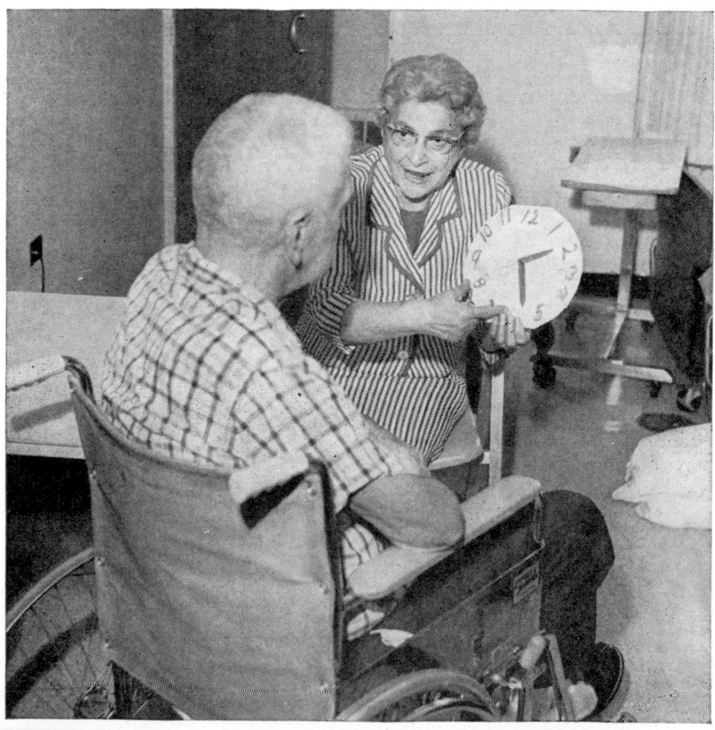

Fig. 5-12. The speech therapist uses a visual aid while treating a patient.

a. A speech therapy program for an individual patient must be prescribed in writing monthly by the attending physician.
b. At the onset of treatment and at intervals thereafter, diagnostic tests should be conducted jointly by the physician and the speech therapist to evaluate the patient's level of speech function.
c. The physician should review the progress of his patient on a monthly basis from the speech therapy progress report and by consultation with the speech therapist to make revisions in the treatment program if the patient's condition so warrants.

2. Family or Responsible Person
a. Written family or sponsor approval for private patients should be obtained before a speech therapy program is initiated.
b. Discussions with the family
(1) The speech therapist should discuss the treatment of the patient, the program, and the established goals (a) at the beginning of treatment and (b) at intervals thereafter.
(2) The social service director should arrange for these interviews conducted by the speech therapist alone or in cooperation with the social service director.
c. Demonstrations for family: The speech therapist, upon request, should conduct patient demonstrations for families to show progress or lack of progress in speech therapy.

B. Within the Institution

1. The speech therapist should meet regularly with the medical director and various department heads for appraisal of the total speech therapy program and for evaluation of individual patients under treatment.

2. The speech therapist should transmit information on patients' progress to the staff at meetings or through department heads to encourage personnel cooperation in carrying through the efforts of the therapist in daily staff contacts with patients receiving speech therapy.

3. Specific interdepartmental activity with the:
a. Medical director
(1) The attending speech therapist is selected by the medical director.
(2) The medical director and the speech therapist should consult frequently concerning (*a*) the overall treatment of patients, (*b*) specific treatment of individual patients, and (*c*) patient load.
b. Administrative director. The administrative director and the speech therapist periodically should meet to discuss the speech therapy program, scheduling, equipment, location of treatments, record keeping, and billing.

c. Nursing Department

(1) Director of nursing. Conflicts in scheduling should be worked out between the director of nursing and the speech therapist.

(2) Charge nurse on each unit. The charge nurse should verify regularly the patients receiving speech therapy to (*a*) ascertain the availability of patients for treatment and (*b*) note the progress, problems, and reactions of the patients to their speech therapy.

d. Business Department. The Business Department should be notified by the speech therapist of the names of patients and the number of treatments rendered to them for billing purposes.

e. Director of social service

(1) In conjuction with the director of nursing, the social service director should obtain the written prescription for speech therapy from the attending physician and written permission from patient's family or the responsible individual (in the case of private patients).

(2) The speech therapist may be contacted by the social service director to examine the patient and to design and implement a speech program.

(3) The social service director and the speech therapist should meet as needed (*a*) to discuss patient progress within the speech therapy program and (*b*) to transmit recommendations for changes in aspects of the program received from other members of the staff.

(4) The liaison between the speech therapist and the patient's family is effected by the social service director by (*a*) keeping the family informed as to the patient's program and progress in speech therapy, (*b*) making appointments with the family for interviews with the speech therapist, and for patient demonstrations in speech therapy, and (*c*) interpreting the recommendations and opinions of the patient's family to the speech therapist.

f. In-service training sessions for the Nursing Department. The speech therapist should be present at these weekly sessions when patients under his treatment are being observed, to participate and demonstrate the progress of his patients and to train the nursing staff to help the patients to express themselves and to understand more effectively.

g. Interdisciplinary clinical conferences. The attending speech therapist should participate in the interdisciplinary clinical conferences held weekly.

X. EDUCATION AND RESEARCH

A. The speech therapist should attend the annual convention of the American Speech and Hearing Association and meetings of the local association.

B. He should contribute and read various professional publications, such as:

1. *The Journal of Speech and Hearing Disorders*
2. *The Journal of Speech and Hearing Research*

Section 6

Recreation and Volunteers

Introduction

In an extended care facility recreation is an important segment of the total rehabilitation program in assisting patients to function socially in the pursuit of a meaningful way of life. To this end the recreation program should relate to the patients, the institution, and the general community.

A planned and diversified schedule of recreational and social activities should be designed to help patients use their physical and mental capabilities to the fullest possible extent. Successful diversional therapy should engender self-confidence and should preclude the withdrawn attitude often typical of the aged ill by encouraging participation in group activities commensurate with the individual patient's ability to perform.

An active department of recreation and volunteers should aid in the creation and maintenance of an atmosphere of harmony, stimulation, and optimism throughout the facility.

When an extended care facility encourages individuals and groups in the community to entertain, to give information, to hold discussions, and to socialize with patients, the patients and institution are benefited and the members of the community are alerted to the needs and problems of the patient population therein.

I. STAFFING PATTERN

A. For a 65-bed extended care facility, the recreation and volunteer staff should comprise:

1. One full-time director of recreation and volunteers
2. One part-time assistant
3. Three clerical representatives

B. Agencies with 150 beds or more should give serious consideration to the employment also of a full-time director of volunteers.

C. The following pattern of clothing is suggested for this department:

1. Colorful smocks for a female director and assistant with the word "recreation" embroidered on the sleeve, pocket, or elsewhere

2. The traditional pink pinafores over white blouses or pink smocks for adult female volunteers

3. Pink and white striped pinafores and white blouses for teen-age female volunteers

4. Appropriate ecclestiastical garb for clerical representatives in accordance with their tradition and preference

5. Colored coats, appropriately embroidered, for male professional staff

6. Colored jackets for male volunteers, adult and teen-age

II. RECORDS

The records for this department should include:

A. Biographical patient admission cards

B. A monthly planning calendar

C. Daily recreation program record forms

D. Monthly program summary

E. Card file of entertainers, volunteers, and contacts

F. A file containing regular correspondence plus letters of requests to performers for appearance and letters of appreciation

G. Release of responsibility form for patients leaving the premises for a recreational activity

H. A record of volunteer hours and completed application and health forms

I. Senior citizen and discharged patients' attendance list

J. Discharged patients and senior citizen activities book

K. Library card file on the she'f of the bookmobile

L. Film receipts file

M. File of clippings, photos, and posters

N. Petty cash records

O. A chronological birthday book of inpatients and discharged patients

III. THE PATIENT, THE VISITOR, AND RECREATION

The recreation program in an extended care institution should be a cooperative effort among patients, families, staff, and volunteers.

A. The transportaton to and from the recreation room for social and recreational programs should be carried out by the auxiliary nursing staff and volunteers supervised by the recreation director.

B. The recreation director should keep informed of patient care programs medical visits, and other factors in order to coordinate the recreational activities schedule with other patient routines.

C. The recreation director should be apprised of the background, interests, and special abilities of newly admitted patients by:

1. Referring to the biographical patients admission card
2. Conferences wth the social worker and nurses
3. Conversations with the patient and his relatives

D. In the absence of specific medical orders pertaining to patient participation in activities, the recreation director is required to use her considered judgment in patient selection, and she must determine which patients to encourage, how far to go in coaxing reluctant patients, and when to desist.

E. Should the recreation director be in doubt about the desirability of any patient's participation in activities, she should consult with the charge nurse and/or the director of social service.

F. The recreation director should encourage family and visitor participation in patient recreational activities, thereby maintaining the intactness of the program and educating outsiders to the significant use of recreation as a tool for the social rehabilitation of patients.

IV. THE VOLUNTEER

Volunteers in the extended care facility should relate primarily to recreational activities, the recreation director supervising their work among the patients and assisting as needed.

A. Types of Volunteers

1. Volunteer Leaders. Experts in the fields of music, painting, sculpture, gardening, flower arranging, and reading should be recruited to conduct programs for patients on a regular once- or twice-a-week basis.

2. Volunteer Aides. Volunteer aides are carefully selected, untrained men and women who wish to devote a few hours per week to volunteer work with patients, such as friendly visiting, letter writing, and other assisting roles.

B. Recruitment and Interviewing

1. The extended care facility, and particularly a private organization, must take the initiative in recruiting volunteers from student and women's clubs, social and church organizations, and volunteer service bureaus, and by word of mouth.

2. The volunteer candidate is invited to the facility by the recreation director or, when applicable, the director of volunteers for an interview and to complete an application.

a. At the interview, the prospective volunteer is asked to describe her background, abilities, and interests (Fig. 6-1).

b. In turn, the recreation director should brief the volunteer on the patients, the philosophy of the institution, and the recreational program.

c. A tour of the facility is made.

d. In addition to the traditional volunteer handbook, written

Fig. 6-1. The director of recreation and volunteers confers with each volunteer on a regular basis.

guidelines to visitors and volunteers should be presented to the prospective volunteer for study (Fig. 6-2).

3. The actual decision on the acceptance of the volunteer candidate is made after the interview, giving both parties time to consider the situation, and, if both approve, final arrangements should be made either by telephone or after another visit to the nursing center.

Fig. 6-2

GUIDELINES TO VISITORS AND VOLUNTEERS

THE WELCOME MAT is out for you at our nursing facility. By coming here to visit, entertain, or assist patients, you do them—and us—an invaluable service. As the majority of our men and women patients currently are too ill to participate in any local activities outside the extended care facility, they are forced to lead completely shut-in lives. They cannot go out into the community, but you bring the community *in* to them. For this, we are most grateful to you.

In order to make your efforts even more beneficial and pleasurable for everyone concerned, there are certain facts that you should know about our patient population, our staff, and our general routine. It is in a spirit of genuine helpfulness and appreciation, therefore, that we offer the following information and advice. Please take a few minutes to read it through.

First, Specifics about Patients

The following specifics will serve to guide you in your activities and programs and will give you some knowledge of the daily problems which must be faced in caring for geriatric patients.

1. *Hearing and visual disabilities,* frequent among geriatric patients, must be met with patience and understanding by performers, visitors, and volunteers. Speech should be distinct; slides and movies shown should be of good size, with strong contrasts.
2. *Interruptions* are often caused by these disabilities, by sudden illness, or by certain mental difficulties. Patients may seem restless, may change positions, may even speak out during a performance or a program. Try not to let any such interruptions bother you; carry on as smoothly and calmly as possible. If the interruption cannot be ignored, handle the situation with humor and good spirit.
3. *Mental confusion* is not always immediately apparent. Remember, even though a patient may appear to be normal and responsive, he could be suffering from some degree of brain damage following a stroke or other medical problem that could cause vagueness, memory lapses, or distortions. It may be necessary for you to clarify or repeat what you are saying or doing.

Fig. 6-2 (Continued)

4. *Occasional complaints* may be heard about treatment by staff, administration, and relatives. No one truly wants to be sick, widowed, and confined to an institution. Patients may feel frightened, depressed, abandoned by families and friends. These feelings are sometimes expressed by resentment toward the facility, the food, the staff, and families, and should be understood in that light.
5. *Short attention span.* Plan your program, activity, or conversation keeping always in mind that a sick, elderly person cannot maintain interest and attention for a great length of time. Make allowances for wandering attention, and try to vary your material sufficiently to hold interest.
6. *Schedules.* Each patient undergoes certain treatments, medications, and therapy important to his general health and improvement. Please do not be disturbed if a patient must be called away for any such purposes.
7. *Visiting families and friends.* If visitors arrive to see a patient during a program, volunteers should encourage them to take part in the activity rather than have the patient called away to see them. In this way, visitors can not only be helpful, but can also gain better understanding of the rehabilitation work that is being carried on at the extended care institution.
8. *Emergencies.* If any emergency or sudden illness should occur to a patient during your stay, it is important to keep calm. Do not attempt to handle the situation yourself, but ask the nearest staff member for assistance.
9. *Serving refreshments.* Some patients, such as diabetics, are not permitted to eat certain foods. Always check with the recreation staff member in charge when you are helping serve refreshments, to make certain just which persons are to be omitted.
10. *Shopping and errands.* A patient may ask you to shop for him or to perform some outside service. If it is convenient for you to give such a service, be sure to check with a recreation or administrative staff member first. If you cannot help the patient, let a staff member know about his request.

Next, The General Picture

There are now approximately nineteen million people more than sixty-five years of age in these United States. Less than 6 percent of these men and women live permanently in medically supervised congregate settings. The patient picture here is of sick old people no longer requiring acute hospital care but needing concentrated around-the-clock nursing care and rehabilitative services. Here are a few helpful facts.

About Our Patients

The average age of our men and women patients is eighty, the usual range being from seventy-five to eighty-five. Generally, there are more women than men patients.

Fig. 6-2 (Continued)

Patient Disabilities. Patients suffer a variety of disabilities, primarily of the chronic type. A great number of patients are confined to wheelchairs; many have limited use of arms and legs. Hearing and visual difficulties are common. Mentally, some patients are alert and intact. Others have varying degrees of senility—hardening of the arteries of the brain—causing them to become moderately to severely confused in their behavior.

Our patients fall into two groups. Those requiring concentrated nursing care live on the first floor in a hospital-like setting. Less disabled patients possessing certain self-help abilities are housed on the second floor.

About Our Staff

The ratio of total staff to total patient population is about one to one. Major departments are as follows: Administrative, Nursing, Restorative and Social Services, Recreation and Volunteers, Dietary, Housekeeping, Maintenance, Business and Health Records. Though as a visitor, a volunteer, or an entertainer, you will be mainly concerned with the Recreation Department, you may have occasion to contact members of other departments such as nurses, aides, or administrative personnel. Room directions and information about the locations of patients may be obtained from the receptionist.

Responsibility of Staff. All personnel are educated to be constantly aware of the great responsibility we bear for the safety, the health, and the peace of mind of patients. For these reasons, if one of our staffers sometimes seems unnecessarily firm with a patient, this is done for the sole purpose of that patient's welfare and should be taken in that spirit. Then, staff sometimes address patients, and vice versa, by first names. This practice is permitted with the sole and specific aim of helping certain confused patients feel warmth and friendliness, and must not be judged as over-familiarity or disrespect.

Policy with Patients. Every patient has important physical, social, and emotional needs. The effort of our staff is devoted to keeping these needs alive and preventing the withdrawal symptoms common to the aged ill. No patient is allowed to remain in bed, except in emergencies and under physician's orders. For we believe that the patient who stays in bed unnecessarily, or who remains secluded in his room, withers and dies—spiritually as well as physically. Whether he shows it or not, every patient derives some measure of benefit from personal contact with his peers, with visitors, and with volunteers.

About Our Facility

Architecturally, our structure is designed to closely relate the physical environment to patient function and needs. Ramps have been used wherever possible; living accommodations are designed to encourage independence of function; outdoor areas are easily accessible yet provide maximuf safety. Walls, doors, and furnishings are in bright colors which, together with carefully planned lighting, help patients with impaired vision to move about more confidently.

The Nursing Center conducts its programmed entertainment and activities

Fig. 6-2 (Continued)

in a large, glass-walled room on the first floor. Unsupervised recreation is enjoyed by less disabled patients in community rooms, where they may chat, read, write, watch television, and dine together in a therapeutic community atmosphere. In addition, outdoor living areas are provided in balconies and in the garden.

About Our Activities

The Recreation Department figures importantly in our patient program. To help patients function to the best of their abilities, both physically and mentally, a carefully planned program of recreational activities is conducted mornings, afternoons, and occasionally during the evenings. Every effort is made to keep this program fresh and varied. And that's where you, our visitors and volunteers, enter the scene. By coming here to entertain, to converse, to read to patients, you are drawing them away from themselves and their problems. By assisting patients with painting and crafts, indoor gardening, and flower arranging, you are giving them a sense of accomplishment. By holding regular meetings of your local club or organization at our facility and welcoming patients who are able to participate, you are making them feel that they belong. In short, with your cooperation and efforts, they become involved with *living* rather than dying!

A Word to Performing Groups

Performing groups often find our facilities useful for rehearsal purposes, for you might rightly liken the men and women patients to theater audiences in such tough try-out towns as Boston or Philadelphia. They are hard to please, critical, seemingly unresponsive. Some may even walk out during a performance. Yet these men and women are often far more aware than they appear to be. Long after the performance, the lecture, film, or visit is over and the visitors have departed, many delight in reliving what they have seen, heard, and done.

In Closing, we want to again impress upon you the importance of your work on behalf of our patients. Your visits are a vital part of our rehabilitation program, which could not be successful without your cooperation. On behalf of administrators, staff, patients, and their families, therefore, we express our deep appreciation.

C. Orientation

1. The volunteer should be introduced to staff and patients on her first day.
2. The volunteer aide should work closely with the recreation director, observing appropriate procedures with the patients, visitors, and staff.
3. The volunteer aide should gradually be given greater responsibility as she becomes more knowledgeable about her role.

4. The work of all volunteers, leaders, and aides is performed under the supervision of the recreation director or her assistant.
5. When a group of adult or teen-age volunteers is recruited at about the same time, a formal orientation program with the participation of key department heads should be planned for several consecutive days.

D. Volunteer Activities

1. Volunteer Leaders. Programs directed by volunteer leaders are fully described later in this section.
2. Volunteer Aides
a. Within the extended care facility they should:
(1) Help to physically set up planned programs
(2) Assist in transporting patients to planned activities
(3) Aid patients when necessary in arts and crafts; games such as bingo, checkers; and other programs (Fig. 6-3)
(4) Serve as companion to those unable or unwilling to participate and attempt to stimulate their interest in an activity
(5) Help with serving of juice or other refreshments
(6) Help clear and straighten the recreation room after a program is finished
b. Outside the extended care facility they may on occasion do

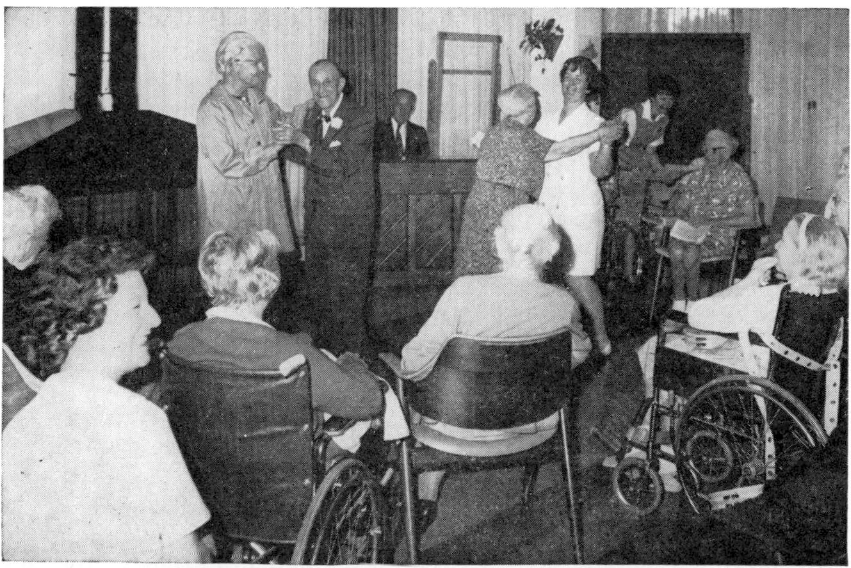

Fig. 6-3. A volunteer aide is in the background ready to assist patients during a musical program.

special shopping, prepare arts and crafts materials, or do some typing at home only at the request of the director of recreation and volunteers.

E. Attendance

1. On each visit to the facility, the volunteer should sign her name, the date, and the times of her arrival and departure in the volunteer book.
2. Punctuality and dependability should be stressed if volunteers are to be useful to the nursing center.
3. Should a volunteer be unable to appear as scheduled, she would be expected to inform the recreation director as far in advance as possible.
4. Should a volunteer fail to report as expected or discontinue her work without explanation, the recreation director or assistant should follow up with a telephone call to determine the reason for her absence.

F. Uniforms. Volunteers are expected to be neat in appearance and to wear the official volunteer pinafore or smock, which should be laundered after each wearing.

G. Relationships

1. With Patients
- *a.* Should a volunteer be unsure of a patient's ability to participate, she should contact the recreation director immediately.
- *b.* In an emergency, the charge nurse should be notified immediately.
- *c.* When a volunteer is requested by a patient to do some shopping or another special service, she first should consult with the recreation director concerning the appropriateness of the activity.

2. With Staff. All interdepartmental associations for recreational activities should be handled by the recreation director, and the volunteer should be engaged in interdepartmental relations only under the direction of the recreation director, except in an unforeseen situation.
3. With Visitors and Staff
- *a.* All volunteers should be clearly instructed that any medical or personal information learned about patients is confidential.
- *b.* Volunteers should engage in only cursory comments about patients with staff and visitors.

H. Recognition

1. At the annual senior citizens' month celebration in May, volunteers of all ages should be recognized for their services, and one outstanding senior citizen volunteer should be honored and given a citation (Fig. 6-4).

2. From time to time, volunteers should be named in the monthly newsletter.

V. PROGRAMS FOR PATIENTS

A. Entertainment by Community Groups and Individuals

1. Obtaining Programs

a. The recreation director should keep informed on available local programs of entertainment and information:

(1) Through newspapers and radio

(2) Through social and professional gatherings, church meetings, etc.

b. She should follow through on all promising leads via telephone calls and letters such as the one in Fig. 6-5.

c. She should continually be on the lookout for new material to use in building and maintaining a complete and up-to-date resource file.

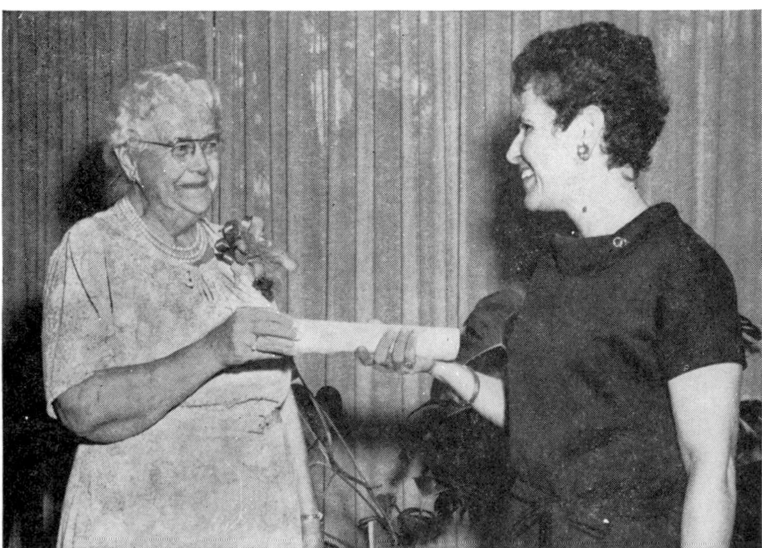

Fig. 6-4. An outstanding senior citizen receives a citation for service to patients from the administrative director at a special celebration in May.

Fig. 6-5

Mrs. George A. Grant
15 Mason Road
White Plains, New York

Dear Mrs. Grant:

Recently I spoke to you regarding the possibility of bringing your group to entertain the patients of the community extended care facility. You very kindly agreed to come and asked me to let you know which days would most conveniently fit in with the ongoing programs at the institution.

May I suggest that you schedule your performance for some Wednesday or Thursday afternoon during either January or February? Please contact me as soon as you decide on the particular day so that we may discuss further details and make definite plans.

We appreciate your cooperation in bringing pleasure and stimulation to our ill and handicapped patients. These men and women are currently unable to leave the nursing center to participate in any community activities, and it means a great deal to them to know that the outside community cares enough to come to entertain them.

I will look forward to hearing from you soon regarding the scheduling of your program at the community extended care facility.

Very truly yours,

Mary Jones
Recreation Director

d. If a letter or a call is received from an unknown group or individual, the recreation director should request that an audition performance be given at the extended care facility to determine the program's suitability.

2. Description of Programs

a. Whenever possible, patients should be encouraged to play an important role in the planning process by the use of a committee, a suggestion box, or other means.

b. A minimum of twice a week the extended care facility should enjoy programs by individual volunteers and groups from the community in the following categories:

Fig. 6-6. Patients in wheelchairs benefit from rhythmic exercises.

(1) Plays and dramatic readings
(2) Movies and slides
(3) Musicales
(4) Dancing and variety shows
(5) Instructive demonstrations (Fig. 6-6)
(6) Talks on travel, art, music, and civic affairs

c. The programs should take place during weekday mornings, afternoons, and evenings, occasionally on weekends.

3. Arrangements

a. A definite date and time should be set and a final verification call made a day or two before the scheduled day of the program. (Calls may have to be made nights and weekends from the recreation director's home, depending upon the availability of the person to be contacted.)

b. The recreation director should brief all performing individuals and groups on patients' behavior, attitudes, interests, and disabilities, and should distribute copies of Guidelines to Visitors and Volunteers prior to performance.

c. All possible information about the program should be obtained beforehand; e.g., if a group is expected, the number of persons included should be carefully noted so that necessary spatial and other arrangements may be made, particularly in the case of dancing or dramatic groups, when a room for changing costumes may be required.

d. With the help of the porters, the recreation room should be prepared for the event with:
   (1) Chairs placed according to the type of program
   (2) Projector and screen positioned, if needed
   (3) Extra chairs borrowed if required
   (4) Tables and utensils set up for serving refreshments
   (5) The Dietary Department notified of the type of refreshments needed and the number of people anticipated, including performers, patients, and visitors

e. The receptionist should be alerted to details of the event by the director of recreation:
   (1) The name of the performer or group
   (2) The time that the program is scheduled
   (3) The number of anticipated guests

f. The receptionist should greet the performers and visitors and announce their arrival to the recreation director or, if the program is held in the evening when the receptionist is off duty, the recreation director, or, in her absence, an appointed member of the staff should be posted at the entrance to receive and announce the visitors and performers.

4. Conduct of Program

a. The recreation director should conduct the recreational programs and should attend to all details.

b. She should supervise the escorting of patients to the recreation room and should direct and assist in their seating arrangements to achieve good viewing and hearing positions for patients with visual and auditory deficits.

c. She should welcome visitors and help them find comfortable chairs.

d. She should greet entertainers and give them any needed assistance and, when appropriate, introduce the administrative director to the entertainers.

e. When guests and patients are comfortable and the entertainers are ready, the recreation director should launch the program with brief introductory remarks.

f. Should a program be delayed or should there be a last-minute cancellation, the recreation director should fill in time with such spontaneous activities as group singing, dancing with patients, and simple word games to keep patients from becoming restless and drifting away.

g. During the program, the recreation director should remain alert to late arrivals and to any patients needing assistance.

h. At the conclusion of the program, she should make appropriate closing remarks to express appreciation on behalf of the extended care facility.
i. The serving of refreshments by nursing aides, volunteers, and able patients is supervised by the recreation director.
j. When the guests and patients have departed, the empty recreation room should be cleaned and straightened by the housekeeping staff in cooperation with the recreation director.

5. Follow-up
a. At the completion of each program, the recreation director should write a letter of appreciation on behalf of the administration, the staff, and the patients in the following way (Fig. 6-7):

Fig. 6-7

Mrs. George A. Grant
15 Mason Road
White Plains, New York

Dear Mrs. Grant:

On behalf of the patients and staff of the community extended care facility, I want to express our appreciation to you and your group for the splendid performance given here last Friday afternoon. We are deeply and sincerely grateful to you for bringing so much pleasure to our patients.

The entire program was a joyous and memorable experience for our people. This type of musical entertainment is particularly suited to their interests and has a beneficial effect. In fact, so stimulated were they by the fine performance that the program was a main topic of conversation for several days.

Please convey our thanks to each member of your group, and best wishes to all. We at the extended care center would be most pleased if at some time in the future you would find it possible to return for a repeat performance.

Very truly yours,

Mary Jones
Recreation Director

b. The recreation director should maintain cards in her file box concerning all performers and volunteers, with appropriate notes on their effectiveness.

B. Special Events

1. Birthday Parties

a. All patients whose birthdays occur during the current month are to be honored at a "birthday of the month" party.

b. The names of these patients should be displayed on decorative and timely posters in conjunction with a "Happy Birthday" sign in the recreation room.

c. Special entertainment should be planned for that afternoon, volunteer performers being invited to the extended care facility.

d. The recreation director should alert the Dietary Department for extra juice or coffee to be served to visitors.

e. A birthday cake is either baked by the chef or contributed by family or friends of one of the honored patients who have been invited in advance to participate in the event.

f. A long table should be set with a cloth, birthday napkins, plates, flowers (if available), and utensils. The cake should be cut and refreshments served after the program by the recreation director, aided by staff members and/or volunteers, relatives, and able patients (Fig. 6-8).

g. At the conclusion of the celebration when the recreation room is empty, it should be cleared and straightened by the recreation director assisted by the Housekeeping Department.

2. Holiday Parties

a. The following holidays should be celebrated at the extended care institution:

Thanksgiving	Valentine's Day	Mother's Day
Christmas	St. Patrick's Day	Father's Day
Easter	Halloween	Fourth of July
Jewish holidays	New Year's	

Senior Citizens' Day (a day in May selected for commemoration of senior citizens' month)

b. Special entertainment should be planned for these occasions.

c. When appropriate, patients should participate in making decorative menus and decorations for these holidays, supervised by the recreation director and/or volunteers.

d. The recreation director should inform the Dietary Department of the need for refreshments during the afternoon, and a long table should be set and decorated.

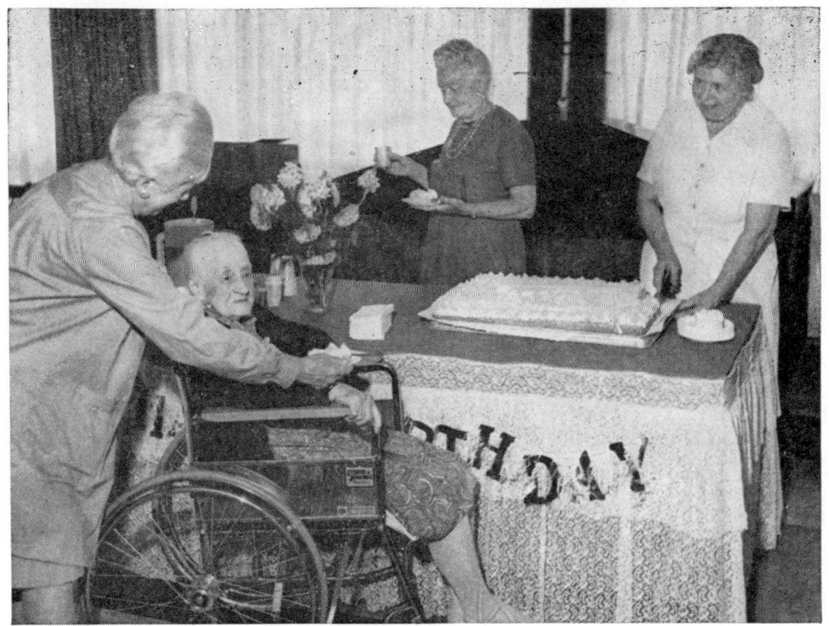

Fig. 6-8. Staff and visitors assist at the monthly birthday party.

e. At the conclusion of the program the refreshments are served by staff members and/or volunteers and able patients.

f. When guests and patients have left the recreation room, it is cleared and straightened by the recreation director assisted by housekeeping staff.

3. Gatherings for Discharged Patients and Neighborhood Senior Citizens

a. A program of social afternoons for discharged patients and local senior citizens can be conducted on a weekly or monthly basis (Fig. 6-9).

b. This program may be co-sponsored by the municipal department of recreation and parks and the extended care facility.

c. The purpose of this program would be to maintain contact with the discharged patients and to bring relatively well older people to mingle with their institutionalized peers in the extended care facility and lessen the fear of the neighborhood aged of confinement to an extended care facility.

d. Participants in the program could include elderly men and women who reside in the area, together with discharged and current patients.

e. Programs should include entertainment, talks by experts in various fields, bingo parties, and other group activities, speakers and performers to be procured by both the recreation director and the city recreation department.

f. The staff writer should design fliers announcing the programs, to be prepared for mailing by the receptionist and patients and mailed to a list of discharged patients and senior citizens prior to the program.

g. The recreation director should arrange the recreation room for the gatherings, setting chairs and tables according to the program or activity planned.

h. The Dietary Department should be alerted to the type of refreshments required and the approximate quantity.

i. During the arrival of visitors, the recreation director should supervise the receptionist in checking attendance in the record book of gatherings for discharged patients and senior citizens.

j. Following the program, the recreation director should supervise the serving of refreshments, aided by recreation leaders, volunteers, and senior citizen group members.

Fig. 6-9. A social afternoon for patients, alumni of the extended care facility, and neighborhood senior citizens.

k. After visitors and patients have left, the area should be cleared and straightened.

l. At appropriate times a committee meeting should be held to discuss future plans and programs for the gatherings. The committee should be composed of the following members:

(1) Recreation director, serving as chairman
(2) Staff writer
(3) Municipal recreation department representative
(4) One senior citizen guest
(5) One resident patient and one discharged patient

m. Records of both programs and committee meetings should be maintained by the recreation director in the discharged patients and senior citizens record book, fliers and clippings to be kept in the discharged patients and senior citizens activities book.

C. Religious Services. Patients are escorted to the recreation room for the services by the recreation director and/or nursing aides and volunteers, but should the patient be too ill to attend services, arrangements to have him visited in his room by the clerical representative following the service should be made.

1. To conform to the Jewish Sabbath, Jewish services should be held on Friday afternoons, if possible.

a. Preparations should include setting a table with a cloth, candles, and flowers; arranging chairs; and putting out prayer books.

b. The recreation director should ascertain that refreshments are being prepared by the Dietary Department to serve following the services.

c. The recreation room should be tidied following the service and collation.

2. Protestant services may take place on Sunday afternoons to conform to the Christian Sabbath and, as the recreation director is off duty on this day, the following arrangements should be made in her absence:

a. The minister should be given special information about patient deaths, transfers, etc., prior to the service.

b. The names of any guest speakers for the services should be listed on the program of the weekly calendar.

c. The Dietary Department should be notified of any change in timing for the post-service collation of coffee and cake or cookies.

d. The Housekeeping Department should be reminded of the need to set up chairs prior to the service and to tidy the room at the completion of the service.

3. Catholic services generally will be held on a weekday to conform to the schedule of the clerical representative.

a. The recreation director should set a table with a cloth, candles, and flowers (if available).

b. The chairs should be arranged so that the Catholic patients are seated in the front line for convenience in receiving communion.

c. After the collation has been served, the recreation area should be put in order by the recreation director.

4. Special holiday religious services for patients and visitors may be conducted by the three clerical representatives by prior arrangement with the recreation director.

5. Storage of Religious Articles

a. For convenient use in emergencies, an additional, labeled box of religious articles, such as candles and the holy water container, should be stored at the main nursing station.

b. The tablecloth, the Jewish and Protestant prayer books, and the articles for the Catholic services should be kept in the storage closets of the recreation room.

6. Prayer Books and Programs

a. The clerical representative may wish to prepare a weekly printed program for use in place of prayer books.

b. When prayer books are used regularly, those with large print should be ordered.

c. Programs or hymn sheets should be typed in capital letters to accommodate the visual deficits of the patients.

D. Informative Speakers

1. Prior to Elections

a. The League of Women Voters should be requested to send a representative to talk to the patients about election procedures and help them to register and to make out their absentee ballots.

b. During this period, local and state candidates for office should be invited by the recreation director to come to talk about pertinent issues to the patients.

2. At other times, leaders in various fields should be invited to speak on such topics as:

a. Medicare (Fig. 6-10)

b. Urban renewal

c. Investments

d. Underdeveloped countries

e. Current affairs

Fig. 6-10. A representative of local government speaks about new legislation for the elderly.

VI. PATIENT ACTIVITIES

A. Activities Directed by Volunteer Leaders

1. Music

a. Twice weekly, preferably in the morning, a music program in which patients participate should be conducted by a volunteer playing the piano and directing group singing (Fig. 6-11).

b. The recreation director should group the chairs in a close circle around the piano before the patients are transported to the recreation room for the music program.

c. The volunteer and the recreation director should discuss the selection of music prior to the commencement of the activity.

d. Throughout the period, the recreation director should work closely with the volunteer, encouraging and helping the patients and, because of their short attention span, interrupting the musical part of the program by such devices as:

(1) Discussions of the music, composers, or musicians

(2) Dancing with certain patients

(3) Encouraging patients to sing solos or recite poems

e. Further variations may be afforded by having an occasional visiting artist sing or play an instrument.

2. Painting and Sculpture
   a. Once or twice weekly, morning or afternoon, a volunteer artist should be invited to conduct a painting or sculpture class for the patients (Fig. 6-12).
   b. The recreation director should arrange easels and tables with painting and sculpture materials in the corner of the recreation room.
   c. The recreation director should check this activity frequently and should lend assistance where needed.
   d. At the end of the art sessions, the recreation director should encourage able patients to help in cleaning up and unfinished work should be put away for the next session.
   e. Patients' completed work should be displayed.
3. Gardening and Flower Arranging
   a. The garden cart. A mobile garden cart, complete with fluorescent lights to encourage blooming, should be used for indoor gardening (Fig. 6-13).
   (1) On a biweekly basis an expert from the Federation of Garden Clubs should be asked to instruct and guide patients on indoor gardening procedures.
   (2) Gardening supplies should be brought in or ordered

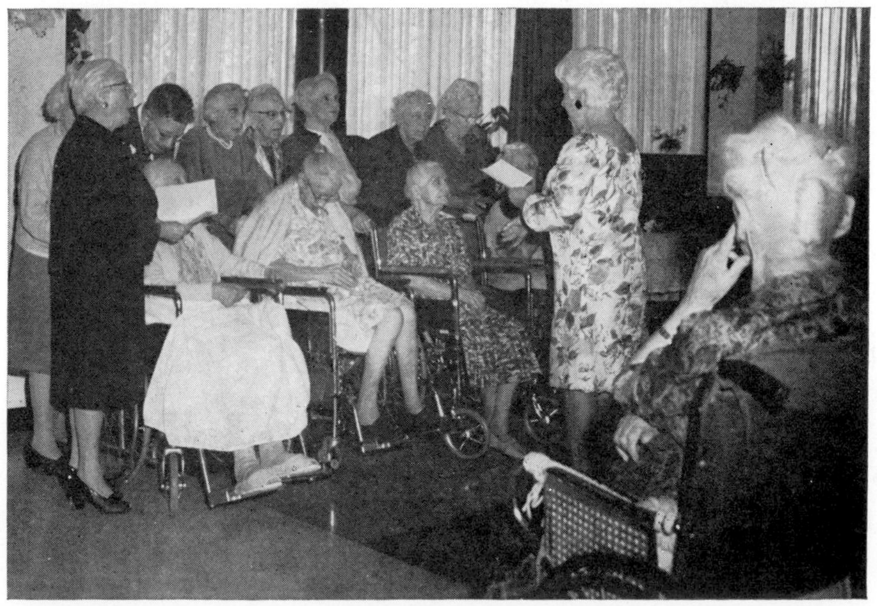

Fig 6-11. Rehearsal of the choral group.

through the volunteer leader or should be grown from slips cut from the plants on the cart.

(3) Prior to the gardening session, the recreation director should set up two tables in a community room, lined with cloth or newspaper, with chairs grouped around for the patients.

(4) Throughout the instruction she should lend any needed assistance.

(5) At the end of the session, the volunteer leader should encourage all able patients to help in the clean-up process.

b. In a similar fashion, waist-high tubs may be used for outdoor gardening during the fair weather.

c. Flower arranging

(1) Every other week, alternating with the garden cart sessions, a flower-arrangement expert from a local garden club should be asked to instruct patients on flower arranging (Fig. 6-14).

(2) Prior to her visit, the recreation director should group four tables in the recreation room, lined with cloths or newspaper, with chairs for the patients.

(3) All necessary equipment, including bowls, clippers, and pin-holders, should be made available.

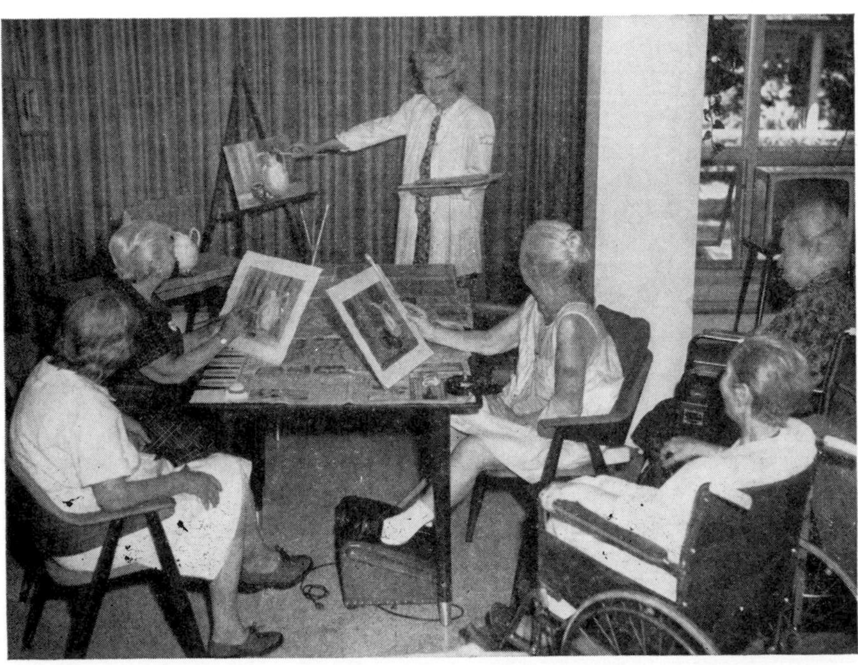

Fig. 6-12. A volunteer artist conducts a painting class.

Fig. 6-13. A mobile garden cart is useful for indoor gardening.

(4) The garden club volunteer should be reimbursed by the extended care facility for the purchase of flowers or decorations.
(5) Flower arrangements should be used as centerpieces on dining tables and for nurses' stations, with special arrangements created for holidays.
(6) At the conclusion of the session, the volunteer leader should encourage all able patients to help in cleaning up.
(7) During the summer months and in the anticipated absence of the volunteers, the flower-arranging program should be continued by the recreation director.

4. Reading Therapy
   a. Once weekly, preferably in the mornings, a volunteer reader should be asked to visit and conduct a read-aloud session for the patients (Fig. 6-15).
   b. The reader should attempt to relate the reading to the special interests of the patients and to the selections and authors represented in the mobile library.
   c. The recreation director should group a circle of patients in a

Fig. 6-14. Floral centerpieces are arranged for the dining tables.

corner of the recreation room, the hard-of-hearing being placed nearest the reader.

d. The recreation director should replace the chairs at the conclusion of the read-aloud.

5. Other programs may be added as volunteers with different talents and abilities are recruited.

B. Arts and Crafts

1. Arts and crafts sessions should be conducted two afternoons a week, articles made by the patients to include the following: tile ashtrays and hot plates, ceramics, ornamental wastebaskets, decorated soap, holiday trimmings, sewing and embroidery, rug weaving, and decorative articles.

2. Completed arts and crafts articles may be presented to visiting performers as tokens of appreciation.

3. Able patients should be asked to help the recreation director at the end of each session by putting away arts and crafts materials.

C. Games

1. Bingo

a. Bingo is generally enjoyed by patients once a week, in the afternoon or evening (Fig. 6-16).

b. Tables should be set up in the recreation room by the recreation director, who conducts the games, sometimes aided by a volunteer.

c. Each week several small prizes and one larger prize purchased by the recreation director from her petty cash funds, including items like handkerchiefs, earrings, perfume, scarves, rain bonnets, pens, or writing paper, are presented to the winners.

2. Bowling

a. Bowling should be played on a weekly basis in the recreation room.

b. The patients who can be involved in this activity include ambulatory and wheelchair patients. Others who do not wish to bowl referee, keep score, help in retrieving balls, and enjoy being spectators.

c. Weekly scores should be posted on the bulletin board.

Fig. 6-15. Patients with visual deficits benefit from a read-aloud session.

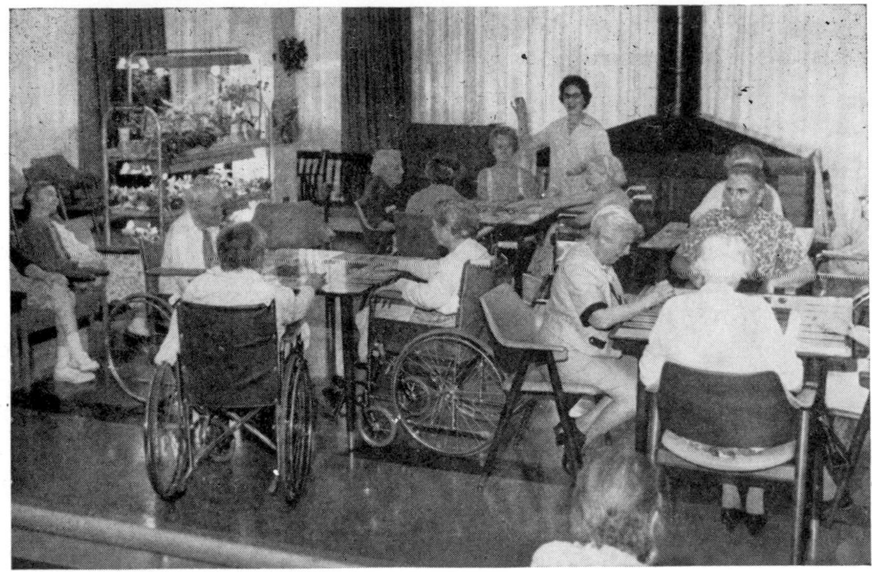

Fig. 6-16. Bingo is a popular activity.

3. Shuffle Board. Occasional games of schuffle board should be played, led by the recreation workers, either on a shuffle board court marked out on the floor of the recreation room or on an outdoor marked court in fair weather.

4. Other Games

a. Occasional card or checker games are played at tables in the recreation room, the recreation worker participating.

b. A game of ball may occasionally be enjoyed by the mentally impaired patients.

c. Dancing to recorded music should be promoted by the recreation staff.

D. Library Services

1. A circulating library should be composed of books loaned to the extended care facility by the public library, via its Shut-in Reader Service, preselected by the library's Readers Advisory Service in consonance with the physical, emotional, social, and intellectual needs of patients, a portion to be special, large-print books for patients with visual difficulties.

2. Members of the public library staff should be invited to write book reviews of two of the books loaned each month to be included in the patient newsletter.

3. For a 65-bed institution approximately 100 books should be stocked on a bookmobile and separated into well-marked subject categories for the convenience of patients and volunteers.

4. The bookmobile should be circulated twice or three times a week among patients by the recreation director or a volunteer in the following manner (Fig. 6-17):

a. An alphabetical card file box should be kept on the bookmobile.

b. When a selection has been made, the card from the back of the book should be removed, marked with the date and the name of the patient, and placed in the file box.

c. Upon the return of a book, the card should be removed from the file box, the return date written in, and the card returned to the book, which then should be replaced on the bookmobile in the proper category.

5. Once a month the recreation director should check the books for exchange, working with a list provided by the library.

6. Thereafter the library volunteer should be contacted to check on the day she will visit the nursing center and to give any special requests for books or records.

7. Once a month the volunteer library representative should visit to

Fig. 6-17. A volunteer librarian assists patients in making a selection.

bring in fresh supplies of books and to remove books no longer wanted.

8. The recreation director should indicate the books being returned on her list and should receive a list of new acquisitions from the volunteer library representative.

9. The contents of the bookmobile should also be available to the staff.

10. A similar procedure should be used for the borrowing of records from the library, with the maintenance of appropriate lists.

E. Films and Slides

1. Films

a. Films should be shown to patients once a week, usually in the afternoon or evening.

b. Preferred subjects will be travelogues, adventure stories, or full-length comedies or musicals.

c. Films may be obtained from the following sources:

(1) Public library

(2) State government departments of commerce, conservation, education, and health

(3) Commercial film companies

(4) Telephone company

(5) Educational organizations

d. The recreation director should be responsible for receiving and returning films, using the address card supplied in each container for mailing purposes and obtaining receipts from the post office for the business office.

e. The recreation workers should be familiar with the operation of a 16-mm sound projector and the rewinding of the film on the original reel for replacement in the mailing case.

f. A reserve supply of appropriate bulbs for the 16-mm sound projector should be maintained by the Recreation Department.

2. Slides

a. Individual volunteers frequently should be invited to show slides.

b. A list of volunteers available to show slides should be maintained in the Recreation Department file box.

c. Slides are also available from a number of educational and commercial organizations.

3. Photos and Movies of Patients. Snapshots and movies of patients and guest performers should be taken by the recreation worker or volunteers, to be shown on the projector or displayed on the bulletin boards.

F. Record Playing

1. The Recreation Department should maintain a supply of records selected to suit the tastes of the patients.
2. A procedure for the borrowing of records from the pub'ic library similar to that for books should be used, with the maintenance of appropriate lists as previously described.
3. A stationary and portable record player should be available.
4. Records frequently should be played in the recreation room, in conjunction with other activities, or alone to create a pleasant ambience.

G. Occasional Activities

1. Community Services. Community service activities can prove to be particularly beneficial to patients who had customarily engaged in volunteer activities prior to their illness, affording a sense of continued usefulness.

a. The handling of special mailings for philanthropic community organizations sometimes should be effected by patients under the supervision of the recreation director.

b. On occasion, handiwork should be done by patients, discharged patients, and senior citizen neighbors for the benefit of needy children or charitable organizations, such as:

(1) An Easter egg tree, with eggs hand-decorated for presentation to a children's hospital

(2) A Christmas fair conducted at the extended care facility and articles made by patients and senior citizens sold for the benefit of a camp fund for needy children

2. Cook-ins. Occasionally the recreation director should plan and direct cook-in parties in the recreation room or special pantry or, weather permitting, out of doors.

a. Food supplies and cooking equipment (including an electric skillet) should be arranged before the patients are transported from their rooms.

b. Aided by able patients, senior citizen guests, and other visitors, the cooking of such items as pizzas, potato pancakes, and the baking of cakes and cookies should be carefully supervised.

c. When the activity has a functional purpose, the occupational therapist should direct the cooking program.

d. Prior to the activity, special dietary problems of the patient participants should be noted.

3. Outings

a. Bus trips should be arranged with the local department of recreation and parks for senior citizen outings.

(1) Announcements of the proposed outings should be mailed to discharged patients and to neighborhood senior citizens.
(2) A record of responses should be kept for the recreation and parks department.
(3) The recreation director should arrange for an accompanying nurse (and other supportive personnel depending upon the size of the group) from the extended care institution and should provide the nurse with a complete list of all passengers.
(4) Name tags should be pinned on the coats or dresses of the participants, names to be checked at departure and return.
(5) People who have accepted the invitation should be alerted to any change in plans by the recreation director.

b. Car rides. Occasionally the recreation director may take or arrange for selected groups of patients to attend special activities outside the facility or to take rides to points of interest.

c. For any activity conducted off the premises of the extended care institution, a signed release of responsibility form must be completed by the patient or his sponsor in order for him to be permitted to engage in the proposed activity.

d. The attending physician must give an appropriate medical order.

VII. ACTIVITIES SCHEDULES

A. For the Month. The recreation director should attempt to schedule a minimum of a month in advance all programs and activities, notations to be made on a monthly planning calendar (Fig. 6-18).

B. For the Week. A calendar showing the schedule of activities for an entire week should be located at the main bulletin board for perusal by patients, staff, and visitors, and should be changed on Fridays by the recreation workers or volunteers (Fig. 6-19).

C. Preview program highlights may be promoted in the monthly newsletter.

VIII. REFRESHMENTS

A. Each afternoon at 3:00 P.M., juice should be brought to the recreation room from the kitchen and served by the recreation director, often helped by able patients, staff members, and/or volunteers.

B. For special programs, birthday parties, and gatherings of discharged patients and senior citizens, coffee and cookies or cake should be served instead of, or in addition to, the juice.

DECEMBER 196_

SUNDAY	MONDAY	TUESDAY	WEDNESDAY	THURSDAY	FRIDAY	SATURDAY
				1 10:30 Setting up of Christmas Fair 2:00 to 4:00 Senior Citizens Meeting Christmas Fair	**2** 10:00 Story Hour Mobile Library 2:00 Arts and Crafts 3:30 Jewish Service	**3** 2:30 Christmas Party with entertainment by the Timbrer Group
4 1:30 Presbyterian Service	**5** 10:30 Group Discussion Group Singing and Dancing Mobile Library 2:00 Bingo—Special Prizes 6:45 Christmas Carols by Mercy College Students	**6** 10:00 Garden Club 11:00 Choir Practice 2:00 Arts and Crafts 7:00 Patients' Group Meeting 8:00 Family Orientation Meeting	**7** 10:30 Catholic Service 11:00 Game Hour: Bowling 2:00 Sculpture Arts and Crafts 7:00 Music: Classical and B Sharp Group	**8** 10:30 Group Discussion Group Singing and Dancing 2:00 to 4:00 Senior Citizens Meeting Party Entertainment by Scarsdale Elks Entertainers	**9** 10:00 Story Hour Mobile Library 2:00 Arts and Crafts 3:30 Special Jewish Service 7:00 Christmas Carols	**10** Visiting—Refreshments
11 1:30 Presbyterian Service	**12** 10:30 Group Discussion Group Singing and Dancing Mobile Library 2:00 Bingo-Special Prizes	**13** 10:30 Flower Arranging with Potpourri Garden Club 11:00 Choir Practice 2:00 Arts and Crafts-Painting 3:30 Chanukah Party with Entertainment 7:00 Patients' Group Meeting 8:00 Family Orientation Mtg.	**14** 10:30 Catholic Service 11:00 Game Hour: Bowling 2:45 Christmas Carols by Manhattanville Students Birthday Party	**15** 10:30 Group Discussion Group Singing and Dancing 2:00 to 4:00 Senior Citizens Meeting 2:25 Christmas Stories told with slides	**16** 10:00 Story Hour Mobile Library 2:00 Arts and Crafts 3:30 Jewish Service	**17** Visiting—Refreshments
18 1:30 Presbyterian Service	**19** 10:30 Group Singing Mobile Library 2:15 Christmas Program by Mrs. Dickie	**20** 10:30 Garden Club 11:00 Choir Practice 2:00 Arts and Crafts 7:00 Patients' Group Mtg. 8:00 Family Orientation Meeting	**21** 10:30 Special Catholic Service 11:00 Game Hour: Bowling 2:00 Nestle Company Caroliers	**22** 10:30 Group Discussion Group Singing and Dancing 2:00 to 4:00 Senior Citizens Meeting 3:00 Christmas Party with Entertainment Glee Club	**23** 10:00 Story Hour Mobile Library 2:00 Arts and Crafts 3:30 Jewish Service	**24** Visiting—Refreshments
25 1:30 Special Christmas Presbyterian Service	**26** 10:30 Group Singing and Dancing Mobile Library 2:00 Bingo	**27** 10:30 Flower Arranging 11:00 Choir Practice 2:00 Motet Carol Crusaders and Highland Bell Ringers 6:00 Patients' Group Meeting	**28** 10:30 Catholic Service 11:00 Game Hour: Bowling 2:00 Painting Arts and Crafts Cox Sister Variety Show	**29** 10:30 Group Discussion Group Singing and Dancing 2:00 to 4:00 Senior Citizens Meeting New Year Party 2:15 Variety Show by Miss Margaret Dance Studio	**30** 10:30 Story Hour Mobile Library 2:00 Arts and Crafts 3:30 Jewish Service	**31** Visiting—Refreshments

Fig. 6-18. Monthly planning calendar.

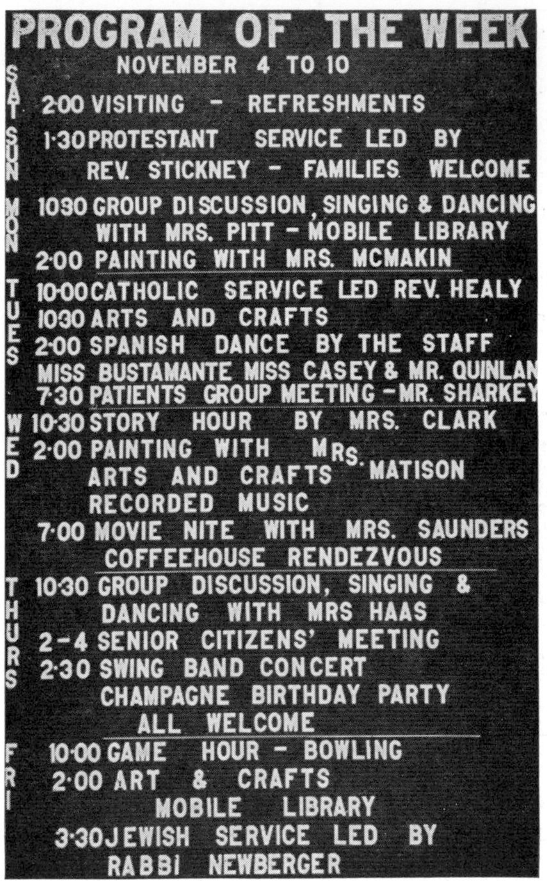

Fig. 6-19. A weekly calendar of activities should be easily visible to patients, families, and staff.

C. When a night program is scheduled, the recreation director may be required to bring in juice and cookies or cake, purchased from petty cash funds, as the kitchen in the extended care facility generally is closed in the evening.

D. At the completion of the daytime programs when visitors and patients have left the recreation room, the recreation director and an assigned housekeeping staff member, able patients, and volunteers should always tidy the area. Dirty dishes, cups, utensils, and napkins should be loaded on a serving truck and returned to the kitchen by dietary personnel.

IX. DISPLAYS

It should be within the purview of the recreation director to maintain changing, interesting, and attractive bulletin boards and decorations in the recreation room, with particular reference to holidays, special occasions, and new seasons.

A. Felt Activity Board. The schedule of the entire week's activities should be displayed on a lettered felt board conveniently placed to be observed by patients, staff, and visitors, with the following information affixed to the bulletin board on which the activity board is mounted:

1. Photographs and biographical information on guest speakers and entertainers scheduled to appear at the extended care facility
2. Special announcements
3. Bowling scores

B. Centrally Located Bulletin Board. This board should be changed monthly and should display a variety of objects arranged by the recreation director:

1. Exhibits of paintings and arts and crafts by patients, each clearly labeled with the name of the patient
2. Photographs of patients, taken by the recreation staff or volunteers
3. Distinctive holiday cards and ornaments
4. Newspaper clippings, cartoons, and poems
5. The most recent issue of the newsletter of the institution

C. Ornaments and Decorations

1. The walls of the lobby and recreation areas should be used for displaying paintings by patients, as well as birthday names and greetings, holiday signs, posters, and other decorations.
2. Ceiling hangings should be created for special holidays, such as Christmas and Halloween, and appropriate ornaments may sometimes be hung from the ceiling by thin 2-in. wires.
3. The counter in the recreation room should hold a bowl or vase of fresh flowers, and at holiday time it should be used to display ornamental figures made by the patients, such as angels and choir boys at Christmas time.

D. Showcases

1. Arts and Crafts Showcase. A covered showcase, with the contents changed monthly by the occupational therapist and recreation director, should be situated at the main entrance to display small arts and crafts articles made by patients.

2. Gift Showcase. A local philanthropic organization could be invited to maintain a showcase filled with gift items to sell to patients and visitors, profits from these sales to be used for civic activities by this club. The extended care facility itself could administer this project.

a. The receptionist could be asked to handle and record sales and to keep a list of special requests.

b. The club director or recreation representative could visit weekly to:

(1) Bring fresh supplies for the showcase and to give a list of these supplies to the receptionist to be used for her sales records

(2) Check over the sales records from the preceding week

(3) Collect all funds in excess of $5 and sign for the amount taken and the date of her visit

c. A balance of $5 should always be maintained for the purpose of providing change and should be kept in the locked showcase for convenient accessibility by the receptionists.

X. WORKING SCHEDULES

A. Recreation Director

1. Typical Daily Schedule: Though the recreation director's hours should be 9:00 A.M. to 5:00 P.M. and her work week Monday through Friday, when special programs for evenings or weekends are planned, she or an assistant should be present to supervise and to serve refreshments.

9:00 A.M. She should check discharges and admissions; biographical patient record cards of new admissions should be studied; birthdays should be noted in the chronological birthday book; cards of newly admitted patients should be filed alphabetically, cards of discharged patients removed from the file, and the discharge noted in the chronological birthday book.

9:00–10:00 A.M. Programs should be planned, telephone calls made, records brought up to date, material filed, arts and crafts materials prepared, patients' watering of plants supervised; work should be distributed for patients to do in their rooms; when appropriate, letters should be dictated; she should introduce herself to newly admitted patients.

10:00–11:30 A.M. The recreation room should be prepared for morning activities; patients should be escorted to the recreation room; the scheduled program should be conducted or supervised and the daily program record completed (Fig. 6-20).

Fig. 6-20

DAILY PROGRAM RECORD
RECREATION DEPARTMENT

Date____________________

Type of program____

Time of program____________________________

Conducted by:

Recreation Department Staff ____________________
Individual Volunteer ____________________
Volunteer Group ____________________
Other (Specify) ____________________

Number of Patients Participating ____________________

Number of Families Participating ____________________

Comments:

11:30 A.M.–12:00 NOON. The patients should be escorted back to their rooms to prepare for lunch; recreation room should be arranged for the afternoon activities.

12:00 NOON–12:30 P.M. Lunch break.

12:30–1:30 P.M. The recreation director should consult with nursing and social work staff about recreational needs of newly admitted patients, continue duties performed earlier, such as calls, records, correspondence, etc.

1:30–2:00 P.M. Patients should be escorted to the recreation room.

2:00–4:00 or 4:30 P.M. She should conduct or supervise the afternoon recreation program or activities; the daily program record should be completed; juice or refreshments should be served; patients should be returned to their rooms.

4:30–5:00 P.M. Recreation room should be tidied, the storage cabinets straightened, and the inventory of recreation supplies checked; birthday cards to discharged patients and neighborhood senior citizens should be addressed and mailed.

2. Weekly and Semiweekly Schedule

Monday

10:30–11:45 A.M. The music program for the patients should be supervised.

12:00 NOON–1:30 P.M. The bookmobile should be circulated among patients on both units.

2:00–4:00 P.M. The bingo game for patients should be conducted.

The money collected for showcase sales should be given to the club representative.

Tuesday

10:30–11:30 A.M. The alternating gardening and flower arranging programs for patients should be supervised.

2:00–4:00 P.M. Arts and crafts

Wednesday

10:30–11:00 A.M. The recreation director should assist with Catholic services.

11:00 A.M.–12:00 NOON. The bowling game for patients should be conducted.

2:00–4:00 P.M. She should oversee the painting or sculpture and arts and crafts programs for patients.

Thursday

10:30–11:45 A.M. The music program for patients should be directed.

2:00–4:00 P.M. She should lead the program for discharged patients and senior citizen neighbors; the attendance record should be kept current.

Friday

10:00–11:00 A.M. The patients should be assembled for the reading-aloud program.

12:00 NOON–1:30 P.M. The bookmobile should be circulated among patients on both units.

2:00–4:00 P.M. Arts and crafts.

3:30–4:30 P.M. The recreation director should assist with the Jewish services.

The weekly schedule on the felt board should be prepared for the forthcoming week.

Other Weekly Activities

Two afternoons a week (sometimes in evening or during weekend). Programs of entertainment should be supervised; conferences should be held with the administrative director for planning purposes.

Before the weekend. Films should be mailed to the supplier.

The accuracy of the volunteers' names and hours in the record book should be verified.

Final plans should be made and coordinated for the recreation program during the coming week.

One afternoon a week, occasionally in the evening. Films should be shown to patients.

3. Monthly Schedule

First of month. The recreation director should work with the volunteer public library representative in exchanging books and records and marking lists.

End of month. She should plan and conduct the monthly birthday party for the patients; change the birthday-of-the month names displayed in the recreation room to the names of patients having birthdays during the forthcoming month.

With the assistance of the occupational therapist, the exhibits in the arts and crafts showcase and the exhibit on right-hand bulletin board should be replaced.

The monthly hours of volunteers should be totaled in the record book.

The activities for the forthcoming month should be added to the calendar.

The monthly program summary should be completed.

All itemized bills and receipts for the month should be turned over to the business office in order to receive the petty cash funds for the coming month.

She should consult with the staff writer regarding program and volunteer news for the monthly newsletter.

4. Periodical Duties

Holidays. Special parties to celebrate each holiday of the year should be planned and conducted.

Other times. Other special programs and outings should be planned, conducted, or supervised.

Weekends and evenings. Special programs of entertainment should be devised, managed, and directed.

Miscellaneous. Supplies should be checked and ordered as needed; the piano tuner should be contacted when needed.

5. Yearly Duties

May. The recreation director should plan and administer the senior citizens' month celebration during the month of May.

September. She should obtain registration forms and absentee ballots for patients and request representatives from the League of Women Voters to assist patients in their voting.

October. She should arrange for candidates from each political party to speak on election issues to the patients and interested staff.

End of Year. She should complete the contract with film company for entire coming year's supply of films prior to January 1.

B. Assistant to the Recreation Director

The recreation director should be helped 2 or 3 days a week by an assistant, whose typical day should be planned by the recreation director to free her for administrative tasks and might include:

9:00–10:00 A.M. Assisting the recreation director by typing letters

10:00–11:30 A.M. Escorting patients to the recreation room and conducting the program or scheduled activity

11:30 A.M. Escorting patients back to their rooms

1:30–2:00 P.M. Escorting patients to the recreation room

2:00–4:00 P.M. Assisting with the afternoon recreation program or activities; transporting patients back to their rooms

4:00–5:00 P.M. Completing specific tasks assigned to her by the recreation director

C. Clerical Representatives. Representatives of each of the three major faiths should conduct regular weekly services as well as special services for holidays, the following schedules being suggested:

Jewish services—Friday afternoons from 3:30 to 4:30 P.M.
Catholic services—Wednesday mornings from 10:30 to 11:00 A.M.
Protestant services—Sunday afternoons from 1:30 to 2:30 P.M.
Staff choir practice—Tuesday mornings from 11:00 A.M. to 12:00 noon

D. Volunteer Leaders

1. Music Therapy. Monday and Thursday mornings, from 10:30 to 11:45 A.M.
2. Painting and Sculpture. Wednesday afternoon, from 2:00 to 4:00 P.M.
3. Gardening and Flower Arranging. Alternating sessions every Tuesday morning, from 10:30 to 11:30 A.M.
4. Reading. Friday morning, from 10:00 to 11:00 A.M.

XI. PURCHASING

A. Types of Purchasing

1. Decorations
2. Arts and crafts supplies
3. Special refreshments
4. Special paper plates, cups, and napkins
5. Flowers and accessories
6. Plastic forks and spoons
7. Games and equipment
8. Prizes for bingo; door prizes
9. Film postage

B. Vendors. Purchases by the recreation director should be made at various wholesale and retail stores and paid for from petty cash funds with charge accounts maintained at a few shops for:

1. Arts and crafts supplies
2. Paper articles and associated supplies
3. Flowers
4. Notions

C. Expenses

1. Each month the recreation director should receive a petty cash fund from the business office to cover her routine and miscellaneous cash expenditures for the month, including travel expenses for special speakers.

2. Bills for items charged to the extended care facility should be given to the business office for payment along with receipts for all items paid for from the petty cash funds.

XII. FACILITIES AND EQUIPMENT

A. Recreation Room Cabinets. These cabinets should provide sufficient, convenient storage for Recreation Department equipment and supplies, the recreation director being responsible for maintaining the equipment in proper working condition, for keeping sufficient supplies on hand, and for organizing equipment and supplies in such a fashion that the following items are ready for use when needed:

Folding chairs
Record players (2)
Records
Games
Decorations
Flower holders and pins
Paper supplies
Plastic utensils
Arts and crafts supplies
Arts and crafts tools
Tablecloth
Prayer books
Prizes
Bulletin board lettering
Miscellaneous items

B. Recreation Room

Loom
Screen for films
Garden cart
Game tables (4)
Shuffle board court
Piano

C. Main Nursing Station

Candles for religious services
Holy water container

D. The Recreation and Volunteer Office

Bookmobile
Movie projector
Slide projector
Desk and chairs
Telephone
Bookshelves
2 or 3 comfortable chairs
A small portable screen
File drawers
Monthly calendar of activities
Bulletin board
Rack to accommodate volunteers' uniforms and coats

E. Maintenance Room

Holiday decorations
Kiln
Extra folding chairs

XIII. RECREATION SUPPLIES (SEE TABLE 3)

TABLE 3. RECREATION SUPPLIES

Articles	Reorder Point	Reorder Quantity
Tiles	1 sheet	4 sheets
Ashtrays	4	1 doz
Trivets	1	6
Paper pads	3	donated
Brushes	when needed	3 or 4
Fabric	when needed	determined by job
Glue	when needed	1 large jar
Rubber cement	when needed	1 small jar
Turpentine	when needed	1 medium jar
Paper goods		
Plates	50	100
Napkins	3 pkg of 24	3 pkg of 24
Plastic utensils	when needed	determined by occasion
Candles		
Birthday	2	box of 12
Jewish services	when ¼ left	2 (donated)
Prizes	weekly order	1 doz or more
Special decorations	when needed	determined by occasion
Wool, cotton, yarn	when needed	determined by job
Crayons, paints, magic markers	when needed	determined by job
Beads	when needed	donated
Cat gut	when needed	donated
Wire	when needed	donated
Sewing equipment	when needed	determined by job
Sticks for boxes	when needed	determined by job
Sterilized potting soil	¼ sack	½-bushel sack
Vermiculite	¼ sack	(1) 25-lb sack
Pebbles	¼ sack	(1) 25-lb sack

XIV. INTERDEPARTMENTAL COOPERATION

A. Administration. The recreation director should keep the administration informed on planned programs and activities.

1. The weekly program should be discussed with the administrative director.

2. The recreation director should keep the administrative director advised in advance of any special projected programs or activities.

3. Together they should consider special need for supplies, equipment, space for activities, and extra personnel.

4. The Recreation Department records should be periodically reviewed with the administrative director.

5. Long-term planning for unmet needs in the light of current patient requirements should occur at regular intervals.

B. Nursing Department

1. When necessary, the recreation director should discuss patient needs with the director of nursing or, in her absence, with the appropriate charge nurse, to determine which patients should participate in the day's or evening's activities and to emphasize special refreshment diet restrictions.

2. Nursing aides assigned from each unit should care for patients' needs when they are attending programs or participating in activities in the recreation room (Fig. 6-21).

3. Nursing aides should assist with the transporting of patients to and from the recreation room for programs and with serving of refreshments under the direction of the recreation director.

C. The Occupational Therapist. The director of recreation shou'd consult with the occupational therapist in program planning, assist in showcase display with particular respect to arts and crafts, and on occasion should work with her on special projects for exhibitions and fairs.

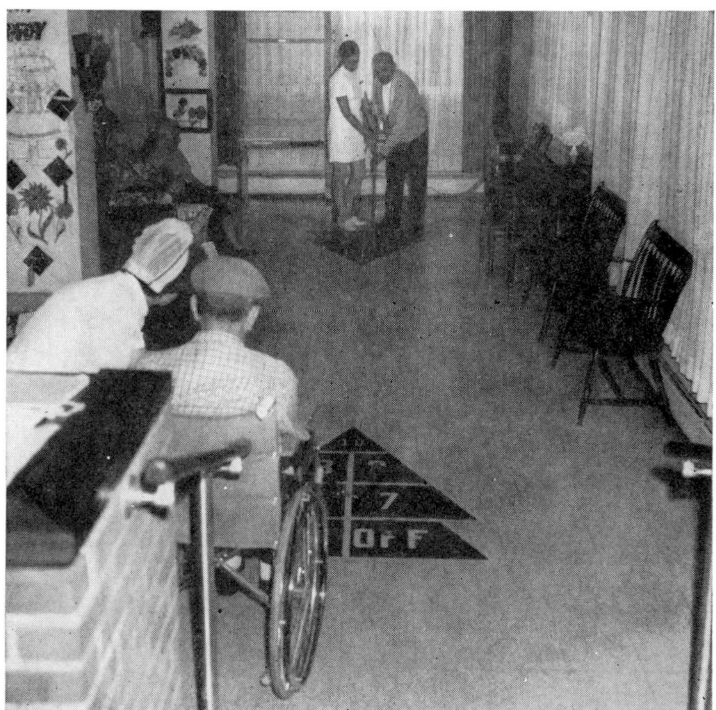

Fig. 6-21. Nurses encourage patient participation in the recreation program.

D. Social Service Department

1. The director of social service may volunteer background information about patients and families which could be helpful in planning recreational activities.
2. The recreation director should meet with the social service director frequently to discuss recreational plans for new patients and to evaluate the recreational participation of patients in residence.
3. The social work students may be assigned to observe the patients, families, and visitors during diversional programs.

E. Dietary Department

1. The recreation director should arrange with the Dietary Department for juice to be available for patients and guests every afternoon at 3:00 P.M., and the soiled utensils should be placed on the serving cart to be taken to the kitchen by dietary personnel.
2. The recreation director should arrange with the dietary director for extra refreshments and coffee when special programs are planned, and the same cleaning-up procedure previously described should be followed when the program has been completed.
3. The recreation director should obtain the menu details for holidays in advance from the dietary director to help patients to make specially decorated and printed menus and place mats for these occasions.

F. Business Department

1. Once a month at the end of the month, the recreation director should receive a petty cash fund from the business office to take care of her routine cash purchases.
2. Any bills for recreational items charged to the extended care facility should be given to the business office for payment.
3. Receipts for cash purchases should be submitted to the business office by the recreation director.
4. Stationery supplies should be obtained from the business office.
5. Announcements, menus, and other special items should be mimeographed for the recreation director by the business office.

G. Maintenance Department. This department should complete small tasks for the Recreation Department whenever necessary, such as repairing the televisions, record players, or projector, and the maintenance director should be notified of a problem by means of a written note placed on his clipboard.

H. Housekeeping Department

1. When needed, the porters should assist in setting up chairs and tables for programs.

2. Heavy pieces of equipment or furniture should be transported by the porters when rearrangement is necessary.
3. The porters should assist the recreation director in decorating high points that are reachable only by using a ladder.
4. Members of the Housekeeping Department should assist in straightening and tidying the recreation areas at the conclusion of the activities.

I. Publications

1. The recreation director should give information on the month's program to the staff writer to be used for the newsletter and for releases to news media.
2. The staff writer should prepare fliers for the weekly gatherings of discharged patients and senior citizens, and, when required, special announcements, using information on programs obtained from the recreation director.
3. The staff writer should participate in the monthly steering committee meetings for planning programs for discharged patients and neighborhood senior citizen gatherings.
4. The staff writer should prepare special handbooks for volunteers, birthday greeting cards, and form letters to families requesting their participation in the monthly birthday celebration.

J. Weekly Interdisciplinary Clinical Conferences. Weekly, the recreation director should attend the interdisciplinary clinical conferences with other staff members.

XV. COMMUNITY RELATIONS

The recreation director should devote an important part of her time to community relations with community leaders and directors of various community volunteer groups in her program planning, and she is involved in community relations in the following other ways:

A. Displays of patients' paintings and handiwork for exhibition in local shows and exhibits are arranged by the recreation director.

B. She should attend meetings of the county recreation and parks society.

C. With other staff members, she should attend monthly meetings of the steering committee for planning the senior citizen programs in cooperation with the municipal department of recreation and parks.

D. With other staff members she should attend conventions and meetings of the state recreation and parks society.

XVI. TRAINING AND EDUCATION

A master's degree in therapeutic recreation and/or group social work is desirable but not mandatory for the director of recreation.

A. The recreation director should be present at conferences, meetings, and classes on subjects pertinent to her work, including such courses as:

1. Creative Recreation: Program Building
2. Leadership Training

B. She should study professional journals on recreational and volunteer activities maintained on the reference shelf of the staff room, and she should develop a recreation and volunteer reference library for the recreation and volunteer office.

Section 7

Dietary

Introduction

Patients generally remain longer in the extended care facility than in the general hospital and, thus, food will assume a more important role for the patient during his period of extended care.

The dietary service should be committed to the preparation of attractive, well-balanced, and varied meals in accordance with the special and nutritional needs of the patient population. The food should be cooked so as to maintain maximum food value, distributed in a sanitary, orderly, and efficient manner, and served at the proper temperature.

Particular attention should be directed to following physicians' orders concerning modified diets as well as patients' individual preferences.

When feasible, community dining should be encouraged to increase the social aspects of mealtime. Dining tables, preferably accommodating four congenial patients, should appear visually inviting with the efficacious use of gay china, colorful place mats, centerpieces, and napkins. The decor, service, and companionship can augment or detract from the beneficial effect of group dining.

I. STAFFING PATTERNS

A. Staff Complement. A 65-bed extended care institution should require the following staff members for efficient preparation and distribution of food:

1 consulting ADA dietitian
1 food-service manager (working chef)
1 assistant chef
2 kitchen assistants
1 relief kitchen worker (to cover for kitchen assistants when off duty)
1 combination dishwasher and kitchen man
1 part-time kitchen assistant
(If the dietary staff are expected to participate in distributing individual trays and waiting on tables, additional personnel will be required.)

B. Recruitment. The recruitment of the Dietary Department staff should be the responsibility of the director of the department following the staffing pattern established by the dietitian and approved by the administrative director. When personnel are engaged, careful consideration should be given to the special physical requirements of kitchen work, involving long hours of standing, lifting, and handling of hot, heavy pots and pans, scrubbing and cleaning.

C. Work Schedule

1. General Work Schedule. In cooperation with the executive housekeeper, a weekly housekeeping and dietary schedule should be prepared and posted on the staff room bulletin board which, at the conclusion of the week, should be put into the staff schedules looseleaf notebook to be kept for a minimum of six months.

2. Time Cards. A monthly time card should be provided for each member of the Dietary Department staff showing a daily record of time signed in and out.

D. Orientation

1. To the Dietary Department. The food-service manager should instruct new employees in all duties of food preparation and distribution, outlining procedures for sanitation of food-service trucks and utensils and storing and cleaning duties.

2. To the Institution. Each new staff member should be given a copy of the personnel handbook, a tour of the building, and an explanation of the goals and purposes of the facility with particular reference to the importance of food service.

E. Uniforms. White jackets and trousers should be required for men and white uniforms and hair nets (or spray net) for female employees.

F. Personal Hygiene. Prior to and during employment the food-service manager should stress the importance of maintaining immaculate hands, fingernails, and hair for all people handling food, hands to be washed before touching any food and frequently during the preparation process.

G. Health Employment Practices. A preemployment physical, including blood work, stool cultures, and chest x-ray, should be required before a new person is permitted to join the dietary staff, and thereafter should be done on an annual basis.

II. RECORDS

The following records should be used in the management of an efficient Dietary Department:

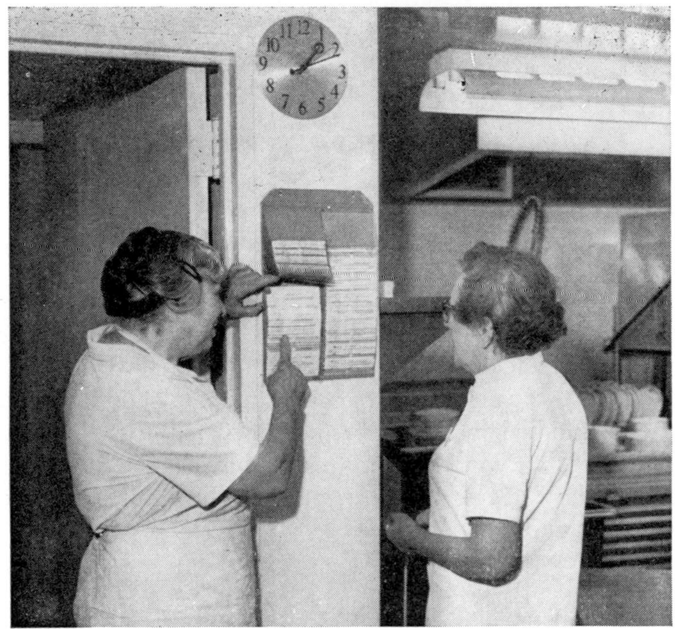

Fig. 7-1. The diet checklist for newly admitted patients is kept in a Kardex in the kitchen.

A. Diet checklist for newly admitted patients (Fig. 7-1)

B. Supper menu choice form

C. Floor supply list

D. Inventory form

E. Purchase orders

F. Sample menu sheet

G. Individual diet card in three colors to designate soft, regular, or puree diet

H. Tested recipe file adjusted to the number of patient and staff meals served

I. Record of meals served to patients, staff, and visitors, including number and types of modified diets

J. Schedule of special forthcoming functions such as parties, luncheons, meals for visiting students and dignitaries

K. Purchase records of foods and supplies to demonstrate price rises and declines of each item

L. Weekly report of the consulting dietitian to the administrative director

III. PATIENTS' MEALS

A. Time Schedule (starting)

1. Meal Service. Meal service should be scheduled according to the needs of the patients and the total program, with breakfast starting at 7:45 A.M., dinner at 12:30 P.M., and supper at 5:45 P.M., so that no more than 14 hr elapse between supper and breakfast.
2. Snacks. The floor pantries should be stocked with milk, juices, tea, coffee, crackers, and cookies for between-meal snacks.

B. Cycle Menus. Cycle menus for a 3-week period should be prepared by the dietitian for each season of the year.

IV. DUTIES AND PROCEDURES

A. Consulting Dietitian

1. A 3-week cycle of menus for each season of the year, with alternate suggestions for salads, desserts, and supper combinations, should be formulated by the dietitian in consultation with the food-service manager and posted in the kitchen and on those patients' charts with written physicians' orders for modified diets (Figs. 7-2 to 7-4).
2. The dietitian should observe and supervise the preparation of food and the use of new recipes.
3. She should assist with food purchasing, should offer suggestions for specifications of fresh foods, staples, meat, etc.
4. She should make rounds during meal hours to observe the:
- *a.* Food service
- *b.* Likes and dislikes of patients
- *c.* Amounts to be served
- *d.* Changes in service
- *e.* Modified diets

5. She should offer suggestions for safety and sanitary practices in the kitchen, with particular attention to dishhandling and dishwashing.
6. She should be consulted in the selection of new supplies and equipment.
7. The dietitian should meet with the medical director, the administrative director, the food-service manager, and the director of nursing periodically.
8. She should develop and supervise an orientation and in-service

Fig. 7-2

CYCLE MENU First week

Date:
Week of ________ to ________

MENU

	PATTERN	SUNDAY	MONDAY	TUESDAY	WEDNESDAY	THURSDAY	FRIDAY	SATURDAY
BREAKFAST	Fruit or juice	Unsweetened orange juice	Unsweetened pineapple juice	Unsweetened orange/ grapefruit juice	Unsweetened grapefruit juice	Unsweetened pineapple juice	Prune juice or Stewed prunes	Unsweetened apple juice
	Cereal with milk	Dry cereals as requested Farina	Dry cereals as requested Ralston	Dry cereals as requested Oatmeal	Dry cereals as requested Cream of rice	Dry cereals as requested Ralston	Dry cereals as requested Farina	Dry cereals as requested Oatmeal
	Egg and/or meat	Eggs	Eggs	Eggs	Eggs	Eggs	Eggs	Eggs
	Toast with margarine, marmalade, jam, or jelly	Danish pastry	Danish pastry	Muffins	Corn muffins	Cinnamon buns	Danish pastry	Sweet rolls
	Beverage	Tea, coffee, milk	Tea, coffee, milk	Tea, coffee, milk	Tea, coffee, milk	Tea, coffee, milk	Tea, coffee, milk	Tea, coffee, milk

Fig. 7-2 (Continued)

	SNACK							
DINNER	Meat, poultry, or fish	Roast chicken with pineapple glaze	Fresh ham with stuffing, apple sauce or Steak	Meat loaf	Roast sirloin of beef au jus	Lamb stew	Swordfish with lemon and tartar sauce	Smoked tongue with raisin sauce
	Potato or substitute	Baked mashed sweet potatoes with marshmallow topping	Mashed potatoes	Baked potatoes	Oven brown potatoes	Potatoes	Parsley boiled potatoes	Small potatoes in jacket
	Cooked vegetable	Peas and fresh carrots	Green beans	Broccoli or Wax beans	Creamed spinach	Onions and turnips	Harvard beets Plain beets (diabetic)	Boiled cabbage Fried eggplant
	Salad, cooked vegetable, or soup	Grapefruit salad	Cabbage, pineapple, orange salad	Green salad with fresh spinach	Tossed salad	Marinated bean salad	Tomato aspic with cabbage	Shredded lettuce and dressing
	Bread or rolls with margarine							
	Fruit or simple dessert	Pear halves and vanilla cookies	Gelatin with whipped cream	Sherbert and cookies	Fruit cup and date cookies	Baked apple	Lemon meringue pie	Butterscotch pudding
	Beverage	Tea, coffee, milk	Tea, coffee, milk	Tea, coffee, milk	Tea, coffee, milk	Tea, coffee, milk	Tea, coffee, milk	Tea, coffee, milk

Fig. 7-2 (Continued)

	SNACK							
SUPPER	Main dish—meat, poultry, fish, cheese, or eggs	Gefilte fish or salmon salad plate or Fruit plate with cottage cheese	Bacon, lettuce, and tomato sandwiches or Chicken salad	Grilled cheese sandwiches or Bologna sandwiches	Herring in wine sauce plate or Spanish rice with meat sauce	Franks in buns or Potato salad with cold cuts	Tunafish salad or Cheese omelets	Macaroni and cheese or Peanut butter and jelly sandwiches
	Salad, cooked vegetable, or soup	Chicken noodle soup	Minestrone soup	Beef noodle soup	Cream of mushroom soup	Green salad or Chicken noodle soup	Corn chowder	Tomato soup or Waldorf salad
	Bread with margarine							
	Fruit or dessert	Whipped gelatin and cookies	Baked custard	Canned apricots and cookies	Sour cream cake	Bananas in orange juice	Canned peaches and cookies	Fruit gelatin and cookies
	Beverage	Tea, coffee, milk	Tea, coffee, milk	Tea, coffee, milk	Tea, coffee, milk	Tea, coffee, milk	Tea, coffee, milk	Tea, coffee, milk
	SNACK							

Fig. 7-3

CYCLE MENU Second week

Date:
Week of ________ to ________

MENU

	PATTERN	SUNDAY	MONDAY	TUESDAY	WEDNESDAY	THURSDAY	FRIDAY	SATURDAY
BREAKFAST	Fruit or juice	Unsweetened citrus fruit juice	Unsweetened citrus fruit juice	Unsweetened citrus fruit juice	Unsweetened citrus fruit juice	Unsweetened citrus fruit juice	Unsweetened citrus fruit juice	Unsweetened citrus fruit juice
	Cereal with milk	Dry cereals as requested Various cooked cereals	Dry cereals as requested Various cooked cereals	Dry cereals as requested Various cooked cereals	Dry cereals as requested Various cooked cereals	Dry cereals as requested Various cooked cereals	Dry cereals as requested Various cooked cereals	Dry cereals as requested Various cooked cereals
	Egg and/or meat	Eggs	Eggs	Eggs	Eggs	Eggs	Eggs	Eggs
	Toast with margarine, marmalade, jam, or jelly	Cinnamon rolls	Cinnamon rolls	Cinnamon rolls	Raisin bread	Doughnut	Danish pastry	Raisin bread
	Beverage	Tea, coffee, milk	Tea, coffee, milk	Tea, coffee, milk	Tea, coffee, milk	Tea, coffee, milk	Tea, coffee, milk	Tea, coffee, milk

Fig. 7-3 (Continued)

	SNACK							
DINNER	Meat, poultry, or fish	Beef pot roast with gravy	Liver and bacon	Swedish meat balls	Baked chicken with gravy	Corn beef	Fried scallops with lemon and tartar sauce	Roast leg of lamb with gravy
	Potato or substitute	Potato pancake	Baked potatoes or Yellow turnips	Mashed potatoes	Rice	Small potatoes in jacket	Parsley boiled potatoes	Mashed potatoes
	Cooked vegetable	Buttered green beans	Spinach	Peas	Fresh carrots	Boiled cabbage Baked squash	Plain beets (diabetic) Harvard beets	Wax beans
	Salad, cooked vegetable, or soup	Cheese salad	Waldorf salad	Tossed salad	Grapefruit salad	Pineapple, orange, cabbage salad	Tossed salad	Green salad
	Bread or rolls with margarine							
	Fruit or simple dessert	Prune whip	Blueberry cobbler	Banana cream pie with cornflake crust	Ice cream and plain cookies	Angel food cake	Fruit cup and cookies	Bread custard
	Beverage	Tea, coffee, milk	Tea, coffee, milk	Tea, coffee, milk	Tea, coffee, milk	Tea, coffee, milk	Tea, coffee milk	Tea, coffee, milk

Fig. 7-3 (Continued)

	SNACK							
SUPPER	Main dish—meat, poultry, fish, cheese, or eggs	Sardine platter or Ham sandwiches	Manicotti with tomato sauce or Fruit salad with cottage cheese	Tongue sandwiches or Hash	Grilled cheese sandwiches or Chef salad	Creamed chicken and peas on toast or Blueberry pancakes	Creamed herring plate or Macaroni and cheese	Cheese-burgers in buns or Salmon salad
	Salad, cooked vegetable, or soup	Vegetable soup	Cream of asparagus soup	Chicken gumbo soup	Minestrone soup	Vegetable beef soup or Gelatin with fruit and cottage cheese	Clam chowder or Fruit salad with cottage cheese	Chicken noodle soup
	Bread with margarine							
	Fruit or dessert	Frosted shortcake	Fresh fruit and butterscotch cookies	Baked apple	Fruit cup and date cookies	Prune whip with custard sauce	Coconut cake with lemon filling	Brown betty
	Beverage	Tea, coffee, milk	Tea, coffee, milk	Tea, coffee, milk	Tea, coffee, milk	Tea, coffee, milk	Tea, coffee, milk	Tea, coffee, milk
	SNACK							

Fig. 7-4

CYCLE MENU Third week

Date:
Week of __________ to __________

MENU

	PATTERN	SUNDAY	MONDAY	TUESDAY	WEDNESDAY	THURSDAY	FRIDAY	SATURDAY
BREAKFAST	Fruit or juice	Unsweetened citrus fruit juice	Unsweetened citrus fruit juice	Unsweetened citrus fruit juice	Unsweetened citrus fruit juice	Unsweetened citrus fruit juice	Unsweetened citrus fruit juice	Unsweetened citrus fruit juice
	Cereal with milk	Dry cereals as requested Various cooked cereals	Dry cereals as requested Various cooked cereals	Dry cereals as requested Various cooked cereals	Dry cereals as requested Various cooked cereals	Dry cereals as requested Various cooked cereals	Dry cereals as requested Various cooked cereals	Dry cereals as requested Various cooked cereals
	Egg and/or meat	Eggs	Eggs	Eggs	Eggs	Eggs	Eggs	Eggs
	Toast with margarine, marmalade, jam, or jelly	Danish pastry	Danish pastry	Danish pastry	Cinnamon rolls	Cinnamon rolls	Muffins	Muffins
	Beverage	Tea, coffee, milk	Tea, coffee, milk	Tea, coffee, milk	Tea, coffee, milk	Tea, coffee, milk	Tea, coffee, milk	Tea, coffee, milk

Fig. 7-4 (Continued)

	SNACK							
DINNER	Meat, poultry, or fish	Roast turkey with dressing	Baked ham or Steak	Beef stew with carrots and celery	Beef pot roast with gravy	Veal parmesan	Filet of flounder with lemon and tartar sauce	Hamburgers with tomato sauce
	Potato or substitute	Parsley boiled potatoes	Baked potatoes	Parsley boiled potatoes	Mashed potatoes	Noodles or Yellow turnips	Baked potatoes	Parsley boiled potatoes
	Cooked vegetable	Broccoli or Wax beans	Spinach	Green beans	Peas	Zucchini squash	Stewed tomatoes or Fried eggplant	Beets
	Salad, cooked vegetable, or soup	Fruit salad	Cabbage, orange, pineapple salad	Tossed salad	Marinated bean salad	Canned peas in lime gelatin salad	Cole slaw	Green salad
	Bread or rolls with margarine							
	Fruit or simple dessert	Ice cream	Baked apple	Chocolate eclairs	Jewish apple cake	Fruit cup and cookies	Lemon custard	Peach pie
	Beverage	Tea, coffee, milk	Tea, coffee, milk	Tea, coffee, milk	Tea, coffee, milk	Tea, coffee, milk	Tea, coffee, milk	Tea, coffee, milk

Fig. 7-4 (Continued)

	SNACK							
SUPPER	Main dish—meat, poultry, fish, cheese, or eggs	Tuna salad plate or Fruit plate with cottage cheese	Turkey chow mein on rice or Grilled cheese sandwiches	Hamburgers in buns or French toast with syrup	Hash or Ham sandwiches or Pancakes with syrup	Cheese rarebit or Hot roast beef sandwiches	Sardines or Egg salad with vegetable garnish	Gefilte fish or Grilled cheese sandwiches or Potato salad and cold cuts
	Salad, cooked vegetable, or soup	Chicken and rice soup	Tomato salad or Chicken gumbo soup	Cream of asparagus soup or Green salad	Tomato soup or Vegetable salad	Vegetable beef soup	Corn chowder	Split pea soup
	Bread with margarine							
	Fruit or dessert	Baked custard	Whipped gelatin	Orange sections with banana cookies	Vanilla pudding	Pineapple upside down cake	Sherbet and cookies	Orange sections with banana cookies
	Beverage	Tea, coffee, milk	Tea, coffee, milk	Tea, coffee, milk	Tea, coffee, milk	Tea, coffee, milk	Tea, coffee, milk	Tea, coffee, milk
	SNACK							

training program for dietary personnel in conjunction with the food-service manager.

9. She should attend the interdisciplinary conferences.

10. She should prepare written weekly reports of the dietary service for the administrative director.

B. The Food-service Manager. Although the food-service manager in a 65-bed institution should also function as a working chef, the following specific functions should be her sole responsibility:

1. Food purchasing of high-quality merchandise should be done by the food-service manager, with attention to seasonal buys and special values in quantities carefully planned to maintain sufficient inventories, with the exception of perishables such as meats, fish, poultry, fresh fruits and vegetables, eggs, and dairy products.

a. Vendors. Vendors should be selected on the basis of quality of goods, dependability, and frequency of delivery service, local vendors being given preference. Prices of items listed below should be checked on a weekly basis, and all articles verified and weighed upon delivery:

(1) Meat, fish, and poultry
(2) Groceries
(3) Frozen foods and vegetables
(4) Milk, cream, cottage cheese
(5) Bread, rolls
(6) Eggs, butter
(7) Fresh fruit, vegetables
(8) Coffee, tea
(9) Ice cream
(10) Special groceries (or emergency items), such as instant decaffeinated coffee, should be purchased from a local grocer using a charge account, not cash.

b. Ordering schedule. Since deliveries generally are not made from Saturday to Monday, the food-service manager should plan accordingly, continuously watching food marked for special buys. Specialty items for unexpected needs should be ordered from the local grocer.

(1) Daily: Milk and bread should be ordered and delivered every day except Sunday.

(2) Semiweekly:

Monday and Thursday. Fresh fruits and vegetables should be ordered and delivered the same day.

Monday and Thursday. Meat, fish, and poultry should be ordered for delivery on the folowing day. Eggs and butter should be ordered and delivered the same day.

(3) Weekly:
Wednesday. Coffee should be ordered and delivered. The ice cream company should call for an order to be delivered on Friday. Frozen foods should be ordered weekly, including turkey, fish, vegetables, orange and grapefruit sections, and juice; staples should be ordered weekly.
(4) Monthly: Cookies and crackers should be ordered monthly.

c. Floor supply list (Fig. 7-5). The daily floor supply list, completed by assigned nursing aides on each unit, should be brought to the kitchen and should include items for daily use by patients on the floors, such as eggnog, bread, butter, tea, catsup, mustard, mayonnaise, sugar, French dressing, salt, pepper, and also margarine.

d. Quantities and inventories. These quantities listed below are based on the needs of a 65-bed facility, including 10 members of the staff, and correspondingly larger quantities will be required for larger institutions.
(1) Food staples kept in stock (see Table 4).

Fig. 7-5

FLOOR SUPPLY LIST FOR______________________________

Date ____________________

Tube feeding________________
Patient____________________
Patient____________________
Patient____________________
Eggnog____________________
Juice____________________
Sugar____________________
Bread____________________
Butter____________________
Milk____________________
Instant coffee________________
Tea bags____________________
Napkins____________________
Salad dressing________________
Mayonnaise__________________
Catsup____________________
Mustard____________________
Salt Substitute________________
Lemons____________________
Other (specify)________________

TABLE 4. FOOD STAPLES KEPT IN STOCK

Food Items	Quantity per Meal	Reorder Point	Reorder Quantity
Cereals	**Packages**		
Oatmeal	(1) 2 lb 10 oz	6 pkg	1 case (18)
Maltex	(2) 20 oz	6 pkg	1 case (18)
Cream of wheat	(1) 28 oz	6 pkg	1 case (18)
Farina	(1) 28 oz	6 pkg	1 case (18)
Brown cereal	(2) 22 oz	6 pkg	1 case (18)
Dry Cereals			
Special K	(10) ⅝ oz	2 cases	6 cases (50)
Canned Fruit (All No. 10 cans—6 cans per case)			
Peaches (halves)	2 cans	6 cans	1 case
Peaches (sliced)	2 cans	6 cans	2 cases
Pears (halves)	2 cans	6 cans	1 case
Pears (salad cut)	2 cans	6 cans	2 cases
Fruit cocktail	2 cans	6 cans	2 cases
Apricots (halves)	2 cans	3 cans	1 case
Pineapple (sliced)	2 cans	3 cans	1 case
Pineapple (tidbits)	2 cans	3 cans	2 cases
Pineapple (crushed)	1 can	3 cans	1 case
Plums (purple)	2 cans	3 cans	1 case
Applesauce	2 cans	6 cans	2 cases
Canned Vegetables (All No. 10 cans—6 cans per case)			
Asparagus center cut (3 sieve)	2 cans	2 cans	1 case
Green beans—cut (4 sieve)	2 cans	4 cans	2 cases
Blue Lake beans (4 sieve)	2 cans	4 cans	2 cases
Wax beans	2 cans	2 cans	1 case
Beets (sliced)	2 cans	2 cans	1 case
Beets (small, whole)	1 can	2 cans	1 case
Beets (shoestring)	1 can	2 cans	1 case
Carrots (sliced)	2 cans	4 cans	2 cases
Corn (whole, vacuum-packed for regular diets)	1 can	2 cans	1 case
Peas (3 sieve)	2 cans	4 cans	2 cases
Peas (mixed sizes)	1 can	2 cans	1 case
Tomatoes (whole)	4 cans	1 case	3 cases
Tomatoes (Italian)	2 cans	1 case	2 cases
Tomatoes (crushed)	3 cans	1 case	3 cases
Potatoes (tiny whole)	2 cans	4 cans	2 cases
Potatoes (dehydrated, sliced)	(1) 5-lb pkg	2 pkg	1 case
Potatoes (instant whipped)	½ No. 10 can	2 cans	1 case
Potatoes (sliced)	2½ lb	3 lb	1 case
Sweet potatoes	2 No. 10 cans	2 cans	1 case
Whole Irish potatoes	2 No. 10 cans	2 cans	1 case
Frozen Items (ordered bimonthly)			
Green beans	4 pkg	4 pkg	1 case
Green peas	4 pkg	4 pkg	1 case
Cut broccoli	4 pkg	3 pkg	1 case
Cauliflower	4 pkg	3 pkg	1 case
Cut spinach	4 pkg	3 pkg	1 case

TABLE 4. FOOD STAPLES KEPT IN STOCK (Continued)

Food Items	Quantity per Meal	Reorder Point	Reorder Quantity
Frozen Items (Continued)			
Baby lima beans	3 pkg	3 pkg	1 case
Fish	4 pkg	4 pkg	1 case
Turkey	1 turkey	2 turkeys	4 turkeys
Strawberries	1 No. 10 can	2 cans	1 case
Starches			
Rice (long grain)	3 lb	10 lb	6 to 10 lb
Noodles (medium or broad)	6 lb	5 lb	10 lb
Spaghetti	8 lb	5 lb	20 lb
Liquids			
Soups			
Tomato	(2) 50-oz cans	12 cans	2 cases
Mushroom (cream)	(3) 50-oz cans	12 cans	2 cases
Others	(3) 50-oz cans	12 cans	1 case each
Punch drinks			
Grape	according to need	(12) 24 oz	1 case
Fruit	according to need	(12) 24 oz	1 case
Juices			
Concentrated orange	(2) 24-oz cans	12 cans	2 cases
Grapefruit	(5) 50-oz cans	6 cans	2 cases
Orange	(5) 50-oz cans	6 cans	2 cases
Others	(5) 50-oz cans	6 cans	1 case each
Coffee	$2\frac{1}{4}$ lb	weekly	25 lb
Prune juice	(6) 24-oz cans	6 cans	1 case
Mixes, Canned Fish, etc.			
Biscuit, cake, and pancake	(1) 5-lb pkg	2 pkg	1 case
Muffin	(1) 3-oz pkg	2 pkg	1 case
Jello	(2) 24-oz pkg	2 pkg	1 case
Pudding	(2) 24-oz pkg	2 pkg	1 case
Basic custard mix (dry)	16 oz	3 No. 10 cans	1 case
Dzerta (modified diet)	(1) 3-oz pkg	(2) pkg	1 case
Diabetic pudding	(1) 3-oz pkg	(2) pkg	1 case
Tea	according to need	300 bags	1000 bags
Sugar (granulated bulk)	according to need	30 lb	100 lb
Sugar (individual pkg)	according to need	300 envelopes	3,000 envelopes
Powdered milk	according to need	20 lb	50 lb
Pickles (sweet)	according to need	1 jar	1 case
Pickles (kosher)	according to need	1 jar	1 case
Catsup	according to need	(6) 14-oz bottles	1 case
Mustard	according to need	(6) 2-oz jars	1 case
French dressing	according to need	2 gal	1 case
Peanut butter	according to need	(3) 3-lb pails	1 case
Jelly	according to need	(3) 4-lb jars	1 case
Marmalade	according to need	(3) 4-lb jars	2 cases
Gefilte fish	according to need	(3) 28-oz jars	1 case
Herring in cream	according to need	$\frac{1}{2}$ gal	1 gal
Herring in wine	according to need	$\frac{1}{2}$ gal	1 gal

TABLE 4. FOOD STAPLES KEPT IN STOCK (Continued)

Food Items	Quantity per Meal	Reorder Point	Reorder Quantity
Mixes, Canned Fish, etc. (Continued)			
Sardines in tomato sauce	according to need	(6) 12-oz cans	1 case
Sardines (skinless)	according to need	(6) 7-oz cans	½ case
Salmon, red sockeye	according to need	(6) 1-lb cans	½ case
Tuna fish	according to need	(3) 66½-oz cans	1 case
Instant coffee	according to need	(3) 10-oz jars	6 jars
Margarine	according to need	2 lb	30 lb
Premium crackers (salt-free)	according to need	2 lb	6 lb
Cookies (mixed)	according to need	2 lb	6 lb
Salt (iodized)	according to need	1 lb	24 lb
Pepper	according to need	as needed	1 lb
Diet Fruits			
Pineapple	according to need	6 cans	1 case
Fruit cocktail	according to need	6 cans	1 case
Peaches	according to need	6 cans	1 case
Pears	according to need	6 cans	1 case
Applesauce	according to need	6 cans	1 case

Note: Quantities herein listed are for usual orders and may be altered by opportunities for special buys of broken sizes, by seasonal trends, and by special needs, including the accessibility of vendors to the institution.

(2) *Fresh foods* required for daily use:

Fresh eggs: Should be delivered at least twice a week, the suggested quantity per day to be 10 doz, 8 doz served as meal fare and 2 doz used for cooking purposes.

Fresh milk: Should be delivered daily with the suggested quantity per day to be 20 qt, not including 8 to 10 qt of skimmed milk; reconstituted dried milk to be used to supplement fresh milk in cooking.

Butter: Should be delivered twice a week, the suggested quantity per day to be 7 lb—5 lb for patient trays and 2 lb for cooking purposes.

Cottage cheese: 2½ lb should be delivered daily.

Sweet cream: 1½ gal of half and half should be delivered daily.

Sour cream: 1 pt of sour cream should be delivered daily.

Bread: Should be delivered daily, the suggested quantity per day to be 6 to 8 loaves of the cake pullman texture, 3 loaves of whole wheat, 1 loaf of rye, and the suggested quantity per week to be 2 loaves or raisin bread, 6 doz Danish pastry, 4 3-lb pound cakes, 2 3-lb raisin cakes, 6 doz small doughnuts, and 6 doz bran muffins.

TABLE 5. FRESH FOOD REQUIRED FOR FREQUENT USE

Food Items	Quantity per Meal for 65 Patients, 10 Staff	Description
Meats		
Roast beef	24 lb	Split and tied top round
Corned beef	23–25 lb	Mild cured brisket
Pot roast	23–25 lb	
Roast lamb	20 lb net	3 legs, boned and tied; gross wt. 25 lb
Roast veal	20 lb	
Stew beef	20 lb	
Stew veal	20 lb	
Stew lamb	20 lb	
Chopped beef	20 lb	
Poultry		
Chicken (oven baked, cacciatore and breaded baked)	18 2¾-lb broilers	Cut in quarters, making 72 pieces
Turkey (for roasting)	(1) 24–26-lb bird (1) 8-lb whole breast	
Turkey (for à la king, pot pie, and chow mein)	(1) 24–26-lb bird	
Fish		
Cod, swordfish, halibut, filet of sole	16 lb	Cut to order in 72 4-oz portions
Rolls	6 doz	Small rolls ordered; served hot
Doughnuts, Danish	6 doz	For all patients, except those on modified diets
Ice cream	2 gal	2½-gal containers

(3) Fresh food required for frequent use (see Table 5).

2. Purchasing Equipment and Supplies

a. Major equipment. Major dietary equipment should be bought or replaced by a competitive bidding method that takes both quality and availability of service into consideration, with the consulting dietitian, the food-service manager, the administrative director, and the director of maintenance working together in ordering this equipment.

b. Small equipment should be chosen by the consulting dietitian, food-service manager, and administrative director, with items available in open stock selected for replacement purposes. The food-service manager should prepare purchase orders for items such as china, silverware, glassware, salt and pepper holders, sugar containers, trays, plate covers, napkin dispensers, and paper supplies.

c. Cleansers. Supplies for specific kitchen-cleaning equipment should be ordered biweekly by the food-service manager, with general duty cleansers, such as powder, bleach, and ammonia, obtained from the Housekeeping Department for Dietary Department use.

d. Equipment and supplies vendors. At least two vendors should be used, with frequent spot checking of accuracy, costs, reliability in delivery, and agreeability to keeping stock items required by the extended care facility.

3. Budget. The Dietary Department should run on a budget set up by the administrative director in consultation with the dietitian and food-service manager; the number of patients, food cost per patient, department maintenance cost, and labor expenses should all be taken into consideration when working out the budget.

4. Purchase Order Forms. Purchase order forms should be used for all orders of kitchen equipment and supplies by the food-service manager, and one copy of the purchase order should be kept by the Dietary Department for use in checking items ordered as they are delivered.

5. Billing. All bills should be received and paid monthly by the business office.

6. Inventory (Fig. 7-6). A physical inventory should be taken every 3 months during the year, the first inventory each year to be done on January 1, the second on April 1, the third on July 1, and the final on October 1.

7. Direction of Staff. The food-service manager should work closely with the dietitian and should supervise the assistant chef, kitchen assistants, and dishwasher, directing such special jobs as storing incoming stock and cleaning storage areas, walls, stove hoods, window screens, food trucks, toaster, mixer, and grill. She should maintain an accident-free department by carefully instructing staff on the dangers of a greasy, slippery floor, by warning about burns caused by steam sprays from coffee urns or boiling water on stoves, and by teaching staff to deflect steam when removing the cover of a boiling pot.

8. Scheduling of Staff (Fig. 7-7). The food-service manager should schedule staff for a 5-day straight-shift work week, alternating weekend free time, implemented by:

a. The dietary director (food-service manager) and assistant chef serving as relief for each other

b. The assignment of one person to serve as relief when the kitchen assistants and dishwasher are not on duty

Fig. 7-6

FOOD INVENTORY

Item	Unit Size	Unit Price	In Stock	Value
Apricot halves	No. 10 can			
Applesauce	No. 10 can			
Cherries: sweet	1 gal			
sour pitted	No. 10 can			
Peaches: sliced	No. 10 can			
halves	No. 10 can			
Pears: halves	No. 10 can			
sliced	No. 10 can			
Cranberry sauce	1 lb			
Fruit cocktail:				
Diet	No. 10 can			
Regular	1 lb			
Grapefruit sections	No. 4602			
Pineapple: tidbits	No. 10 can			
crushed	No. 10 can			
sliced	No. 10 can			
Prunes: whole	1 lb			
Plums: purple	No. 10 can			
Beans: baked	No. 5002			
cut green	No. 10 can			
wax	No. 10 can			
Beets: small, whole	No. 10 can			
shoestring	No. 10 can			
Cabbage: red	No. 10 can			
Carrots: diced	No. 10 can			
sliced	No. 10 can			
Asparagus: center cut	No. 10 can			
Corn: whole kernel	No. 10 can			
Onion: whole white	No. 10 can			
Peas: sweet	No. 10 can			
Pimentoes	4 oz			
Potatoes: instant whipped	No. 10 can			
Irish	No. 10 can			
sweet	No. 10 can			
sliced (dehydrated)	5 lb			
sliced	2½ lb			
Lentils	1 lb			
Tomatoes: Italian	No. 10 can			
crushed	No. 10 can			
whole	No. 10 can			

Fig. 7-6 (Continued)

Item	Unit Size	Unit Price	In Stock	Value
Gefilte fish	1 qt			
Salmon	1 lb			
Ham	lb			
Liverwurst	lb			
Salami	lb			
Frankfurters	lb			
Chicken, cooked pieces	lb			
Cereal: brown	lb			
Farina	lb			
Oatmeal	lb			
Maltex	24 oz			
Special K	5/8 oz			
Cream of wheat	28 oz			
Corn flake crumbs	5 lb			
Chili sauce	No. 10 can			
Catsup	14 oz			
French dressing	gal			
Mustard, dry	lb			
Mustard, jar	3 oz			
Worcestershire				
Tomato sauce				
Pickles: kosher	gal			
sweet	gal			
relish	gal			
Mayonnaise	gal			
Peanut butter	5 lb			
Vinegar	gal			
Crackers: unsalted	lb			
Cookies:				
Cinnamon-sugar				
Shortbread				
Butter thins				
Jello: all red				
Pudding: vanilla	24 oz			
chocolate	24 oz			
butterscotch	24 oz			
lemon	24 oz			
Pie filling:				
lemon	No. 10 can			
apple	No. 10 can			
mince meat	No. 10 can			
Custard mix				

Fig. 7-6 (Continued)

Item	Unit Size	Unit Price	In Stock	Value
Apples, sliced	No. 10 can			
Fresh vegetables:				
Potatoes	lb			
Carrots	lb			
Lettuce	head			
Cucumbers				
Cauliflcwer	lb			
Onions	lb			
Celery	bunch			
Tomatoes	lb			
Frozen vegetables:				
Cut broccoli	lb			
Beans, French cut	lb			
Chopped spinach	lb			
Peas	lb			
Lima beans	lb			
Strawberries	lb			
Ice cream	gal			
Milk	qt			
Cottage cheese	lb			
Sour cream	pt			
Breads: white				
whole wheat				
rye				
Pancake syrup	gal			
Raisins	15 oz			
Olives				
Swordfish	lb			
Shrimp	lb			
Scallops	lb			
Filet of sole	lb			
Soups:				
Beef base				
Chicken base				
Chicken broth				
Chicken noodle				
Clam chowder				
Beef consomme				
Minestrone				
Chicken/mushroom				
Green pea				
Tomato				
Vegetable beef				

Fig. 7-6 (Continued)

Item	Unit Size	Unit Price	In Stock	Value
Cracker meal	5 lb			
Oysterettes				
Sugar:				
brown				
confectionary				
granulated				
envelopes				
Cornstarch				
Baking soda				
Salt				
Evaporated milk				
Nonfat dry milk				
Coffee cream				
Chocolate syrup				
Oleo margarine chips				
Oleo margarine (solid)				
Oleo margarine (unsalted)				
Cheese, grated				
Horseradich				
Coconut				
Real lemon				
Topping whip				
Tart shells				
Olive oil				
Herring in cream				
Clams				
Chow mein				
Mushrooms				
Sauerkraut				
Punch:				
Grape				
Fruit				
Juices:				
Apple	No. 5 can			
Apricot nectar	No. 5 can			
Orange concentrate	No. 2402			
Prune	1 qt			
Prune concentrate	No. 2502			
Orange	No. 5 can			
Tomato	No. 5 can			
Grapefruit	No. 5 can			
Pineapple	No. 5 can			

Fig. 7-6 (Continued)

Item	Unit Size	Unit Price	In Stock	Value
Nuts:				
Almonds	1 lb			
Walnuts	1 lb			
Coffee: Instant	10 lb			
Regular grind	lb			
Tea bags	100			
Brown bread	lb			
Mixes:				
Bran muffin	5 lb			
Plain muffin	5 lb			
Devils food	5 lb			
Ginger bread	5 lb			
French crumb	5 lb			
Golden mix	5 lb			
Yellow cake	5 lb			
Orange cake	5 lb			
Biscuit mix	5 lb			
Corn muffin	5 lb			
Pancake mix	5 lb			
Extracts:				
Egg shade	1 qt			
Orange	1 qt			
Red shade	1 qt			
Almond	1 qt			
Rum	1 qt			
Lemon	1 qt			
Vanilla	1 qt			
Apple currant jelly	4 lb			
Marmalade	4 lb			
Pizza sauce	No. 10 can			
Spaghetti sauce	gal			
Meat balls	No. 10 can			
Noodles: medium	lb			
Elbow macaroni	lb			
Spaghetti	lb			
Soya oil	gal			
Cheese: sliced	lb			
cheddar	lb			
mozzarella	lb			
Turkey, whole	lb			
breasts	lb			
Bacon	lb			

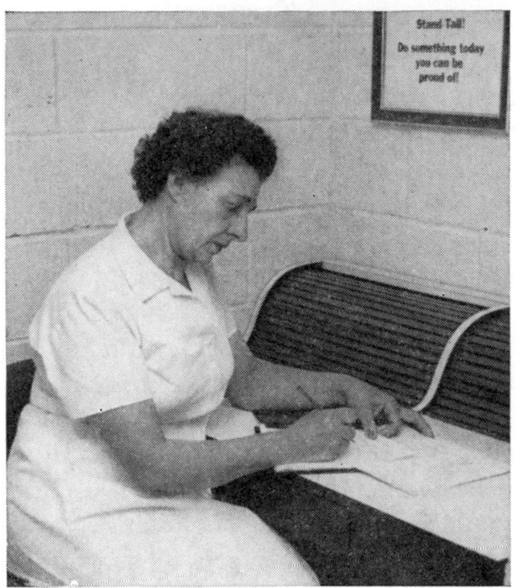

Fig. 7-7. The food-service manager works on the weekly schedule for the dietary staff.

C. Dietary Director. In a 65-bed institution the food-service manager should perform these functions listed below, although in a larger facility these duties should be separated from the purchasing and administrative responsibilities of the food-service manager.

1. Regular Duties

a. Food service

(1) The diet checklist should be prepared by a staff member on the admission of each patient that should be kept in a Kardex posted on the wall of the kitchen for convenient reference by the dietitian, food-service manager, chefs, and kitchen assistants (Fig. 7-8).

(2) General duties: The main types of diets to be prepared include regular, soft, puree, liquid, and salt-poor. Herbs are used to season food. Some canned and frozen foods are used daily; cured meat is served for dinner weekly, and occasionally as an alternate at the evening meal.

(3) Modified diets: Modified diets should be provided only under the written orders of physicians.

(4) Menus: The dietary director should assist the dietitian in planning a 3-week cycle of menus for each season, with a list of comparable items used to substitute for meat, desserts, and supper alternates to provide more variety in the cycle menus.

b. Food preparation and serving

(1) The dietary director should be responsible for the supervision or preparation of three regular meals and/or modified diets for patients and staff meals in addition to tube feeding formulas, daily nourishments for nursing units, and daily refreshments sent to the Recreation Department for patients and guests.

(2) For the concentrated care unit the meals should be served on individual preheated covered plates set on trays and on individual preheated plates served at dining tables in the skilled nursing care unit. Desserts should be taken to both units following the main course of the meal.

(3) The cooking schedule should relate to the types and variety of food to be prepared, the size and capability of the staff, and the equipment in the kitchen. The following constitute suggested methods of food preparation for a 65-bed extended care facility:

(*a*) In deciding the cooking time for meat, poultry, and fish, the size, quality, and amount of fat should represent determining factors, and each should be carefully tested for completion of

Fig. 7-8

Date:______________________________ Time:______________

DIET CHECKLIST*

Regular ( )
Soft ( )
Puree ( )
Liquid ( )
Salt-poor ( )
Other
Note below special likes or dislikes of patient

(Last) (First)

ROOM__________NAME______________________________

* To be sent to kitchen immediately after admission of new patient.

cooking; all fish should be served filleted. *Leg of lamb:* For 8 lb, roast for 3½ hr at 300–325°F uncovered. *Top sirloin beef:* 12 lb, boned and tied, roast 3 hr at least, at 300–350°F., uncovered. *Fresh ham:* rolled and tied, roast covered for 4½–5 hr, at 350°F. *Loin of pork:* 10 lb, halved and split, roast for a minimum of 4 hr, at 350°F. *Baked ham:* 12–13 lb, precooked, bake 1–1¼ hr, at 300°F; add glaze last half hour. *Corned beef:* 2 pieces, 12–13 lbs, simmer 4–5 hr until tender, at 185°F. *Meat loaf:* 4 loafs, 4–5 lbs each; bake 2 hr, or until done, at 325–350°F, depending upon meats used. *Pot roast:* 25 lb bottom round, boned and tied (split ¼ is used); flour and brown in oven; simmer 4½–5 hr until tender, covered; check. *Chicken legs and breasts:* bake breaded or unbreaded for 1–1¼ hrs, at 325–350°F. *Roast turkey:* 24–26 lb bird used at room temperature, roast 5–6 hr, at 325°F, checking after 5 hr. *Turkey à la king:* pot pie; chow mein; 24–26 lb bird, simmer day before using; cool in liquid; store in refrigerator; or may be roasted in oven with juice and seasoning, covered. *Fish (cod, swordfish, halibut, filet of sole):* cut into 4-oz portions; bake ¼ hr at 400°F; check. (*b*) Fresh coffee should be prepared for each usage, approximately 10 gal of coffee cooked daily in the quantity per meal and coffee break determined by patient and staff preference, for patient's meals, and for coffee served in the recreation room on weekends, afternoons, and at special events, such as evening programs, seminars, and senior citizen gatherings. It should be prepared in the kitchen with setup as follows: milk, hot foam cups, bulk sugar, napkins, teaspoons, cookies or small cakes. Patients who wish to remain in their rooms should be served coffee individually by nursing aides, the recreation director, or volunteers. (*c*) Other liquids: *Soups:* Soup and crackers should be available as a supper choice at the extended care institution 7 nights a week during cold weather, prepared in a 22-qt aluminum pot, and seasoned carefully, using fresh soup with chicken or beef stock base for modified diets. *Fruit juice:* For the two nursing units, 8 qt of unsweetened prune or citrus fruit juice should be used for breakfast and/or supper for 65 patients. *Fruit punch:* Two 2-qt pitchers of punch should be kept in the salad refrigerator for serving to patients daily by the recreation director at 3:00 P.M. in the recreation room, with grape punch substituted for the Jewish services. Punch also should be available for other occasions by special request of the administrative director. *Eggnog:* Should eggnog be required for modified diets, the charge nurse should send a special order to the kitchen; otherwise, 2 qt of eggnog should be maintained in the salad refrigerator, 1 qt to be kept in the refrigerator of each floor pantry. (*d*) *Whole milk:* It can be anticipated that more milk will be required for breakfast than for dinner or supper, varying according to the tastes of the patient population. (*e*) *Cottage cheese:* A No. 16 scoop should be used for cottage cheese served with fruit, such as half a peach and orange sections, on luncheon plates. (*f*) *Jelly and marmalade:* Should be served with each patient's breakfast. (*g*) *Sugar:* When feasible, sugar may be placed in sugar bowls for group dining, or two envelopes of sugar may be placed on each tray in the kitchen when tray service is to be used. (*h*) *Cereal:* Hot cereal should be served to patients in individual bowls with pitchers of milk placed on individual trays or tables, according to the type of food service employed. (*i*) *Desserts:* Pie: Two No. 10 cans of fruit should make 7 pies; 10 portions per pie with fruit is prepared by adding liquid to the proper consistency; then sweetening, thickening, and adding seasoning. Cobbler and brown betty: Two No. 10 cans of fruit, plus liquid sweetening and seasoning are used, and a No. 16 scoop should be used for serving. Custard (rice or bread puddings): 2 gal of basic custard mix should be used with 2 qt of rice or cubed bread and a No. 16 scoop used for serving with the following basic custard recipe:

1 qt milk
½ cup sugar
4½–5 eggs
1 teaspoon of vanilla

Bake in water bath at 350°F. Ice cream: A No. 16 scoop should be used to serve the 2½ gal required per meal. Jello: Two gal of water (1 hot, 1 cold) should be used for two 24-oz pkg and should be served with a No. 16 scoop, employing fruit juices in place of water when available. Junket: 1 qt milk, warmed to body temperature, should be added to the ½ cup of junket powder and let set for 5 to 10 min.

c. Cleaning and checking. The dietary director should be expected to maintain clean stoves, blender, and food slicer, and she should regularly inspect the freezers and refrigerators, checking their sanitary condition, temperature, and the condition of of foods stored therein; she should inspect the coffee urns daily and hood exhaust screens weekly, and should supervise their cleaning.

2. Typical Daily Schedule of Dietary Director and Assistant Chef

(Hours may be interchanged with the assistant chef arriving at 7:30 A.M. and departing at 3:30 P.M. or arriving at 10:30 A.M. and leaving at 6:30 P.M.)

7:30 A.M. Breakfast preparation and serving should be supervised.

8:45 A.M. Record of breakfasts served should be noted.

9:00 A.M. Dinner preparations should be started.

10:00 A.M. Paper work, including inspection of the inventory, planning food purchases for the coming week, and writing purchase orders, should be done while assistant chef completes dinner preparations.

11:00 A.M. The food warmer should be turned on to 170°F, and the water in the dehumidifier should be checked.

11:15 A.M.–12:15 P.M. With help of the assistant chef and the kitchen assistant, staff dinners should be served in two half-hour shifts.

12:25 P.M. With help of assistant chef and kitchen assistant, dinner for patients in both units should be portioned.

12:55 P.M. Record of dinners served should be noted.

1:00 P.M. The food-service area and stove should be cleaned.

2:00 P.M. All baking and special dessert making should be done.

3:30 P.M. Either the dietary director or assistant chef should go off duty.

4:30–5:30 P.M. Staff suppers should be served in two half-hour shifts.

5:45 P.M. Suppers should be portioned, and trucks loaded to be taken to both units.

6:00 P.M. Record of suppers served should be noted.

6:05 P.M. The food-service area and stove should be tidied. The dietary director should be relieved by the assistant chef assisted by the P.M. kitchen assistant.

3. Weekly and Semiweekly Duties

Monday: The special scrubbing of cups and bowls to remove stubborn stains and the weekly cleaning of silverware and the refrigerators should be supervised.

Tuesday: The cleaning of the chinaware racks and the scrubbing and hosing of the wooden flour racks, and the cleaning of the stove hood exhaust screens should be directed.

Wednesday: The day should be utilized for consultation with the dietitian.

Thursday and Friday: The overnight soaking and next-day scouring of coffee pots should be overseen, rounds should be made to patient units to determine continuity of food service, floor pantries should be inspected, and the weekly staff work schedule for the Dietary Department should be made and posted.

4. Monthly and Periodic Duties. The kitchen assistant's washing of the kitchen and staff dining-room window screens and the cleaning of the walls and ceiling in the kitchen and dining areas should be verified.

D. Kitchen Assistants (A.M. and P.M.)

1. Regular Duties

a. Setting up for meals: The kitchen assistants should set up trays on food trucks for both units twice a day in the following manner:

(1) After dishes have been washed and food trucks cleaned, a tray doily, napkin, silverware, cup and saucer, and bread and butter plate should be placed on each tray for the concentrated care unit.

(2) The china, silverware, and table linens for the skilled nursing care unit should be placed on small trucks for nursing aides to use in setting dining room tables.

b. Distribution of meals:

(1) Meals should be placed on individually set-up trays for service to patients in the concentrated care unit.

(2) Covered plates of food should be placed directly on trucks for patients to be served in dining rooms in the skilled nursing care unit.

(*a*) Breakfast

The A.M. kitchen assistant, in cooperation with the dietary director or his assistant, should prepare and serve breakfast, assisted by the kitchen man.

The A.M. kitchen assistant should transport the food truck to the skilled nursing care unit loaded with items to be used by the aides for the final setting of community room tables, including cold cereals, milk, butter, fruit juice, sugar, jelly, and special items ordered by the charge nurse, such as tea or cocoa.

The A.M. kitchen assistant should return the food trucks to the kitchen upon the completion of beakfast.

(*b*) Midmorning deliveries

After receiving the completed floor supply lists from the nursing aides, special drinks such as eggnogs and juices, as well as butter, bread, and milk, should be taken by the A.M. kitchen assistant to the pantries on both units and placed in the refrigerators.

(*c*) Menu choice

Menus with choices listed for supper should be delivered to the patient units.

(*d*) Dinner

Both kitchen assistants should assist the dietary director in portioning out meat, potatoes, and vegetables onto hot plates, should deliver the food trucks to the patient units, and should return the trucks to the kitchen upon the completion of the dinner meal.

c. Dishwashing: The actual dishwashing process should be performed by the kitchen man. The A.M. kitchen assistant and the kitchen man should strip the breakfast food trucks (dirty dishes, napkins, tray covers, etc.) and should place the trays in the sink for washing and place the soiled linens in laundry bags, the first assistant washing and cleaning the food trucks. The above process should be repeated for dinner by both kitchen assistants, and for supper by the P.M. kitchen assistant and the part-time assistant.

d. Food preparation: The A.M. kitchen assistant should aid the dietary director in the preparation of salads and diet and regular desserts for staff and patients.

e. Cleaning and checking: The P.M. kitchen assistant should be responsible for the proper maintenance of the salad refrigerator and the food service trucks with regard to cleanliness and for checking chipped glassware and china. Both kitchen assistants according to their schedules, should clean the staff dining area, the tables, chairs, and coffee service equipment.

2. Daily Schedule (A.M. Kitchen Assistant)

7:00 A.M. Should report to work and sign in; should transport the food truck with items for final community room settings to the proper unit; should prepare and serve breakfast, assisted by the kitchen man in cooperation with the dietary director or the assistant chef.

8:30 A.M. Should take coffee to the staff dining room and check requests for supper alternates with the patients (if Nursing does not do so).

8:45 A.M. Should bring the food trucks from the floors; should clean the trays and food truck and set up the food trucks for dinner.

10:00 A.M. Should deliver by cart special diet needs and other items to the pantry refrigerator.

10:30 A.M. Should assist dietary director in the preparation of the modified and regular salads.

10:45–11:15 A.M. Should eat dinner.

11:15 A.M.–12:00 noon. Special cleanup before the service of staff dinners should be done.

12:25 P.M. Should assist the dietary director in serving food.

12:30 P.M. Should deliver the food carts to the patient areas.

1:15 P.M. With the P.M. kitchen assistant, should bring the food trucks to the kitchen, strip the trays, and clean and set up the food trucks for supper.

2:00–2:30 P.M. With the P.M. kitchen assistant, should help prepare the afternoon patient snacks for distribution by the recreation director, and the dietary director should be assisted with food storage and checking of stock.

3:00 P.M. Should sign out.

3. Daily Schedule (P.M. Kitchen Assistant)

11:00 A.M. Should report to work and sign in; should clean the salad refrigerator, woodwork in kitchen, and the tables in the staff dining room; should prepare the setups for the staff dinner.

12:00 noon. Should deliver milk and salads to the floors.
Should assist the dietary director and the A.M. kitchen assistant in serving dinner.

12:45–1:15 P.M. Should eat dinner.

1:15 P.M. With the A.M. kitchen assistant, should remove the food trucks from the floors, strip the trays, clean and set up the food carts for supper.

2:00–2:30 P.M. Should assist in the preparation and delivery of afternoon patient snacks with A.M. kitchen assistant.

2:30–4:30 P.M. Should assist with cleaning stockrooms, food storage, and checking of deliveries.

4:30 P.M. With part-time kitchen assistant, should assist the assistant chef in the preparation and portioning of supper; should place the covered plates on trays and food trucks and deliver them to both units.

4:30–5:30 P.M. Should serve staff suppers in two half-hour shifts.

6:00–6:30 P.M. Special cleanup should be done.

6:30–6:50 P.M. With the part-time assistant, should bring the trucks from the floors, should strip trays, and clean food carts.

6:50 P.M. Should deliver breakfast china, silverware, table mats, and napkins to the skilled nursing care unit for use in setting breakfast tables in the dining rooms; should stock the floor pantries with milk, juice, crackers, and cookies for patient snacks.

7:00 P.M. Should sign out.

4. Weekly and Semiweekly Duties—A.M. and P.M. Kitchen Assistants (in addition to regular daily work)

Monday: The kitchen assistants should give a special scrubbing to the cups and bowls to remove stubborn stains.

Wednesday: The kitchen assistants should give a special weekly cleaning and polishing to all silverware.

Thursday: The kitchen assistants should clean the chinaware rack and provide fresh underlying mats.

Friday: The P.M. kitchen assistant should prepare grape juice and cookies, to be taken to the recreation room for nursing aides to serve after the Jewish services.

Weekends: The P.M. kitchen assistant should help the dietary director in the preparation of coffee and cookies to serve patients and visitors from 2:00 to 4:00 P.M. in the recreation room.

5. Monthly Duties—The Kitchen Assistants. Both kitchen assistants should wash the kitchen and staff dining room window screens once each month.

E. Kitchen Man

1. Regular Duties. It should be the kitchen man's responsibility to keep the kitchen and all eating and cooking utensils spotless, to assist in the delivery of breakfast and dinner to the patient units, and to weigh in and place newly arrived orders.

- *a.* Equipment needed. Dishwashing powder, rinse-all, dish towels, commercial detergent for pots and pans, pot brushes, stainless steel pads and cleanser, broom, wet mop, rags, and plastic bags.
- *b.* Dishwashing. After the serving of each meal, the pots and pans should be cleaned, dishes scraped, sprayed, and put into dish-

washer with rinsed silverware (except for egg dishes, which should be soaked), the same process to be repeated for all meals.

c. Cleaning. The kitchen man should be responsible for keeping the dishwashing machine and area clean at all times, as well as keeping the mixer, blendor, and toaster clean. The kitchen floor and the walk-in refrigerator, including racks, doors, and floor should be swept daily after breakfast and dinner; the storeroom floors should be cleaned with lukewarm water; a strong detergent should not be used; the wooden racks should be cleaned daily and scrubbed and hosed weekly.

d. Food trucks. The kitchen man should assist in the delivery of food trucks for breakfast and dinner; the part-time assistant should take up supper trucks; and P.M. and part-time assistants should bring the trucks down from the floors following supper.

e. Garbage cans. The garbage cans should be emptied twice a day, morning and noon, into large covered dumpster; the pails should be cleaned out, relined with plastic liners; the trash should be burned as accumulated; the part-time kitchen assistant should do this after the supper meal.

2. Typical Daily Schedule

7:30 A.M. Should report to work and sign in; should assist the dietary director and the first kitchen assistant in serving breakfast; should place filled plates and bowls on the food carts; should assist in delivering breakfast food trucks; should clean service area; should wash pots and pans.

8:45 A.M. Should help A.M. kitchen assistant return food carts from the floors; should help strip the trays, and should wash the dishes.

9:30 A.M. Should clean dishwasher and area and sweep kitchen floor; should do general cleaning and polishing.

12 noon–12:30 P.M. Should eat dinner.

12:30 P.M. Should deliver first food truck to patient floors.

12:45 P.M. Should deliver second food truck to patient floors; should clean service area; should wash pots and pans.

1:15 P.M. Should wash dinner dishes.

2:15–3:30 P.M. Should clean the dishwasher and area; should empty and wash and line garbage cans; should complete general kitchen cleaning and cleaning of floors of stockrooms and walk-in refrigerator.

3:30 P.M. Should sign out.

3. Weekly and Semiweekly Duties

Wednesday: The walk-in refrigerator should be cleaned.

Thursday: Wooden floor racks should be scrubbed and hosed.

Sunday: The stove hood and exhaust screens should be thoroughly cleaned.

Tuesday and Friday: The coffee urns should be soaked overnight and scoured the next day.

4. Other Periodic Work

a. The floors of storerooms should be wet-mopped when necessary.
b. The walls and ceiling of the kitchen should be scrubbed.

F. Part-time Kitchen Assistant

Daily Schedule:

4:30 P.M. Should report to duty and sign in; the kitchen towels should be laundered, dried, and folded; coffee for patient and staff suppers should be prepared.

5:00 P.M. Should take small truck to patient units with bread, crackers, butter, and juices, if ordered; should assist dietary director and/or P.M. kitchen assistant with final supper preparations.

5:30 P.M. Should clean up after staff suppers.

5:40 P.M. Should deliver soup, juice, and milk to pantries; should assist in the distribution of food carts.

6:00 P.M. Should clean the service area and wash the pots and pans.

6:30–7:15 P.M. With the P.M. kitchen assistant, should return the food trucks, strip the trays, and clean the food carts.

7:15–8:00 P.M. Should wash the supper dishes, empty the garbage cans, wash and line cans, and burn the trash; should hose and scrub the kitchen floor and the staff dining area; should examine the entire kitchen and staff dining area for cleanliness and safety; should lock the kitchen.

8:00 P.M. Should sign out.

V. FACILITIES AND MAJOR EQUIPMENT

A. Staff Dining Room: Tables, chairs, coffee maker, and bulletin board

B. Pantry on Each Patient Unit: Hot plates, refrigerators, sinks, heavy-duty toasters

C. Storage

1. Stock Rooms

a. Food items. Staple stocks such as groceries, condiments, canned goods, dry goods, and certain cereals should be stored in a cool and ventilated storeroom adjacent to the kitchen area on rust-proof metal shelves arranged at least 1 ft from the floor, with opened packages of dry items stored in carefully labeled stainless steel and/or plastic containers.

b. Cleaning items. Cleaning stock should be stored in a separate metal closet in the storeroom, removed from the food storage shelves.

c. An inventory of china, glassware, and silver should be maintained in a locked cabinet in the storeroom.

d. Paper goods should be stored in a special section of the storage area.

2. Freezer. Frozen foods should be stored in an upright compartment freezer.

3. Walk-in Refrigerator. Dairy products, unfrozen meats, cold cuts, fruit juices, fresh fruit, and vegetables should be stored in the walk-in refrigerator or in a compartment refrigerator.

4. Salad Refrigerator. A six-compartment, upright salad refrigerator should hold individual salads, relishes, etc., for use during the day.

5. Scale. A scale to verify weights of meat, fish, and fresh produce should be conveniently located.

D. Cooking Equipment—Major

1. Whenever feasible, two gas ranges—one with flat-top heating surface; the other with four individual, grated heating surfaces

2. Appropriate ventilating fans and an automatic fire extinguisher

3. 1 attached oven, used dually for baking and roasting

4. 1 convection oven for more rapid baking and roasting (Fig. 7-9)

5. 1 gas grill

6. two 6-gal coffee makers, gas heated

7. 1 steamer

8. 1 four-slice, heavy-duty electric toaster (toasters should also be located in floor pantries)

9. 2 heavy-duty 2-quart Waring Blendors

10. 1 floor-mounted mixer with attachments for grinding, grating, etc.

11. 1 heavy-duty electric food slicer

E. Serving Equipment

1. 1 electric or steam serving table

2. Two 15-tray food trucks, enclosed on four sides, for delivering individual trays to concentrated care unit

Fig. 7-9. The chef instructs her assistant in the use of the steamer and convection oven.

3. 4 two-tier food delivery carts for meal service to tables in the skilled nursing care unit

4. 1 electric plate warmer

5. A covered plate system should be used for soups, cereals, and main courses.

6. A stem thermometer should be used to test food temperatures—cold foods to be below 45° when served and hot foods to be above 140°.

F. China, Glassware, and Cutlery. The selection of these items should be based on proper balance and weight for patients' safety, durability, ease in reordering, and beauty.

G. Dishwashing Equipment

1. A 24- × 24-in. dishwasher with automatic rinse and booster heater (the temperature of the water for washing to be 150°F, for rinsing 180°F)

2. Appropriate ventilating fan

3. Dish, silverware, glass, and tray racks

H. Cleaning Equipment. Cleaning equipment for the kitchen area should be stored in a separate ventilated closet.

I. Office Area. An office area complete with a desk, two chairs, files, a bulletin board, and bookshelves for diet and training dietary aide manuals, diet and equipment manuals, special diets, and other reference material used by the dietitian and/or the food-service manager should be contiguous to the dietary area.

VI. RELATIONS WITH GOVERNMENT AGENCIES

In addition to usual supervisory visits by regulatory agencies, the Dietary Department in an extended care institution generally is inspected by the county department of health in order to qualify for an eating place permit, which should be posted on the kitchen bulletin board along with the weekly menu, the record of meals served, and special timely information.

VII. INTERDEPARTMENTAL COOPERATION

The dietary director and/or food-service manager should have contact with all other departments of the extended care facility.

A. Housekeeping Department

1. The executive housekeeper should inspect the refrigerators in pantries on both units to verify their sanitary condition (duty of nursing aides).
2. When appropriate, the executive housekeeper should arrange for the rental from a linen rental company of mens' uniforms and aprons for Dietary Department personnel.
3. Supplies such as bleach and ammonia should be obtained from the Housekeeping Department.
4. Certain cleaning tasks such as the laundering of napkins, table cloths, and kitchen curtains should be the responsibility of the Housekeeping Department.

B. Nursing Department

1. Individual Diets: The Nursing Department should also provide the Dietary Department with an individual diet checklist on the admission of a new patient, to be kept with current diet orders in a Kardex in the kitchen, giving information about modified diets that may be prescribed by patient's physician.
2. A diet manual should be placed at each nurses' station for physicians' use in ordering modified diets, to be transmitted by the charge nurse to the dietary director.

3. Charge nurses may circulate and return completed supper menu-choice forms to the kitchen by 2:00 P.M. or this may be handled by representatives of the Dietary Department.

4. Notice of Absence

a. Permanent. Notices of discharge or death of patients should be furnished by the Nursing Department to the Dietary Department.

b. Temporary. Should a patient be away for any meals, the Nursing Department should so inform the Dietary Department.

c. Room change or transfer of a patient to a different room and/or unit should be reported promptly to the kitchen.

5. Distribution of Meals

a. Concentrated care unit. The dietary staff should deliver food trucks loaded with individual trays to the concentrated care floor for the nursing aides to serve to individual patients at drop-leaf tables in patients' rooms or, when necessary, at overbed tables.

b. Skilled nursing care unit. The Dietary Department should deliver the setups and food carts for the community room dining areas, the nursing aides doing the actual table settings and the serving of individual plates to patients (Fig. 7-10).

6. Refrigerators. The refrigerators in the pantries should be kept stocked by the Dietary Department with supplies of bread, butter, milk, eggnog, jelly, catsup, mustard, and salad dressings.

7. Food Preparation. Toast should be prepared by the nursing aides in floor pantries, and soup sent to the community dining area should be heated there before serving.

C. Maintenance Department

1. Repairs. The maintenance director should repair or supervise the repairing of any equipment in the Dietary Department, such as refrigerators, freezers, stoves, dishwashers, plumbing, electricity, etc.

2. Major Cleaning. Painting and once-a-year washing down of kitchen walls should be completed under supervision of the maintenance director.

3. Safety. The maintenance director should check all kitchen equipment weekly.

D. Recreation Department

1. Afternoon Refreshments. Each afternoon at 3:00 P.M. juice should be prepared for the director of recreation to serve in the recreation room.

2. Religious Services. Juice and cookies should be served by the

Fig. 7-10. Individual covered plates rather than individual trays are distributed to community dining areas.

nursing aides on Friday afternoons at 3:30 P.M., after the Jewish services, under the direction of the recreation director.

3. Weekends. Saturday and Sunday afternoons from 2:00 to 4:00 P.M., cookies and coffee may be served to patients and visitors in the recreation room.

4. Special Events. The dietary director should be notified at least one day in advance when refreshments will be required for special afternoon and evening events.

E. All Departments

Staff members should inform the dietary director at least one day in advance when mealtime visitors of patients or personnel are expected.

F. Interdisciplinary Conferences

The consulting dietitian should attend the weekly interdisciplinary staff conferences together with other professional staff.

G. Staff Meals and Coffee Breaks

1. Coffee should be provided for use in staff dining rooms mornings and afternoons.

2. Live-in staff members should be able to have three meals a day, and other staff members have the option of eating one meal per day at a nominal fee.

VIII. TRAINING AND EDUCATION

A. Within the Extended Care Facility

1. Departmental Meetings. The extended care facility periodically should hold staff training sessions for the Dietary Department for the purpose of presenting and exploring new methods in food preparation and distribution, and maintenance of equipment and sanitation.

2. Reference Shelf. Written material on food service should be maintained in the staff room.

3. Publications. The dietitian and dietary director should use a diet manual and should review professional journals for suggestions on food preparation and service.

B. Outside the Extended Care Facility

1. Courses. The food-service manager and/or the dietary director should take special courses by mail or in person and should attend seminars or meetings to broaden knowledge in the field of nutrition and food service as well as leadership skills.

2. Professional Societies

- *a.* The consulting dietitian should be a member of the American Dietetic Association.
- *b.* The food-service manager and/or the dietary director should be a member of the American Society for Hospital Food Service Administration.

Section 8

Housekeeping

Introduction

In a health care facility, the quality of the Housekeeping Department cannot be measured only by the esthetic appearance of the building, equipment, furniture, and linens, for in a larger sense the quality of housekeeping is reflected in patient health and well-being. The Housekeeping Department should strive to maintain safe, sanitary, orderly, and pleasant surroundings, essential to the proper care and welfare of patients, and to effect this in an efficient and economical manner.

The laundry, in an institution of 100 beds or less, should be the responsibility of the Housekeeping Department. During the rehabilitation process at the extended care facility, patients should be encouraged to dress in street clothes in contrast to the sleepwear customarily worn by patients in the general hospital and, thus, there should be provision for caring for patients' personal laundry in addition to the operation of the usual institutional laundry service.

Other functions of the Housekeeping Department in the extended care institution should include the regulation of noise, the control of the use of heat and electric illumination, the furthering of safety by the diligent reporting of potentially dangerous conditions, and the ability to work harmoniously within the department and with other members of the staff in all departments.

I. STAFFING PATTERN

A. Recruitment. Recruiting, engaging, and terminating the employment of the housekeeping staff should be the responsibility of the executive housekeeper in accordance with the staffing pattern established in conjunction with the administrative director.

B. Staff Complement. The staff complement of a 65-bed institution, depending upon the square footage, finishes, building design, and amount of laundry to be done, usually should be composed of an executive housekeeper, a consultant interior designer, two porters, a relief porter, two maids, and a relief maid.

C. Work Schedule. In a small facility with only five or six on staff, it is helpful to develop a standardized plan and to distribute staff time in the following manner to allow for a more flexible schedule:

1. The maids should work 5 days a week with one on duty from 7:00 A.M. to 3:00 P.M. and the second from 7:30 A.M. to 3:30 P.M.
2. The porters should work a 5-day week, with one on duty from 8:00 A.M. to 4:00 P.M. and the second beginning at 8:30 A.M. and concluding at 4:30 P.M., half an hour mealtime for maids and porters.

D. Orientation. At the first interview, the executive housekeeper should stipulate the rules of conduct and personal hygiene expected of new personnel outlining the duties and giving the new staff member a daily work schedule and a personnel handbook along with the following reminders:

1. The significance of the Housekeeping Department to the morale of patients, staff, families, and visitors should be described in detail, as the quality and importance of effective housekeeping cannot be overemphasized.
2. Although scheduling is important, it is imperative that the Housekeeping Department respond immediately to emergency cleaning situations.
3. Consistency of housekeeping is often the measure of the quality of the extended care facility to patients, personnel, and visitors.

E. Uniforms. The advisability of providing uniforms for members of the housekeeping staff should be determined by administration, but maids should wear white or pastel uniforms with white shoes, and porters washable khaki trousers and white shirts.

II. RECORDS

A. Time Card. Monthly time cards should be maintained for members of the housekeeping staff and should show a daily record of the time signed in and the time signed out.

B. Weekly Time Schedule. A weekly time schedule for the Housekeeping Department, possibly together with the Dietary Department, should be posted on the bulletin board of the staff room and should be kept for 6 months in a loose-leaf notebook in the administrative offices.

C. Laundry Count List. Should a linen rental service be retained, a count of outgoing laundry by the linen rental company should be maintained in a list on the laundry room bulletin board, and incoming clean laundry checked against this list.

D. Housekeeping Supply Inventory. An inventory for all housekeeping supplies, listing each item used, category, amount in stock, supplier, and price information, should be employed.

III. DUTIES AND PROCEDURES

A. Executive Housekeeper

1. Regular Duties

a. Supervision of staff. Careful and frequent supervision is particularly important in the Housekeeping Department where the maids and porters generally work alone in various parts of the building in contrast to dietary and nursing personnel, who work together in special areas.

(1) The maids and porters should be checked on the neatness of their personal appearance and the condition and suitability of their equipment.

(2) They should be instructed to begin their daily work on schedule but without interfering with the patients' breakfasts, dressing, or care.

(3) The staff should be alerted to any special job that is to be done.

b. Inspection. The building should be toured and surveyed at least twice a day:

(1) Checking all exit lights (Fig. 8-1)

(2) Inspecting refrigerators in pantries

(3) Noting the sanitary condition of the wet mops and cleaning cloths in the housekeeping closets

(4) Inspecting elevator for cleanliness, particularly after meal periods

(5) Scrutinizing outside porches for cleanliness and orderliness

(6) Examining the interiors of garbage pails for tidiness and the use of plastic liners

(7) Verifying the supply of toilet paper and paper towels in the visitors' and staff lavatories

(8) Checking the cleanliness of air vents

(9) Ascertaining that all storage areas and housekeeping closets are in order and locked

(10) Checking incinerator room

(11) Scrutinizing all linen to detect damages

Fig. 8-1. Exit lights must be checked twice daily by the housekeeper.

c. Laundry. In an extended care facility of 65 beds where a linen rental service is used and no ironing is required, the maids on the housekeeping staff should be able to handle the patients' personal laundry and the other linen requiring washing by working together as a team.

(1) General procedure. On a semiweekly pickup and delivery basis, sheets, pillowcases, and bath towels may be rented from a commercial laundry with one-third of the linens used per day to be laundered on the premises ready for emergencies during day or night; blankets, bath blankets, bedspreads, and facecloths should be owned by the facility and laundered on the premises, and patients' personal laundry not requiring ironing should be done on the premises, to avoid accumulation of soiled and odoriferous clothing.

(2) Sorting and checking. The executive housekeeper should count out the linens for the rental service, placing aside damaged linens for replacement, and a careful record of all outgoing soiled linens and all incoming clean linens should be maintained. (Soiled and clean linen should be handled in separate areas.)

(3) Apportioning of linens. The housekeeper should determine that a proper amount of bed and bath linens is distributed to the nursing units during the day, particularly ensuring an ample supply for use during the night.

(4) Care of patients' personal laundry. When a new patient is admitted, the executive housekeeper should check his clothing to determine that the patient's name is written clearly in indelible ink, and she should supervise the washing and distribution of patients' personal clothing twice daily (Fig. 8-2).

Fig. 8-2. Patients' personal laundry is sorted into individual baskets for easy distribution.

(5) Contaminated laundry should receive separate and special handling.

d. Outside services. The executive housekeeper should supervise the outside services, including garbage pickup, extermination, linen rental, and window cleaning.

e. Flowers. She regularly arranges cut flowers brought in by visitors and should discard all dead flowers.

f. Illumination and heat control. She should be responsible for a continuing program of controlling the use of unnecessary artificial illumination and heat.

g. Noise control. She should plan departmental activities in such a way to minimize excessive noise at times inappropriate for the program of patient care.

h. Planning. The schedule of the Housekeeping Department should be planned in accordance with patient activities such as mealtime, bathing, and recreation.

i. Lockers. Lockers should be assigned by the housekeeper to all new personnel.

2. Typical Daily Schedule

8:00 A.M. She should report to work. Maids and porters should be checked on their daily routine.

8:55 A.M. She should examine and, if necessary, clean lint trap in the clothes dryer.

9:00 A.M. and at intervals throughout the morning. She should note soiled linens and patients' personal laundry brought by maids to the laundry room and should sort, count, and put aside laundry to be picked up and done outside.

10:00 A.M. She should verify cleanliness of all pantry refrigerators. During A.M. The entire building should be toured to determine that the maids and porters are on schedule, checking exit lights, paper towels, and toilet paper in staff and visitors' bathrooms, housekeeping closets, outside porches, garbage pails, and air vents.

12:00 noon. The washed, folded patients' personal laundry should be placed in the appropriate drawers and closets of the patient bedrooms by the housekeeper.

1:00 P.M. She should eat her dinner.

1:30–2:00 P.M. She should care for the patients' cut flowers and the plants scattered throughout the building.

3:00 P.M. She should assist with laundering if needed and should distribute extra folded linens to patient units to be stored in the linen closets for emergency use.

4:00 P.M. The schedule for the following day should be planned, the recreation director should be assisted in tidying the recreation room, and the storage areas and incinerator room should be checked.

4:30 P.M. She should sign out for the day.

3. Weekly Schedule (in addition to regular daily work)
Monday: In the absence of visitors, Monday should be devoted to extensive cleaning.

a. The tidiness of the storage room should be noted.
b. Supplies should be checked and orders for the week placed with the purchasing agent, including all cleaning supplies, paper goods, and laundry supplies.
c. The maids should be directed in washing and disinfecting patient room closets and in thorough cleaning of patients' rooms and bathrooms.
d. The thorough cleaning of the floors in the patient rooms by the porters should be supervised.

Tuesday: She should count the laundry delivered in the clean laundry area and the laundry taken out by the commercial laundry in the soiled linen area. Clean linens should be stored in the linen room.
Wednesday: She should take this day off.
Thursday: She should check the removal of fingermarks from the walls, mirrors, woodwork, and elevator.
Friday:

a. She should count the laundry brought in and taken out by the linen rental company.
b. A careful pre-weekend inspection of the building and of all supplies should be made.

Saturday and Sunday: In lieu of taking one full day off on weekends, it is suggested that the executive housekeeper work 4 hr on each day.

a. The cleaning, laundry, and exit lights should be checked.
b. In consultation with the food-service manager, the weekly housekeeping and dietary schedule should be prepared and posted on the bulletin board of the staff room.
c. The recreation room should be prepared for the Protestant services in the absence of the director of recreation.

4. Special Work. The executive housekeeper should be responsible for all work done in her department, and certain monthly and periodic duties performed by her staff or outside help require her assistance and/or supervision.

a. Monthly duties

(1) Floors: Once a month, under the executive housekeeper's supervision, all resilient floors should be lightly finished and buffed by porters, and all carpets should be dry-shampooed.

(2) Exterminating: On his regular visits the exterminator should be accompanied by the executive housekeeper in his rounds.

(3) Windows: The executive housekeeper should arrange for and should oversee the work of the window washer once a month.

b. Periodic work

(1) Lights: The executive housekeeper should direct the thorough cleaning of all electrical fixtures twice a year with ammonia, soap, and water, and the cleaning of the piping by the porters at the same time.

(2) Curtain laundering: All window curtains of synthetic fiber should be laundered by the Housekeeping Department twice a year, with the exception of cubicle, shower, kitchen, and dining area curtains, which require more frequent laundering.

(3) Window screens: The window screens should be removed and washed by the contract window-washing service quarterly, or more frequently should the housekeeper deem it appropriate.

(4) Heat ducts: The heat ducts on all floors should be cleaned by the porters every 4 months under the supervision of the housekeeper.

(5) Floors: At least once a year, resilient floors should be stripped of all finish and should be dried, refinished, and buffed for a permanent finish; with daily cleaning and monthly finishing, the resilient floors should remain attractive looking.

(6) Periodic inspection: Periodically the executive housekeeper should inspect the upholstery, blankets, pillows, bedspreads, curtains, mattresses, wastebaskets, and all furnishings and should consult with the administrative director to reorder these items when necessary. (See Part IV.)

(7) All plants should be hosed or sprayed and repotted when necessary.

B. Maid in Concentrated Care Unit

1. Regular Duties

a. Cleaning

(1) Equipment needed: The following items should be assembled on a cleaning cart: a plastic bag for emptying wastebaskets, clean lintless dusting cloths, rags, creme cleaner (a liquid containing disinfectant) for all porcelain, tile, enamel, and

metal surfaces, and for woodwork, Formica tables, and bureau tops; odorless disinfectant germicide for bathrooms, chairs, lavatories, and certain utensils used for patients' care; glass cleaner spray for mirrors, glass doors, and all glass surfaces; wet mop and plastic pail; stainless steel polish for chrome and steel; a Johnny mop; a sponge.

(2) General rooms: Early in the morning the general rooms such as the conference and recreation rooms should be cleaned, going over all table tops, counters, chairs, and other furnishings; emptying and cleaning out ashtrays; the visitors' lavatory and the nurses' lavatory should be cleaned, replenishing needed supplies. By early afternoon the fingermarks on the woodwork and the glass doors should be removed, and the pantry and utility rooms should be thoroughly scoured.

(3) Patients' rooms: The cleaning of patients' rooms should not begin until patients have been dressed and have left their rooms. In the morning the mirrors should be cleaned; table and bureau tops, all lights, window sills, tops and bottoms of beds should be dusted; bedroom sinks should be scrubbed; patients' bathrooms should be cleaned and disinfected. In the afternoon the maid should return to patients' rooms to clean tables and to remove any spots left from spillages of the noontime meal; the furniture should be lightly polished, the bathrooms rechecked, and toilet paper, towels, and soap replenished. The patients' rooms should be examined to see that all is in order for the evening before the maid goes off duty.

b. Wastebaskets. All wastebaskets on her assigned floor should be emptied every morning into a large plastic bag attached to the maid's cart, which should be transported to the incinerator room for the contents to be burned by the porters.

c. Laundry. The following procedure should be observed by the maid:

(1) Collecting: About six times a day all soiled linens on her assigned unit should be collected and taken to the dirty-linen room to be sorted.

(2) Laundering process: After the sorting, the soiled items should be placed in the washing machine, following the instructions for the particular machine, and then loaded into the dryer, cleaning out the lint trap before each use.

(3) Folding: Assisted by the other maid, she should fold the patients' personal laundry in early afternoon on a table in the clean-linen room; the linens folded later in the afternoon, for the executive housekeeper to deliver to the patient units.

d. Care of equipment. The cleaning cloths and rags should be washed, and all equipment returned to the housekeeping areas at end of her day.

2. Typical Daily Schedule

7:00 A.M. She should report to work. The soiled linens and patients' personal laundry should be collected, and the laundry process begun.

7:45 A.M. The wastebaskets should be emptied and new liners inserted.

8:00 A.M. The daily cleaning routine should be started; the conference room and recreation room should be tidied.

8:30 A.M. The visitors' lavatories should be scoured and supplies replenished.

8:45 A.M. The nurses' utility areas and lavatory should be cleaned and supplies restocked.

9:00 A.M. The patients' rooms should be given the morning cleaning.

11:30 A.M. She should eat dinner.

12:00 noon. Assisted by the other maid, the patients' personal laundry should be folded, sorted, and distributed.

1:00 P.M. The patients' rooms should be rechecked after the noontime meal, the furniture should be polished, the bathroom supplies should be checked, and the pantry and utility rooms should be thoroughly cleaned.

1:30 P.M. The fingermarks on the woodwork and on the glass doors should be removed.

2:00 P.M. Assisted by the other maid, clean linens for executive housekeeper to deliver upstairs should be folded.

2:30 P.M. The cleaning cloths and rags should be washed, equipment should be put away, the patients' bedrooms and bathrooms should be given the final survey of the day.

3:00 P.M. She should sign out.

3. Weekly Schedule (in addition to regular daily work)

Monday:

a. Patients' bedrooms should be cleaned thoroughly.

b. Bathrooms should be scrubbed and bowl cleaner used in the toilets.

c. Everything should be removed from the clothes closets; the floors and shelves should be washed, disinfected, and dried, and all clothing rehung and all articles replaced on shelves.

Tuesday:

a. Tile walls of bathing areas should be washed down.

b. Fingermarks on woodwork and walls should be removed.

c. All mirrors, bed lights, and lights over sinks in bathroom should be polished or washed.

Wednesday: Routine work.

Thursday: Off duty.

Friday:

a. Fingermarks should be removed from the woodwork and walls.

b. Mirrors and glass doors should be cleaned.

c. Everything should be in order for the weekend.

Saturday and Sunday: One week, the maid should be off duty on Saturday and should work on Sunday, the schedule being reversed the following weekend.

4. Periodic Work: Upon notification from the Nursing Department of the discharge of a patient, the maid should give terminal disinfecting to the room and bath formerly occupied by the discharged patient.

C. Maid for the Skilled Nursing Care Unit

1. Regular Duties

a. Cleaning

(1) Equipment needed: The same items of equipment and supplies previously enumerated for the maid in the concentrated care area should be made available on a housekeeping cart.

(2) Community rooms: The community dining areas should be cleaned twice daily and then again after dinner, the tables and chairs being washed with an odorless disinfectant germicide mixed with water.

(3) Service areas: The floor pantry, utility rooms, and nurses' lavatory should be kept immaculate and stocked with appropriate supplies.

(4) Patients' rooms: During the breakfast period when patients are out of their bedrooms in the community rooms, the maid should begin to clean the bedrooms and bathrooms, cleaning mirrors and dusting table and bureau tops, lights, window sills, tops and bottoms of beds, cleaning bedroom sinks, cleaning and disinfecting patients' bathrooms. In the afternoon furniture should be lightly polished, rooms straightened, bathrooms checked, and toilet paper, towels, and soap replenished. Once

again before leaving, patients' rooms and bathrooms should be rechecked to see that all is in order for the evening.

(5) Medical director's offices: The medical offices, including the x-ray, laboratory, dark room, examining room, dental treatment room, lavatories, and medical secretary's office, should be cleaned daily, dusting and polishing furniture and scrubbing.

b. Wastebaskets. All wastebaskets should be emptied every morning, following the same procedure previously outlined for the maid in the concentrated care area.

c. Laundry. The laundry procedure for this maid should be as follows:

(1) All soiled linens and patients' personal laundry to be collected in separate hampers and taken to the laundry room

(2) Items from the Medical and Physical Therapy Departments to be taken to the laundry

(3) The patients' personal laundry to be folded early in the afternoon and the linens later in afternoon

d. Care of equipment. The cleaning cloths and rags should be thoroughly washed and all equipment placed in housekeeping closet at the end of her day.

2. Typical Daily Schedule

7:30 A.M. She should report to work. Soiled linens, patients' personal laundry, and medical and physical therapy dirty linens should be gathered, and the laundry process should begin.

8:00 A.M. The wastebaskets in patient and medical areas should be emptied and relined.

8:15 A.M. The medical area should be cleaned.

8:30 A.M. The cleaning of patient bedrooms and bathrooms should be started.

10:30 A.M. The community rooms should be cleaned and straightened.

11:15 A.M. The pantry and utility areas should be deterged.

11:30 A.M. Dinner should be eaten.

12:00 noon. More soiled laundry should be collected and washed.

12:30 P.M. The patients' personal laundry should be folded, sorted, and distributed.

1:15 P.M. The dining tables and chairs should be washed.

1:30 P.M. The bedroom furniture should be polished.

2:00 P.M. Assisted by the other maid, the clean linens for the executive housekeeper to deliver to the patient floors should be folded.

2:30 P.M. The patients' bedrooms and bathrooms should be visited for a final check; soiled clothing should be collected and taken to the laundry room.

3:00 P.M. The balance of the laundry should be transported to the laundry room.

3:15 P.M. The cleaning cloths and rags should be washed, and the equipment stored for the night.

3:30 P.M. She should sign out for the day.

3. Weekly Schedule (in addition to regular daily work). The same weekly schedule should be followed by the maid in this unit as in the concentrated care area except that the days off should be different for both maids.

4. Periodic Work. This too should parallel the periodic work of the other maid.

D. Relief Maid. The relief maid should relieve the other two maids on their 4 days off, and on her fifth working day she should be assigned to thoroughly clean the medical and dental area and to wash window and cubicle curtains on a continuous schedule.

E. Porter 1

1. Regular Duties. This porter should be responsible for the care of all floors in one unit of the building, including the recreation room, conference room, front entrance, patients' bedrooms, corridors, bathing area, pantry and utility rooms, certain specified stairwells, and the front steps and porches, regardless of the composition of the flooring or floor covering, and he should always be available for emergency cleanups throughout his assigned unit.

2. Daily Floor Care. The following articles are required for daily floor care: germicidal detergent, a set of pails for washing floors, a vacuum cleaner, a cotton dry mop, a nylon wet mop, clean sponges and rags, and a wet floor sign.

a. Cleaning

(1) Early in the day the large recreation room should be dry-mopped, using a washable cotton dust mop that has been pretreated with a spray to absorb dust.

(2) Then the vacuum cleaner should be used to pick up excess dirt.

(3) Next, a nylon wet mop should be used to wash the floor, and for the first washing ¼ cup of neutral germicidal detergent should be mixed with 2 gal of warm water, and a second pailful of clear, lukewarm water should then be used with a clean, wet mop (the mop should be just damp wet, as too much water spoils the finish).

(4) The same procedure should be followed for the front entrance floor and the front corridor.

(5) The front steps and porches should be swept, the conference room should be dust-mopped and washed, and the carpet vacuumed.

(6) After patients in the concentrated care unit have had their breakfast and the beds have been made, the porter should dry-mop all bedrooms.

(7) After vacuuming excess dust, each bedroom should be wet-mopped.

(8) The floors of staff locker rooms, the corridors, and lavatories in the basement should be wet-mopped.

(9) The staff dining room should be dry- and wet-mopped.

(10) All corridors in the concentrated-care area should be dry- and wet-mopped, half the width at one time to permit safe passage, with signs used to indicate wet floors.

(11) The bathing area floor should be scrubbed daily.

3. Weekly Floor Care

a. Special equipment needed. The following equipment should be available for weekly floor care: a buffing machine with light-duty pads for polishing, a cotton wet mop for washing porches and stairwells, and a strap-on vacuum or push broom for sweeping same.

b. Thorough cleaning. Once weekly all furniture in patients' bedrooms should be moved so the porter may wet-mop each room, taking care to clean and mop all corners and moldings.

c. Buffing. The floors should be buffed, using the buffing machine for rooms on one side of corridor one day, and the other side of corridor the next day. He buffs the floors of the corridors, entrance hall, and large recreation room on another day with light-duty pads used for these weekly buffing jobs.

d. Porches. The porches should be swept with a push broom, and when needed, washed with the cotton wet mop used for outside areas.

e. Stairwell. Three times a week the stairwell should be swept or vacuumed and washed with a cotton wet mop.

4. Monthly Floor Care

a. Special equipment needed. For this task applications, finish, and heavy-duty buffing pads are required.

b. Procedure. Once a month a small amount of finish should be applied to all resilient floors in this unit; the buffing machine should be used, with a heavy-duty buffing pad added to its brush to clean the floor and lightly finish at the same time; a light-duty buffing pad would be attached to the brush and the floors polished.

5. Yearly Floor Care. If floors are kept clean daily and lightly finished monthly, a stripping job need be done only annually.

a. Special equipment needed. Finish remover, disinfectant solution, floor sealer liquid, sponge, finish.

b. Floor stripping. All finish and scuff marks should be removed with a disinfectant solution mixed with water, then rinsed thoroughly; and after floors are perfectly dry, a coat of floor sealer should be applied with a sponge and permitted to dry, and a thin coat of finish should be spread on with the buffer and polished for a permanent finish.

6. Other Daily Jobs

a. Equipment needed. Sponges for sinks, Johnny mops for toilet bowls, plastic bag for emptying trash.

b. Trash. The porter daily should empty and clean the large trash can in the dirty utility room as well as the sand urns placed in selected areas in his assigned unit.

c. Lavatories. The lavatories in the men's and women's locker rooms and visitors' lavatory in basement should be cleaned, using a sponge with creme cleaner to wash out the sinks and a Johnny mop for the toilet bowls.

d. Care of equipment. At the end of each day's work, the porter should wash out the mops, pails, sponges, and rags, and return everything to the proper closet.

7. Typical Daily Schedule

8:00 A.M. He should report to work.

8:05 A.M. The trash and sand urn receptacles should be emptied.

8:20 A.M. He should dry- and wet-mop the recreation and conference room floors and should vacuum the rug.

8:40 A.M. The front steps, front entrance, and porches should be swept, and the entrance and porches wet-mopped, if needed.

9:00 A.M. The front corridor should be dry- and wet-mopped.

9:15 A.M. He should dry- and wet-mop the floors of the patients' bedrooms.

11:30 A.M. He should eat dinner.

12:00 noon. He should dry- and wet-mop the floor of the staff dining room and should clean the basement locker rooms, the visitors' lavatory, and the basement corridors.

1:30 P.M. The corridors in the concentrated care unit should be dry- and wet-mopped.

2:30 P.M. The bathing area floor and pantry should be scrubbed.

3:00 P.M. The patients' rooms should be surveyed for spillage; after patients and visitors have left, the recreation room and lobby should be rechecked; all equipment should be washed and put away.

4:00 P.M. He should sign out for the day.

8. Weekly Schedule (in addition to regular daily work)
Monday: The furniture in patients' rooms should be moved and the floors thoroughly cleaned; the porches should be scrubbed.
Tuesday: Half of the patients' rooms in the unit should be buffed.
Wednesday: Off duty.
Thursday: The balance of patients' rooms in the unit should be buffed.
Friday: Corridors and recreation room floors should be buffed.
Saturday and Sunday: Corridors and recreation room floors should be buffed. One week this porter should be free on Saturday and on duty on Sunday; the following week, the process should be reversed with the second porter; all offices not in use should be cleaned and buffed; he should assist in preparing the recreation room for the services and should straighten the recreation room later in the afternoon.
Tuesday and Friday: All resilient floors in the basement should be lightly finished and buffed.
Monday, Wednesday, and Friday: The stairwell should be vacuumed and wet-mopped.

9. Periodic Work

a. Exit lights. All exit lights in this unit should be replaced by the porter under the supervision of the housekeeper.

b. Minor repairs. When necessary, the porter should make minor repairs, such as fixing broken toilet-paper holders in lavatories or attaching side rails to patients' beds (major repairs should be made by the head of the Maintenance Department, sometimes with the help of the porters).

c. Wall washing. Yearly all walls in the unit should be washed down.

d. Snow removal. In the wintertime, the porter in this unit should remove ice and snow from the front steps and the front walk.

F. Porter 2

1. Regular Duties. This porter should be responsible for the care of all floors in the skilled nursing care unit of the building, including the community rooms, patients' bedrooms, corridors, bathing areas, and the medical director's offices, specified stairwells, and porches contiguous to this unit, and should be available for emergency floor cleanups throughout his tour of duty.

2. Daily Floor Care

a. Equipment needed. The same equipment will be needed as indicated for porter 1, including germicidal detergent, a pail, a vacuum, a cotton dry mop, a nylon wet mop, clean sponges, a wet floor sign, rags, and a carpet shampoo machine.

b. Cleaning

(1) The floors of patients' bedrooms should be vacuumed and spot cleaned (if carpeted) or dry-mopped while the patients are breakfasting in community dining rooms.

(2) Carpeted corridors and community rooms should be vacuumed and spot cleaned or resilient floors dry-mopped, using the same procedure previously described, and subsequently vacuumed and wet-mopped.

(3) The pantry, utility, and bathing area floors should be scrubbed daily.

3. Weekly Floor Care

a. Special equipment needed. A buffing machine with light-duty pads for polishing, a cotton wet mop for washing porches and stairwells, and a push broom for sweeping same should be used.

b. Thorough cleaning. Once a week all furniture in patients' bedrooms should be moved for thorough vacuuming (if carpeted) or wet-mopping of each room, taking care to clean all corners and moldings.

c. Buffing. The daily dusting and wet-mopping of the floors should be supplemented with buffing, using the buffing machine for rooms on one side of corridor one day, the other side of corridor the next day. On another day the floors of the two north community rooms plus the medical director's offices should be buffed, and on still another day, the corridors and other community rooms should be buffed with light-duty pads used for these weekly buffing jobs.

d. Porches. Once weekly the porches next to this unit should be cleaned and the floors swept with a push broom, and outside areas only washed with the cotton wet mop.

e. Stairwell. Three times a week the porter should vacuum or sweep, and wet-mop, his assigned stairwells.

4. Monthly and Interim Floor Care

a. Special equipment needed. Carpet shampoo machine with proper detergent or floor finish and heavy-duty buffing pads for polishing resilient floors.

b. Process. Every 4 to 6 months or more often if necessary, all carpeted patient areas should be shampooed, and every month all resilient floors in this unit should be lightly finished, buffed, and polished.

5. Yearly Floor Care. All resilient floors in this unit should be stripped according to the previously described method for porter 1.

6. Other Daily Jobs

a. Trash

(1) The large trash cans in the utility rooms and the sand urns should be emptied and cleaned.

(2) All trash collected by the maids and other porter should be brought to the incinerator room, including newspapers, paper napkins, cups, cleansing tissues, milk cartons, and general debris, to be burned.

(3) Porter 2 should keep the incinerator room tidy and clean.

b. Care of equipment. At end of each day's work the porter should wash out the mops, pails, sponges, and rags, and should place everything in the proper closet.

7. Typical Daily Schedule

8:30 A.M. He should report to work.

8:35 A.M. He should empty and burn trash.

9:00 A.M. He should vacuum and spot clean (if carpeted) or dry- and wet-mop corridors and floors of patients' rooms.

11:30 A.M. He should have dinner.

12:00 noon. Floors of the bathing area, pantry, and utility rooms should be scrubbed.

1:30 P.M. Community room floors should be vacuumed or wet-mopped.

2:30 P.M. The patients' rooms should be rechecked for spillage and cleaned when needed.

3:50 P.M. He should clean lint trap of the clothes dryer.

4:00 P.M. He should tidy the recreation areas after patients and visitors have departed.

4:15 P.M. He should wash and clean his equipment before putting it away.

4:30 P.M. He should sign out.

8. Weekly Schedule (in addition to regular daily work)
Monday: He should hose area after the garbage pick-up; the furniture in patients' rooms should be moved in order to give the floors a thorough cleaning; the porches should be thoroughly cleaned.
Tuesday: Porter is off duty.
Wednesday: He should hose area after the garbage pick-up; when resilient floors are used, the floors of patients' rooms should be buffed.
Thusday: When resilient floors are used, the public rooms in this unit should be buffed.
Friday: He should hose the area after the garbage pick-up; the balance of the resilient floors in this unit should be buffed; he should assist the housekeeper with cleaning and storage of articles in the housekeeping and laundry areas.
Saturday and Sunday: These days off should be alternated with the other porter; offices not in use should be wet-mopped or the carpet shampooed when indicated.

9. Periodic Jobs

a. Curtains. The porter should help the executive housekeeper rehang cubicle and window curtains throughout the building after they have been laundered.

b. Exit lights. The bulbs in exit lights should be replaced by the porter.

c. Repairs. The porter should effect minor repairs, such as fixing broken toilet-paper holders, attaching rails onto patients' beds, etc. (Major repairs should be made by the head of the Maintenance Department, sometimes with the help of the porter.)

d. Heat ducts. Every 4 months the porter should clean all heat ducts.

e. Wall washing. Annually all walls of the unit should be washed down.

f. Light fixtures. Twice a year all fixtures in the building should be taken down and, with the help of the executive housekeeper, cleaned with ammonia, detergent, and water; the tops of the overhead pipes should be cleaned and the fixtures replaced.

G. Relief Porter. The relief porter should fill in on the 4 days that the two porters are off duty and on the fifth day should be available for special housekeeping projects as directed by the housekeeper.

H. Interior Designer. The services of a consulting interior designer should be used when furnishings are to be selected and when environmental changes are contemplated.

IV. FURNISHINGS, EQUIPMENT, AND SUPPLIES

The executive housekeeper should be responsible for the proper and economical use and maintenance of all furnishings, equipment, and supplies described in this section, and all necessary replacements should be requisitioned by the executive housekeeper. Major purchases first should be approved by the administrative director, and needed repairs brought to the attention of the maintenance director in writing.

A. Control Record. A control record listing all furniture and equipment, the date of the purchase, source, and cost should be retained by administration and be available for reference by the housekeeper.

B. Furnishings. Furnishings should be listed in the control record according to manufacturer, catalog number, and any other identifying material as used in the following areas: recreation and community and dining rooms, patient bedrooms, nurses' stations, staff rooms, terraces and garden, medical, social service, recreation, business, and administrative offices, x-ray and laboratory, treatment and examining rooms.

C. Linens and Curtains. The following quantities of bed and bath linens and curtains are suggested for a 65-bed extended care facility:

1. 600 bed sheets
2. 72 cotton flannel sheets
3. 450 pillowcases (allowing for the use of 2 pillows by a large proportion of patients)
4. 150 blankets
5. 100 bedspreads
6. 350 towels
7. 500 washcloths
8. 12 spare cubicle curtains
9. 12 pairs of additional window curtains
10. 3 extra shower curtains

D. Equipment. The following stock of equipment and supplies is indicated to implement an effective housekeeping program in a 65-bed extended care facility:

1. Housekeeping
2 vacuum cleaners
1 strap-on vacuum

1 floor polishing machine and parts
1 carpet shampoo machine
4 ladders of various sizes
3 push brooms
2 regular brooms
4 galvanized pails on wheels
4 wringers
3 dustpans and brushes
1 sand strainer
3 floor knife scrapers
6 wastebaskets
6 mattresses
1 mattress carrier
carpet runners for all entrances
1 carpet sweeper
3 wet-floor signs

2. Laundry

2 12-lb washing machines
1 25-lb dryer
1 large table for folding laundry
6 receptacles for soiled linen with foot-operated cover
2 clean laundry carts
A plastic container on wheels for the soap powder

E. Supplies. All housekeeping, cleaning, and laundry supplies and materials should be requisitioned by the executive housekeeper and ordered by the purchasing agent.

1. Housekeeping

Item	*Reorder Point*	*Reorder Quantity*
Blankets	12	24
Bedspreads	6	12
Sheets—72 in.	Rented	Rented
Sheets—54 in.	Rented	Rented
Pillowcases	Rented	Rented
Pillows	6	12
Washcloths	5 doz	10 doz
Towels	Rented	Rented
Flannel bath sheets	3 doz	6 doz
Wet mops	4	6
Dry mops	4	1 doz
Heavy-duty stripping pads	1 case of 3	1 case of 3
Buffing pads	6	1 case of 10
Filters for vacuum cleaner	½ case of 24	1 case of 24
Germicidal floor solution	2 gal	5-gal can

Stripper	2 gal	5-gal can
Floor sealer	1 gal	5-gal can
Floor finish	½ gal	5-gal can
Mop dressing	1 gal	5-gal can
Floor finish remover	2 pt	6 pt
Chair brushes	2	12
Furniture polish	1 qt	3 1-qt
Sponges	4	1 case of 12
Creme cleaner	3 qt	1 case of 24 qt
Disinfectant	3 qt	1 case of 24 qt
Glass wax	3 tins	1 case of 24 tins
Cleanser powder	4 tins	1 case of 24 tins
Toilet bowl cleaner	4 qt	1 case of 24 qt
Steel wool pads	1 bolt	1 case 6 bolts
Metal polish	2-qt tin	1 case 12 tins
Ammonia	3-qt bottles	1 case 24 qt
Johnny mops	3	6
Carpet cleaner	1 gal	6-gal can
Ashtrays	6	2 doz
Hand soap (bars)	¼ case	5 cases
Liquid soap	3 qt	1 case of 24 qt

2. Laundry

Item	*Reorder Point*	*Reorder Quantity*
Laundry powder	1 100-lb bag	8 100-lb bags
Bleach	(3) ½-gal jars	1 case (6) ½ gal

3. Kitchen (may be requisitioned from Housekeeping or ordered by Dietary)

Item	*Reorder Point*	*Reorder Quantity*
Soap powder for dishwasher	1 100-lb drum	2 100-lb drums
Steel wool pads	3 pkg of 12	6 pkg of 12
Kitchen pot brushes	4	1 pkg of 12
Pot-washing solution	1 gal	1 case of 4 gal
Rinse solution for dishwasher	¼ case	1 case of 24 bottles

4. Paper and Other Plastic Items

Item	*Reorder Point*	*Reorder Quantity*
Toilet tissue	¼ case	1 case
Bathroom and kitchen dispenser towels	¼ case	1 case
Plastic wastebasket liners	¼ case	1 case 500 bags
Plastic garbage liners	¼ case	1 case 250 bags

V. OUTSIDE SERVICES

The supervision of several outside services should be the responsibility of the executive housekeeper, including:

A. Extermination. The exterminating should be done on a monthly basis or as frequently as necessary, and the serviceman should be accompanied by the executive housekeeper to make certain that the entire building has been serviced properly.

B. Garbage Removal. Although city garbage service may be available, the use of a private waste pickup may be tailored according to the needs of the extended care facility, with more frequent visits and the use of a dumpster in place of numerous untidy-looking garbage cans.

C. Linen Rental Service. The following factors should be taken into consideration before a decision is made concerning the installation of an institutional laundry or the development of a contract for a linen rental service:

1. The size of the extended care facility
2. The amount of linen used
3. The number of machines and the amount of space required for their placement
4. The number and cost of staff needed to operate the laundry
5. The other costs such as water, gas, electricity, soap supplies, and the cash outlay required for the machines
6. The cost of stocking and replacing an adequate supply of bed linens and towels, assuming four sets of linen per patient—one in use, one in the laundry, one in stock, and one in reserve
7. The cost of the contract service and the duration of the contract
8. The frequency of regular and emergency deliveries
9. The ability to launder the rented linen on the premises of the extended care facility when necessary
10. The maintenance of quality performance and reliability by the outside service

D. Window Washing. In a Housekeeping Department employing only three porters, the advisability of in-house window cleaning should be questioned, and the use of an experienced outside service should be investigated:

1. The cost of engaging an additional man solely to wash windows would prove to be more than the cost of using a professional window cleaner.
2. The quality of window cleaning can be maintained by careful supervision on the part of the executive housekeeper.
3. The service contract can stipulate certain provisions of performance such as the type of weather conditions under which the window washing may take place, the time of day appropriate for washing

kitchen and patients' bedroom windows, and a provision for washing screens and window trim.

E. Upholstery. A reupholstery plan for all furniture based on a projection of its useful life should be developed utilizing:

1. A local upholsterer on a continuing regular basis, particularly during his slow periods
2. A careful record of the upholstery fabrics used on all furniture in sufficient detail to permit easy ordering of fabrics
3. Consultation with an interior designer when changes are contemplated

VI. ORDERING

A. Vendors. In addition to the original control records, a shelf of catalogues should be maintained for the purpose of reordering:

1. Furnishings
- *a.* Curtains and draperies
- *b.* Bedroom furniture
- *c.* Tables and chairs
- *d.* Rugs and carpets
- *e.* Swivel chairs for nurses' stations
- *f.* Lounge furniture
- *g.* Outdoor furniture
- *h.* Office furniture

2. Equipment and Supplies
- *a.* Bedspreads
- *b.* Blankets
- *c.* Pillows and mattresses
- *d.* Paper goods
- *e.* Carpet runners, large wet and dry mops, waxes, housekeeping cleaning supplies, such as buffing pads, brushes, etc.
- *f.* Small equipment (mops, brooms, pails, waste baskets, brushes, rubber gloves, towel and soap dispensers)
- *g.* Cleaning materials
- *h.* Patients' soap
- *i.* Laundry detergent and bleaches

B. Budget. The complete cost of materials over a 1-year period should be kept within 6 percent of the total cleaning cost. The housekeeping budget, set up by the housekeeper in consultation with the administrative director, should include the purchase of supplies and equipment, the rental of laundry, other contract services, and all salaries.

C. Purchasing. Purchasing should be done in cooperation with the purchasing agent with order forms in triplicate—one color for suppliers; one for the Housekeeping Department; the third attached to invoices, which should be turned over to the business office.

D. Bills. All bills should be received by the business office to be paid monthly, the executive housekeeper verifying delivery invoices before they are turned over to the business office.

E. Inventory. Inventory should be taken on housekeeping supplies every 3 months, items to be replenished as needed.

VII. FACILITIES

A. Storage. The following safe storage areas should be provided for all housekeeping equipment and supplies, accessible to authorized personnel only, precautions being taken for the proper storage of flammable materials:

1. Laundry-Room Closet. This should be used for soaps, bleaches, and other cleaning aids used in the laundry.
2. Clean-Linen Storage Room. This spacious dry area should be provided with:

- *a.* Shelves for clean linens such as sheets, blankets, bedspreads, towels, facecloths, underpads for beds, pillowcases, pillows, and rubber sheets
- *b.* A plastic bag for clean rags
- *c.* Laundry bags for soiled and clean linens
- *d.* Sheepskin pads for patients' use
- *e.* Rubber or plastic mattress protectors

3. Soiled-Linen Storage Area. Soiled linen should be kept in covered receptacles in a well-ventilated room before laundering or linen pick-up.
4. Housekeeping Room. In this room all staple supplies such as scouring pads, steel wool pads, waxes, garbage liners, clean dry and wet mops, pails, buffing machine, vacuum cleaners, carpet shampooer, cases of toilet paper, paper towels, folding chairs, and portable coat racks should be stored.
5. Housekeeping Closets (in each nursing unit). Pails, sponges, mops, a sink, and all items for daily use should be kept here.

B. Housekeeping Office. Adjacent to the housekeeping and laundry areas, a nook should be provided with a desk, chairs, files, and a bulletin board for the housekeeper to use for desk work and to store equipment manuals, inventories, forms, and vendors' telephone numbers.

C. Laundry Room. Besides the washing machines and dryer, this room should contain two sinks and a large table for folding linens, a bulletin board for linen count, messages, instructions for laundering curtains, and patients' names and room numbers for simplifying distribution of clean personal laundry.

VIII. INTERDEPARTMENTAL COOPERATION

A. Nursing Department. The executive housekeeper should cooperate with the charge nurses:

1. By cleaning schedules which are planned so that patients' rooms may be cleaned without interfering with their treatment or activities of daily living
2. By supplying clean linens and caring for patients' personal laundry
3. By laundering sheepskin pads used for patients' beds whenever necessary (Fig. 8-3)
4. By terminal disinfection of patient's room and bath upon notification of discharge

B. Dietary Department. The executive housekeeper should be responsible for the ordering of tablecloths, napkins, and uniforms for male kitchen staff from the linen rental service, and the kitchen cleaning items used should be billed to the Dietary Department.

C. Maintenance Department. The porters are directed by the head of the Maintenance Department:

1. In the cleaning of the incinerator
2. In some minor repair jobs
3. In the annual wall washing

Fig. 8-3

INSTRUCTIONS FOR LAUNDERING SHEEPSKIN PADS

Temperature of water in washing machine must be kept at 90°F, or below, and washing machine set at the slowest cycle; then proceed with a regular *wool wash* routine, which is as follows:

Wash with mild soap and lukewarm water in washing machine. Then place skins in dryer for 5 min, with indicator dial set for *synthetic.*

Take out of dryer and hang in warm room or in sun for an hour. Hand-stretch to natural size during drying process.

4. In the reporting of major repairs in writing
5. In the removal of snow and the spreading of deicer

D. Medical and Physical Therapy Departments. Fresh linens for use in physical therapy, medicine, and dentistry should be supplied by the Housekeeping Department.

E. Recreation and Volunteers Department. Housekeeping should assist the recreation director:

1. By rearranging furniture for special events in the recreation room
2. By straightening and cleaning the room at the conclusion of programs (Fig. 8-4)
3. By providing extra folding chairs and portable coat racks when required for special events

F. Special Events. The executive housekeeper should prepare rooms in cooperation with appropriate department heads for special events by supervising the setting up of chairs and tables, extra clothes racks, etc.

Fig. 8-4. Housekeeping cooperates with Recreation by straightening the room at the conclusion of the program.

IX. TRAINING AND EDUCATION

A. Within the Extended Care Facility

1. Departmental Meeting. Once a month the members of the Housekeeping Department should hold a meeting to discuss any problems that may have arisen and suggestions for improvements.
2. Reference Shelf in Staff Room. *The Manual of Hospital Housekeeping* and housekeeping and laundry periodicals should be kept on this shelf for reference.
3. Interdepartmental Conferences. Once a week the executive housekeeper, along with other department heads, should meet with the administrative director for the purpose of improving services and discussing goals and fresh approaches to realize the objectives.

B. Outside the Extended Care Facility

1. Courses

a. Appropriate courses and seminars on housekeeping and supervision should be attended by members of the Housekeeping Department, including the executive housekeeper.
b. Correspondence courses may be taken by the housekeeper to improve her skills.

2. Memberships. The housekeeper should be encouraged to become a member of the National Executive Housekeepers Association.

Section 9

Maintenance

Introduction

An inpatient care facility must be functional, comfortable, and kept free from hazards day and night, 365 days a year. To keep all major equipment and appliances operating efficiently and economically, an ongoing program of preventive maintenance, interior and exterior, should be instituted. Maintenance should not be a crisis-oriented procedure, but a planned, orderly, continuing process.

In some aspects a small extended care facility presents a greater challenge than larger institutions because more versatility is expected of the lesser number of maintenance staff employed. Irrespective of the size, the complexity of contemporary equipment in an extended care facility necessitates close communication and cooperation among service departments and personnel to maintain all the mechanical aspects of the institution at the maximum level of performance.

Of equal importance is the instruction of staff and the education of patients and visitors in safety measures at all times and emergency procedures to be followed during periods of disaster or other unforeseen events.

I. STAFFING PATTERN

A. Staff Complement. In a 65-bed facility the size of the maintenance staff should be related to the scope and the amount of work to be performed on the premises by the staff and the amount to be completed by outside specialists.

1. With the majority of assignments carried out by the full-time staff, the director of maintenance should be assisted by:

a. Full-time assistant and/or relief maintenance worker

b. Part or full-time grounds man, depending upon the amount of gardening

c. When appropriate, a watchman

d. Porters on a part-time basis, when needed
e. Safety and fire prevention consultant
f. Part-time outside technician for certain emergency and/or highly technical work

2. Should the in-house maintenance program be severely restricted, the director of maintenance should work alone, functioning as a liaison between the institution and the outside technicians for all mechanical repairs, assisted by:
a. Porters on a part-time basis
b. Safety and fire prevention consultant

B. Work Schedule

1. The maintenance director and his relief assistant should work a regular work day, but they should alternate being on 24-hour call for emergency situations.

2. The schedule of the grounds man should be planned according to the specific acreage surrounding the institution and the elaborateness of the gardens.

3. The work assignment of the watchman should reflect the particular security needs of the institution with respect to location, the floor plan, and the availability of local police officers.

C. Uniforms. Maintenance staff should wear washable tan slacks and white shirts.

II. RECORDS

A. A log book, recording all activities and all expenditures, should be kept on a daily basis.

B. A weekly work schedule, a plan of activities for the forthcoming week, should be prepared and followed.

C. "Danger" tags should be used to identify machinery and equipment to be repaired and should be removed upon completion of the repairs.

D. A paint color plan for the entire building, including walls, ceilings, doors, and floors, should be accessible.

E. A listing of all other finishes, together with the brand names of such items as counter tops, acoustic tiles, resilient flooring, carpeting, and ceramic tile, should be available.

F. A schedule of all equipment, the date of purchase, the cost, operating instructions, and upkeep should be prepared for the ready reference of the maintenance director and should be kept current by him.

G. Warranties and guarantees on equipment and machinery should be on file.

H. Service instruction manuals for equipment and machinery should be retained in the maintenance office.

I. A set of the working plans of the structure, both mechanical and structural, should be filed in the maintenance office.

J. A key control list should be kept up to date by the maintenance director.

K. A record of fire drills and safety meetings should be written.

L. The record of inspections notebook and the record of meetings of the safety committee should be the responsibility of the maintenance director, but may be located in the administrative office.

III. DUTIES AND PROCEDURES

A. Scope of Duties. The maintenance director, aided by his relief assistant, should be accountable for:

1. All the mechanical workings of the building including:
- *a.* Boilers
- *b.* Electrical system
- *c.* Plumbing
- *d.* Refrigeration system
- *e.* Communications
- *f.* Atmosphere control
- *g.* Auxiliary machinery

2. Implementing the safety program
3. Distribution of keys
4. Transportation, both vertical and surface
5. Painting
6. Carpentry
7. Water supply
8. Exterior condition of the structure
9. Grounds
10. Security program

B. Regular Duties

1. The Electrical System. The maintenance director should maintain the facility's vital electrical system in condition, checking regularly to verify the working order of the:
- *a.* Electrical service

b. Secondary circuit breakers
c. Emergency generator
d. Heat detection system
e. Fire alarm
f. Sprinkler flow control valves
g. Nurses' call equipment
h. Telephone system
i. Public address system
j. Intercommunication units

2. Auxiliary Machinery. Smooth, dependable operation of all machinery, major equipment, and appliances should be supervised by the maintenance director, including the:

a. Sewage ejection pumps

(1) When used, the pump shafts should be greased at the base zerk fitting quarterly in the absence of a sealed bearing.

(2) The floats and electrical arm switches should be checked daily.

b. Should the shut-off valve for sprinklered areas such as the laundry, linen, incinerator, maintenance, and high-hazard rooms be hand-operated, it should be checked daily to ensure that the valve is turned on and that the sprinkler head is not obstructed.

c. Elevator

(1) The control room and pit should be checked twice daily.

(2) In a hydraulic elevator, the oil level should be inspected daily.

(3) The temperature of the windings and bearings of the motors should be examined daily for undue heat.

(4) The pump packing (of the hydraulic type) should be checked daily for excessive drip-off.

(5) The contacts and wiring in the control cabinet should be scrutinized weekly.

(6) Every week the safety devices, such as the emergency stop switches and the governor, should be tested.

(7) The control mechanism and motors should be inspected every 3 months.

d. The following parts of the dishwasher should be tested weekly:

(1) Spray tubes should be checked and cleaned.

(2) The door counter balance should be checked to ensure that it rides within the slotted track.

(3) The overflow should be noted to determine that there is no blockage.

(4) The automatic timer should be checked.

(5) The solenoid-operated fill valve should be checked to verify

that the diaphragm in the valve is not allowing the water to leak when it is shut off.

(6) The booster heater should be tested for 180°F rinse temperature.

(7) A booster-heater air cushion chamber should be added to prevent blow-off of the safety valve, and the chamber should be checked to determine that there is air in the chamber.

(8) The emersion heater should be tested to ensure that reset light is indicating.

e. Freezers and coolers

(1) All refrigeration units whether water- or air-cooled should be checked daily to ensure proper operating temperatures.

(2) All air-cooled condensers and evaporators should be cleaned monthly.

f. Washers and dryers

(1) The machines should be examined daily to ensure good operating condition.

(2) The air-flow switch and main gas solenoid valve of the dryers should be tested out weekly to ensure proper trip-out when the gas burner is used.

(3) The motor areas of the washers and dryers should be vacuumed out weekly.

(4) The oil level of the dryer transmission should be inspected weekly.

g. Incinerator

(1) The fire box and ash-emission collector should be cleaned daily by the porters.

(2) With a gas-fired burner, the maintenance director should verify that the stack is preheated for 5 min before use.

h. Generator

(1) The generator should be test-operated weekly to ascertain proper functioning of the automatic transfer needed to activate the generator, whether fueled by natural gas, gasoline, or diesel.

(2) The size of the standby plant should be measured by the power requirements needed to supply emergency power to vital functions such as corridor and exit lights, elevators, boiler room, kitchen equipment, and nurses' call system.

(3) The engine generator and control should be serviced according to the manufacturer's instructions.

3. Heat and Hot Water

a. At least two boilers should be provided for each edifice to ensure a continuous supply of heat and hot water during periods of repair or breakdown of one boiler.

b. Various fuels may be used to fire the boilers, including oil, natural gas, coal, and electricity in accordance with preference, local availability, and cost.

(1) In the preponderance of contemporary structures, the preferential fuels are oil and natural gas as electricity for heating begins to emerge more frequently and coal diminishes in importance.

(2) Electrical heating generally requires the least maintenance—periodic vacuuming of the convectors and fin tubes by the maintenance staff and service by the local utility company.

(3) Boilers fired by coal will be of the high-pressure type and must be continuously attended by trained staff.

(4) Boilers fired by oil and natural gas require the same type of maintenance program except that the tubes of oil-fired boilers should be punched quarterly, and the tubes of gas-fired boilers require only annual punching.

c. High-pressure boilers should have continuous attention by staff properly trained and licensed.

d. The proper interior temperature of the building should be maintained at 74 to 76°F, and the thermostats checked in the various zones every morning.

e. Procedure for the daily checking of boilers

(1) The burner nozzle and the flame-view cylinder should be checked for slag.

(2) The boiler pressure should be noted, and, if necessary, the expansion tank should be bled.

(3) The ignition should be checked to safeguard against flareback.

(4) When appropriate, the motor modulator and linkage should be viewed to ensure that the primary and secondary air dampers are operating and that the fuel pump is functioning in the correct range.

(5) The flareback string to the safety switch should be scrutinized on oil-fired units.

(6) The fuel level in the burner-gear housing and circulating water pumps should be investigated weekly.

(7) The fan belts and draft-inducer chain links should be inspected on induced draft systems.

(8) The circulators should be checked to determine that they are running in agreement with the thermostats.

(9) When oil is used as the fuel, the fuel bunker should be inspected to ascertain that sufficient oil is on hand for bunkers.

(10) The hot water recirculating pump should be examined to guarantee 120°F water throughout the building.

f. Procedure for the monthly checking of the boilers

(1) The boiler safety valves should be jacked over to ensure the proper operating condition.
(2) The boiler feed water analysis report should be studied and chemicals induced, if needed, through the boiler blowdown valve with the use of chemical feed pump.
(3) If oil No. 4 grade is used, 1 gal of soot solve should be added to the fuel bunker upon delivery to lessen soot accumulation.
(4) The oil-stainer baskets should be cleaned.

g. Procedure for the quarterly checking of boilers
(1) The tubes should be punched (on oil-burning units): (*a*) The burner and all inlet and outlet valves should be shut down; (*b*) the tube sheet inspection door, the induced draft fan, housing inspection doors, and burner box should be opened; (*c*) a proper-sized cutter and a brush on a motor-driven flex table should be used; (*d*) soot from the tube sheets should be vacuumed at the same time.
(2) While the above work is being done, the refractory should be inspected.
(3) After the tubes have been punched, the boiler should be closed up, and the stack and breeching vacuumed.
(4) Upon completion, the valving should be lined up, and the boiler lighted.

4. Atmospheric Control. In addition to heating, the air within a structure may be cooled, ventilated, humidified or dehumidified, filtered, and circulated centrally or sometimes individually, depending upon the needs of the patients and staff and the climatic conditions prevalent at the location of the extended care facility.

a. Exhaust fans
(1) A daily inspection should be made to ensure proper operation.
(2) Duct grills should be cleaned monthly.
(3) Fans with unsealed bearings should be greased quarterly.

b. Air conditioners
(1) A temperature reading should be taken daily on central air conditioners.
(2) The filters should be cleaned or replaced bimonthly.
(3) The screens and duct grills should be freed from soil each month.
(4) The fans, fan housing, and motors should be oiled, cleaned and brush-renewed quarterly.
(5) In all instances the specific instructions given in the manufacturer's brochure concerning air conditioners should be followed.

5. Walls

a. Under the direction of the maintenance director, the walls of the facility should be washed once a year, during the winter months, by the porters.

b. Each year, following the washing, half the walls should be painted by the maintenance director, aided by his part-time relief man, according to the color plan selected by the interior design consultant.

6. Floors. All concrete floors should be repainted annually, directly after a careful scrubbing.

7. Hardware and Keys

a. Distribution of keys to authorized personnel should be directed by the maintenance director.

b. Proper functioning of all hardware should be noted on a quarterly basis.

8. Exterior Work

a. Care of grounds: The maintenance director should direct the maintenance of the grounds and parking areas throughout the year, consideration being given to the employment of an outside gardening service.

(1) The grounds should be watered regularly.

(2) The grounds should be cleaned biweekly, and paper, trash, tree limbs, and branches removed.

(3) Lawns should be mowed weekly during the growing season, and gardens weeded and cleaned.

(4) Leaves should be raked, lawns seeded and fertilized, shrubs trimmed, trees pruned and sprayed.

(5) During the winter, snow should be removed by the porters and maintenance director from the steps, parking lot, and sidewalks surrounding the facility.

(6) The parking lot should be blown weekly to remove accumulated debris.

b. Monthly and periodic exterior work

(1) The roof should be cleared of leaves and trash monthly and more often in the spring and fall.

(2) Debris should be removed from all water down spouts.

(3) The masonry of the building should be inspected regularly and cracks caulked where necessary.

(4) Any cantilevered areas, porches, walks, and steps should be examined regularly for cracks, and new mortar floated where needed.

(5) The ramp and exit drains and trap baskets should be freed of foreign matter regularly.

(6) Sunken areas in the blacktop of the parking areas should be filled with cold patch blacktop.

(7) Exterior doors, roof and step handrails, and fences should be regularly inspected for rust and primed and painted when necessary.

(8) Exterior walls constructed of porous material should be waterproofed at regular intervals.

C. Surface Transportation. The responsibility for planning a transportation program and directing the maintenance of the vehicles required for this activity should be assigned to the maintenance director.

1. Depending upon the following factors, the institution may decide to embark upon a transportation program for staff and patients:

a. Local transportation conditions

b. Location of the extended care facility in relation to public transportation

c. Staff safety and welfare

d. Staff recruitment

2. The transportation plan may be concerned with:

a. A standard pickup and delivery procedure for staff coming on or terminating duty in the evening or night tours

b. Regular bus service between the institution and a central point, such as a railroad or bus station

c. Periodic transportation during episodes of an emergency nature such as strikes, blizzards, and disasters

d. Occasional or regular conveying of patients to special medical and/or recreational events

3. The number and type of vehicles needed by the extended care facility will depend upon the scope of the transportation program, but the basic requirements should encompass:

a. A four-wheel drive pickup truck with a snowplow attachment to be used by the maintenance director or his assistant for the Maintenance Department exclusively (Fig. 9-1).

b. A station wagon or small bus to be used by the Maintenance Department primarily, and other staff such as:

(1) The recreation director to drive patients

(2) The nursing director to convey members of the nursing staff to educational sessions outside the facility

4. Special consideration should be given to:

a. The selection of a passenger vehicle appropriate to the needs of the disabled patients affording easy ingress and egress of wheelchairs through doors of sufficient width

Fig. 9-1. A four-wheel-drive pickup truck can also be used for snowplowing.

b. Carrying ample insurance for the vehicles and passengers in question

c. Requirement of medical orders before patients are free to leave the institution

d. Written family permission to allow the patient to be driven to special activities by staff members

e. Authorization of specific personnel permitted to drive the station wagon or bus

f. Administrative approval prior to planning special projects necessitating transportation

5. The maintenance director or his assistant should direct:

a. The proper advance scheduling for the use of vehicles

b. The appropriate care and servicing of the vehicles

c. The use of specified service stations for the purchase of fuel and repairs

6. The acquisition of vehicles should be a joint decision by the administrative director and the maintenance director relating to:

a. The determination to rent or to purchase the conveyances

b. The selection of the particular type of vehicle

c. The time schedule for trading or changing models

D. Fire and Safety Procedures. In a 65-bed extended care facility, when an assistant administrator is not employed, the maintenance director, assisted by a safety and fire-prevention consultant, should direct a safety program that is composed of the following components:

Fig. 9-2. The maintenance director demonstrates the proper use of various types of fire extinguishers.

1. An easily understandable evacuation diagram should be posted on all nursing unit and service area bulletin boards, indicating the exits, the fire alarms, and the fire extinguishers in the particular area.

2. In consultation with the safety expert and the administrative director, written emergency and utility interruption plans should be developed, explained, and distributed to all personnel.

3. On a quarterly basis the entire staff should be required to attend a safety meeting, devoted to a discussion and demonstration of preventive safety, evacuation procedures, and the proper use of fire-fighting equipment.

a. The fire extinguishers should be used for teaching purposes for staff and to be replaced by spare extinguishers while the originals are being refilled.

b. The types of extinguishers and their uses should be explained (Fig. 9-2).

c. The three classes of fires should be described.

4. All new staff members should be required to pass a written safety quiz administered by the maintenance director as a condition of permanent employment (Fig. 9-3).

5. Monthly fire drills should be conducted by the maintenance director and/or the safety consultant on a rotating basis so that staff on each of the three tours of duty have the opportunity to learn and participate.

Fig. 9-3

OUR SAFETY

While we are always alert to correct conditions that cause fires, we must be prepared to meet an emergency should it occur. In case of emergency, every staff member must take proper action *quickly* and *calmly*. Only in this way can we properly protect our patients.

Did you know that our fire alarms are connected directly to the fire department? In an emergency:

1. Pull the fire alarm.
2. Telephone the fire department and report the fire, making sure to give our address.

Our fire extinguishers are all the easy-to-use trigger type—to work our fire extinguishers, just pull the trigger. They do not have to be turned upside down.

On our two patient floors, most fire extinguishers are the pressurized-water type—pressurized-water extinguishers will put out paper, cloth, and wood fires.

In the kitchen and next to the pantries the fire extinguishers are the dry chemical type to be used for grease, oil, and electrical fires.

One fire extinguisher in the boiler room is foam; this is for an oil fire.

The second fire extinguisher in the boiler room is a dry chemical for ash, oil, and electrical fires.

Complete the following quiz, even if you have to leave the meeting to check a few things you cannot remember.

SAFETY QUIZ

I. The Basement:

1. The one fire alarm box in the basement is located________________.
2. One fire extinguisher in the kitchen is located over the stove. The other one is located__________. It is a dry chemical and will extinguish__________, _______________, and______________fires.
3. The two fire extinguishers in the boiler room are located______________ and______________. One is the foam type for________________fires, and the other is a dry chemical for_________________,_________________, and ________________fires.
4. The three exits in the basement are:
   a.______________________
   b.______________________
   c.______________________

II. The First Floor:

1. The three fire extinguishers on the first floor are located______________, ______________, and______________. Two are pressurized water extinguishers and will put out______________, ______________, and__________fires. The

Fig. 9-3 (Continued)

third is dry chemical and will extinguish fires caused by ________, ________, and________.

2. The two fire alarm boxes on this floor are located________________ and________________.

3. There are five exits on the first floor. They are located:

a.________________
b.________________
c.________________
d.________________
e.________________

4. Is there a fire extinguisher in the x-ray room? If so, where is it located? ________________.

III. The Second Floor:

1. The two fire alarm boxes on the second floor are located________________ and________________.

2. The three fire extinguishers on the second floor are located, ____________, ____________, and____________. Two are pressurized water and will put out __________, __________, and__________fires.

3. Besides the elevator, there are three exits on the second floor. They are:

a.________________
b.________________
c.________________

IV. Doors and Windows in a Fire Emergency:

1. In case of fire, doors to patient rooms should be opened____________ closed____________?

2. In case of fire, windows should be opened____________, closed ____________?

6. In a crisis situation, the procedure outlined in the emergency and utility interruption plans should be followed, with the maintenance director acting as fire marshal and assisting staff, patients, visitors, and the fire department by:

a. Disconnecting the power and gas lines under the direction of the fire department
b. Closing windows and doors
c. Restoring service on the power and gas lines when directed by the fire department at the conclusion of the emergency

7. Frequent building inspections should ascertain the proper storage and disposal procedures of oxygen, paints, and other flammable agents in appropriate containers and locations.

8. A safety committee should be organized:

a. To be composed of department heads, the consultant on safety, and chaired by the maintenance director

b. To concern itself with all phases of safety such as lifting, the use of approved areas for smoking, prevention of falls, elimination of slipping in bathing areas, visitor safety, the storage of oxygen cylinders, and the training of staff in safety measures

c. To analyze the accident reports of patients, staff, and visitors in order to preclude future similar episodes

9. The fire alarm system should be tested weekly by the maintenance director by operating it manually with:

a. The auxiliary master switch and trouble bell turned off

b. Any one of the local station alarms pulled

c. The alarm and clock reset and the auxiliary master switch reactivated at the conclusion of the test

10. The company servicing the fire extinguishers should be reminded to check them on a quarterly basis.

E. Procedure during Major Emergency Repairs

1. Electrical Repairs

a. The director of nursing, or, in her absence, the charge nurse should be notified about prospective repair work and the approximate time that the equipment or appliance would be out of service.

b. A danger tag should be attached to the circuit breaker of the machine to be repaired (Fig. 9-4).

c. A test lamp should be used to ensure that the hot lines to the circuit are broken.

d. The repair work should be completed.

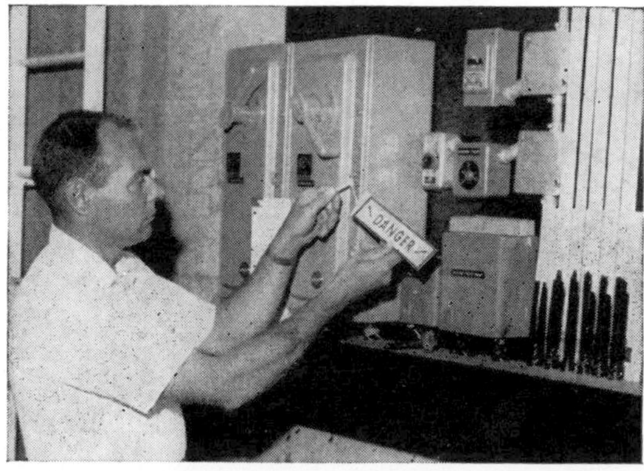

Fig. 9-4. A danger tag is affixed to the mechanical part of a machine to be repaired.

e. The tag should be removed, and the director of nursing or charge nurse should be informed of the completion of the work.

2. Plumbing and Radiation Repairs

a. The director of nursing, or in her absence, the charge nurse should be notified about the repair work and the approximate time that the equipment or appliance should be out of service.

b. The valves connected with work should be disconnected and marked with danger tags.

c. The repair work should proceed.

d. Tags should be removed, and the director of nursing or charge nurse notified upon the completion of the work.

F. Typical Daily Schedule. The maintenance director should make a daily inspection of the building and grounds including:

1. The Service Area

a. Starting at the boiler room to determine that the boilers are operating, that the circulating pumps are running, and that the hot water recirculating pump is maintaining 120°F

b. Verifying the proper functioning of the incinerator

c. Ascertaining that the sewage ejection pumps are operating, and that the floats are moving

d. Checking all refrigeration and air conditioners to ensure the correct operating temperatures

e. Inspecting the laundry room equipment

f. Testing the emergency generator

g. Checking all lighting

h. Examining all flushometers, faucets, and traps

i. Inspecting any sprinkler shutoff valves

j. Checking all piping for leaks

2. Patient Areas

a. Inspecting all flushometers, sink traps, and faucets

b. Checking all lighting

c. Examining the toasters, refrigerators, and hot plates in the pantries

d. Checking the traps, piping, ventilation, and faucets in the shower and bathing areas

e. Inspecting refrigerators in medication rooms

f. Testing the television sets in the recreation areas

3. General Areas

a. Inspecting all fans

b. Checking all exit lights

c. Touring all stairwells to check lighting and the proper closing of exit doors

d. Testing elevator for a smooth ride, correct floor leveling, and proper functioning of indicator lights
e. Examining time clock and condition of exterior lighting
f. Checking radiation throughout the building
g. Viewing the exterior and grounds for orderliness
h. Checking lighting, faucets, and flushometers in medical and dental areas

G. Special Weekly Duties. On a weekly basis, the following guide should be used:

1. The dishwasher spray tubes to be checked and cleaned
2. The airflow switch and main gas solenoid valve of the dryer to be tested
3. The emergency generator to be checked thoroughly
4. The fire alarm system to be tested
5. The cleanup of grounds and lawn mowing to be supervised

H. Special Monthly Duties. Monthly tasks should include:

1. Cleaning the air-cooled condensers and evaporators of the freezers and coolers
2. Removing the dirt from the exhaust duct grills of the fans, emptying down spouts
3. Checking the boiler safety valves and feed water analysis report
4. Cleaning the roof of leaves and debris (more often in spring and fall)
5. Changing or cleaning the air-conditioner filters
6. Conducting and evaluating, together with the safety consultant, fire drills
7. Meeting with the safety committee

I. Special Quarterly Duties. Every 3 months:

1. The sewage pump shafts shou'd be greased.
2. The ventilating fans should be greased.
3. The boliers should be cleaned.
4. The fire and safety demonstration for the entire staff should be conducted.
5. Rusted metal should be treated.
6. The service company for the fire extinguishers should be contacted.
7. All hardware should be inspected.

J. Annual Duties. Once a year:

1. In the winter, the maintenance director should direct the washing down of all walls of the facility by the porters.

2. Following washing, the maintenance director, aided by his relief man, should paint half the walls so that the entire facility will be repainted every two years.
3. All concrete floors should be repainted.
4. The caulking of masonry where required should be completed.

K. Assistant and/or Relief Maintenance Man. The assistant and/or relief maintenance man should be assigned duties by the maintenance director according to the needs of the extended care facility and commensurate with his abilities and skills in order to free the maintenance director for tasks of an administrative and preventive nature.

IV. PURCHASING, OUTSIDE CONTRACT MAINTENANCE, AND SUPPLIES

Explicit information concerning major repairs, after the receipt of bona fide bids, should be presented to the administrative director for the final decision.

A. Vendors and Outside Contract Maintenance

1. Parts. The maintenance director should conduct an investigation to determine appropriate sources for the purchase of fixtures and standardized parts for the mechanical equipment such as:
a. Plumbing
b. Dishwasher
c. Refrigerators
d. Incinerator
e. Washers and dryer

2. Supplies and Equipment. The maintenance director and the person designated to serve as purchasing agent should develop convenient, reliable, and economical vendors of uniform supplies and equipment in the following categories:
a. Electrical
b. Fuel
c. Paints
d. Light bulbs
e. Small tools
f. Major tools

3. Outside Contract Maintenance
a. Whenever possible repairs should be completed by the maintenance director or his alternate, but, should he be unable to solve the problem or should he not be available, the following outside service agencies should be called:
(1) Television, public address, and intercommunication system specialist

(2) Boiler installation and service company
(3) Utility companies
(4) Plumbing contractor
(5) Refrigerator service company
(6) Garage to service the truck

b. Annual contracts should be developed by the maintenance director with the assistance of the administrative director to assure proper functioning of:
(1) Elevator
(2) Fire extinguishers
(3) Boiler, by the analysis of the water by a chemical engineer

c. Maintenance of the grounds may be handled by an outside contract whereby no garden equipment would have to be purchased or serviced by the extended care institution (or by the addition of a part-time person to the maintenance staff, requiring also the purchase and maintenance of lawn mowers, leaf blowers, spreaders, etc.).

4. Other Repairs. The x-ray machine and other equipment used by the medical director, the telephones, and office equipment should be repaired by outside technicians, usually contacted by department heads, but as the maintenance director may be called upon to assume responsibility for making contacts for emergency repairs of this equipment in the absence of department heads, sources for repairing the equipment below should be known and listed by him:

a. Medical equipment
(1) Electrocardiogram machine
(2) X-ray apparatus
(3) Fluoroscope

b. Telephones and station-to-station intercom

c. Office equipment
(1) Electric typewriters
(2) Adding machines
(3) Mimeograph machine
(4) Electrostatic copier
(5) Dictating machines
(6) Postage meter

d. Recreation equipment
(1) Movie projector
(2) Slide projector

B. Quantities and Inventories. For a 65-bed extended care facility the following schedule of quantities is suggested:

Item	Reorder Point	Reorder Quantity
Light bulbs		
F40 CW (fluorescent)	6 bulbs	Case of 24
40-watt utility (for inside exit and outside stairwells)	1 doz	4 doz
60-watt (for inside stairwells and room lamps)	1 doz	4 doz
100-watt (for interior and exterior incandescent globes)	1 doz	4 doz
150-watt (for medical suite, maintenance, and boiler rooms)	1 doz	4 doz
Oil	19 in.	2,800 gal of No. 4
Deicer	100 lb	400 lb

C. Items Kept in Stock. The items listed below should be kept in stock to permit prompt repairs of mechanical equipment, to ensure safe practices and to limit the loss of personnel time:

1. For the Clothes Washers
- *a.* 2 spare fluid drives
- *b.* 6 fluid drive clutches
- *c.* 1 agitator post assembly, complete
- *d.* 6 agitator shift clutches
- *e.* 1 spare timer
- *f.* 2 spare water pumps
- *g.* 3 spare belts

2. For the Dryer
- *a.* 2 spare air-flow switches
- *b.* 1 spare relay
- *c.* 1 spare motor, rewound
- *d.* 1 spare pulley
- *e.* 1 spare belt

3. For Faucets: 4 dozen washers

4. For Sinks
- *a.* 1 dozen pop-up stoppers
- *b.* Spindles

5. For Fluorescent Lights: 4 rapid-start ballasts

6. For Flushometers (Toilets)
- *a.* 1 spare flushometer, complete
- *b.* 6 rebuilding kits

7. For Television: six 5-ft lengths of TV lead-in wires to master antenna

8. A portable carrying chest to be used by the maintenance director with a front-hinged door and drawers containing:

a. Faucet washers
b. Assortment of stove bolts, nuts, and screws
c. Assortment of fiber washers
d. Assortment of mollies
e. Assortment of self-tapping sheet metal screws
f. Wire nut insulators
g. An assortment of bayonets, spades, and connectors
h. Eyelets and electrical forks varying from ⅛ to ¼ in.
i. An assortment of lock washers and flat washers
j. An assortment of insulated wire nuts from $\frac{1}{16}$ in. to number 12
k. A selection of running and starting capacitators

D. Purchasing. Purchasing should be effected by the maintenance director in consultation with the designated purchasing agent and, when capital expenditures are involved, the administrative director.

V. FACILITIES AND MAJOR EQUIPMENT

A. Facilities:

1. Workshop
2. Boiler Room
3. Maintenance Room
4. Elevator Room
5. Incinerator Room
6. Electrical Room
7. High-Hazard Room
8. Emergency Generator Room
9. Maintenance Garage

B. Equipment. Generally, the skilled maintenance director will provide his own tools, but the following equipment should be provided by the extended care facility to guarantee a smooth-functioning department:

1. Workshop

a. Desk, chairs, and files
b. 12-amp welder, a.c.
c. Radical arm Dewalt saw
d. Tilt Arbor table saw
e. Joiner
f. A floor-mounted drill press
g. Grinder
h. Small tools

i. An oxyacetylene set
j. Storage cabinets
k. Workbench and stool
l. Master key control cabinet

2. Boiler Room
a. 2 boilers
b. Circulating pumps
c. Feed pump (for a high-pressure system)
d. Tube-punching gear

3. Maintenance Room
a. 1 cement mixer
b. 1 gasoline-driven compressor for spraying paint
c. 1 portable pump for emergency work
d. 2 snow shovels
e. 2 rakes
f. 1 weeder
g. Hosing
h. Shelving and racks to accommodate the storage of supplies
i. 2 dollies
j. 2 hand trucks
k. 1 5-ft stepladder
l. 1 8-ft stepladder
m. 1 industrial vacuum cleaner
n. Spare fire extinguishers

4. Elevator Room
a. Oil reservoir
b. Pumping unit
c. Other elevator controls

5. Incinerator Room
a. Incinerator
b. Service sink
c. Rake, shovel, and broom

6. Electrical Room
a. Fire alarm system
b. Heat-detection unit
c. Main service

7. High-hazard Room. A sealed room for the storage of flammable and/or combustible materials with particular reference to paints

8. Emergency Generator Room. A separate room, preferably adjoining the electrical room, for ease of functioning of the automatic transfer needed to effect the self-starting generator

9. Maintenance Garage
a. 1 snow blower

b. 1 lawn mower
c. 1 hydraulic snowplow
d. 1 4-wheel drive unit truck, which is kept stocked with tools and spare parts for both normal and emergency repairs, as well as current supply of parts
e. 1 wheelbarrow
f. 1 20-ft extension ladder
g. 1 30-ft extension ladder
h. 1 40-ft extension ladder

VI. INSPECTION BY GOVERNMENTAL AND INSURANCE AGENCIES

The conduction of inspections of the physical facility by various agencies should be the responsibility of the maintenance director, written record maintained of each inspection by any agency to be kept, including the signature of the person making the inspection, his position, the date, in the appropriate loose-leaf notebook kept in the administrative office.

A. City Departments

1. Department of Buildings generally has the responsibility for:
a. Annual plumbing inspection
b. Annual multiple-residence inspection
c. Annual boiler inspection
d. Quarterly elevator inspection

2. Department of Public Safety
a. The fire prevention bureau of the fire department should make a quarterly inspection of the building for any fire hazards.
b. Monthly unannounced fire drills may be held by the fire department.
c. The police department should make an annual safety inspection.

B. County Health Department

1. Department of Air Pollution (where appropriate). This department should inspect the chimney for smog and fly ash emission, caused by use of boiler and/or the incinerator.
2. The Health Department may survey the building annually.
3. The Health Department should effect a quarterly sanitation inspection of the kitchen.

C. Medicare Certification. The state agency designated by the governor should survey the extended care facility annually to determine continued eligibility to receive Title 18 patients and should make its report available to the Social Security Administration before January.

D. Insurance Companies. At least two annual inspections should be made by the insurance carriers prior to the expiration dates of the policies covering:

1. Boilers
2. Liability of the building and elevator

VII. INTERDEPARTMENTAL COOPERATION

A. Housekeeping Department. Cooperation should be afforded by the maintenance director in the following areas:

1. Curtains. Ringlets for the curtains should be stapled after laundering.
2. Walls. The maintenance director should direct the annual washing down of the walls by the porters.
3. Lights. New bulbs should be installed by the Housekeeping Department, but the fixtures should be maintained by the maintenance director.
4. Laundry Room. The washers and dryer should be regularly examined and maintained in good working condition by the maintenance director.
5. Incinerator Room. This room should be cleaned by the porter, but the incinerator itself should be serviced by the maintenance director.
6. Sewage Traps. The sewage traps should be cleaned by the porters and kept in working condition by the maintenance director.
7. Exterior Work. Outside work may be shared by the maintenance director and porters, grounds and lawns being cared for by a gardening service, and snow removal effected by the maintenance director and porters.
8. Cleaning equipment used by Housekeeping such as vacuums should be serviced by the maintenance director.

B. Nursing Department

1. Bed Rails. Bed rails should be installed or removed by the maintenance director.
2. Signal Systems. The nurses' call system should be kept in working order and tested regularly by the maintenance director.
3. Small Equipment. Drug refrigerators, autoclaves, and sterilizers should be kept in good condition by the maintenance director.
4. Patient Lifter and Other Equipment. The maintenance director should inspect and maintain patient lifters and other equipment such as shower chairs used by the Nursing Department.

C. Dietary Department

1. Major Equipment. All repairs on major equipment such as the range, freezers, coolers, and dishwasher should be completed at the direction of the maintenance director.
2. Filters. Range hood filters should be examined regularly by the maintenance director and cleaned by the Dietary Department.
3. Temperatures. The maintenance director should scrutinize all coolers and freezers daily to see that the proper degrees of temperature are maintained.

D. Recreation Department

1. Equipment. Repairs on phonographs, projector, flower cart, etc., should be effected by the maintenance director when requested in writing by the recreation director.
2. Fireplace. Should there be a wood-burning fireplace in a recreation area, only the maintenance director should be permitted to light the fire.

E. Restorative Services

1. Repairs of equipment for physical and occupational therapy should be completed by the Maintenance Department.
2. On occasion the maintenance director may be requested to devise or build special self-help equipment for disabled patients.

F. Medical and Dental. When possible, repairs should be accomplished on medical and dental equipment by the maintenance director.

G. Business. Simple repairs may be attempted by Maintenance on the office machines.

H. All Departments

1. A listing of outside service agencies should be provided to all department heads to be used in an emergency in the absence of the maintenance director and his assistant.
2. A safety committee composed of the heads of all departments and the safety consultant should be chaired by the maintenance director.

VIII. TRAINING AND EDUCATION

The director of maintenance and his assistant should keep up to date on new equipment and machinery and safety methods by:

A. Careful study of service manuals

B. Regular reading of periodicals and publications relating to safety and maintenance

C. Perusal of all material distributed by the National Safety Council

D. Attendance at appropriate meetings and seminars

E. Maintaining a complete catalog file

Section 10

Business

Introduction

The extended care facility represents big business in relationship to funds expended and people served. With the anticipated continued growth in the population over sixty-five and the consequent increase in the number of Medicare beneficiaries, the extended care institution can be expected to become a larger and more important agency in the constellation of health care facilities.

Whether the institution be nonprofit or proprietary, whether it be directed by a private corporation or a governmental agency, management must be informed regarding the financial position of the institution to aid in the decision-making process.

Accurate statistical information must be obtained for the purposes of:

1. Administrative control
2. Acquisition of data to be used in budget preparation
3. Computation of costs and proper charges
4. Completion of reports to owners, governing boards, third-party payors, insurance companies, fiscal intermediaries, governmental agencies, patients, families, and the community
5. Development of long-range plans with reference to replacement and expansion

The Business Department has the responsibility of maintaining complete and current financial records of all patients, employees, and accounts in an orderly and efficient manner, thus contributing to the economical management of the facility in accordance with the operating budget.

I. STAFFING PATTERN

A. Staff Complement. In a 65-bed extended care facility the business office staff should consist of:

1. Business Manager
2. Bookkeeper
3. Consulting Certified Public Accountant

B. Work Schedule. The business manager and bookkeeper should work a 5-day week, and the certified public accountant routinely should spend approximately 2 days a month in the facility except when the preparation of unusual financial studies requires more time.

II. RECORDS

Records for this department may be subdivided into:

A. Business Records

Title:

Annual operating budget
Monthly statistical data
Monthly financial data
Statement of income and capital
Monthly billing statement
Distribution journal
Departmental distribution card
Vendor card
Purchase and cash disbursements journal
Charges and receipts journal
Payroll summary journal
General checking account check
Payroll check
Purchase order
General deposit ticket
Payroll deposit ticket

B. Employee Records

Title:

Completed employee application
Social security information
Employee time cards
Employee payroll cards
Employee health examination
X-ray reports
Completed educational tests
Reference forms
Other pertinent information about employees

C. Patient Records

Title:

Completed family responsibility sheet
Accounts receivable card
Medicare billing form
Laboratory and x-ray patient billing book
Restorative services book
Special services book

D. Accounting Records

Title:

Balance sheets
Statement of income, expenses, and net gain or loss
Budget control and comparative expenses
Statistical data for month and cumulative period of months for present year as compared with data for the same cumulative period of months for previous year

III. ACCOUNTING

A. General Principles. The process of accounting in an extended care facility should be concerned with an effective procedure of recording, classifying, summarizing, and interpreting the financial activities of the institution with adherence to:

1. Accrual Rather than the Cash System

a. Accrual referring to the recording of revenue received or expenses incurred in the period of earning or spending

b. Cash relating to the recording of revenue received or expenses incurred when actually deposited or disbursed

2. Fund Accounting. The act of financially separating each distinct phase of the program of the extended care facility

3. Uniform Accounting Cycle

a. The period may follow the calendar year.

b. Or the fiscal year of the institution may be selected according to:

(1) Due dates of reports to government agencies

(2) Less busy intervals affording business office staff ample time to summarize

4. Operating Budget

a. An operating budget is a forecast and plan of operation based on the goals of the facility with regard to patients, families, staff, and the community, taking into account:

(1) The anticipated income based on an assessment of the market for extended care services, possible seasonal fluctuations, and trends in the health care field

(2) The planned program allowing for the expansion of activities and the development of new services, the anticipated increase in the general cost of living and in health care salaries, and reserves for unexpected expenditures

b. An annual operating budget, although not a sacred document, should control the proper handling of income and expenditures, and should serve as an adjunct to good management.

c. The budget should by planned by Administration and Business in consultation with department heads after careful study of activities related to income and expenditures of the previous year.

5. Operating capital will be required by the extended care facility to provide for the time lag caused by the practice of fiscal intermediaries, public assistance agencies, and other third-party payors providing reimbursement after the provision of services.

a. To allow for possible delays in payment, sufficient operating capital for a period of 2 to 3 months should be available.

b. Interim financing for Medicare patients from fiscal intermediaries may be sought by institutions using a monthly billing cycle.

6. Depreciation should be funded to provide for future replacement and expansion.

B. Functions of the Business Department. The Business Department in the extended care facility should be staffed, organized, and designed to provide the following services:

1. Collection and recording of income
2. Disbursement and recording of expenditures
3. Chronicling of assets, liabilities, and equities
4. Accumulation of statistical data
5. Development of an itemized estimate of income and expenses for the operating budget
6. Protection of personal valuables of patients
7. Purchase and notation of purchase of supplies and equipment
8. Control of inventory
9. Maintenance of employee records

C. Responsibilities of the Consulting Accountant. At the completion of the journalizing and posting process by the Business Department, a summary of the financial transactions of the extended care facility

Fig. 10-1

STATISTICAL PATIENT COST DATA

Statistical Data	Current Year Month of ___	Current Year Months	Prior Year Month of ___	Prior Year Months
Patients at beginning of period	______ To	______	______ To	______
New admissions	______	______	______	______
Patients discharged or deceased	( )	( )	( )	( )
Patients at end of period	======	======	======	======
Patient days	______	______	______	______
Number of days in period	______	______	______	______
Daily average number of patients	______	______	______	______
Patient capacity	______	______	______	______
Average patient days—percent of capacity	______	______	______	______
Cost per Patient Day (days) ______Months to__________:				
Administrative and general	$	$	$	$
Education				
Plant operation and maintenance				
Dietary				
Housekeeping and Laundry				
Nursing				
Pharmacy				
Laboratory and x-ray				
Recreation and volunteers				
Social service				
Communications				
Physical and occupational therapy	______	______	______	______
Total	$======	======	======	======
Average income per patient day	$______	______	______	______
Cost per meal				
Total cost of dietary for _____months to__________	$______			$______
Divided by number of meals served ( )	______			______
Average cost per meal				
Food	$______			$______
Salaries	______			______

Fig. 10-2

BALANCE SHEET

ASSETS		
Cash		
Accounts receivable		
Deposit		
Prepaid expenses		
Equipment:		
Building furniture		
Medical and kitchen equipment		
Automobiles		
Less accumulated depreciation	$____	
	Total Assets	$____
LIABILITIES AND CAPITAL		
Accounts payable		
Accrued expenses		
Notes payable		
Payroll taxes payable		
Capital:		
Capital stock or net worth		
Accumulated earnings		
	Total Liabilities and Capital	$____

may be prepared by the accountant for a period of a year, month, week, or day, to include:

1. Statistical patient cost data (Fig. 10-1)
2. A balance sheet showing the financial position of the institution at the end of an accounting period by listing what is owed and what is owned by the organization, the difference representing the net worth or capital of the extended care facility (Fig. 10-2)
3. A statement of revenue and expense demonstrating the results of operations during an accounting period (Fig. 10-3)
4. A study of income and expenditures in relation to the cumulative period of the preceding year and the current annual operating budget (Fig. 10-4)
5. Pertinent data for monthly conferences with Administration to assess progress and discuss future plans

D. Technology Employed by the Business Department. The size of the extended care facility and the complexity of the financial data desired should determine the specific hardware employed in the

Fig. 10-3

STATEMENT OF INCOME, EXPENSES AND NET GAIN OR LOSS

	Current Year		Prior Year	
	Month of	Period from	Month of	Period from
Income	______	____to____	______	____to____
Accommodations	$	$	$	$
Coinsurance				
Special attendants				
Personal grooming				
Employees' room and food				
Employees' gift fund				
Other contributions	______	______	______	______
Total Revenue	$______	$______	$______	$______
Expenses				
Administrative and general	$	$	$	$
Education				
Plant operation and maintenance				
Dietary				
Housekeeping and laundry				
Nursing				
Pharmacy				
Laboratory and x-ray				
Recreation and volunteers				
Social service				
Communications				
Physical and occupational therapy	______	______	______	______
Total Expenditures	$______	$______	$______	$______
Net Gain or (Loss)	$______	$______	$______	$______

operation of the Business Department although the overall plan should not vary, including the use of:

1. A semimechanical system whereby a posting board forms the basis of all bookkeeping procedures, recommended as adequate for a 65-bed facility (Fig. 10-5)

2. An appropriately selected and versatile business machine, suggested for an institution of 100 beds or more

3. A shared computer for a group of extended care facilities averaging over 200 beds when the cost of the computer time will be offset by the need for fewer business office employees

4. A combination method whereby certain procedures such as pay-

Fig. 10-4

BUDGET CONTROL AND COMPARATIVE EXPENSES
FOR THE PERIOD FROM ______ TO ____________________

	Total Current Budget	Total Disbursed To ____	Salaries Month of ___	Salaries Months To ____	Other Than Salaries Month of ___	Other Than Salaries Months To ____	Budgetary Balance At ____	Prior Year Month of ___	Prior Year Months To ____
ADMINISTRATIVE									
Salary—administrative director	$	$	$	$	$	$	$	$	$
Salary—assistant director									
Medical director									
Administrative salaries									
Office supplies and postage									
Telephone									
Auto expenses									
Travel expenses									
Subscription, license, and dues									
Legal, accounting, and clergy									
Advertising									
Insurance									
Depreciation—furniture									
Depreciation—equipment									
Depreciation—auto									
Hospitalization									
Payroll taxes—social security									
Payroll taxes—state unemployment									
Payroll taxes—federal unemployment									
Payroll taxes—disability									
Personal grooming									
Miscellaneous expenses									
	$____	$____	$____	$____	$____	$____	$____	$____	$____

Education									
Tuition	$	$	$	$	$	$	$	$	$
	$____	$____	$____	$____	$____	$____	$____	$____	$____
Plant Operation and Maintenance									
Salaries	$	$	$	$	$	$	$	$	$
Fuel, heat									
Gas									
Electricity									
Maintenance supplies									
Outside maintenance services									
Rent									
	$____	$____	$____	$____	$____	$____	$____	$____	$____
Dietary									
Salaries	$	$	$	$	$	$	$	$	$
Food									
Kitchen supplies and other									
	$____	$____	$____	$____	$____	$____	$____	$____	$____
Housekeeping and Laundry									
Salaries	$	$	$	$	$	$	$	$	$
Linen rentals									
Laundry supplies									
Laundry equipment—repairs									
Housekeeping supplies									
	$____	$____	$____	$____	$____	$____	$____	$____	$____
Nursing									
Salaries—professional nurses	$	$	$	$	$	$	$	$	$
Salaries—licensed practical nurses									
Salaries—attendants									
Supplies									
	$____	$____	$____	$____	$____	$____	$____	$____	$____

Fig. 10-4 (Continued)

BUDGET CONTROL AND COMPARATIVE EXPENSES
FOR THE PERIOD FROM_____ TO ____________

	Total Current Budget	Total Disbursed To____	Salaries: Month of__	Salaries: Months To____	Other Than Salaries: Month of__	Other Than Salaries: Months To____	Budgetary Balance At____	Prior Year: Month of__	Prior Year: Months To____
	$____	$____	$____	$____	$____	$____	$____	$____	$____
Pharmacy									
Medical supplies	$	$	$	$	$	$	$	$	$
	$____	$____	$____	$____	$____	$____	$____	$____	$____
Laboratory and X-ray									
Salaries	$	$	$	$	$	$	$	$	$
Supplies									
	$____	$____	$____	$____	$____	$____	$____	$____	$____
Recreation and Volunteers									
Salaries	$	$	$	$	$	$	$	$	$
Supplies									
	$____	$____	$____	$____	$____	$____	$____	$____	$____
Social Service									
Salaries	$	$	$	$	$	$	$	$	$
Supplies									
Consultants									
	$____	$____	$____	$____	$____	$____	$____	$____	$____

Communications									
Public relations	$	$	$	$	$	$	$	$	$
	$	$	$	$	$	$	$	$	$
Physical and Occupational Therapy									
Salaries	$	$	$	$	$	$	$	$	$
Supplies									
Personal purchases									
	$	$	$	$	$	$	$	$	$
Combined Totals	$	$	$	$	$	$	$	$	$

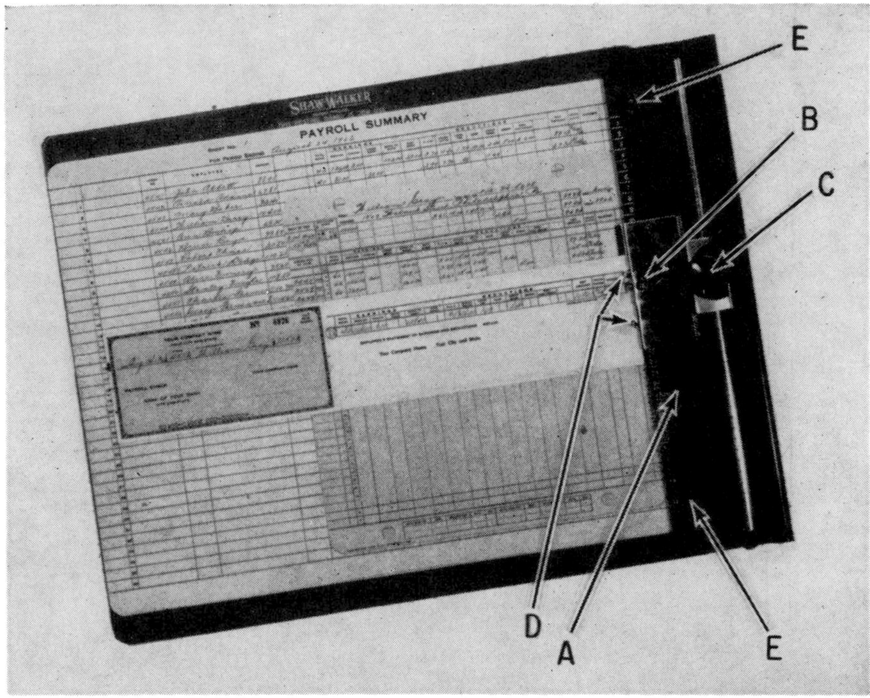

Fig. 10-5. The Shaw-Walker posting board is used in all the bookkeeping procedures described in this chapter. The arrows depict the locations of the operative parts, including the:

A. Clamp—All journal sheets are inserted under the clamp for the purpose of security.
B. Traveler—The traveler is a guide to enable proper lining up of the sheets.
C. Lock—The lock holds the traveler in place.
D. Check posts—All checks are placed over these posts.
E. Journals posts—All journal sheets are placed over these posts.

rolls or accounts payable are completed by a computer service, and the balance of business office activities are effected by the posting board or business machine technique

IV. PROCEDURES

A. Admission of Patients

1. Alphabetical File. When a patient is admitted, a file should be started including the following records:

a. The completed family responsibility sheet
b. Correspondence regarding the patient's billing or address changes of the family
c. Medicare information

2. Readmissions should be treated as new admissions unless the bed was held for the patient.

B. Accounts Receivable

1. Types of Rates. Rates may be structured to be inclusive, partially inclusive, or separate for each unit of service rendered to patients, with the following advantages and disadvantages:

- *a.* The inclusive rate should encourage the use of all services in the extended care facility, irrespective of the ability of the patients to pay.
- *b.* With an inclusive rate Social Service can predetermine the cost for patient care and thus develop an effective financial plan prior to admission.
- *c.* Inclusive rates should conserve staff time by eliminating the need for the preparation of charge slips for special services.
- *d.* However, lack of charge slips will preclude accurate financial measurement of work performed by the various services.
- *e.* Complaints regarding extra charges will be avoided with inclusive rates.
- *f.* Inclusive rates may incite some patients to complain that they are paying for services rendered to other patients.
- *g.* Inclusive rates may tend to encourage wastefulness in the utilization of special services.

2. Patients' Accounts

- *a.* All patient bills should be submitted on a weekly, biweekly, or monthly basis, depending upon the usual length of patient stays.
- *b.* Statements should be presented after services have been rendered, charges being classified according to accommodations, special attendants, laboratory, x-ray, restorative services, coinsurance, and personal grooming.
- *c.* The account balances should be maintained on an accrual basis with the income for services rendered charged to the patient and recorded as gross revenue when earned (not when paid).

3. Procedure for Patient Charges (Billings)

- *a.* Preparing the charges journal sheet

  (1) On the posting board, a charges journal sheet should be placed.

  (2) The sheet should be headed with the page number, and the month and year of the charge period added.

  (3) The letter "C" should be placed before the page number, to indicate the use of this sheet as a charges journal sheet.

  (4) A sheet of special carbon paper should be placed on top of the charges journal sheet.

Fig. 10-6. A separate accounts receivable card is maintained for each patient, using the same classification of charges as the charges journal sheet and the monthly billing statement.

NAME________________ ACCOUNT NO.________________

ADDRESS________________________________

	Date	Charges						Total Charges	Credits			New Balance	
		Accommo-dations	Co-insurance	Laboratory and X-ray	Pharmacy	Code	Amount		On Account	Code	Other		
1													1
2													2
3													3
4													4
5													5
6													6

(5) The accounts receivable card for the first patient to be billed should be removed from the accounts receivable file tray (Fig. 10-6).

(6) The name of the patient and the old balance of the patient should be listed on the charges journal sheet, as noted from the patient's individual accounts receivable card.

b. The monthly billing statement

(1) The billing statement should be prepared as follows: addressed and headed; positioned on the posting board above the carbon paper, which, in turn, should be on top of the charges journal sheet with the card and the statement aligned with the corresponding name on the charges journal sheet. This material should be inserted under the traveler and locked.

(2) Patient charges should be classified according to the procedures described below:

All patients should be charged for accommodations. Other charges may include, coinsurance, equipment rental, speech therapy, pharmacy, podiatry, or other extra-cost services.

Special attendants—These charges should be obtained from the employee time cards located at the main nurses' station.

Laboratory and x-ray—The original laboratory and x-ray orders should be brought to the business office daily to record the laboratory and x-ray services rendered in the laboratory and x-ray patient billing book for purposes of billing.

Physical therapy—Charges for physical therapy should be obtained from the "restorative services book" at the nurses' station.

Personal grooming—Charges for personal grooming should be determined by referring to the special services book kept at the main nurses' station (provided that the barber and/or beautician do not do their own billing).

(3) The billing statement should be completed by recording the patient billings on the billing statement, stapling the previous period's receipted bill for each patient to the back of the current bill, placing both bills into a window envelope with the name of the person being billed showing through the window, and mailing.

c. Completion of charges journal sheet

(1) Credits. Credits issued during the billing period for early discharges or rate adjustments are to be recorded in the charges journal as a negative charge, and the individual account card should be posted at the same time to record the patient credit and adjusted balance.

(2) Balancing. At the end of each previously determined billing

Fig. 10-7. The same journal sheet may be used for cash receipts and charges by placing a "C" after page no. for charges and an "R" to indicate cash receipts.

Code: A—Equipment Rental
B—Personal Grooming
C—Physical Therapy
X—Special Attendants
Y—
Z—
D—Speech Therapy
E—Occupational Therapy
F—Podiatry

Page No. R
Date

						Charges							Credits				
Number	Name					Accommo-dations	Coinsur-ance	Laboratory and X-ray	Pharmacy	Code			On Account	Code	Other	New Balance	
		1															
		2															
		3															
		4															
		5															
		6															

period, every page of the charges journal is to be footed and cross-footed: the individual charges columns must equal the total charges; the old balance, plus the total charges less credits, if any, must equal the new balance; and should a page total not cross-foot, the error can be found by reviewing each posting made on the page (to localize errors within one page).

(3) The charges journal should be summarized and posted to the general ledger and the accounts receivable control card tray.

4. Procedure for Recording Income

a. When checks are received in the mail:

(1) On two general deposit tickets the last name of the patient for whom the check is made out, the date that appears on the check, and the amount of the check should be listed.

(2) Medicare checks should be noted on separate deposit slips.

(3) The back of the check should be rubber-stamped "For Deposit."

b. After having deposited the checks in the bank, the duplicate deposit ticket is used for completion of the cash receipts journal.

5. The Cash Receipts Journal Sheet

a. On the posting board a cash receipts journal sheet should be placed (Fig. 10-7).

b. The page should be numbered to run consecutively from one sheet to the next.

c. The month and the year should be written.

d. The patients' names should be listed as they appear on the duplicate deposit ticket in the column headed Name.

e. A piece of special carbon paper should be placed above the journal sheet.

f. On top of the carbon paper the patient's accounts receivable card, corresponding to the first name listed on the journal sheet, should be placed.

g. The last balance from the accounts receivable card should be transferred to the Old Balance column of the cash receipts journal sheet.

h. The date of the deposit ticket should be entered on the accounts receivable card under the column labeled Date and the amount from the deposit ticket should be entered under the column labeled On Account (under the credit columns).

i. The new balance should be written under the column labeled New Balance.

j. After having completed the above process for all the names listed, the following procedure should be employed:

(1) On the next empty line of the cash receipts journal the date and the amount of the deposit ticket should be entered.
(2) The cash receipts journal sheet should be footed and cross-footed, whereby the total old balance less the total of the On Account column should equal the New Balance column, and the amount of the deposit ticket should equal the total of the On Account column.

C. Procedure for Medicare Patients

1. Billing

a. A patient may be covered by Medicare only after an approved report of eligibility form has been returned by the fiscal intermediary.

b. The Extended Care Admissions and Billing form of the Department of Health, Education, and Welfare should be completed monthly (or at the customary billing interval), after services have been rendered to the Medicare patient, and sent to the fiscal intermediary.

c. Medicare billing should consist of two accounts receivable cards, one marked "Medicare" and one marked "Regular Account."

d. The Medicare card should be completed with all the information from the billing form, following the same procedure used for the regular patient billing, but it should be kept in a separate charges journal marked "Medicare Account."

e. Coinsurance and other charges not covered by Medicare should be added to the regular accounts receivable card and to the regular charges journal.

2. Receipts of Medicare Payments

a. Medicare payments received should be deposited with separate deposit slips.

b. The provider reimbursement statement, attached to the check received from the fiscal intermediary, should be used to record payments on Medicare accounts receivable and Medicare receipts journal with the same procedure as that followed for the regular accounts receivable.

c. The provider reimbursement statement should also be used to prove gain or loss on each individual Medicare patient.

3. Accounts Receivable Distribution. At the end of each billing period or month:

a. All columns of the charges journal summary sheet should be totaled.

b. Below each total, a number should be placed corresponding to the title on the top of the column.

c. From this summary sheet the following accounts receivable distribution is devised, using the titles at the top of each column and the numbers below the totals:

Classification of Income	*Distribution Number*
Accommodations	301
Coinsurance	302
Laboratory and x-ray	331
Personal grooming	392
Employees' room and food	391
Physical therapy	397

d. The above distribution along with the corresponding totals of each classifiication should then be posted (transferring information from the journal—the book of original entry—to a second record called a ledger) to the general ledger control record.

D. Purchasing. Effective purchasing can make a substantial contribution to management, patient care, and employee utilization by providing quality material and services at reasonable costs.

1. Types of Purchasing

a. The feasibility of a joint or group purchasing plan with other area institutions should be explored for the purpose of effecting savings resulting from enlarged purchasing potential.

b. Within the individual institution, the question of departmental or centralized purchasing should be resolved with:

(1) Centralized being the preferred method to establish uniformity and effective controls

(2) Departmental purchasing affording department heads the opportunity to utilize their particular expertise in departmental purchasing

(3) A combination plan, with centralized purchasing the practice except for separate purchasing by departments, such as dietary, pharmacy, x-ray, and laboratory.

2. Person Designated to Purchase

a. An institution of 200 beds or more can justify the employment of a person with the sole responsibility for purchasing and stores control.

b. A 65-bed facility with a partially centralized purchasing program cannot economically employ one person to function only as the purchasing agent.

c. In a small organization the purchasing role may be assumed by an assistant administrator, the administrator, the business manager, the pharmacist, or other qualified personnel.

3. Stores Control

a. The person designated to purchase may also act as the receiving and issuing clerk when a central storage system is employed.

b. In larger institutions an additional person may be employed for this post to establish centralized control on purchases and issues.

c. Whether the storage method be centralized or departmentalized, a stores control system should be employed with:

(1) The use of stores requisition slips

(2) The maintenance of a perpetual inventory in the central storage area

(3) The institution of regularly scheduled departmental inventories

(4) Careful study of inventory patterns pointing up problems such as hoarding

(5) Maintenance of low inventory by rapid turnover of merchandise

d. A system for platform receipt, inspection, and storage of goods should be developed with:

(1) Merchandise stored in original unbroken cartons

(2) Goods received checked against samples and/or specifications

(3) Unapproved substitutes rejected

4. Purchasing Records

a. A clear system of record keeping should be employed for purchasing to assist in identifying and correcting errors in methods of purchasing, distribution, and storage of wares by using:

(1) Purchases recording system to verify charges

(2) Purchase requisitions cleared only by the person designated to purchase

(3) Purchase orders issued exclusively by the purchasing agent or other authorized person

(4) A system for vendors' bills of lading and packing slips

b. A current catalog file should be maintained.

c. A categorized index of vendors should be developed.

d. Purchasing forms should be indexed and numbered.

e. Each piece of equipment over $50 should be listed on a file card with cost price, description, vendor, date of purchase, where used, dates, cost of maintenance, and estimated period of usefulness.

5. Selection of Vendors

a. The number of vendors for regular business should be kept to a minimum, but their prices should be checked regularly.

b. For expensive and extensive orders, bids should be sought, and the order should be given to the lowest bidder consistent with all prestated criteria.

c. Policies should be developed vis-à-vis the selection of local versus outside vendors, taking into consideration transportation costs, unit prices, accessibility of parts and service, delivery time, and community relations.

6. Guidelines for Quality and Quantity Purchasing

a. A price range should be developed in consultation with appropriate department heads for particular items in accordance with low maintenance costs.

b. The purchasing agent or designated person should confer regularly with department heads to keep informed about new products on the market.

c. Standard specifications should be developed jointly by department heads and the purchasing agent for equipment and supplies, including such criteria as:

(1) Measurement
(2) Shrinkage
(3) Weight
(4) Thread count
(5) Odor
(6) Performance
(7) Colorfastness
(8) Resistance to heat
(9) Tensile strength
(10) Visual qualities

d. When appropriate, an annual contract for the purchases of items like milk, bread, fuel or services such as linen rental and elevator maintenance should be investigated.

e. Quantities to order should be determined by:

(1) Knowledge of speed of use of the merchandise
(2) Storage space required
(3) Economy
(4) Cognizance of changing trends in medical care
(5) Understanding of the wastefulness of having money tied up in inventory

7. Emergency Orders

a. When absolutely necessary, emergency orders should be telephoned and purchase orders mailed the following day to the vendor by the purchasing agent or designated person.

b. A subsequent investigation should be made to determine the reason for the emergency order to preclude future exigencies by the purchasing agent and appropriate department head.

E. Accounts Payable

1. General Description

a. All bills should be paid between the tenth and the fifteenth of the month except when a discount is afforded by earlier payment.

b. Recording of accounts payable

(1) All costs and expenses should be recorded on an accrual basis whereby the liabilities or services and purchases are written as incurred and charged to the operations of the applicable month, the actual date of payment of the liabilities having no bearing on the accurate operating results for any period.

(2) Under this accrual system, the expenses are recorded on a historical basis and are properly matched to revenues earned for the same period.

(3) Accounts should be classified, numbered, and distributed according to departmental expenditures.

2. Procedure

a. Purchase orders

(1) Triplicate order forms should be used by the person charged with the responsibility for purchasing with one sheet for the supplier, one sheet kept by the person delegated to purchase, the third sheet attached to the invoice and kept by the Business Department.

(2) After the completion of each purchase order, the ordering information should be entered in a purchase recorder binder to verify costs according to past experience.

(3) Each department should be assigned purchase numbers, such as:

Dietary	520
Housekeeping and Laundry	530 and 540
Plant Operation and Maintenance	510
Administrative and General	410
Nursing	600
Social Service	760
Recreation and Volunteers	750
Physical and Occupational Therapy	790

b. Handling the invoices

(1) Collection. Three to five times per week the Dietary-checked invoices should be delivered or collected by the busi-

Fig. 10-8. The same journal sheet may be interchangeable for use as a purchases journal sheet or a cash disbursements journal sheet by placing an "X" to signify purchases or cash disbursements in the appropriate box.

Page No. P
Date

JOURNAL

Purchases ☐P Cash Disbursements ☐

		New Balance	Invoice Number	Date	Vendor	Payments & Purchases		Discount	Allow-ance	Net Amount	Check Number
						Debit	Credit				
1		P	P	P	P		P				
2											
3											
4											
5											
6											

ness office; invoices for all other departments should be checked by the purchasing agent and brought to the business office for completion of the "received" section of the purchase recorder, or invoices may be received through the mail.

(2) Checking. All invoices should be checked against purchase orders for the significance of recipients and accuracy of their totals with an appropriate mark placed below a correct total. Should there be an error, the invoice should be corrected, a notation of the error made on the company statement, and a check sent for the correct amount with a request for a corrected statement; or the check may be withheld until the arrival of the corrected statement.

(3) Totaling. After all invoices have been checked for accuracy, all invoices from the same company should be collected, totaled, and stapled together, the adding machine tape being attached to the front of each.

c. Preparing the purchases journal

(1) A purchases journal sheet should be placed on the posting board (Fig. 10-8).

(2) The pages should be numbered to run consecutively from one sheet to the next.

(3) After the word Date, only the month and the year applicable at the time the work is being done should be written.

(4) Next to the word Purchases at the top of the page is a small box for an "X" to signify a purchases journal sheet.

(5) In the first large box to the left of the box labeled Invoice Number, the heading New Balance should be noted.

(6) In the large box to the right of the box labeled Date, the heading Vendor should be written.

(7) When this form is used as a purchases journal sheet, only the columns in which a "P" appears should be used.

(8) A piece of special carbon paper should be placed over the purchases journal sheet.

d. The vendor card

(1) Over the carbon paper, the vendor card corresponding to the invoice being noted at the time should be placed (Fig. 10-9).

(2) The purchases journal sheet, the carbon paper, and the vendor card should be locked under the traveler.

(3) On the vendor card the invoice number appearing on the invoice, the date, the name of the vendor, and the amount of the invoice (this last to be written in the column headed Credit) should be written.

Fig. 10-9. A vendor card.

NAME ______________________ ACCT. NO. ________________
ADDRESS ____________________ PHONE ________________

Old Balance	New Balance		Invoice Number	Date	Name	Payments & Purchases		Discount	Allow-ance	Net Amount	Check No.		
						Debit	Credit						
		1											1
		2											2
		3											3
		4											4
		5											5
		6											6

(4) The amount which appears in the credit column should be added to the old balance, the new balance to be written in the column so headed.

(5) The invoice should be placed to one side, the vendor card replaced in the vendor tray, the next invoice and vendor card to which it refers selected, and the above procedure repeated until all purchases for the month have been recorded.

e. Distribution of accounts payable. Each invoice recorded in the purchases journal must be recorded in the distribution journal in the same order as in the purchases journal according to the following procedure:

(1) Preparation of the distribution journal sheet to be effected by placing a distribution journal sheet on the posting board and at the top left-hand corner writing the page number and date, with page numbers to run consecutively from one sheet to the next, and placing a piece of special carbon paper over the distribution journal sheet (Fig. 10-10).

(2) The departmental distribution card (located in departmental distribution tray) should be prepared by placing the departmental distribution card referring to the department to which the first invoice is to be allocated and writing the following information on the card: the date of the invoice, the vendor's name, and the amount of the charge (Fig. 10-11).

(3) The current charges should be completed by adding to the previous total to date the current charges, the total of these two figures to be written on the same line as the current charge, in the column headed Total to Date. Without removing the card from the board, move across the board to the left to locate the account number on the distribution journal sheet corresponding to the number at the top of the departmental distribution card and write the account number noted from the top of the departmental distribution card in the appropriate column under the heading Account No. on the distribution journal sheet. Next to this, write the current charge, also noted from the departmental distribution card, and then, removing the departmental distribution card only from the posting board, refile it and place the next departmental distribution card on the board. The entire process should be repeated until all invoices for the month have been noted on the departmental distribution cards and the distribution journal sheet.

(4) Footing and cross-footing. The distribution journal sheet should then be footed and cross-footed by totaling all charges columns totals, and if this total equals the total of the credits

Fig. 10-10. A section of a distribution journal sheet.

Page no._____
Date_______

					790		720		710		700		450	
					Physical and Occ'l. Therapy		Pharmacy		Consulting		Other Services		Education	
	Acct. No.	Amount	Acct. No.	Amount	Acct. No.	Amount	Acct. No.	Amount	Acct. No.	Amount	Acct. No.	Amount	Acct. No.	Amount
1														
2														
3														
4														
5														
6														

Fig. 10-10 (Continued)

730–740		770		780			750		760		600		410	
Laboratory and X-ray		Religion		Communications			Recreation and Volunteers		Social Service		Nursing		Administrative and General	
Acct. No.	Amount	Acct. No.	Amount	Acct. No.	Amount		Acct. No.	Amount	Acct. No.	Amount	Acct. No.	Amount	Acct. No.	Amount
						1								
						2								
						3								
						4								
						5								
						6								

Fig. 10-10 (Continued)

510		530–540		520								
Plant Operation and Maintenance		Housekeeping and Laundry		Dietary		General						
Acct. No.	Amount	Acct. No.	Amount	Acct. No.	Amount	Acct. No.	Amount	Invoice Date	Vendor	Opening Balance	Charge	Total to Date

Fig. 10-11. A departmental distribution card.

Account No.

	Invoice Date	Vendor	Opening Balance	Charge	Total to Date		
1							1
2							2
3							3
4							4
5							5
6							6

on the purchases journal sheet, the invoices should be placed in the bills payable folder.

(5) Invoices should be checked against the vendors' monthly statements, following which each invoice should be attached behind each corresponding vendor card in the vendor tray for future cash disbursement or payment.

f. Cash disbursements

(1) A cash disbursements journal sheet may be prepared by placing a cash disbursements journal sheet on the posting board the same sheet as is used for a purchases journal sheet (Fig. 10-8), writing an X in the block next to the words Cash Disbursements to indicate its use for cash disbursements, numbering the page to run consecutively from one sheet to the next, and after the word Date, indicating the month and year of payment of the bills, and writing in the first seven blocks from the left of the sheet the word General, and in the eighth block, the words Patient Refunds, and in the ninth block, the word Transfer.

(2) Bills with no vendor cards should be paid by placing a blank check directly on top of the cash disbursements journal sheet, after the word Pay noting the amount of the check, and in the blocks at the upper left-hand corner writing the date of the invoice in the column under Invoice and the amount of the invoice in the column headed Amount and under the word Date indicating the date the check is being written and under

the words To The Order Of writing the name of the person or company to whom the check is to be sent in the block between the two black lines, entering the net amount of the check (in figures) in the block so labeled, writing the check number which appears at the top of the check in the bclok labeled Number, On the lines under the name of person or company to whom the check is being rendered, complete the address of the person or company, have the check signed, and align with the name of the person or company to whom the check is being made out, moving across the cash disbursements sheet to one of the labeled columns at the left and entering the amount of the check in the appropriate column. Write an explanation of the purpose of any check entered into the general column and finally insert the check in a window envelope to be mailed.
(3) Bills with vendor cards should be paid by placing a piece of special carbon paper over the cash disbursements journal sheet and on top of the carbon paper putting the vendor card corresponding to the statement to be paid; arranging a check over the vendor card (over the two posts on the traveler), completing only the shaded area of the check while attached to the board, including the date, to the order of, gross (referring to the total of the statement received), and a discount or allowance to be noted in the blocks that have these labels, making the net amount of check (the gross less the discount or allowance) and the check number. Move across to the left to the vendor card aligned with the shaded area of the check and write the new balance for this vendor in the column labeled New Balance, always writing a new balance even if it is "0" (when using a vendor card, no entries are to be made in the left-hand columns of the cash disbursements journal). Remove the check from the board, completing the remaining sections of the check (invoice, amount, pay, the address, authorized signature), and inserting the check in a window envelope to be mailed, and on the statement writing the check number and the date of the check. File the paid statement and the attached invoices alphabetically according to the vendor's last name, a miscellaneous file to be maintained for bills not received regularly.

g. Procedure for annual storage of bills
(1) All bills for the year should be arranged according to their distribution titles in the distribution journals in separate envelopes or folders.
(2) All envelopes should be filed with the year noted on the outside of the file.

(3) Bills should be kept for the number of years determined by the records supervisor in cooperation with the business manager and administrative director.

F. The Payroll

1. General Information. Personnel should be thoroughly exposed to payroll procedures by oral explanation by their supervisors and by study of:

a. Information written in the employee handbook, including items such as:
(1) Definitions of the work week
(2) Day of distribution of payroll
(3) Payroll deductions
(4) Method of payroll distribution to the employee or his designee
(5) Fringe benefits
(6) Stipulated holidays
(7) Vacations
(8) Sick leave
(9) System of reporting on and off duty
(10) Method of payment for employees who leave and/or are discharged before the termination of the payroll period

b. Sample salary charts illustrating:
(1) Hourly and daily rates compounded on the basis of an annual salary for the nonprofessional staff
(2) The differences between staff and per-diem salaries for the professional nursing staff

2. Pay Period

a. The preferred payroll period should relate to the needs of the majority of the staff, the nonprofessional workers, who generally can plan their budget more effectively on a weekly basis.

b. Payroll may be distributed weekly to nonprofessionals and/or biweekly or monthly to professional staff.

c. The fiscal pay week should follow the work week of the institution, generally beginning on Sunday morning and ending at midnight Saturday.

3. Procedure

a. Preparation of the payroll summary journal sheet. A payroll summary journal sheet should be set on the posting board using the following procedure (Fig. 10-12):
(1) Headings. The top of the sheet or sheets should be headed with the next consecutive number referring to the week number of the completed payroll, with an "A" after the number of the

Fig. 10-12. Payroll summary sheet.

Sheet No.

For Period Ending

	Hours Worked								Employee				Earnings				Deductions				Net Amount	Period Ending	Number
								Total	Name		Breakdown	No.											
1																							
2																							
3																							
4																							
5																							
6																							

week on the second sheet and the date when the pay period ends to be noted at the top of the sheet after the words, For Period Ending. (Two rubber stamps may be used to fill in the two blocks under the headings Earnings and Deductions.)

(2) Employee information. The employee time cards (Fig. 10-13) should be collected and under the heading Employee on the payroll summary sheet, the names of all employees listed in the order in which they appear in the employees' weekly pay binder (the binder containing employee payroll cards maintained for each employee), writing the hours worked and the total number of hours to the left of each employee's name on the payroll summary sheet, and then placing a sheet of special carbon paper over the payroll summary sheet, the employee payroll card corresponding to the first name on the payroll summary sheet placed over the carbon paper (Fig. 10-14).

(3) Placement of payroll check. A payroll check should then be placed over the employee payroll card and all forms inserted under the traveler and locked, except the payroll check, which should be placed over the spindles on top of the lock.

b. Pay statement. At the upper left of each payroll check a summary of the pay statement should be completed, indicating the following information:

(1) Earnings. First the total number of hours worked should be noted to the left of the employee's name on the payroll summary sheet, in the block headed Hours Worked.

(2) Regular wages. For an employee working on an hourly basis, the regular wages should be calculated by multiplying the total hours worked by the amount earned per hour with the result to be written in the block headed Regular Wages, or for an employee working on a salary basis, the regular weekly salary should be noted in the Regular Wages block.

(3) Room and board. Should an employee obtain lodging and/or meals, the appropriate amount may be subtracted from his regular wages and the remainder of his regular wages written in the block captioned Total Taxable Income, but should there be no deduction from room and/or board, the regular wages figures should be repeated in the Total Taxable Income block.

(4) Deductions. Federal and state taxes: The amounts to be deducted for taxes (F.I.C.A., Federal WH/Tax, State WH/Tax, and State Disability Tax) can be found in the payroll-taxes guidebook, which should be available in all business offices.

(5) Insurance benefits may be paid completely or partially by

Fig. 10-13. Employee time cards may be kept in a separate Kardex for Nursing, Dietary, and Housekeeping.

Sun	Mon	Tue	Wed	Thurs	Fri	Sat
2	3	4	5	6	7	8
9	10	11	12	13	14	15
16	17	18	19	20	21	22
23	24	25	26	27	28	29

Name: April 196_

Fig. 10-14. An individual employee payroll card.

Rate of Pay

Withholding Status

M ☐ F ☐

S ☐ M ☐

Name__________ Soc. Sec. No.

Address__________

Dept.________

Year________

Gross Pay to Date			Earnings			Deductions				Net Amount	Period Ending	Number	
	½ Yr. Tot.												
	1												1
	2												2
	3												3
	4												4
	5												5
	6												6

the institution, and stipulated premiums may be deducted from the payroll checks of those employees requiring family plans, should these premiums not be paid by the extended care facility.

(6) Loans and garnishees. Deductions should be made when applicable but this practice may be discouraged by appropriate statements in the personnel policies.

(7) All the preceding deductions should be totaled and the total placed in the column headed Total Deductions.

(8) Net amount. The total deductions should be subtracted from the regular wages (not from the total taxable income) with the remainder (the net amount) to be so written later on the employee's weekly pay check and now written in the proper pay-statement block.

(9) Period ending and number. The date of the ending of the pay period should be written in the proper block and the number appearing after the letters "PR" at the top of the payroll check in the block headed Number.

(10) The described procedure for the pay statement should be followed for each employee in the order listed on the payroll summary sheet, remembering that the payroll check itself is to be written later and only the pay statements should be written at this point.

c. Balancing the payroll summary sheet. After the pay statements for all employees have been completed, all the columns on the payroll summary sheet should be footed and cross-footed:

(1) "Footing" means adding vertically with the total noted at the bottom of column.

(2) "Cross-footing" means adding horizontally: The total for room and board plus the total taxable income should equal the total regular wages with all deduction totals for various categories equal to the total deductions and the total deductions plus the net amount total to equal the regular wages total.

d. Writing and distributing the payroll check

(1) Writing the check. Only after the payroll summary sheet is balanced may the individual checks be written and signed by using the full name of the employee, ascertaining that the date corresponds to the date appearing on the attached pay statement under Period Ending, and that the amount is the figure that appears under Net Amount on the attached pay statement.

(2) Distributing the checks. Each payroll check should be inserted in an envelope, marked with the employee's name as it appears on the check, sealed, and given to the department head for distribution to the employee, except for Nursing Department pay checks of evening and night staff, which are placed for safekeeping until collected by those members of the nursing staff.

e. Payroll breakdown. The total payroll should be broken down or distributed to determine the amount of money that has been allocated to each department as follows:

(1) On the payroll summary sheet, under the heading Breakdown, departmental breakdowns and distribution numbers should be listed for the categories such as:

Medical director
Administrative director
Administrative salaries
Maintenance

Dietary
Housekeeping and laundry
RN nurses
LPN nurses
Nursing attendants
Recreation and volunteers
Social service
Occupational therapy
Physical therapy

(2) The departmental titles should be written under the word Breakdown in the column headed Employee, and the distribution numbers written in the first block next to the title.

(3) The number corresponding to the department with which the employee is associated (taken from the breakdown) should be written in the first block next to each employee's name.

(4) All the regular wages for each departmental breakdown should be added, and the total placed in the regular wages column aligned with the corresponding department title.

(5) After the breakdowns for all departments have been completed, the figures of the breakdown should be totaled, and this total must equal the total regular wages figure.

(6) The individual breakdown total for each department should be transferred to departmental distribution cards demonstrating the current expenditures for each department.

f. Monthly payroll summary sheet

(1) All totals from the payroll summary sheet should be transferred to a monthly payroll summary sheet.

(2) The monthly payroll summary sheet should be completed immediately after the last pay period each month.

(3) This sheet should use the same sheet number appearing on the last weekly payroll summary sheet of that month with the word Monthly printed before the words Payroll Summary of the heading, and the letter ""B" placed after the number to distinguish the monthly from the weekly sheet.

(4) At the end of the month, the monthly payroll summary sheet should be footed and cross-footed in the same manner described for the weekly sheet for the accountant's use in the monthly analysis.

g. Quarterly and yearly tax returns

(1) All the employee payroll cards should be totaled.

(2) All the payroll summary sheets should be totaled.

(3) The totals of the payroll cards and the payroll summary sheets must correspond.

(4) The above figures should be submitted to the accountant for preparation of the tax returns if a controller is not in the employ of the extended care facility.

G. Bank Accounts

1. Types. A variety of bank accounts for various purposes may be held by the institution, but at least two are required:

a. The general account—All income should be deposited in this account.

b. The payroll account—For payroll exclusively, and the net amount of a payroll should be transferred weekly from the general account to the payroll account, sufficient reserves being maintained between payroll periods.

2. Authorized Signatures. In the event of illness or absences for other reasons of the administrative director, at least two members of the staff should be authorized to sign checks, but in no event should the person writing the checks be permitted to act as the signatory.

3. Deposits

a. Deposits for the general account should be made daily.

b. Deposits should be made to the general account by:

(1) Completing two deposit tickets for regular deposits, two separate deposit slips for Medicare checks

(2) Submitting both deposit tickets to the teller

(3) Returning one ticket listing the individual checks, with the total amount of the deposit stamped on it by the bank, to the business office for further entry

c. Deposits to the payroll account should be made as follows:

(1) Only one deposit ticket should be completed.

(2) Upon making the deposit at the bank, only one slip noting the amount of the deposit will be returned by the teller.

4. Reconciliation of the bank statements should be handled by the bookkeeper at the end of each month.

5. Cash Position

a. Once weekly the business manager should submit to the administrative director a written report of the balances of the general and payroll accounts.

b. On the fifteenth of each month a written list of outstanding accounts receivable should be presented to the administrative director for appropriate action.

c. A written report of the potential income for the month as compared with the budgeted income should be brought to the attention of the administrative director.

H. Handling of Mail (The distribution of patient and staff mail was described previously.)

1. Procedure for Incoming Business Department Mail

a. All bills received should be filed in the tray marked "Bills" in the business office.

b. Incoming checks should be placed in a separate location and should be processed as outlined in the discussion of the section on accounts receivable.

2. Procedure for Sending Out Mail

a. All outgoing mail should be conveyed to the business office.

b. All mail should be weighed, stamped on the postage meter, and placed in the outgoing mail basket.

c. All mail should be deposited in the mail box no later than 5:00 P.M.

3. Procedure for Refilling Postage Meter

a. When the postage meter, with a capacity of $99.99, registers $3, it should be refilled.

b. A check should be written for $96.99 to the order of the postmaster and taken to the bank to be certified.

c. The certified check and the postage meter should be delivered to the post office, where the postage meter will be refilled.

I. Protection of Valuables

1. General. The responsibility for the protection of patient valuables, including cash, jewelry, or other precious items, should be relegated to the business office.

2. Procedure for the Safekeeping of Valuables

a. All valuables belonging to a patient should be inserted in a special valuables envelope before placement in the safe.

b. The name of the patient, the contents, the date, and the initials of the business staff member should be marked on the front of the envelope.

c. A signed receipt for the money and/or articles should be given to the patient or his sponsor.

3. Procedure for the Return of Valuables

a. When items are removed from the safe, the patient or his designee should be required to affix his signature, the date, and the name of the article, the ornament, or the amount of money removed.

b. The receipt should be returned and signed by the recipient.

c. In the event of an unplanned discharge or the death of the patient, the valuables or cash should be mailed, insured and/or registered return receipt requested, to the patient or his sponsor.

V. DUTIES AND RESPONSIBILITIES

A. Business Manager

1. Daily or Regular Duties

a. She should take charge of the outgoing mail.

b. The charges journal should be completed should a patient be admitted and/or discharged.

c. Bank deposits should be made.

d. In cooperation with department heads, she should coordinate all purchasing and should keep the purchases recording journal current.

2. Weekly Duties

a. Employee records should be checked for completeness, including health examinations, x-rays, reasons for discharge, resignation, etc. (Fig. 10-15).

b. All material for duplication should be mimeographed.

c. Cash disbursements should be made.

d. She should inform the administrative director of the cash position.

e. Medicare-eligibility forms should be prepared and transmitted to the fiscal intermediary.

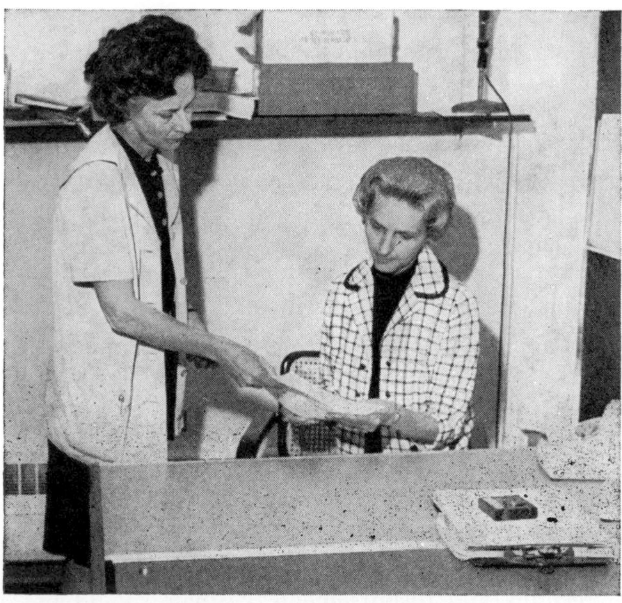

Fig. 10-15. A department head submits a completed employee application form to the office manager.

3. Monthly Duties

a. The state and federal withholding taxes should be paid.

b. Sign-in cards should be prepared for the following month.

c. She should report to the administrative director concerning accounts receivable and potential income in comparison with the budgeted figures.

d. The monthly statistical data should be gathered.

4. Other Responsibilities

a. She should assist whenever government or insurance inspectors come to review the books.

b. She should complete all forms sent by various government agencies concerning employees.

c. She should maintain and refer to the insurance roster.

d. She should administer the safekeeping of valuables.

e. She should complete requests from insurance companies concerning third-party payments for patients.

B. Bookkeeper

1. Weekly Duties

a. The weekly payroll should be prepared.

b. The cash receipt journals should be completed.

c. The purchases and distribution journals should be finished.

d. All paid bills should be filed.

e. Incoming invoices should be verified as to correct figures and totals.

f. She should maintain employee records and keep financial material current on appropriate forms (Fig. 10-16).

g. She should assist in other assignments given by business manager.

2. Monthly Duties

a. All monthly bills should be paid on or before the fifteenth of each month.

b. The patient billings should be prepared and mailed.

c. She should complete and summarize the following:

(1) Accounts receivable journal

(2) Accounts payable journal

(3) Purchases journal

(4) Distribution journal

(5) Payroll journal

d. The bank reconciliation should be done.

e. All receipts and disbursements journals should be analyzed.

f. She should cross-foot all books to determine whether or not they balance.

Fig. 10-16. The bookkeeper can work more efficiently if the business office is removed from the mainstream of activity.

g. Entries should be posted into the general ledger.
h. The control cards on accounts receivable and payable monthly should be maintained.

3. Quarterly Duties
a. The individual employee payroll record cards for the quarter should be totaled.
b. The quarterly payroll tax returns should be figured.

4. Yearly Duties
a. All bills, cancelled checks, and other business records for the year should be filed.
b. New employee payroll record cards should be prepared at the end of the year.
c. Summaries of state and federal income taxes withheld should be prepared and distributed to all personnel employed during the calendar year.

C. Certified Public Accountant

1. The accountant should prepare monthly and quarterly financial reports from the data obtained from the business manager to present to administration.

2. He should close the books by removing the totals of revenues accumulated in the ledger during the accounting period so that the balance will not be confused with income and expenses of future accounting periods.

3. Special financial reports for government agencies, fiscal intermediaries, banks, and the governing body should be completed by the accountant.

4. The accountant should engage in long-range financial planning with the administration and the governing board.

VI. SCHEDULE OF SPECIAL PAYMENTS

Special payments to be made during the year should be listed on a schedule, including such items and time periods as are shown in Table 7.

TABLE 7. SCHEDULE OF SPECIAL PAYMENTS

	Monthly	Quarterly	Annually
Federal			
Depositary receipt*			
940 employer's unemployment tax return			
Corporate income tax			
941 employer's tax return (F.I.C.A. and withholding)		March 31 June 30 Sept. 30 Dec. 31	
State			
Employer's contribution for unemployment insurance		usually March 31 June 30 Sept. 30 Dec. 31	
Disability insurance premiums			
Deposit premiums for Workmen's Compensation			Jan. 1 (or fiscal year)
Franchise tax	according to state regulation		
Withholding tax	according to state regulation		
Unincorporated business tax	according to state regulation		
Other			
Rent	according to lease		
Honoraria to clergy	by the 15th of each month		
Recreation petty cash ($25)	by the 30th of each month		

* May be weekly or biweekly.

VII. INSURANCE PLAN

A. Agent and/or Consultant

1. Due to the diverse and unusual circumstances related to insuring health care institutions, the use of a consultant to assist in the development of the insurance program should be considered.
2. The advice of insurance company representatives should also be heeded.

B. Purposes of Insurance

1. To protect and preserve the assets of the extended care facility, such as plant, equipment, and income, which are subject to risks of destruction, breakdown, legal risk, or theft
2. To protect the facility against claims for any injuries that may be sustained by patients, visitors, and staff
3. To provide for losses due to personal injury, sickness, or death suffered by personnel in the course of employment
4. To provide for losses due to personal injury, sickness, or death of personnel suffered not in the course of employment

C. General Principles. The following general principles should be considered prior to the development of a formal insurance program in the extended care facility:

1. All policies should be stored in a safe, fireproof, yet accessible area.
2. Wherever feasible, policies should be consolidated to afford maximum safety and coverage.
3. The installation of devices to reduce insurance costs, such as sprinklers and fire-detection systems should be studied.
4. A roster of insurance coverage should be prepared to provide for uninterrupted coverage and quick analysis of present protection, listing policies, due dates, amounts of premiums, and their exact time of expiration.
5. All staff members, full and part-time, should be provided with workmen's compensation insurance.
6. Outside contractors should be required to provide workmen's compensation insurance for their employees.
7. All staff, board members, and volunteers should be insured against injury suits.
8. The pharmacist should be compelled to carry liability insurance.
9. The extended care facility should be covered by products' liability insurance.
10. The property of patients, staff, and visitors should be insured against theft or other harm.

11. The extended care facility should investigate the possibility of group insurance plans with other health and welfare agencies.
12. All descriptions of the property must be correct.
13. The proper name and address of the insured should appear on all policies.

D. Types of Insurance Carried

1. Property Insurance. Fire and extended coverage should include all-risk physical damage to the building and contents.
(This type of policy will not cover the loss of staff's or patient's property in the event of fire or other loss.)

a. Plate glass coverage should be unlimited except for a moderate sum per incident in case of fire, war, or nuclear explosion.
b. Boiler coverage should include machinery, equipment, and boilers on a blanket basis with simple or furnace explosion unless this coverage is contained under the fire insurance policy.
c. Other property insurance. Other property coverage might be concerned with:
(1) Sprinkler leakage or water damage
(2) Aircraft damage
(3) Earthquake, windstorm, cyclone, tornado damage
(4) Riot and civil commotion
(5) Lightning damage
(6) Vandalism and malicious mischief

2. Legal and Liability Insurance
a. Workmen's compensation insurance
(1) Coverage: This insurance should cover loss due to statutory liability as a result of personal injury, sickness, or death suffered by employees in the course of their employment.
(2) The amount is prescribed by law: (*a*) It is two-thirds of the weekly salary, but not in excess of a stipulated amount. (*b*) Weekly payments are payable after the eighth day of disability but should the disability continue beyond 14 days, payments will be made dating from the first day of disability. (*c*) All medical expenses will be reimbursed and worker is free to elect his own doctor and/or hospital. (*d*) In the event that the Workmen's Compensation Board should determine that an injured employee is entitled to a specific award, such award will be made in addition to the above benefits. (*e*) An accident form must be completed by a charge nurse.
b. Comprehensive general liability
This should cover liability:

(1) Imposed by law for damages because of bodily injury, sickness, or disease, (including death) at any time resulting therefrom, and including damages for the care and loss of services sustained by any person, caused as a result of an accident arising out of maintenance or use of the premises or property and all operations which are necessary or incidental thereto

(2) For an accident caused by an employee while on or off the premises, if such act is committed while in the course of employment

(3) For mishaps caused by elevator and products' usage

(4) With the exception of accidents caused by automobiles or other vehicles which generally are excluded from this type of policy

c. Hospital professional liability (malpractice). This coverage should:

(1) Protect the extended care facility against claims brought as a result of error of omission or commission in the rendering of professional care to a patient, including the furnishing of food and beverage

(2) Include all sums that the facility may become obligated to pay because of injury (including death) sustained by any patient resulting from error of omission or commission in the rendering or failing to render of medical or nursing treatment

d. Automobile

Vehicle policies should afford protection:

(1) For auto ownership and nonownership liability, including leased or hired cars, covering liability under any operator

(2) Relating to individual and/or groups of patients and employees

3. Burglary

The following categories should be covered by burglary insurance:

a. Equipment in the medical and dental areas

b. Patients' personal effects

c. Belongings of staff members

d. Property of visitors

4. Disability

This coverage should provide:

a. For loss due to statutory liability as a result of personal injury or sickness suffered by employees not in the course of their employment

b. A weekly income in amounts prescribed by law, the law presently requiring weekly indemnity of 50 percent of the average weekly wages, not to exceed a maximum of a stipulated amount for a maximum of 26 weeks

c. Benefits to begin 8 days after the accident or the onset of illness

5. Hospitalization and Medical Benefits

a. Hospitalization benefits with specific reference to hospitals within and outside the serviced area for the stated period or a minimum of 21 days in a 180-day contract, meaning room and board at the hospital's average semiprivate rate for the first 21 days and 50 percent of such charge for the next 180 days, to include coverage for:

(1) Obstetric deliveries
(2) Communicable diseases
(3) Mental and nervous disorders
(4) Pulmonary tuberculosis
(5) First aid

b. Medical benefits with sufficient minimum coverage and realistic sums allocated for:

(1) Surgery
(2) In-hospital medical care
(3) Electroshock therapy
(4) Maternity care
(5) In-hospital consultation
(6) Radiation therapy
(7) Anesthesia
(8) Diagnostic x-ray

VIII. EQUIPMENT AND SUPPLIES

A. Business Office Equipment

1 safe
1 mimeograph machine
Two 10-key adding machines
2 electric typewriters
3 posting boards
4 file trays
5 ledger binders
1 postage meter
1 check writer
1 postage scale
1 paper cutter
1 adjustable hand punch
1 DYMO

TABLE 8. BUSINESS OFFICE SUPPLIES

Item	Reorder Point	Reorder Quantity
Forms		
Billing statement	150	500
Employee payroll card	1 doz	1 box (50 cards)
Patients accounts receivable card	25	50
Departmental distribution card	25	50
Accounts payable vendor card	25	50
Purchases—Cash disbursements journal sheets	25	50
Purchases—Recorder sheets	25	50
Charges and receipts journal sheets	25	50
Payroll summary journal sheets	25	50
General checking account check	200	1,000
Payroll account check	500	2,000
Special carbon paper	25 sheets	1 box (100 sheets)
Mimeograph paper		
White	1 ream	5 reams
Salmon	1 ream	5 reams
Blue	1 ream	5 reams
Green	1 ream	5 reams
Pink	1 ream	5 reams
Yellow	1 ream	5 reams
Buff	1 ream	5 reams
Other Mimeograph Materials		
Hand cleaning pads	1 can	12 cans
Mimeograph ink	1 can	10 cans
Mimeograph stencil sheets	1 box	10 boxes
Mimeograph protective covers	1 box	10 boxes
Colored ink (red, green) and correction fluid	1 bottle	1 bottle
Mimeograph ink pads	1 pad	1 box
Reinforced mimeograph paper	1 box	6 boxes
Envelopes		
Plain windowed (with return address) $3\frac{3}{4} \times 6\frac{1}{2}$ in.	$\frac{1}{2}$ box	1,000
Plain (with return address) $3\frac{3}{4} \times 6\frac{1}{2}$ in.	$\frac{1}{2}$ box	500
No. 10 blank envelopes	$\frac{1}{2}$ box	500
No. 10 envelope with blue logo return address	1 box	
No. 10 envelope with black logo return address	1 box	
Brown envelopes 6×12	50	1,000
Pencils		
No. 2	2 pencils	1 doz
No. 4	2 pencils	1 doz
Colorbrite medium red	1 pencil	3 pencils
Oxford File Cards		
White plain 3×5	50	1,000
White plain 5×8	50	1,000
Typing Material		
Heavy bond typing paper	$\frac{1}{4}$ box	1 box
Medium-weight bond typing paper	$\frac{1}{4}$ box	1 box
Black carbon paper	10 sheets	1 box
Miscellaneous		
Files	5 files	1 box

Table 8. BUSINESS OFFICE SUPPLIES (Continued)

Item	Reorder Point	Reorder Quantity
Purchase order forms	50	1,000
Accountant extra-fine point pens—blue	1 pen	1 doz
Paper clips	1 box	3 boxes
Typewriter erasers	2	6
Rubber bands	2 boxes	6 boxes
Reinforcements	2 boxes	6 boxes
Staples	¼ box	1 box
DYMO tape	4 rolls	6 boxes
Manila file folders	10 folders	1 box
Scotch Tape	1 roll	2 rolls
Adding machine tape	1 roll	1 doz
Reinforced indexes (black A-Z tabs)	1 set	6 sets
Purchase index stock sheets	50	500

2 staplers
Two 5 x 8 file boxes
1 purchase recorder binder

B. Business Office Supplies (see Table 8)

IX. INTERDEPARTMENTAL COOPERATION

A. Administrative Director

1. The business manager should submit a weekly written report of the cash position of the facility to the administrative director.

2. The business manager should present a written report of the outstanding accounts and the potential income for the month.

3. She should consult with the administrative director whenever equipment costing over a stipulated amount is to be purchased.

B. Social Service Department

1. Admission of New Patients

a. The director of social service should inform the business office of the admission of a new patient and should supply information on the patient's sponsorship status, including Medicare, private or third party, plus any arrangements for special services.

b. The director of social service should submit a signed family responsibility form to the business office, indicating the name and Medicare number of the newly admitted patient, the name and address of the responsible family member, the patient's daily charges, and written permission for special charges if the patient is to receive special services.

2. Handling of Patient Finances during Residence

a. Once a month during patient residence, the business manager should meet with the director of social service to discuss the status of patient financial accounts and to bring accounts judged delinquent to her attention for appropriate action.

b. Should the responsible family member request an explanation of patient billing procedures or account status, the director of social service should refer the family to the business manager to provide the necessary explanatory services.

c. Requests for completion of third-party payments forms may be directed to the director of social service by the responsible family member, and these forms should be completed by the business manager.

3. Patient Discharge. The director of social service should notify the business office of planned patient discharges and should cooperate with the business manager to check on patient financial accounts so that the correct bills may be submitted to the responsible family member prior to patient discharge.

4. Files on Patients and Families. The following files on patients and families should be maintained in the business office:

a. Signed family responsibility forms

b. Written permission to purchase services

c. Written permission to leave the premises (a copy to be put on the patient's chart)

d. Medicare records

C. Nursing. Patients ready for discharge must present the charge nurse with a slip from the business office indicating no outstanding bills.

D. Health-Records Librarian. When a patient is discharged, the data kept in the business office may be incorporated with other material by the health-records librarian and filed in the health-records room.

E. All Other Departments

1. Upon hiring a new employee, all department heads should submit to the business office, a completed application for employment, a W-4 form, and any other pertinent information concerning the new employee.

2. When requiring the purchase of merchandise, the department heads should submit a completed requisition slip to the business manager.

3. Verified invoices should be submitted regularly to the business office.

X. TRAINING AND EDUCATION

The business staff should attend the following meetings:

A. Monthly Staff Meetings

B. Quarterly Safety Education Meetings

C. Appropriate Workshops and Seminars

Section 11

Records

Introduction

An extended care facility is a complex organization. It comprises a minimum of 10 departments and/or services and a total staff equal to or in excess of the number of patients accommodated. With the incessant activity typical of a modern health care facility, it is virtually impossible for anyone—the administrator, the president of the governing body, or the medical director—to trust to his memory relevant material concerning the operation of the institution.

Thus, pertinent records, including correspondence, contracts, reports, executed forms, card and sheets, medical records, minutes of meetings, insurance policies, blueprints and specifications, and corporate data, become an essential tool of management, similar to a budget or a table of organization. Not only should the above-mentioned materials be retained for future reference, but they must be retained in a systematic form for easy accessibility.

With the passage of time it must be assumed that the extended care facility will serve a continuing number of patients, employ a successive stream of personnel, add to the medical staff, and engage in business with an increasing number of vendors. To preclude unnecessary effort and expense at some future date, it is imperative that the facility develop a systematic plan for the organization and coordination of all institutional records.

I. STAFFING PATTERN

A. An extended care facility of 100 beds or more should employ a full-time health-records librarian, and this person should be designated to act as a supervisor of health and administrative records.

B. In an institution of less than 100 beds, too small to justify the post of a full-time health-records librarian, the secretary of the administrative director may be assigned to organize, maintain, and supervise all files.

II. ADMINISTRATIVE RECORDS

A. Scope of Responsibility of Records Supervisor. The records supervisor should develop a standard method of indexing and filing all records with the exception of patient and accounting material.

B. Duties and Procedures. The records supervisor should:

1. In conjunction with the administrative director and all department heads prepare a master list of subject captions
2. Determine the arrangement of filing captions and records according to subject matter or name
3. Select an additional filing caption to locate data for the purpose of developing a cross-reference file
4. Train personnel to index and file in accordance with a predetermined plan
5. Permit changes, additions, and deletions in the design only with the express approval of the administrative director, the department heads, and herself
6. Evolve meaningful criteria for records' retention and disposal with full knowledge that records:
- *a.* Should be kept to the limit of their potential use
- *b.* Should be destroyed when no longer useful in order to eliminate crowding and shorten the time required to search through voluminous files
- *c.* Should be kept varying lengths of time according to the suggested guidelines in Table 9

7. Develop a program for the preservation of records by:
- *a.* Use of a charge-out method for all material removed from the files and a periodic checking procedure to verify the return of all data
- *b.* Storing records to be kept over 5 years in their original form
- *c.* Microfilming original records with the following benefits and disadvantages:
  - (1) Disposal of the original cumbersome records.
  - (2) A consequent saving in space for records and file cabinets.
  - (3) The permissibility of microfilm records in courts of law.
  - (4) The elimination of refiling of specific records and the resultant diminution of misfiling.
  - (5) Records preserved on microfilm should last longer.
  - (6) The initial cost for a microfilm installation is considerable.
  - (7) Microfilming may require the preparation of a totally new indexing and filing system.
  - (8) Microfilmed records may be used less frequently by professional staff.

Table 9. SUGGESTED PERIOD OF RECORD RETENTION

Length of Time to be Kept	Type of Record
1 year	Information desk file
	Telephone index
2 years	Departmental reports
	Purchasing records
5 years beyond expiration	Insurance policies
5 years	Budget reports
	Record of food costs and meals served
	Tax statements
Statute of limitations	Employee records
	Patient records*
10 years	Cost statements
	Medical audits
Until revised	Admission policies
	Personnel policies
Until new approval received	Joint Commission for the Accreditation of Hospitals reports
As long as useful	Publications and reports of other agencies
As long as active	Committee reports
Until superseded	Codes
	Emergency and utility interruption plans
	Rules for libraries
	Rules for visitors
Indefinite	Annual reports
	Audit reports
	Balance sheets
	Bank records
	Income and expense statements
	Legal suits
	License numbers of personnel
	Licenses and permits
	Minutes of meetings
	Organizational charts
	Rates and charges
Permanent	Specifications and plans
	Certificate of doing business
	Certificate of occupancy
	Certificate of incorporation
	Constitution and bylaws
	History of the institution
	Medical staff appointments
	Medical staff bylaws

* May be kept permanently for research purposes.

8. Decide upon the development of a centralized, partially centralized, or decentralized file system on the basis of:

a. The size of the extended care facility

b. The number and location of departments lending themselves to decentralization where:

(1) The departments and administration are physically separated.

(2) The nature of work in the department may be dependent upon easily accessible records.

c. The volume of records:

(1) Sufficient magnitude would justify the employment of a full-time file clerk.

(2) One person filing records uniformly under the close direction of the records supervisor should eliminate errors.

d. The architectural design of the building or buildings:

(1) Should all offices be in close proximity, a centralized file system will be effective.

(2) When departments and administration are not in close proximity, a decentralized file system should ensure more usage due to physical accessibility and no time loss resulting from transportation.

e. The frequency of reference to the records

f. The nature of the intercommunication system in the institution:

(1) Provision of a messenger service

(2) Use of a public address system

(3) Practice of telephone intercommunication

9. Establish standardized sizes for all types of records to:

a. Expedite the handling process

b. Eliminate the added expense of special supplies and filing and storage cabinets

10. Number and date all newly developed and/or revised record forms for purposes of:

a. Easy identification

b. Scheduling periodic review for correction and/or deletion

c. Adding to the master records list

11. Set up a master list of records used in the extended care facility (see Table 10):

a. In departmentalized form for quick reference

b. To be able to ascertain the exact number and types of records in use at any given time

III. HEALTH RECORDS

A. Functions of Health Records. In an extended care facility, records:

1. Serve as tools of communication between various professionals involved in the care of patients

2. Furnish relevant data in the event of patient readmission

3. Offer information for medicolegal problems

4. Are useful for purposes of education and research

5. Assist the institution in evaluating its own services

TABLE 10. SUGGESTED MASTER LIST OF RECORDS

Name of Record
Administration Department
Annual report of general and statistical information
Notification of patient movement
Patients alphabetical index cards
Patient register forms
Record of patient admission (for health department)
Record of patient discharge (for health department)
Release form for news stories and photographs
Room information card for receptionist
Release form for patient outings
Tally sheet of sociologic statistics of discharged patients
Business Department
Accounts receivable card
Annual budget
Billing statement
Balance sheet
Budget control and comparative expenses
Charges and receipts journal sheet
Departmental distribution card
Discharge approval slip for nursing
Distribution journal vendor card
Employee payroll card
General checking account check
General deposit ticket
Monthly billing statement
Monthly financial data
Monthly statistical data
Patients' accounts receivable card
Payroll check
Payroll deposit ticket
Payroll summary journal sheet
Purchases-cash disbursements journal sheet
Purchase orders
Purchases recording journal sheets
Release for valuables
Requisition slip
Statement of income and expenses
Valuables envelope
Dietary Department
Cycle menu
Diet checklist
Floor supply lists
Food inventory
Individual diet card
Menu choice
Menu planner
Record of meals served
Reports
Weekly schedule of hours
Housekeeping Department
Laundry count list
Supply inventory
Reports
Maintenance Department
Architectural plans and specifications
Danger tags
Index of equipment purchases and maintenance
Log book
Reports
Safety quiz
Medicare
Certification and recertification forms
Extended care admission and billing form
Medicare patient register for utilization review
Provider reimbursement statement
Summary sheet of Medicare patients for review by the utilization review committee
Transfer forms
Utilization review forms
Medical Staff and Allied Health Professionals
Application for the medical staff
Contracts for allied health professionals
Curriculum vitae for allied health professionals
Dentists orders and progress notes
Initial physical examination
Laboratory report
Permission for the patient to leave the premises
Physician's orders and progress notes
Podiatrist's orders and progress notes
Reports
Urinalysis report
Utilization review form
X-ray report
Nursing Department
Admission and discharge information
Census sheet
Check sheet
Control record of narcotics and sedatives
Incident or accident report
Intake and output record (bedside copy)
Intake and output record (chart copy)
Inventory of drugs surrendered (state narcotics control bureau)
Inventory of nurses' supply room
Nursing care plan and progress notes
Nursing care plan cards
Record of patient care by nursing attendants

TABLE 10. SUGGESTED MASTER LIST OF RECORDS (Continued)

Name of Record	Name of Record
Nursing Department (continued)	Letter of request
Release of responsibility for discharge against advice	Monthly calendar
Reports	Monthly program summary
Special services	Patient admission card
Transfer and referral record	Record of volunteer hours
Personnel	**Restorative Services**
Annual record of earnings and deductions	Occupational therapy prescription
Application for employment	Record of occupational therapy treatment and monthly progress report
Application for hospitalization insurance	Physical therapy prescription
Health examination forms	Record of physical therapy treatment and monthly progress report
List of nurses and state registration numbers	Record of speech therapy treatment and monthly progress report
Payroll cards	**Social Service Department**
Reference forms	Daily record for social work activities
Reports	Information for families form
Social security information	Monthly family integration meeting record
Time cards	Monthly patient group meeting sheet
Weekly schedule of hours	Monthly social service summary
Weekly time and floor schedules	Patient admission card
Recreation and Volunteers	Preadmission questionnaire
Application for volunteers	Record of inquiry
Daily recreation program record form	Record of patient status changes
Health form for volunteers	Reminder of Medicine expiration date
Letter of appreciation	

6. Aid the public health agencies in community planning by the information provided in the record materials

B. Treatment of Health Records

1. All personal health records of patients should remain confidential, the originals never leaving the premises and release of copies for medicolegal purposes sanctioned in writing by the patient or the responsible family member, or authorized by court subpoena.
2. Records as impersonal documents may be used for purposes of scientific research and education.
3. The record of each patient should be kept for a period of time prescribed as the statute of limitations by state law following the discharge of that patient.

C. Scope of Responsibility of the Health-records Librarian

1. The librarian should coordinate all medical and nursing records.
2. These records should be checked during patients' stays at the facility and upon their discharge.
3. The necessary indexes should be developed.

4. All records should be filed completely and in the properly designated order.

D. Specific Responsibility for Records. The completion of the records listed below should be the chief responsibility of the health-records librarian:

1. Certification and recertification form, to be completed by the attending physician (see Fig. 3-3)
2. Remainder of Medicare expiration date form, to be completed by Director of Social Service at the request of the health-records librarian (Fig. 11-1).
3. Record of patient status changes, to be maintained on a daily basis together with the patient census sheet (Fig. 11-2).
4. Medicare patients register for the utilization review committee (Fig. 11-3)

Fig. 11-1

REMINDER OF MEDICARE EXPIRATION DATE

____
Date

To Sponsor____________________

Address____________________

____

Medicare benefits for______________________________expire at
Patient's Name
____________________________on____________________. Please
Name of Facility Date
let us know if you plan to have the patient remain on private status. May we have your decision no later than one (1) week prior to the above date.

Thank you.

Patient's Medicare number____________________

Date of admission____________________

____
Director of Social Service

RECORD OF PATIENT STATUS CHANGES

Month____________________

Date	ON			OFF		
	Medicare	Medicaid	Private	Medicare	Medicaid	Private

5. Utilization review form for each Medicare patient [See Section 2 and utilization review committee notification form (Fig. 11-4).]
6. Summary sheet of Medicare patients for review by the utilization review committee (Fig 11-5)
7. Tally sheet of sociologic statistics of discharged patients (Fig. 11-6)
8. Notification of patient movement (Fig. 11-7)

E. Duties and Procedures

1. Regular Duties

a. Admissions

(1) The librarian should verify prospective admissions with the Social Service Department daily in order to prepare charts for new patients using the unit (original number for all read-

Fig. 11-3

MEDICARE PATIENTS

Name	Admission No.	Room	Admission Certification	Recerti-fication	Second Certification	Third Certification	Expiration Date	Disposition	Remarks

Fig. 11-4

UTILIZATION REVIEW COMMITTEE NOTIFICATION

To: Attending Physician
Extended Care Facility
Responsible Relative

Re: ______________________
Patient's Name

From: Utilization Review Committee

We have completed a review of the above patient's case with respect to approval or disapproval for benefits under the health insurance program.

__________patient is approved for admission to this ECF.

__________patient is disapproved for admission to this ECF.

__________patient is approved for extended stay.

__________patient is disapproved for extended stay.

____
Date of Next Review

____
Secretary of Committee

____
Date

missions) or the serial method (new numbers for each patient readmission).

(2) Charts should be arranged for new patients with as complete information as possible at the time.

(3) While admitting new patients and meeting their families, she should complete the new patient charts and subsequently deliver the appropriate sections to the business office, the proper nursing units, the receptionist, and the recreation and social work offices.

b. Patient movement notification

(1) Utilizing the notification of patient movement slips, she

Fig. 11-5

SUMMARY SHEET OF MEDICARE PATIENTS

Utilization Review Committee ______________ Date of Meeting

Patients for review:

Name	OASI No.	Number	Diagnosis	Disposition

should make the appropriate entries in the patient register and on the Medicare list and should correct the patient roster.

(2) She should transmit information on the notification of patient movement slips to the Dietary Department to verify the previous verbal notifications of the Nursing Department.

(3) The notification of patient movement slips should then be given to the business office.

c. Medicare records. The librarian should bring the Medicare records up to date by conferring with Social Service, Nursing, Recreation, the dietitian, and Restorative Services.

d. Other records and files

(1) The librarian should inspect the charts of discharged patients transferred to the record room after processing by the Business Department.

(2) She should file the patients' index cards in alphabetical order.

(3) She should arrange the chart material in proper order, precisely as follows: admission and discharge information (face sheet); medical abstract, if any; initial physical examination;

Fig. 11-6

TALLY SHEET OF SOCIOLOGIC STATISTICS OF DISCHARGED PATIENTS

Patient	Sex	Marital Status	Religion	Birth Place	Occupation	Last Residence	Length of Stay	Admission Diagnosis	Source Finance	No. Living Relatives	No. Times Transferred

Fig. 11-7

NOTIFICATION OF PATIENT MOVEMENT

Name:________________________________Room____________Date:____________

1. Moved to room__________________________Time________________
2. Transferred to___________________________Time________________
3. Discharged to___________________________Time________________
4. Died____________________________________Time________________

Kitchen notified__________________(Initials of Nurse)

Please take to health-records office as soon as possible.

social service notes; physician's orders and progress notes; electrocardiogram; laboratory and x-ray reports; dental and podiatry treatments; check sheets; nursing care plan and progress notes; narcotic and sedative records; intake and output records; accident report; physical, speech, and occupational therapy records.

(4) She should locate any missing sheets and arrange for appropriate additions.

(5) She should complete and file charts in numerical order (Fig. 11-8).

2. Monthly Duties. The health-record librarian's monthly duties should be directed to work related to the meetings of the utilization review committee.

a. Preparatory work for meetings. Considerable advance preparation for the monthly meetings of this committee is required, keeping all records up to date and thus avoiding an unduly heavy work load immediately preceding the meeting.

(1) Nurses should be encouraged to have certification and recertification forms signed properly by physicians and a check made about 4 days before the meeting, followed by phone calls to physicians whose records are delinquent.

(2) If necessary, forms should be mailed to physicians who cannot visit the facility, or on rare occasions these forms may be collected at the physicians' offices.

(3) Utilizing the corrected previous month's summary sheet of Medicare patients for the utilization review committee, a list of all patients to be considered at the meeting should be typed, and names of new patients obtained from individual utilization review forms should be added.

Fig. 11-8. The health-records librarian works in the health records room.

(4) Individual patient records should be prepared and submitted to the proper nurse for her comments and signature.
(5) The physical therapists should be consulted for additional information on treatments being given to patients on the list.
(6) The director of recreation and/or the occupational therapist should be interviewed, and notes should be made on special progress or marked regression shown by specific patients.
(7) Members of the medical staff who serve on the committee should be contacted to remind them of the date and hour of the meeting.

b. Work following meeting
(1) Appropriate records should be completed with material filed in a special Medicare file in the health-records room.
(2) A monthly report should be made for Medicare patients indicating admissions and discharges and should be kept in the loose-leaf notebook in the record office labeled Utilization Review Committee.
(3) The business office should be notified of members of the committee in attendance at the meeting for purpose of reimbursement.

c. The health-records librarian should complete the tally sheet of sociologic statistics of discharged patients and present a written report to the administration.

F. Special Meetings and Projects

1. Meetings. The health-records librarian should attend meetings both inside and outside the facility.

a. Meetings inside the facility

(1) Weekly in-service training program for the nursing staff

(2) Weekly clinical rounds and interdisciplinary conferences

b. Meetings outside the facility

(1) Monthly meeting of the city or county medical record librarians association

(2) Other professional meetings and conferences

2. Projects. The health-records librarian should prepare special reports at the request of the administrative staff, medical director, or other professional staff members.

G. Facilities and Equipment. The health-records librarian should make her headquarters in the record room, containing the following equipment:

1. Files
2. Worktable and chair
3. Desk and chair
4. Typewriter
5. Photocopy machine
6. Shelves
7. Medical dictionary and index of diseases

H. Interdepartmental Cooperation

1. Administration

a. The librarian should gather special data for reports to governmental or health care agencies.

b. She should cooperate with the administration in research and educational projects by making material available.

c. The receptionist should be given a copy of the patient admission card.

2. Social Service Department. The librarian should perform record functions associated with admissions, discharges, transfers, and patient movement and should confer with the social service director concerning information for Medicare records.

3. Nursing Department

a. The librarian should arrange, complete, and deliver new patient charts to the proper nursing units.

b. She should coordinate all medical and nursing records and should check them during patients' stays at the facility and upon their discharge or transfer.

c. She should confer with members of the nursing staff to gather data for Medicare records.

4. Dietary Department

a. The librarian should transmit diet check lists and notification of patient movement slips to the Dietary Department.

b. She should consult with the dietitian for Medicare records.

5. Recreation Department

a. The librarian should be informed by the Recreation Department of patient activities for Medicare records.

b. The recreation director should be given her copy of the patient admission card.

6. Restorative Services. The librarian should meet with representatives of Restorative Services for completion of Medicare records.

7. Business Office

a. The librarian should deliver appropriate sections of information from the charts of new patients to the business office.

b. She should transmit notification of patient movement slips to the business office.

c. She should order needed office supplies through the business manager.

References

American Hospital Association, Chicago, Ill., publications:

Accounting Manual for Long-term Care Institutions, 1968.

Classification of Health Care Institutions, 1968.

Developing Policies and Procedures for Long-term Care Institutions, 1968.

Diet and Menu Guide for Extended Care Facilities, 1967.

Emergency Removal of Patients and First-aid Fire Fighting in Hospitals, 1956.

The Extended Care Unit in a General Hospital, 1966.

Food Service Manual for Health Care Institutions, 1966.

Guide for Preparation of Medical Staff Bylaws, Rules and Regulations for Inpatient Care Institutions other than Hospitals, 1961.

Horty, John F.: *Q and A on Agreements between General Hospitals and Long-term Care Facilities,* 1964.

Hospital Accreditation References, 1964 revision, 1965.

Hospital Records Administration, Manual of Procedures, 1949.

Hospital Safety Manual, 1954.

Housekeeping Manual for Health Care Facilities, 1966.

Manual of Hospital Maintenance, 1952.

Manual on Insurance for Hospitals and Related Health Care Facilities, 1965.

Model Constitution and Bylaws for a Voluntary Hospital, rev. November, 1956. (New revision: *Suggested Constitution and Bylaws for a Voluntary Hospital,* 1968.)

Preventive Maintenance Guide, 1959.

The Teen-age Volunteer in the Hospital and Other Health Care Facilities, 1965.

Transfer Agreements between Extended Care Facilities and Hospitals, 1966.

The Volunteer in Long-term Care Institutions, 1968.

American Medical Association, Department of Hospitals and Medical Facilities: *The Extended Care Facility: A Handbook for the Medical Society,* Chicago, 1967.

American Nurses' Association: *A Guide for the Establishment of Refresher Courses for Registered Nurses,* New York, July, 1968.

American Nursing Home Association, Washington, D.C., publications:

A Guide to Transfer Agreements and Utilization Review, October, 1966.

National Safety Council, in cooperation with the American Nursing Home Association: *Safety Manual for Nursing Homes and Homes for the Aged,* 1962.

Pharmaceutical Services in the Nursing Home, 2d ed., 1966.

Reese, Dorothy Erickson, R.N., M.P.H.: *How To Be a Nurse's Aide in a Nursing Home.*

Regan, James P.: *Fire and Safety Guide/Checklist for Nursing Homes.*

Baumgarten, Harold, Jr.: *Concepts of Nursing Home Administration,* The Macmillan Company, New York, 1965.

Burling, Temple, M.D., Edith M. Lentz, Ph.D., and Robert N. Wilson, Ph.D.: *The Give and Take in Hospitals,* G. P. Putnam's Sons, New York, 1956.

Harmer, Bertha, rev. by Virginia Henderson: *Textbook of the Principles and Practice of Nursing,* 5th ed., The Macmillan Company, New York, 1955.

Huffman, Edna K.: *Medical Records in Nursing Homes,* Physicians' Record Company, Berwyn, Ill., 1961.

Jacobs, H. Lee, Ph.D., and Woodrow W. Morris, Ph.D., eds.: *Nursing and Retirement Home Administration,* Iowa State University Press, Ames, Iowa, 1966.

Joint Commission on Accreditation of Hospitals: *Model Medical Staff By-Laws, Rules and Regulations,* Chicago, 1964.

Joint Commission on Accreditation of Hospitals: *Standards for Accreditation of Extended Care Facilities, Nursing Care Facilities, and Resident Care Facilities,* Chicago, 1964.

Kurtz, Russell H., ed.: *Manual for Homes for the Aged,* Federation of Protestant Welfare Agencies, Inc., New York, 1965.

MacEachern, Malcolm T.: *Hospital Organization and Management,* 3d ed., Physicians' Record Company, Berwyn, Ill., 1962.

McGibony, John R., M.D.: *Principles of Hospital Administration,* G. P. Putnam's Sons, New York, 1952.

Moore, Joseph A.: *Hospital Public Relations—Why and How,* Becton, Dickinson and Company, Rutherford, N.J., 1967.

Naylor, Harriet H.: *Volunteers To-Day,* Association Press, New York, 1967.

Newton, Kathleen, and Helen C. Anderson: *Geriatric Nursing,* 4th ed., The C. V. Mosby Company, St. Louis, 1966.

O'Brien, Ruth: *Establishing a Volunteer Department in a Rehabilitation Center,* New York University Medical Center, Institute of Rehabilitation Medicine, New York, 1967.

Record Controls, Inc., and American Association of Hospital Accountants: *A Guide for the Retention and Preservation of Records with Destruction Schedules,* 3d hospital ed., Hospital Financial Management Association (formerly American Association of Hospital Accountants), Chicago, 1967.

Seawell, L. Vann: *Principles of Hospital Accounting,* Physicians' Record Company, Berwyn, Ill., 1960.

Stenzel, Anne K., and Helen M. Feeney: *Volunteer Training and Development*, Seabury Press, New York, 1968.

Sutton, Audrey Latshaw, R.N.: *Bedside Nursing Techniques in Medicine and Surgery,* W. B. Saunders Company, Philadelphia, 1964.

U.S. Department of Health, Education, and Welfare, Public Health Service, Washington, D.C., publications:

Elementary Rehabilitation Nursing Care (P.H.S. Publication No. 1436), April, 1966.

A Guide to Nutrition and Food Service for Nursing Homes and Homes for the Aged (P.H.S. Publication No. 1309), June, 1965.

Hospital and Nursing Home Equipment Planning Guide (P.H.S. Publication No. 930-D-4), rev. 1967.

How to Organize a Health Record System: A Guide for Nursing Homes and Homes for the Aged (P.H.S. Publication No. 1429), January, 1966.

McGibony, John R., M.D.: *Hospital Medical Records: Criteria for Administrative Evaluation* (P.H.S. Publication No. 930-C-5), 1963.

U.S. Department of Health, Education, and Welfare, Social Security Administration, Washington, D.C., publications:

Conditions of Participation: Extended Care Facilities (HIR-11), February, 1968.

Extended Care Facility Manual (HIM-12), January, 1967.

Principles of Reimbursement for Provider Costs (HIM-5), rev. January, 1967.

Provider Reimbursement Manual (HIM-15), July, 1968.

Webster, Albert N.: *Personnel Management Materials for Health Care Institutions,* Industrial Relations Counselors Services, Inc., 1270 Avenue of the Americas, New York.

Wiesen, David, ed.: *Administrative Manual of the Beth Abraham Hospital,* Beth Abraham Hospital, Bronx, New York, Dec. 1, 1966.

Wiesen, David: *Medical Manual of the Beth Abraham Home,* Beth Abraham Home, Bronx, New York.

Index

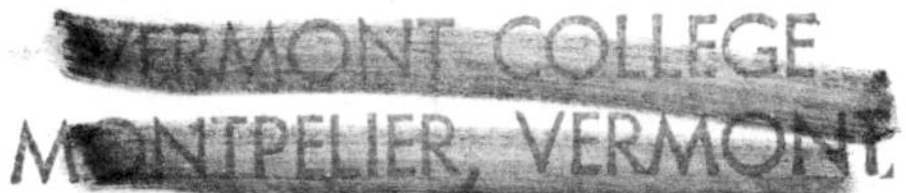
VERMONT COLLEGE
MONTPELIER, VERMONT